THE
GAMBLER
WIFE

THE GAMBLER WIFE

*A True Story
of Love, Risk,
and the Woman Who
Saved Dostoyevsky*

ANDREW D. KAUFMAN

Riverhead Books - New York
2021

RIVERHEAD BOOKS
An imprint of Penguin Random House LLC
penguinrandomhouse.com

Library of Congress Cataloging-in-Publication Data
Names: Kaufman, Andrew, 1969– author.
Title: The gambler wife : a true story of love, risk,
and the woman who saved Dostoyevsky / Andrew D. Kaufman.
Description: New York : Riverhead Books, 2021. | Includes bibliographical references and index.
Identifiers: LCCN 2021009411 (print) | LCCN 2021009412 (ebook) |
ISBN 9780525537144 (hardcover) | ISBN 9780525537168 (ebook)
Subjects: LCSH: Dostoyevsky, Fyodor, 1821–1881. | Novelists, Russian—19th century—Biography. | Dostoevskaîa, Anna Grigor'evna Snitkina, 1846–1918. | Author's spouses—Russia—Biography.
Classification: LCC PG3328.D6 K38 2021 (print) |
LCC PG3328.D6 (ebook) | DDC 891.73/3—dc23
LC record available at https://lccn.loc.gov/2021009411
LC ebook record available at https://lccn.loc.gov/2021009412

Printed in the United States of America
1 3 5 7 9 10 8 6 4 2

BOOK DESIGN BY LUCIA BERNARD

FOR CORINNE,

my gambler wife

and

MY FATHER,

the original gambler

CONTENTS

Anna Snitkina.

Fyodor Dostoyevsky, early 1860s.

Introduction

O n the cold, clear morning of October 4, 1866, a slender twenty-year-old stenography student in a black cotton dress left her mother's apartment in Petersburg. A short distance away, she stopped by Gostiny Dvor, a huge arcade of shops on Nevsky Prospect, to buy some extra pencils and a leather portfolio, hoping to lend a more businesslike air to her youthful appearance. Half an hour later, arriving at a gray-bricked building on the corner of Malaya Meshchanskaya Ulitsa and Stolyarny Pereulok, she ascended the poorly lit staircase to the second floor and rang the doorbell to Apartment 13, where her prospective employer was expecting her. The student's name was Anna Snitkina, and her employer-to-be was a forty-four-year-old former convict and enigmatic widower about town who also happened to be a novelist of some fame: Fyodor Dostoyevsky. Anna looked at her watch and smiled to herself. It was a few minutes before eleven thirty, just as she had been instructed. A prudent young woman, she was not about to take any chances—not on the day she hoped to be hired for her first job.

Almost immediately, a thickset woman in a green checkered shawl opened the door. Having followed the serialized installments of Dostoyevsky's newest work, *Crime and Punishment*, Anna wondered whether this very garment might be the prototype of the worsted shawl that played such an important role in the novel's Marmeladov family. She did not dare ask, of course, and told the maid simply that she had been referred by her stenography instructor, Professor Olkhin, and that the master of the house was expecting her.

The maid, whose name was Fedosya, led Anna down the dark corridor into a dining room, its walls lined with a chest of drawers and two large trunks, all of them draped in intricately crocheted rugs. She asked the young guest to have a seat and said her master would come shortly.

Two minutes later, Dostoyevsky appeared. Without so much as a greeting, he commanded Anna to go to his study while he fetched tea. And then he was gone again.

Anna looked around as she entered the large, gloomy study. Its divan was draped in shabby brown fabric; nearby, a small round cloth-covered table was shared by a lamp and two or three photo albums. Two windows let in a few rays of sunlight.

"It was dim and hushed," she later recalled, "and in the dimness and silence you felt a kind of depression." It was the sort of study she would have expected to find in the home of someone of modest means, not a man rapidly becoming one of Russia's most important authors. She scanned the room for clues about her potential employer—listening in vain for children's voices, wondering whether the painting above the sofa, of a cadaverous woman wearing a black dress and cap, was a portrait of Dostoyevsky's wife, who had died two years earlier. (It was, Anna would later learn.)

A few minutes later, the enigmatic fellow she'd encountered earlier reappeared. Anna tried hard to project confidence; this was a moment she had been anticipating longer than she might have cared to admit.

The name Dostoyevsky had long been familiar in the Snitkin home. He was her father's favorite writer; whenever the subject of modern literature arose, he would inevitably say, "Well now, what kind of writers do we have nowadays? In my time we had Pushkin, Gogol, Zhukovsky. And of the younger writers there was the novelist Dostoyevsky, the author of *Poor Folk*. That was a genuine talent." The past tense was no mistake: "Unfortunately," he continued, "the man got mixed up in politics, landed in Siberia, and vanished there without a trace." Then, in 1859, to the delighted surprise of Anna's father, Dostoyevsky had returned to the capital—after a four-year prison sentence in Siberia followed by five more years of mandatory military service—and resumed his writing with newfound vigor. Anna's father was a devoted reader of *Time*, a journal founded by Dostoyevsky and his brother Mikhail, and before too long the whole Snitkin family was reading Dostoyevsky—though none of them with greater emotional investment than Anna.

The work of Dostoyevsky was well-known among educated readers like Grigory Ivanovich Snitkin, who subscribed to *Time* and the other "thick journals," as they were known. Published weekly or biweekly, these compendia of literary, philosophical, and journalistic material were nineteenth-century Russia's equivalent of *The New Yorker*, *Newsweek*, and *Scientific American* all rolled into one. They included news, book reviews, cultural and literary criticism, scientific articles, and, of course, fiction; in fact, nearly every Russian novelist of the time debuted in these journals. Dostoyevsky's own first original published work, *Poor Folk*, appeared when he was twenty-four, in 1846—the year Anna Snitkina was born.

An epistolary novel, *Poor Folk* traced the love affair between an impoverished forty-seven-year-old copy clerk and his distant relative, a poor orphan girl. Readers recognized the novel as an original and moving take on the social Christianity and sentimental philanthropism that were characteristic of literature of the time. "A new Gogol has arisen!" exclaimed Vissarion Belinsky, the era's most influential literary critic, after reading it. "Do you yourself understand what you have written?" he asked the starstruck writer when they met in person—a day Dostoyevsky would long remember. Belinsky's endorsement gained Dostoyevsky immediate entrée into elite literary circles, and the novel was a great success with the reading public as well.

Yet Dostoyevsky's first taste of celebrity did not last. His next novel, *The Double*, about a minor civil servant lost in the Petersburg bureaucracy, was published just months after *Poor Folk*; it was a critical and commercial failure, as were the short stories that followed. "I really puffed him up, in considering Dostoyevsky a genius!" Belinsky told a critic after reading Dostoyevsky's new work. "I, the leading critic, behaved like an ass to the nth degree." The critic was especially nonplussed by the fantastic elements in *The Double*, whose hero loses touch with reality and strikes up a bizarre relationship with his doppelgänger. Such topics, Belinsky said, "can have a place only in madhouses, but not in literature, being the business of doctors, not poets."

On April 23, 1849, at the age of twenty-seven, Dostoyevsky was arrested for his participation in a revolutionary society known as the Petrashevsky Circle, which led to his disappearance from the literary scene for nearly a decade. After his return, he had resurrected his career with *The Insulted and Injured* (1861), a sentimental melodrama filled with colorful characters and dramatic cliffhangers at the end of each chapter—elements that made him enormously popular among readers, if distasteful to critics. He returned to critical favor with his next major work, *Notes from the House of the Dead* (1860–63), a semifictionalized account of Dostoyevsky's experiences in the Siberian labor camp. A blend of memoir, social exposé, and cultural criticism, *Notes from the House of the Dead* took up several of his familiar themes, such as the plight of the downtrodden man, the cruelty of officialdom, and the supreme value of Christian compassion. But it also explored new ideas that would become central to Dostoyevsky's art and thought in the years to come: the personality's need for inner freedom at any cost, the psychological complexity of the criminal mind—a topic the writer would return to in *Crime and Punishment*—and the spiritual depth of the Russian people.

By the time Anna Snitkina arrived at his door, then, Dostoyevsky had established his reputation as one of Russia's most promising writers. But he was not yet considered one of its greatest. He had exhibited flashes of genius, to be sure, but they were lost on critics like Belinsky, who tended to read Dostoyevsky through a narrowly utilitarian lens, overlooking the psychological acuity that undergirded his social commentary. It was this combination—social realism informed by profound psychological insight—that would make Dostoyevsky not only unique among his Russian contemporaries—"a realist in the higher sense," as he called himself—but vital to the history of Russian literature.

TO ANNA SNITKINA, however, Dostoyevsky was simply an author who fascinated and moved her. As soon as each issue of *Time* arrived at their home, Anna's father would be the first to read it. Then, just as he dozed off in his wingchair, magazine still in hand, fifteen-year-old Anna would sneak up to disengage it from his fingers, and then run out into the garden to lose herself in Dostoyevsky's latest novel—at least until Masha, claiming the elder sister's prerogative, sneaked up and snatched it away for herself.

Dostoyevsky's compassion for society's outcasts resonated with Anna's instincts, and her heart ached for the downtrodden souls he brought to life on the page. "I was quite a daydreamer," she said, "and the heroes of novels were always real people to me." She "hated" the predatory serf owner in *The Insulted and Injured*, who tries to pressure his son into a financially advantageous marriage, and she "despised" his naïve but lovable son almost as much for lacking the courage to stand up to his father and breaking off his relationship with the girl he loves. She shed tears over *Notes from the House of the Dead*, admitting later that "my heart was full of sympathy and pity for Dostoyevsky, who had to endure a horrible life in prison at hard labor."

This gruff, nervous man in front of her, however, seemed a far cry from the dashing, noble-minded author she had read and dreamed so much about. Dostoyevsky's chestnut-colored hair was pomaded and smooth, but his face was pale and sickly against his worn blue cotton frock coat. He seemed distracted and agitated, asking Anna every few minutes to remind him of her name. His eyes troubled her, too. The left was dark brown, while the right had a pupil so dilated you couldn't even see the iris—the result, she would later discover, of an accident many years ago, when he fell against a sharp object during an epileptic seizure.

"How long have you been studying stenography?" he asked.

"Just half a year," Anna replied, holding tight to what she hoped was a professional demeanor.

"And does your teacher have *many* pupils?"

"More than one hundred and fifty were registered for the course at the beginning, but only about twenty-five are left now."

"Ah, and why so few?"

"I suppose many of them found stenography simple enough to learn," Anna said uncertainly, "but hard to keep up beyond a few days, and so they dropped out."

"That's always the way it is in our country, isn't it," he said, "with every new undertaking? We start things off at a fever pitch, only to cool off fast and drop them altogether. Your colleagues see you have to work, and . . . who wants to *work* these days?" He offered her a cigarette.

Dostoyevsky was testing her, as he often did when meeting strangers. To him everything was a test: love, relationships, life itself. He was especially keen to determine whether this Anna Snitkina was like the many progressive young women who had been cropping up throughout Russia in the 1860s, in the wake of Tsar Alexander II's Great Reforms—a series of sweeping political, social, and economic changes introduced after Russia's humiliating defeat during the recent Crimean War.

Anna did, in fact, proudly consider herself an emancipated "girl of the sixties," as the young Russian feminists of her generation often called themselves. "I felt I was setting out on a new road, that I would be earning money by my own labor, that I could become independent," she wrote later, recalling what the prospect of working for Dostoyevsky meant to her. "And the idea of independence for me, as a girl of the sixties, was a very precious idea"—as it was for the vast majority of educated young women.

Taking advantage of the new spirit of openness, socially conscious Russians had begun to express their pent-up desire for thoroughgoing change within the traditional authoritarian family structure. They pushed for women to be given the opportunity to play a more central role in the rebuilding of Russian society after the war. An unprecedented number of books and articles on the family and the role of women in Russia appeared in these years, giving birth to a debate that in time came to be known as the "woman question."

Dostoyevsky was no enemy of this new Russian feminist movement. Indeed, he was one of the few major writers of the time who openly championed the broadening of women's intellectual horizons. "Educated women need a wider thoroughfare," he wrote in the early 1860s, echoing one of the feminists' main tenets, "one which is not cluttered up with needles, threads, chain stitches, and sewing." In the pages of *Time*—in one of the same issues where Anna had been reading *The Insulted and Injured*—Dostoyevsky defended the feminists against conservative critics who dismissed their supporters as "emancipators." In his view, female emancipation was a matter of "Christian love of mankind, of the education of oneself in the name of mutual love—of the love that a woman also has the right to demand herself." Such relations between the sexes, he argued, are perfectly healthy and desirable, and will be inevitable when the level of society itself is elevated. And his sensitivity to the plight of Russian women was evident in Dostoyevsky's fiction, which featured a panoply of female characters who are enslaved by parents, husbands, guardians, or benefactors, or mired in an abject poverty they cannot escape except by marriage, prostitution, or some form of pathological relationship to a man.

For all his sympathies with the aims of feminism, however, Dostoyevsky was put off by the brashness of many radical feminists. The "New Woman," as they called themselves, reminded him of much that he found wrong about the "new Russia"—a country he felt had lost touch with the values of decency, modesty, and, above all, morality. He resented this brave new world, heavily influenced by the West, which valued the "debauch of acquisition, cynicism, and materialism" and, most pointedly, free love. A lonely widower who had been rejected romantically by more than one progressive young woman, he also had personal reasons to be turned off by this brand of feminism.

What intrigued Dostoyevsky about Anna Snitkina was that she seemed different from the more radical feminists of the era: she appeared self-possessed, not rash or impetuous. As she politely declined his cigarette, the novelist was struck by the young woman's "serious, almost stern behavior," and was glad to have met such a "serious and efficient young girl."

Anna would not have known it from Dostoyevsky's gruff demeanor, but he'd taken a liking to this prospective employee. It helped, certainly, that she did not crop her hair, wear spectacles, or smoke—three archetypal anti-bourgeois habits of the "New Woman." With her blend of feminine modesty and professional tact, she made an excellent first impression.

"I was glad when Olkhin suggested a female stenographer, rather than a man," Dostoyevsky told Anna, "and do you know why?"

"No, I don't," she responded.

"Why, because a man would likely start drinking, while *you*—you won't fall into any drinking habits, I hope?"

Wanting to burst out laughing, Anna restrained herself. "I most certainly will not fall into any drinking habits," she said with perfect seriousness, "you may be sure of that."

"Well, then, we'll see how it works out," Dostoyevsky muttered vaguely. "We'll give it a try."

"Sure, why don't we try it," she said. Then, in case Dostoyevsky harbored any lingering doubts about her, she added: "But if it turns out to be inconvenient for you to work with me, you can tell me straight out. Please be assured I won't hold it against you if the job doesn't come to anything."

To test her skills as a stenographer, the writer picked up a copy of *The Russian Messenger*, where *Crime and Punishment* had been coming out in installments that year, and started reading from it—extremely quickly—expecting her to take dictation. Though Anna had been trained in shorthand, she was unable to keep up, and asked him politely if he could dictate at the speed of normal conversation. Annoyed by the interruption, Dostoyevsky leaned over to check her work. He chastised her for omitting a period and writing a hard sign unclearly, and then proceeded to grumble about women's lack of fitness for work.* Shocked and insulted, Anna nevertheless made every effort not to show it. Nothing was more important to her than succeeding professionally and becoming independent. She was not about to jeopardize that.

After a few more minutes, Dostoyevsky told Anna he needed to take

---

*In Russian orthography a hard sign (ъ) makes the preceding letter hard, whereas a soft sign (ь) makes the preceding letter soft. There is a very subtle distinction between the two, so writing one unclearly could cause it to be confused with the other.

a break, but he asked her to return that evening so he could begin dictating his novel to her. Anna was relieved to know he was serious about hiring her, yet her feelings were mixed. "I left Dostoyevsky's apartment in a very low mood," she wrote many years later in her memoir, *Reminiscences*. "I didn't like him; he made me feel depressed." In an unpublished draft, she went even further: "Never had a person before or since made such a difficult, depressing impression on me than Fyodor Mikhailovich did at our first meeting. I saw in front of me a terribly unhappy, broken, tormented man. He had the look of a person who today or yesterday had lost someone close to his heart, a person struck by some terrible misfortune."

The prospect of working for Dostoyevsky—a volatile genius, apparently also a reflexive misogynist—made Anna contemplate what price she was willing to pay for financial independence. "Earning one's own way, when they start saying such unpleasant things, can also sometimes be a bitter experience," she wrote in her diary, recalling her employer's rude remarks, "and this from one of the best people. What would it be like with less developed people? No, it's better to get married, maybe, if it means not having to subject yourself to such unpleasantries." That was the path chosen by the young women of her mother's generation—and even by her older sister, Masha, who had recently married a distinguished young professor. Anna was starting to understand the appeal of that choice, but she was not yet ready to give up her dream.

ANNA RETURNED to Dostoyevsky's apartment later that evening, and again the next day. Over the course of those first few meetings, she noticed a marked change in his behavior. He had grown warmer since their first encounter, more voluble. His speech was still disjointed, jumping from topic to topic, but as soon as he started talking he seemed somehow younger to Anna. She, on the other hand, continued to speak "simply, seriously, almost sternly," resolved to keep their relations "on a businesslike footing," no matter how much more comfortable she was beginning to feel in his presence.

As the hours passed, and Dostoyevsky told her story after story about his life, Anna was charmed by the writer's animated, childlike exuberance. He recounted, in great detail, his arrest for participating in the Petrashevsky Circle and the harrowing ordeal of his near execution. After being informed that the group was intending to publish seditious material, Tsar Nicholas I had sentenced the members of the circle to death. On December 22, 1849, Dostoyevsky was driven to Semyonovsky Square, dressed in a white robe, blindfolded, and lined up alongside his comrades. "As I watched the preparations taking place," he told Anna, "I knew that I had no more than five minutes left to live. But those five minutes seemed years—decades—so much time, it seemed, still lay ahead of me!" They had dressed the prisoners in their death robes and divided them into groups of three. Dostoyevsky was number eight in the third row. The first three had been tied to the execution posts, and it would soon be his turn. "My God," he recalled for Anna, "my God, how I wanted to live!"

Then, suddenly, a retreat was sounded. His comrades were untied and led away from the execution posts. A new sentence was read, condemning him to four years at hard labor. The entire execution had been staged, intended to put a scare into Dostoyevsky and the other members of the group without actually putting them to death. "That was the happiest day of my life," Dostoyevsky told Anna. "I walked back and forth in my cell . . . and kept singing, singing out loud—so glad was I for the gift of life."

Anna could not say which was more shocking: the details of the ordeal, or the fact that this important man had just relayed such intimate stories to his new employee, a near stranger. Like most educated Russians at the time, she'd known that Dostoyevsky had spent time in prison for his political activities. But the details had always been shrouded in mystery. Now he had given his young employee a glimpse behind the veil. "It would seem on the surface that he is a secretive person," she later told her diary, "but then he told me stories in such detail and so sincerely and openly that it even became a bit strange to watch. Oh, but I liked it terribly, this trustfulness and openness of his."

One other story caught Anna's attention. Since the death of his brother Mikhail, he revealed, Dostoyevsky had been in precarious financial straits. The magazine they had founded together—once known as

Time, later reincarnated as *Epoch*—had been liquidated, and though he wasn't legally required to do so, Dostoyevsky had taken it upon himself to pay off the journal's outstanding debts. He had also promised to support Mikhail's widow, Emilya Fyodorovna, and her orphaned children.

These crushing responsibilities left Dostoyevsky in such constant fear of debtors' prison that, in July 1865, he had signed an ill-advised contract with a shady editor and literary speculator named Fyodor Timofeyevich Stellovsky. In exchange for a mere three-thousand-ruble advance (just under thirty thousand dollars in today's money), Dostoyevsky had granted Stellovsky the right to republish in a single edition all of his previously issued works, many of which were still in print. (By comparison, a few years earlier Dostoyevsky's contemporary Ivan Turgenev had received nearly five thousand rubles, or fifty thousand dollars today, for *Fathers and Sons* alone.) What was more, Dostoyevsky was now contractually obligated to provide a new full-length novel by the first of November, 1866. Should he fail to do so, the novelist would forfeit the rights to everything he wrote for the next nine years—including all income. For the equivalent of a year and a half's living wage, Dostoyevsky had risked giving away all potential earnings from nearly a decade's worth of future work.

By the fall of 1865, the author had become so engrossed in churning out new installments of *Crime and Punishment* that he had little time for the novel he owed Stellovsky. At the beginning of October, just a month before this new novel was due, Dostoyevsky had only a few scattered notes and rough plans to show for it. In desperation, he turned to one of his oldest and closest friends, Alexander Milyukov. At first Milyukov suggested assembling a group of writer friends to create the novel together, but Dostoyevsky would not even consider signing his name to somebody else's work. So Milyukov had another idea: Why not put Dostoyevsky in touch with Pavel Olkhin, a well-known professor of stenography in Petersburg, to recommend his best pupil for this job? Dostoyevsky agreed, and that was how he had come to post the job opening that had brought Anna to his rooms.

The stories kept flowing, as Fedosya slipped in and out of the room, serving trays of fresh rolls and hot black tea. As Dostoyevsky meandered from topic to topic, though, Anna grew increasingly concerned that they had not accomplished any actual work. She was just about to remind her employer of her purpose in being there, when suddenly he seemed to recall it himself and asked Anna to begin taking down dictation. As she quickly removed the notebook and pencils from her leather portfolio, Dostoyevsky lit a cigarette, began pacing swiftly between the door and the stove, and started dictating his new novel, to be called *The Gambler*.

DOSTOYEVSKY WAS NOW ANNA'S EMPLOYER, and she his employee. It was her very first job, and she was ecstatic, as any progressive young woman would have been in those heady days of Russia's women's liberation movement. "My cherished dream had come true—I had a job!" she recalled. But those fond notions of independence would soon be complicated by other factors. Though she had come for a job, Anna would soon become a wife—the wife of a writer, and of a gambler. It was an unexpected decision for such a pragmatic, ambitious young woman, one that would afford her a life of both chaos and opportunity.

The story of Anna Snitkina and her employer, lover, husband, and charge, Fyodor Dostoyevsky, occurred against the backdrop of one of Russia's most tumultuous eras, the period that led directly to the Russian Revolution of 1917. It was a time of deep social and political unrest, marked by the growing rift between liberals, who wanted to do away with the autocracy and rebuild Russia along Western democratic principles, and conservatives, who sought to uphold the tsarist regime and preserve the patriarchy that had existed in Russia for centuries. The division was only sharpened by the Great Reforms that Alexander II implemented in the early 1860s—an important slate of structural changes that frightened many conservatives but left liberals restless for more.

The mid–nineteenth century also saw the introduction of capitalism into a society that for centuries had been fundamentally feudal and agrarian—a development vehemently opposed by progressives and traditionalists alike. And alongside Alexander's reforms came the rise of the "woman question"—the debate over what the path to fulfillment for women might look like in this rapidly changing society. First raised by feminists and liberals in the 1850s, the issue caught fire in the 1860s, burning until it was eventually subsumed into the burgeoning revolutionary movement. Anna Snitkina's story represents one woman's effort to find her own answer to the "woman question," while navigating a unique path through the competing ideologies of her time.

Most of Dostoyevsky's literary contemporaries engaged passionately with the issues of their time. Hundreds of thick journals emerged, each a mouthpiece for one faction or another. Most were liberal in their orientation, a vehicle for the era's radical intelligentsia, who argued that revolution was the only viable path forward for Russia. A smaller handful of thick journals espoused a conservative ideology. One leading thinker, Alexander Herzen, captured the mood of the era in his own journal, *The Bell*: "The storm is approaching, it is impossible to be mistaken about that," he wrote. "The Revolutionaries and Reactionaries are at one about it. All men's heads are going round; a weighty question of life and death lies heavy on men's heads."

In founding *Time*, the Dostoyevsky brothers had initially hoped to tow a middle line, offering a venue where the warring groups might be reconciled. Yet by the mid-1860s, as it became clear that the ideological rifts in Russian society were irreparable, Dostoyevsky threw his weight behind the conservatives. While openly acknowledging their blind spots— he himself had once been a member of the Petrashevsky Circle, after all— he preferred the conservative faction to the radical intelligentsia, whose atheism, worship of science, and calls for revolutionary violence were an affront to some of the writer's most deeply held values.

By the time Anna and Dostoyevsky met, the "weighty questions" Herzen referred to had gone beyond Russia's intellectual circles, flooding all corners of society. Russian literature had a major civic role to play in these culture wars, because readers expected their writers to guide them toward a resolution of the burning social questions of the day. And Dostoyevsky's own life experience—and the themes he had been exploring in his work since his first novel, *Poor Folk*, in 1846—placed him, if not at the leading edge, certainly at the center of the action.

Given the circumstances, then, it is little wonder that Anna's appearance in Dostoyevsky's life was of such personal and professional consequence. The young stenographer would not only help him navigate the rockiest patch of his career; she would also, with time, create a structure that enabled him to fulfill his civic mission as a Russian writer—and his ambitions as one of the essential voices of world literature. Anna Dostoyevskaya's spiritual evolution was influenced by her immersion in her husband's artistic world, but in turn Anna helped shape Dostoyevsky's approach to his three most prominent literary themes: the power of compassion, the dangers of intellectual pride, and the abiding possibility of redemption.

THE GAMBLER WIFE is based on decades of research into Dostoyevsky, Russian literature, and the cultural turmoil of the era. The details of the lives of Anna Snitkina and Fyodor Dostoyevsky have been carefully reconstructed from primary and secondary sources, many of which have been mined only by Slavic specialists contributing to scholarly publications. Previous accounts have recognized Snitkina's arrival as a dramatic shift in the novelist's life but failed to acknowledge her agency or the complicated social and cultural background from which she emerged. Readers might come away from such books with the impression that Snitkina was put on this earth for the sole purpose of rescuing a great man from his self-destructive tendencies and bringing glory to his name through the publication of his work. Her own character and complexity, the decisions she made and risks she undertook—these remain peripheral to many biographical works, which present Anna Snitkina in terms of what she meant to Dostoyevsky rather than what their relationship meant to *her*.

That question—what are we to make of Anna Snitkina's own choices, of the way she conducted her own life?—raises complicated issues worthy of nuanced consideration. In dedicating herself to her husband's work, for instance, was Anna betraying her longtime dream of becoming an emancipated woman? Many of Anna's radical feminist contemporaries certainly would have viewed her ardent devotion to her husband, and his work, as a betrayal of the dream of emancipation. Even today readers might find it difficult to view Anna Dostoyevskaya as a liberated woman, given the many sacrifices she made and the hardships she endured for Dostoyevsky's sake. Indeed, in certain moments, Anna did behave in ways that are unlikely to inspire the admiration of contemporary feminist readers. And yet such instances make all the more compelling her ultimate personal triumphs and professional accomplishments, not to mention her ability to rewrite the nineteenth-century Russian feminist script in a voice entirely her own.

Two volatile personalities, Fyodor Dostoyevsky and Anna Snitkina, met at a moment when their lives were profoundly unresolved, when their potential might just as easily have been extinguished as unlocked. Dostoyevsky was a reckless risk-taker, a creative genius, a mercurial writer who veered between inaction and bouts of frenzied productivity rather than consistent, steady work. When Anna arrived, he was on the brink of penury and battling a self-defeating depression so strong that it nearly scuttled his career. Anna, for her part, was personally and professionally ambitious; like the man she married, she was also a kind of gambler—but, as it turned out, a far shrewder and more strategic one than he. Had she never met Dostoyevsky, she would likely have led the simple but professionally secure life of a stenographer, like hundreds of other young women in Russia at the time. With her strong character and intense personality, however, it's doubtful whether such a life could ever have satisfied her.

Their union was as complex as it was deeply imperfect. It left room for Dostoyevsky's narcissism and abusive tendencies to persist unchecked, in ways that should create discomfort in any modern observer. But through a singular combination of patience, judgment, and an almost daredevil-level tolerance of risk, Anna managed to sustain a successful relationship with him when other women in his life had failed or stopped trying. With her tenacity, her resourcefulness, and her ability to absorb both personal mistreatment and professional whiplash in service of Dostoyevsky's career, Anna fostered the stability that allowed him to produce the landmark works of his later career, including *The Idiot* (1868–69), *The Possessed* (1871–72), and *The Brothers Karamazov* (1879–80). Through her example of active love, she also inspired the artistic vision of these late masterpieces.

In the process, through her steadiness, judgment, and ambition, she created for herself the opportunity to found an almost unprecedented and successful business venture of her own, becoming one of the first female publishers in Russian history. This enterprise not only earned her the satisfaction of significant professional accomplishment; it also allowed her husband to abandon his precarious dependence on demanding and sometimes unscrupulous publishers in favor of a stable and rewarding business that they themselves controlled.

"You are the rarest of women," Dostoyevsky told his wife a few years before his death. "You yourself don't suspect your own capabilities." Well aware of how different his own life and career would have been had they never met, Dostoyevsky bestowed upon her the highest possible honor by dedicating to her his last and greatest book, *The Brothers Karamazov*. And he would often tell his wife: "You are the only woman who ever understood me." At long last, readers will now have the opportunity to understand her.

TOP LEFT: *Polina Suslova*. TOP RIGHT: *Anna Dostoyevskaya*.
BOTTOM: *Nevsky Prospect, Petersburg*.

I

THE GAMBLE

1.

The Decent Thing to Do

Anna Grigoryevna Snitkina was born in Petersburg on August 30, 1846, the balmy feast day of the thirteenth-century warrior-prince Saint Alexander Nevsky, amid the sonorous ringing of monastery bells and the solemn strains of a military band. Later in life, she would say that the timing and ceremonial spirit of her arrival in the world were no coincidence. For like her patron saint, who repelled foreign invaders and united the far-flung tribes of the Great Rus', Anna Dostoyevskaya would become a Russian warrior after her own fashion.

She would begin that journey, paradoxically, in the most westernized of Russian cities, the famed capital built by Peter the Great at the beginning of the eighteenth century as part of his project to modernize what he considered a backward society. Peter designed his "window to the West" with charming Venetian-style canals and an orderly grid of narrow streets lined by two- and three-story classical buildings. Adorning the city's center, along the embankment of the Neva River, was the tsar's stately Winter Palace. From here one could see, on the other shore of the Neva, the magnificent Stock Exchange, flanked by two rostral columns and a granite embankment descending to the river, and the Peter and Paul Fortress, the city's original citadel, which by Anna's time had been adapted into a prison for political convicts. (Dostoyevsky himself would be held here for several months in 1849 while awaiting his sentence.) The farther one traveled from the city's center, the seat of its political and cultural power, the dingier the streets and buildings became. It was here, in the cramped, poorly ventilated apartments situated in Petersburg's back alleys, that many of Dostoyevsky's own tormented characters dwelled.

Anna Snitkina enjoyed a comfortable girlhood in her family's two-story brick home not far from the city's center, on a nearly five-acre plot of land at the corner of Kostromskaya and Yaroslavskaya streets. The family owned this and three other houses on the same land, purchased with money inherited from Anna's maternal grandfather, a Finnish landowner. The well-to-do Snitkins lived on the second floor of the largest house, which was adjacent to a giant, shady garden studded with richly scented berry shrubs, and rented out the other rooms to tenants. Anna's enterprising mother managed the rentals, while Anna's father, Grigory Ivanovich Snitkin, served as a civil servant in a government ministry. Here Anna spent her "quiet, measured, and serene" childhood, a period "without quarrels, dramas, or catastrophes."

As a young girl, she was given few children's books. "No one tried to 'develop' us," she would recall—a laissez-faire approach to child-rearing in an era when the influence of English utilitarian philosophy and French social thought had led to a rash of self-improvement fads and theories of social progress, from Socialism to Materialism, Positivism to Pietism. A glance at advertisements in the thick journals of the day, offering everything from cures for venereal disease to supposedly life-changing spiritual seances, suggests a Russian people that believed—or wanted to believe—in the possibility of a panacea for all that ailed mankind. But these utopian dreams and cure-all promises were so much snake oil, as far as the Snitkins were concerned. Proudly holding to their bourgeois ways, they valued above all else hard work, modesty, and the virtuous gratifications of quiet daily service to others.

Although hardly pampered, Anna and her siblings—her older sister, Masha, and younger brother, Ivan—had enjoyable childhoods, playing in the large family garden from morning to night during the summer, and in the winter sledding down the ice hill their father had constructed for them. At Christmastime, the family lighted a fir tree; during Carnival weeks their parents took them for rides in carriages decorated with shiny bells and bright whistles. Twice a year, they went to the theater. On holidays Anna's relatives came to the Snitkins' spacious apartment from near and far to celebrate, often staying until late into the night. Anna's own arrival into the world came during one such celebration, an event the family greeted as a harbinger of future happiness—a prophecy Anna later insisted had come true in the end.

One of her first conscious memories was of an incident that occurred when she was a toddler: a local drayman rode into a collapsing old barn owned by the Snitkins. Two-year-old Anna looked on with her mother and nurse, all of them letting out terror-stricken screams, only to discover moments later, "as luck would have it," that the man had miraculously survived. The same force was at work a year later when she suffered a severe illness. Whether it was the writhing leeches creeping across her naked chest that cured her, or her mother's insistence that she receive communion and pray before the miraculous icon of the All-Compassionate Mother of God hanging in the church on Shpalernaya Ulitsa, Anna could not say. But whatever the source of her healing, from that moment on, she would remain convinced that some divine force was looking over and protecting her.

The Snitkins loved to tell such tales. Anna also recalled the story of how her father, "a man of very exuberant nature, nimble-witted, and given to pranks," enjoyed his youth so thoroughly that he waited until he was forty-two before proposing to Anna Nikolayevna Miltopeus, a slender, strikingly beautiful twenty-nine-year-old whose family descended from a Swedish line of scholars including a Lutheran bishop. At the insistence of Snitkin's parents, the bride-to-be was to convert to Russian Orthodoxy before marrying Snitkin—no small sacrifice for a girl with her lineage. On the evening just before she was to give her final answer, Anna Nikolayevna dropped to her knees before the crucifix in her parents' home, hoping for guidance. After the better part of an hour, she looked up and saw a magical radiance lighting up the entire room above the crucifix before fading again. As she watched, the aura appeared a second time and then a third. Later that same night, in a dream in which she'd entered an Orthodox church to be anointed, Anna Nikolayevna suddenly found herself standing right next to the Shroud of Christ. Together, the two signs—the vision above the crucifix and the dream—sealed her conviction that she was fated to convert to Russian Orthodoxy and marry Snitkin. (Two weeks later, during the actual anointment ritual within the Simyonovskaya church, she was astonished to find herself standing next to the very Shroud of Christ she'd seen in her dream.)

Anna Nikolayevna was never able to read the prayers in Old Church Slavonic, but she brought all the fiery devotion of a recent convert to her adopted Orthodox faith, never regretting her decision. "Otherwise," she used to tell her children, "I would have felt remote from my husband and children, and that would have been painful for me." Her daughter sensed that she was the "real head of the house," while her father "yielded to her willingly," reserving for himself only a few cherished freedoms, such as the right to stop at the local antique markets to buy knickknacks and rare porcelains.

Yet her father could also surprise Anna with random acts of courage that seemed to belie his otherwise pliant nature. As a ten-year-old, he had been stopped on his way to school by a well-dressed gentleman who asked Snitkin to come quickly to his home to serve as the godfather of a new-born boy. The young Snitkin agreed without hesitation, finding out only after the fact that he was fulfilling a popular tradition: in cases where all children in a family have died, then a newborn child must be christened by the first person the child's father encounters. Anna often cited the story as a moving example of her father's easy and spirited generosity.

Anna also inherited from her father a love of fairy tales—his favorite being "Ivan Durachok," or "Ivan the Fool," which he recounted to his children in endless variations each night after dinner. Snuggled between her brother and sister, Anna would listen with delight to find out how Ivan would manage to cleverly extricate himself from yet another misfortune. Without knowing it, Anna was absorbing two essential life skills she would one day need to draw on: storytelling and the art of survival. Indeed, in the playful poetry she and Dostoyevsky would compose many years later, making light of their daily misfortunes during their European travels, one can hear the jaunty rhythms and lighthearted spirit of Mr. Snitkin's favorite fairy tale.

Mr. Snitkin was also a passionate devotee of high art, which he regarded with an almost religious reverence. In his youth he had worshipped the celebrated tragic actress Varvara Asenkova, spending his evenings at the theater to gaze at her in performance, and eventually finagling his way backstage to meet her. To his surprise and delight, Asenkova took an immediate liking to her young admirer, making a point of handing him her bouquet and shawl whenever she took the stage to recite the verses of Racine or Corneille, and allowing him to escort her back to her dressing room after a performance. After the actress's untimely death from consumption, the young Snitkin was so heartbroken that he was unable to enter a theater for years; he paid regular visits to Asenkova's grave. Anna later recalled how her father brought her and her older sister, Masha, to the actress's grave and made his daughters kneel before the gravestone and "pray for the repose of the soul of the greatest artist of our age."

Anna's father was also the one who introduced her to the writings of Fyodor Dostoyevsky. Reading his autobiographical *Notes from the House of the Dead* in *Time* between 1860 and 1863, when she was in her midteens, she was pained to read the convict-narrator's account of his years of hard labor in Siberia. Encountering *The Insulted and Injured* in the same magazine in 1861, Anna commiserated with the dreamy, penniless young writer Ivan Petrovich, whose love for Natasha is scuttled after her parents force him to postpone their marriage until he is more established professionally. Natasha falls in love with Alyosha, the ne'er-do-well son of a cruel, wealthy merchant, until he tries to steer Alyosha away from Natasha into a more lucrative match.

It was a typical early Dostoyevskian plot, with a meek, purehearted dreamer-artist confronting a harsh reality peopled with social predators. Anna Snitkina, who had a lifelong antipathy for egoists, reflexively sided with the underdog, and she was drawn to Dostoyevsky's portraits of personal injustice. "I simply couldn't understand," she admitted to Dostoyevsky after they were engaged, "how Natasha could prefer that worthless

Alyosha to my dear Ivan Petrovich. While I was reading the novel I would think, 'She deserved what she got because she rejected the love of Ivan Petrovich.'" She intuited, rightly, that Ivan Petrovich was a surrogate for the author himself: "It seemed to me that it was Dostoyevsky himself telling his sad story of unsuccessful love." An attentive follower of his work and life story, she recognized the novel's autobiographical overtones—not least the fact that Petrovich was a writer whose first novel bore a striking similarity to Dostoyevsky's own debut, *Poor Folk*, with which Anna was of course familiar.

Anna's passion for Dostoyevsky was so pronounced that, by the time she was sixteen, her family had nicknamed her "Netochka Nezvanova," after one of the author's unfinished novels. *Netochka Nezvanova*—a phrase meaning "Uninvited Nobody," but more commonly interpreted as "Nameless Nobody"—recounts the anguished childhood of a talented, emotionally abused orphan girl, who is shepherded from one "accidental family" and dysfunctional relationship to the next before, at the age of eighteen, she is able to channel her painful experiences into a budding singing career.

Dostoyevsky's work on *Netochka Nezvanova* was cut short after his arrest and imprisonment; the first two installments were published before his arrest in April 1849, and the third appeared a month later. He never completed the project, but if he had, it would have become nineteenth-century Russia's first feminist novel: the very first book, as scholar Joseph Frank noted, to "depict a talented and strong-willed woman who refuses to allow herself to be crushed—who becomes the main *positive* heroine of a major [Russian] novel."

In fashioning such a story, Dostoyevsky was anticipating one of the most dramatic upheavals in Russian culture of the mid-nineteenth century: the rise of a distinct feminist movement. Feminist ideas had circulated within the Russian aristocracy since the late 1700s, but the "woman question" was first elevated to broad public attention in an influential article published in 1856 by the surgeon and pedagogue Nikolai Pirogov. Inspired by the skill and courage of female nurses he had supervised in the Crimean War, Pirogov argued that education was essential to prepare women to become true partners of their husbands in the struggle to defend the material and spiritual well-being of the nation. Pirogov is credited with making education a central goal of the early Russian feminist movement—an objective that bore fruit when the government approved a plan to open the first secondary schools for girls in 1858 and then opened university courses to female students the following year. Another early advocate was the writer Mikhail Mikhailov, who proposed a systematic program for women to achieve emancipation by raising their children early in life before shifting their attention to employment and productive social activity. Mikhailov, himself part of an amicable ménage à trois, was also an early proponent of giving women the freedom to divorce, to ensure that marital unions could be based on love.

In the years that followed, other voices—many of them women—joined the debates. "Ladies. Stop being children. Try to stand on your own two feet!" exhorted Marya Vernadskaya, coeditor with her husband of the *Economic Index*, around 1860. She told women it was time to stop frittering away their days in meaningless activity and start earning their own living. Overnight, it seemed, hundreds of women's societies emerged, in the provinces as well as the big cities, to help women do just that. "Women in Russia have virtually no social significance," complained one organizer in the town of Perm, where she became known for showing up at rallies carelessly dressed, her hair closely cropped. Russian women had too long been valued, she said, "neither as wives nor as mothers, since until now men have had complete power over them." It was up to women, she said, to join in solidarity in order to defend their dignity and their rights. Other feminists poured their energies into charitable causes that specifically supported women. The popular Sunday School movement, for example, offered women the opportunity to teach reading, writing, sewing, and religion to young girls of lower and middle classes—"the very first outlet," recalled one teacher, "for our aspiration for work, for the public good, and for contacts with the people."

By the early 1860s, the "woman question" was a burning issue in the era's thick journals, university lecture halls, student apartments, and literary salons. The movement inspired many short stories and novels, the most famous and influential of which was Nikolai Chernyshevsky's 1863 novel *What Is to Be Done?*, which presents a clear model of the truly liberated woman. The young feminist heroine of Ivan Turgenev's *On the Eve* (1860) marries a consumptive freedom fighter and after his death continues his lofty political cause of the liberation of Bulgaria. Nadezhda Khvoshchinskaya's novel *The Boarding School Girl* (1860) tells the story of Lelenka, the daughter of a provincial noble family, who is inspired by feminist ideas to break free of her parents. After separating from her family and carving out a career as an artist, she declares: "I will never fall in love, never. It's stupid. . . . I swear that I will never again grant someone power over me, that I'll never serve those old, barbaric codes in word or deed. On the contrary, I say to everyone, do as I have done. Liberate yourselves, all you people with hands and a strong will! Live alone. Work, knowledge, and freedom—that's what life is all about." Her words could have served as a blueprint for the radical feminists of the 1860s.

Reactionaries dismissed feminists like Khvoshchinskaya's heroine, Lelenka, as "female Nihilists" for their open disdain for social and cultural norms and their intentionally disruptive behavior and attire, not to mention their frequent support for revolutionary causes. Many of these women enjoyed provoking the ire of polite society by walking about the streets unescorted, smoking in public, and refusing to let men open the door for them. Scorning the muslin, ribbons, parasol, and flowers of the traditional Russian miss, the female Nihilists cropped their hair and sported plain dark woolen dresses that fell straight and loose from the waist, embellished only by a white collar and cuffs. Through dark blue spectacles, they devoured foreign scientific works, rejecting Russian belles lettres as soft and outdated. "Value us as your comrades, your co-workers in life; people that are equal to you," one firebrand demanded. "Try to discern our equality and we will try to remind you less that we are women."

Such calls for cultural or social revolution marked a break from the feminist voices of the 1850s, who were focused not on a complete overhaul of society but on securing concrete professional and educational opportunities for women. The leaders of this earlier strain were Nadezhda Stasova, Marya Trubnikova, and Anna Filosofova—educated and well-connected women who combined a strong social conscience with pragmatism and savoir vivre. Like other enlightened members of the upper classes, they dressed more simply, relied less on servants, and eschewed the formalities that governed polite society, but their familiarity with the milieu helped them gain official approval for their reformist efforts. Together they founded the Society for Cheap Lodgings, which provided housing and other assistance to impoverished gentlewomen. They mobilized women in a campaign to enhance female education. And, in one of their most successful ventures, Trubnikova and Stasova founded an all-woman publishing cooperative in 1863, giving educated women the opportunity to write, translate, and bind books themselves.

More nonconformists than rebels, Stasova, Trubnikova, and Filosofova retained vestiges of their aristocratic upbringing even as they took risks to support progressive women's causes. They kept their activist work largely behind the scenes, advocating for economic and professional opportunity for women without demanding a complete reformation of relations between the sexes. They also saw no contradiction between female emancipation and a satisfying family life. On the contrary, they believed that women needed both domestic happiness and productive outlets outside the home to achieve fulfillment. "Remember," Filosofova cautioned her daughter, "there is no destiny in the world more elevated than the family."

Young Anna Snitkina wouldn't likely have known of Filosofova, Trubnikova, or Stasova, who never became household names like the more radical feminists of the 1860s. Yet these original leaders of the women's liberation movement articulated a vision of feminist empowerment that Anna herself would have recognized and found sympathetic—realizing their potential in much the same way that Dostoyevsky had envisioned for his heroine in his unfinished *Netochka Nezvanova*.

Russia may have forgotten Dostoyevsky's book during his prolonged absence, but the Snitkins certainly had not. They preserved the memory of his heroine, this "uninvited nobody," through the nickname their daughter carried with pride. In *Reminiscences*, Anna maintained that the nickname referred to both her passion for Dostoyevsky and her habit of dropping in on relatives without an invitation. Yet it's hard not to wonder, given the course of her life, whether she might have had deeper reasons to identify with Netochka Nezvanova's story.

IF IT WAS HER FATHER who gave Anna her love of literature, and her mother who was responsible for the young woman's religious inclination and belief in signs and omens, both parents fostered Anna's love of Russian traditions. In 1856, when she was ten years old, Anna and her family traveled to Moscow, where her father's aunt was a nun with a significant position in the Kremlin's Resurrection Monastery. This aunt arranged for the Snitkins to rent a private monastery apartment from which they could view the coronation of Tsar Alexander II. Half a century later, Anna could still vividly remember the majestic procession amid the ringing of the Kremlin bells and the regimental music. She recalled "the military and court personnel in their brilliant, gold-embroidered regimentals," and the sight of the tsar and his wife beneath a great canopy decorated with white ostrich feathers and gold tassels, as the "sounds of the national anthem merged with the deafening cries of 'Hurrah!'"

Anna would recall, too, the behavior of guests a short while later at a ceremonial dinner she attended with her family. As the guests were leaving the enormous, glittering dining hall, many began removing decorative flowers from the vases on each table to keep as souvenirs. Only there were fewer bouquets than guests, and ten-year-old Anna watched in confusion and horror as these ostensibly sophisticated government officials literally tore bouquets and flowers from one another's hands, leaving empty stalks in the vases and scattering petals on the floor. The contrast between the elegant coronation ceremony and this churlish aftermath disturbed Anna, reinforcing her belief in the importance of decency and decorum.

She remembered, as well, her parents' warm business relations with the tenants in their rental properties. Anna's parents were known as kind and scrupulous landlords, a rarity in those rough-and-tumble early days of capitalism in Russia. The Snitkins charged only five to eight rubles per

month for well-kept, spacious apartments overlooking an attractive garden, and the tenants appreciated how all the mothers kept their children
under strict supervision as they played in the common courtyard. Often
staying for years at a time, the tenants were treated by the Snitkins like
members of the family. Lodgers spent Christmas and Easter with the
family, sent them presents on their birthdays and name days,* and invited
their landlords to their own family christenings, weddings, and funerals.
Anna would look back on her parents' behavior as remnants of a "patriarchal" time, "which evidently will never return."

The female tenants especially liked Mrs. Snitkina, who not only offered motherly counsel but also let them borrow her silk dress, Turkish
shawl, and beribboned dress hat for religious holidays. One year, during
Lent, a tenant who had borrowed these items found herself genuflecting
so forcefully in front of the church icons that her head bumped into a
lamp, sending oil pouring out onto her head and down her back. When
she returned home with the bespattered dress and the wax-filled hat
crumpled up in her hands, she fell to her knees before Mrs. Snitkina and
began to sob. Anna's mother comforted the suffering woman, assuring
her that the items could be easily cleaned and repaired. In truth the
clothes were forever ruined, recalled Anna, who never forgot her mother's
example of gracious generosity. "It was easier to live in the world back
then," Anna reflected many years later, "and easier to bear the trials sent
to us by fate."

Anna respected her parents and loved her country, but she also had an
undeniable rebellious streak. The custom of arranged marriages was still
common then—indeed, her elder sister had recently acceded to such a
union—but from the time she was sixteen Anna declared herself disgusted by the practice. "People were not ashamed to speak directly about
[arranged marriage], as in: 'You have a product, we have a buyer' or 'I've
got a young lady, here's a profitable suitor for you.'" The custom made

---

*In Russian culture a name day is the feast day of the Christian saint after whom a person is named. In
nineteenth-century Russia, which was heavily influenced by Orthodox Christianity, name days were
often considered more important than birthdays and accompanied by large celebrations.

Anna feel more like a piece of property than a person; in her view, it encouraged not only parents but their children to engage in the most undignified forms of subterfuge.

Anna remembered all too clearly how she felt when one family friend secretly introduced Anna's mother to a young man who said he was interested in taking one of the Snitkins' rental properties. In reality, he only wanted to inspect the younger Snitkin daughter, whom he was considering taking for a wife. On another occasion, when Anna discovered that a young, handsome, and very rich heir—a young man she actually liked—had contrived to meet her by crashing a wedding party Anna was attending, she refused to take any of his subsequent house calls. "The young man's deception immediately lowered him in my eyes," Anna recalled with prideful rigidity, "and I even started to feel sorry for him. . . . Mama tried to change my mind and lessen the 'groom's' guilt, but I was unyielding and stood by my position."

Anna showed the same determination when it came to her education. From the ages of nine to twelve she attended St. Anna's School, where all subjects except for religion were taught in German—a skill that would prove invaluable years later, as she and her husband traveled through Europe. She then attended the Mariinskaya—an early "gymnasium," or school, for girls—which had opened in Petersburg in 1858 as part of the government's national effort to provide better educational opportunities for women. A talented, hardworking student with a "lively, firm, ardent temperament," according to her classmate and lifelong friend Marya Nikolayevna Stoyunina, Anna was awarded a silver medal, first class, upon her graduation at the age of eighteen. This studious girl, with striking eyes and a passionate nature, was also known among her classmates for her wicked sense of humor, which allowed her to find the comedy in almost any situation and break readily into sudden, contagious laughter.

For all her spirit and energy, though, Anna never quite seemed to fit in with her more worldly classmates. As a member of what was derided by some as a "democratic," or bourgeois, family, she chose not to crop her hair, affect spectacles, or smoke—the archetypal behaviors of aspiring young feminists from the late 1850s onward. Anna was surprisingly far better read than most of her classmates, but "her father and mother were simple people," Stoyunina recalled, and Anna herself was unrefined, awkward to the point of clumsiness. She had

> an oval face, penetrating, deep eyes, an open, slightly jutting forehead, an energetic chin, the sign of a powerful nature, a nose with an elegant Japanese protuberance. She had beautiful teeth, with a bluish tint; sand-colored hair and hands coarse and callused from constant work. The color of her face was unhealthy and pale, the sort of pallor you see in a deeply troubled person. She was one of those fiery natures who have a trembling heart that does not know steady, peaceful beating.

She was also a quick study, with an uncanny ability to read people clearly, to know what to say and when to remain silent. No object of the male gaze, Anna Snitkina was the author of a clear-eyed and intuitive gaze of her own, capable of grasping a situation at a single glance and describing it later with colorful precision. "All she'd have to do," remembered Stoyunina, "was go outside, to the market, with the most ordinary aim, and she'd notice everything: not only a major occurrence, a bright scene, but the smallest, albeit most telling details. Returning home, she'd illustrate everything picturesquely, scenically, from sight. She definitely had a hidden artist's spark."

A social progressive with conservative values, a Russian patriot who happened to be half Swedish, a serious student prone to infectious laughter, a decisive young woman with nerves of steel who nevertheless suffered bouts of mania, a pragmatist and a mystic, Anna was a tangle of contradictions. An acquaintance of later years insisted that "the singularity of her spiritual qualities that aroused surprising and deep interest in her" reflected her status not as "the wife of Dostoyevsky, but in and of herself." Anna, with her "indefatigable energy, subtle and broad mind," and "boundless interest in all her surroundings," was someone who "could love and hate to the end," this acquaintance recalled. Indeed, if she saw someone being unfairly treated, she would "stop at nothing" to defend the person's dignity.

All of which helps to explain why, under the influence of the progressive ideas of the time, Anna made the decision to transfer to the Women's Pedagogical Institute, one of the first Russian institutions of higher learning available to women. We have no record of how Anna's parents felt about her decision, but they would likely have been supportive of their daughter, who had already demonstrated her willingness to work hard to achieve academic success.

At that time the natural sciences were especially popular in Russia, and "physics, chemistry and zoology seemed like a revelation to me," Anna would recall. After fainting in zoology class at the sight of a dead cat, however, she concluded that her fascination with science was not matched by her aptitude; she also realized that she felt like a bit of a black sheep at the Institute, just as she had at the Mariinskaya. Increasingly convinced that literature was her true passion, she started looking for a different career path, one that would allow her to turn her interests into a practical profession.

The opportunity presented itself early in 1866, when she learned of Russia's first stenographic training school, established in Petersburg by an instructor named Pavel Olkhin. In his textbook on the subject, Olkhin emphasized that stenography was more than a profession; it was also a way for young people to develop the essential life skills of patience and perseverance. These were qualities that Anna already possessed in abundance when she enrolled in Olkhin's class in the spring of 1866. It was a perfect match of teacher and student: for Anna, stenography was a path to becoming an emancipated woman. Yet while many other young feminists—inspired by the teachings of the radical intelligentsia—worked hard to escape the restrictions of family, Anna was motivated by a desire to *help* her family. "My whole life," she wrote in her diary, "I had only one passionate desire: to have my slice of bread, to be able to not burden my family, to be useful to them myself, to stand on my own two feet, and in case of need to be able to earn a living myself."

This opportunity presented itself sooner than she had hoped. For several years her father had been battling consumption; by 1865 it was clear that his illness was not responding to treatment and he did not have long to live. Earning a living, then, was a looming necessity for Anna. She was on the verge of dropping out of stenography school, to care for her ailing father, when he insisted that she continue.

On April 28, 1866, Grigory Ivanovich Snitkin died. "It was the first real sorrow I experienced in my life," Anna recalled, "and my grief was stormy. I wept a great deal, spent whole days in the Great Okhta Cemetery at his grave and could not come to terms with this terrible loss." In the end, it was her family who helped her find her way through the grief: "My mother, distraught over my depressed state, begged me to settle down to some kind of work."

Professor Olkhin allowed Anna to make up the classes she had missed via correspondence, and she made great progress over the summer—thanks in part to her brother, Ivan, who gave her dictation every day. By the time courses resumed in September 1866, Anna had become Olkhin's best student.

On the third of October, Olkhin approached her before class to ask how she would feel about doing some stenographic work for pay.

"Who is offering the job?" Anna wanted to know.

"It's the writer, Dostoyevsky. He's working on a new novel and has decided to hire a stenographer." He handed Anna a small piece of paper, folded over double, on which was written: "Stolyarny Pereulok, corner of Malenkaya Meshchanskaya Ulitsa, house of Alonkin, Apartment No. 13."

"Please be there tomorrow at eleven-thirty," said the professor, "no earlier and no later."

2.

The Gambler

W hat's that, 'She returned from Roulettenburg'? Did I mention Roulettenburg at all?"

"Yes, you did, Fyodor Mikhailovich, you dictated the word."

"Impossible!"

"Excuse me, but isn't there a city in your novel by that name?"

"Yes, the action takes place in a gambling town that I call 'Roulettenburg.'"

"But then you must have dictated the word to me—or else where would I have gotten it?"

"You're right," he said. "I've gotten something mixed up here."

Dostoyevsky's head was foggy, as it often was after an epileptic attack, like the one he'd suffered the day before. Roulettenburg *was* the name he'd given to the fictitious gambling resort in the novel he was now dictating. To a nineteenth-century Russian ear, this portmanteau word combining the French *roulette* and the German *-burg* would have sounded funny and made-up, even bizarre, which was precisely Dostoyevsky's intention. He wanted to convey the artificiality of the town itself: a glitzy but soulless locale—like all of Germany, in his view—where people lived and died in obeisance to the flesh-God of money, the symbolic epicenter of the bloodless European materialism he had come to deplore. And here, in his fictional Roulettenburg, he was preparing to lay bare some of the ugliest truths about Europe—and, perhaps inadvertently, about himself as well.

They began to settle into a routine. Anna would come to Dostoyevsky's home at noon and stay until four. Days commenced with tea being served by Fedosya, followed by a dictation session. Smoking and talking anxiously, Dostoyevsky stopped often to ponder some idea at length, then asked her to read back what he had just dictated. On a few occasions he asked Anna for her name again, only to forget it a few minutes later, just as he had at their first meeting. Once or twice, he offered her a cigarette, and she reminded him that she didn't smoke. After an hour or so of work he grew tired and needed a rest. At four o'clock she got ready to leave, promising to return the next day at noon. He handed her a pack of heavy writing paper, ruled almost invisibly, and gave her exact instructions on what margins to leave.

With each day they seemed to grow calmer in each other's presence. He admired Anna's efficiency, her tact, her assertiveness. After about a week, Dostoyevsky stopped dictating orally, improvising on the fly; now he worked at night and then dictated from his manuscript. On some occasions he managed to get so much written that Anna had to stay up past midnight to transcribe her notes. "With what triumph I would announce the number of accumulated pages the next day!" she recalled. "And how pleasant it was to see his happy smile in response to my assurance the work was going successfully and would be finished by the deadline, without a doubt."

They had three dictating sessions or so each day, and in between they talked at length, mostly about him. He grew animated as he told her stories about his literary friendships and rivalries, or about his former travels and gambling sprees in Europe. "Chatting with me like a friend," Anna remembered, "he would recount some unhappy episode from his past. I couldn't help being deeply touched by his accounts of the difficulties from which he never extricated himself, and indeed could not."

DOSTOYEVSKY'S DIFFICULTIES went back many years. When he was seventeen, his father, Mikhail Andreyevich Dostoyevsky, was said to have been murdered by peasants on his estate whom he had mistreated. The elder Dostoyevsky was an unhappy man with a nervous condition that made him severe, mistrustful, and explosive. He was also extremely miserly, a trait some scholars believe may have led his son to overcompensate by becoming a reckless spendthrift. The writer's mother, Marya Fyodorovna Dostoyevskaya, was chronically ill, but she was a loving mother and a rare soothing presence in his boyhood home. She was also a practical woman, an efficient manager of the household affairs.

Given his austere upbringing, it is not surprising that there is virtually no evidence of the young Dostoyevsky ever falling in love. The surviving letters from his twenties reveal a dreamy young man who adored his older brother, Mikhail, with whom he shared a passion for literature and all that was "sublime and beautiful." But there is no mention of any strong romantic attachment—a stark contrast to young Leo Tolstoy, seven years his junior, whose youthful letters and diaries are chock-full of frank descriptions of tormented love affairs and visits to brothels. In her memoirs, Anna says "it seemed strange" that her husband "had never in his youth experienced a really passionate, serious love for any woman. His writing consumed him wholly, and therefore his personal life receded into the background." One exception in these early years, which Dostoyevsky likely never shared with his wife, was a passing liaison with a Petersburg prostitute, mentioned obliquely in a letter to Mikhail.

Dostoyevsky did have one other emotional outlet: As a student at the Petersburg Academy of Military Engineers he became a devotee of card parties, gambling regularly with his flatmates. He also became fascinated by the game of billiards, reportedly losing large sums to professional sharpers. At first he was able to cover his losses out of the regular income he was receiving from his father's small estate. But he was perpetually short on funds, often asking his relatives to lend him money, or taking advances against his modest officer's salary, or borrowing from shady creditors at extortionate rates of interest. One thrifty classmate remarked to Mikhail how appalled he was at Dostoyevsky's financial irresponsibility. This marked the beginning of a gambling habit that would flare up periodically throughout the writer's life, lying dormant for extended periods before recurring in often devastating ways.

Dostoyevsky's early professional life was no less challenging. The first brush with fame that came with the publication of *Poor Folk*, when he was twenty-four, fizzled with the failure of *The Double*, and critic Vissarion Belinsky's sudden reversal of his earlier praise left the young novelist scarred and embittered toward the literary establishment. Worse still, formidable new talents like Ivan Turgenev and Ivan Goncharov were starting to appear on the scene, making it clear to Dostoyevsky that he needed an important new novel to halt his decline and confirm the promise of *Poor Folk*. His third novel, *Netochka Nezvanova*, was to be that work. "I can't help feeling that I've begun a campaign against all our literature, journals, and critics," Dostoyevsky wrote to his brother Mikhail, "and with the three parts of my novel in *Fatherland Notes* [a prominent thick journal] this year I will again affirm my superiority in the teeth of all who wish me bad luck."

It was during this first downturn in his literary career that Dostoyevsky began pouring his energies into the Petrashevsky Circle, a close-knit group of young liberal men who dreamed of emancipating the peasants and instituting utopian socialism in Russia. The writer was twenty-five when he started attending the circle, whose aims resonated with his own deepest humanitarian instincts. "Dostoyevsky never was and could not have been a *revolutionary*," recalled a fellow Petrashevskyite, "but as a man of feeling he could become carried away with feelings of outrage and even anger in the face of violence committed against the humiliated and insulted."

Shortly after the first two parts of *Netochka Nezvanova* appeared in *Fatherland Notes* in 1849, Dostoyevsky was arrested along with the circle's other twenty-one members for his "criminal intentions of overthrowing the existing state order in Russia." The editor of *Fatherland Notes* had to obtain special government permission to publish the next installment he'd already received from the writer, who had now become a political convict. The third installment of *Netochka Nezvanova* was published with no author's name attached, and it received no mention in the press. As he languished in exile, Dostoyevsky's name vanished from the public eye for nearly a decade.

Dostoyevsky would never forget the harrowing ordeal of the mock execution—or the surge of ecstasy he felt on the December day when the tsar commuted his sentence and he realized that his life had been spared. "Life is everywhere," he wrote to his brother Mikhail on that day, "life is in ourselves, not in the exterior." His ordeal was not over: he would have to muster every ounce of strength to hold on to this belief through the four years he spent in prison, where he would undergo not only profound suffering but a metamorphosis of many of his social and spiritual beliefs. Getting to know the Russian peasantry and working classes for the first time, he became convinced that they would never share the utopian so-cialist ideals he and the other members of the Petrashevsky Circle had once preached. At the same time, in watching his fellow inmates, he came to recognize that their coarseness and brutality masked an underlying be-lief in the Christian values of love and self-sacrifice—a faith that many educated Russians had lost.

These prison-camp years also ushered in Dostoyevsky's epilepsy, the disease that would haunt him for the rest of his life. The psychological shock of the mock execution itself and sudden redemption from the grave, which drove some of his fellow Petrashevskyites literally insane, may well have been the initial trigger for his affliction. If there was any silver lining to his illness, however, it was the feeling of spiritual epiphany it afforded him: before his attacks Dostoyevsky often experienced an ecstatic aura that filled him with a rapturous feeling of plenitude, a sense of having merged completely with his fellow man and his surroundings—a vision of uni-versal harmony that would inspire intimations of transcendence in his fic-tion. In his novels, Dostoyevsky's most deeply held spiritual convictions are often voiced by epileptic heroes, including Prince Myshkin in *The Idiot*.

When he was released from prison camp, at the age of thirty-two, Dostoyevsky was transferred to the Seventh Siberian Line Battalion in Semipalatinsk, where he was allowed to leave the barracks and live in pri-vate quarters. There he met Marya Dmitriyevna Isayeva, the unhappy, consumptive wife of a poor, alcoholic civil servant. She felt "pity for an unfortunate man crushed by fate," recalled Dostoyevsky's friend Baron Alexander Egorovich Vrangel. "For his part, Fyodor Mikhailovich took her feeling of pity and compassion as love, and he fell in love with her with all the ardor of youth."

When Marya's husband died a few years later, Dostoyevsky proposed to her, and she accepted. Penniless, he begged his relatives to pay for the wedding and help him support his new young stepson, Pavel Alexandrovich Isayev, known as Pasha to his intimates. This marriage between two high-strung, impractical, financially strapped individuals was unhappy from the start, founded not on mature partnership but rather on an unhealthy codependency that was to become a pattern in Dostoyevsky's relationships with women. "In fact, the more unhappy we became," he told Vrangel, "the closer our bond became."

During his years in Semipalatinsk, the writer's interest in gambling grew into something of an obsession, according to one of the girls he tutored in the town: "At one time," she recalled, "Dostoyevsky seemed to be addicted to gambling. People used to gamble a great deal here." To another companion, Dostoyevsky raved about one exciting turn at billiards: "My, that was a hot game! It's rotten not to have any money. A devil's game like that is like quicksand. I see and understand how vile this monstrous passion is. . . . Yet it draws me, it sucks me in."

In the late 1850s, Dostoyevsky resumed his literary work, producing a few minor short stories that were met with silence. After being allowed to return to Petersburg in 1859, he plunged into a maelstrom of social and political debates about the future of Russia. Encouraged by the Great Reforms of Alexander II, Dostoyevsky believed that some of his earlier social ideals were becoming a reality, but he was disturbed by the emergence of a new brand of radical intelligentsia who worshipped Western ideas, mocked religion, and naively believed that science and reason could solve Russia's social ills. Dostoyevsky's experience with criminals in Siberia had given him a new perspective on the profound mysteries and contradictions of the human personality, and convinced him that the radical intelligentsia not only failed to understand the Russian people but were in many cases ruthless egoists posing as social crusaders.

In 1861, Fyodor and Mikhail Dostoyevsky launched *Time*, their effort to steer a middle course between the radical intelligentsia and the conservatives, who believed that the path to a better future for their country lay in a strong autocracy and a renewed commitment to ancient Russian traditions and values. Through their journal the brothers hoped to reconcile these two warring groups by espousing a kind of mystical Russian populism known as *pochvennichestvo*, or "back to the soil," that would unite the intelligentsia with the people. In a matter of two years, *Time* developed into one of Russia's most important journals, even as the Dostoyevskys grew concerned that the schisms within Russian society had grown so severe as to be unbridgeable.

Time was a commercial success as well, thanks in large part to the skillful editorship and literary contributions of Dostoyevsky himself. It was a time of new triumphs for the writer: within the journal's first two years he debuted the extremely popular *The Insulted and Injured,* his first major work since returning from Siberia, and *Notes from the House of the Dead,* which created a sensation and would forever link Dostoyevsky, in the eyes of the Russian public, with the halo of his past suffering.

Yet the writer himself was barely able to enjoy these successes. He was struggling under the crushing burden of running a magazine, Marya Dmitriyevna was rapidly declining ("My wife is dying, *literally*"), and his financial problems were mounting. "My nerves are shot," he told Mikhail. "I am so grimly tormented by *so many things* that I don't even wish to speak of them." In the two and a half years before he met Anna Snitkina, his professional and personal torments would get worse before they got better.

AS DOSTOYEVSKY'S MONOLOGUES to his new stenographer continued, his disclosures grew bolder. "Anna, I'm standing at a crossroads," he told her one day between dictation sessions. "There are three paths open to me: to go East—to Constantinople and Jerusalem—and remain there, maybe forever; or to go abroad to play roulette and immolate myself in the game I find so utterly engrossing; or maybe to marry again and find joy and happiness in family life. Which would you recommend?"

By all means, she told him, he should marry again and find happiness in a family.

"So you think I can marry again?" he asked. "What kind of wife shall I choose then—an intelligent one or a kind one?"

"An intelligent one, of course."

It was an unusual conversation for a writer to be having with his amanuensis, but Anna didn't seem to mind. It was clear that her lonely employer, "apparently abandoned by everyone," appreciated having someone to talk to. And she happened to enjoy their "utterly fascinating conversations."

As much as Anna learned from Dostoyevsky directly, he revealed as much through the novel he was dictating to her. *The Gambler* was based closely on his own manic gambling sprees in the few years before he met Anna, along with his ongoing secret affair with a woman named Apollinaria Prokofyevna Suslova, known as Polina. The novel stands as an acute psychological portrait of Dostoyevsky himself as a man, a gambler, and an artist.

The Gambler is told as a confession by a young man named Alexei Ivanovich, who works as a tutor in the home of General Zagoryansky, now living abroad. By the time the novel opens, Alexei has left his position with the general to become an inveterate gambler, living hand to mouth among the roulette tables of Europe's most famous spas. Only this Alexei—his name containing in Russian overtones of both nobility and naivete—is no ordinary gambler. Whereas the novel's many polished but passionless European characters come to the casino out of base self-interest, calculating material desire, Alexei is motivated by deeper psychic needs—above all, the need to prove himself at any cost, to prove that he is a man, not a machine: "I think around four hundred friederichs d'or came into my hands in some five minutes," Alexei confesses at one point. "I should have walked away right then, but some strange sensation was born in me, some defiance of fate, some desire to give it a flick, to stick my tongue out at it." Winning at roulette becomes, for him, an assertion of his very humanity: "It came to one thousand seven hundred guldens, and that in less than five minutes!" he exclaims. "But in such moments you forget all your previous failures! For I had obtained it at the risk of more than life, I had dared to risk and—here I was numbered among the human beings again!"

The novel's second major story line involves Alexei's tempestuous affair with the general's stepdaughter, an alluring femme fatale named Polina who toys cruelly with his heart. Alexei does bring his own brand of egotism to their relationship: there are hints that Polina may actually like this daring, noble-hearted gambler, but he is so obsessed with his slavish subservience to her that he eventually drives Polina away with his insistence on his own inferiority. Nevertheless, Alexei falls prey to Polina's exhilarating game of cat and mouse. In his mind, Polina is capable of raising him to the heavens or crushing him, much as the roulette wheel spins, only to deliver, in one irrevocable second, its terrifying verdict: Is he to leave anointed as a king or a pauper?

By the time of Anna's arrival, the dangerous allure of the roulette table was coming back to Dostoyevsky—just as he was embarking on the most serious professional gamble of his career. The stakes could not have been higher: if he failed to deliver the new novel to Fyodor Stellovsky, he would forfeit the rights to any writing income for the next nine years. As Dostoyevsky was well aware, Stellovsky had already proven himself capable of destroying vulnerable artists: he'd acquired the complete works of the composer Mikhail Glinka, for instance, for a paltry sum, financially ruining one of nineteenth-century Russia's musical giants. Clearly, he wasn't above treating Dostoyevsky just as poorly.

And yet . . . if Dostoyevsky won the wager with Stellovsky, it would provide him with that almost metaphysical rush of pleasure he and his hero Alexei so craved—the satisfaction of besting that vile literary speculator through the seemingly impossible feat of producing a full-length novel in less than a month. The only question was: Could he do it?

THREE YEARS BEFORE ANNA'S ARRIVAL, in August 1863, forty-one-year-old Dostoyevsky had gazed out of a train window at the blurry lines of the Rhine Valley's forested hills rushing past. In his portmanteau he carried a picture of a twenty-one-year-old woman with a face as serene as an icon's, marked by deep-set sorrowful black eyes and smoothly parted dark hair lifted into a tight braid. She was wearing a white blouse that revealed her firm, seductive neck. No dainty European princess, this was a pure Russian beauty—intense and sorrowful and unpredictable—with lips, firm and strong, that suggested her peasant ancestry.

Scholars disagree about the exact date and circumstances of the first meeting between Dostoyevsky and Apollinaria Suslova—whether she had written him a "naïve, poetic letter" professing her love, as Dostoyevsky's daughter, Lyubov', later claimed in a book about her father, or he approached her himself after publishing her story "In a While" in 1861. Whatever the circumstances of their initial encounter, the reasons for their attraction are understandable. The passionate and attractive Polina represented, for Dostoyevsky, a needed escape from the rigors of intense creative work, as well as the daily battles of running a journal and the strain of his increasingly unhappy marriage to the ailing Marya Dmitriyevna.

As for Polina, Dostoyevsky was her first serious flame; she had a stern and judgmental character, and he alone seemed capable of satisfying her high expectations. "All my friends are kind people," she told her diary, "but weak and poor in spirit; they are abundant in their words, but poor in their deeds. I haven't met a single one among them who would not be afraid of the truth, or who wouldn't have retreated before the conventions of life." Dostoyevsky was different. This daring man who had once defied the government and suffered for his political beliefs, whose novel *Notes from the House of the Dead* had transformed his own harrowing experiences into art, entranced her. His small frame and morose demeanor were more than outweighed by his very evident spiritual qualities; later, speaking of her love for Dostoyevsky with an acquaintance, Polina would say that "during my first youth I paid no attention to beauty."

By the summer of 1863, their affair was in full swing. Earlier in the year, Dostoyevsky had promised Polina that they would meet up in Italy, but complications kept interfering. For one thing, *Time* had been banned by the government for a piece Mikhail had approved for publication, an article the censors deemed unpatriotic. The brothers Dostoyevsky were now scrambling to resurrect their journal under a different name. The writer's epilepsy was getting steadily worse, rendering him incapable of work for weeks at a time, while his younger brother Nikolai, who had been unwell for most of his adult life, was about to go into the hospital yet again. And Dostoyevsky was worried about his failing wife and his teenage stepson, Pasha, whose financial and academic irresponsibility weighed on him.

Desperate for relief from the stress, but unable to afford the trip to Italy on his own, Dostoyevsky turned to the Society for Aid to Needy Writers and Scholars, also known as the Literary Fund. In July 1863, he applied for a loan of fifteen hundred rubles, purportedly "for the treatment of my health and for consultation with European medical specialists about my falling sickness." So anxious was he to get to Europe that he promised the Society that, should he fail to pay back the loan by the following February, he would cede to them the rights in perpetuity to all of his previously published work. Though aware of the risk, Dostoyevsky was determined to see Polina at any cost. Yet he remained tormented by guilt over his betrayal of his dying wife, and over leaving his brother and stepson, who needed him at home. "To seek happiness after abandoning everything, even what you could have been useful to," he admitted to Mikhail in a letter that summer, "is selfishness, and that thought is now poisoning my happiness (if in fact it even exists)."

And yet here he was, on his way to Paris to meet Polina.

As the train sped through the German countryside, Dostoyevsky's excitement grew until it triggered, or was channeled into, another urge altogether: the urge to gamble.

He dashed off a note to tell Polina that he had decided to stop for a few days in Wiesbaden, a German spa and gambling resort on the outskirts of the Taunus mountain range, in the lush Rhine Valley. It was not the first time Dostoyevsky had visited this famed *Weltkurstadt*, or world-class spa town, long a favorite destination not only of European artists like Goethe, Wagner, and Balzac, but also of Russian literary talent. The previous year, during an extensive European trip, Dostoyevsky had spent a day in Wiesbaden, trying his luck with extraordinary results—at least at first. Almost immediately he'd won eleven thousand francs, or just over sixty-two thousand dollars in today's money, an astronomical sum for a financially strapped writer. But then his fortunes suddenly reversed, and he lost it all.

Now, in August 1863, he decided to return to the tables of Wiesbaden, convincing himself that a stint at roulette would be a surefire way for him to acquire necessary funds quickly—though he surely recognized that other forces were also at work within him. He loved to be in that dangerous and intoxicating place, where in a matter of seconds one could go from nothing to everything, everything to nothing. "The point here is that—one turn of the wheel, and everything changes," says Alexei in *The Gambler*. "What am I now? *Zéro*. What may I be tomorrow? Tomorrow I may rise from the dead and begin to live anew! I may find the man in me before he's lost!" In that stressful summer, weighed down by crushing professional burdens and a guilty conscience over his betrayal of his wife and abandonment of those who relied on him, Dostoyevsky needed just such a resurrection.

As soon as he arrived at the Wiesbaden train station, the novelist hired a cab to the nearby Hotel Victoria, checked into his room, and then walked briskly past the familiar sights of the Wilhelmstrasse to the casino less than a half mile away. The surroundings were magnificent: palatial hotels lining the cobblestone street, a majestic, perfectly manicured park in the English style, picturesque fountains and three cascading waterfalls illuminated from within by gaslight. In the middle of the park, flanked by elegant colonnades, was the famed Kurhaus, or casino, a neoclassical building of red sandstone. Along the colonnades were two rows of small boutiques where wealthy guests could purchase lace and silk fabrics, delicate glassware, and other fine goods beyond Dostoyevsky's means. On the casino grounds, a few hundred feet away from the Kurhaus itself, was a famous theater, hosting stars like the singer Adelina Patti.

As he approached the entrance to the Kurhaus, Dostoyevsky grew alert, alive to each prickling moment. After checking in with the concierge, he headed straight for the vast gaming hall. Inside, hundreds of brilliant chandelier gaslights illuminated orderly piles of gold and silver coins spread out on the green baize of the tables. Elegant men in sport-coats or cutaways and top hats and women in enormous crinolines and ornately decorated hats crowded around the action.

Wasting no time, Dostoyevsky took his place at one of the tables and placed his first bet. Then another. And another. Within an hour he won 10,400 francs, or just under sixty thousand dollars today—enough for him to live decently for over two years and more than he had earned from any book he'd written to date. It was an uncanny replay of his run of good luck the previous summer. "Tell me how I couldn't have been carried away after that," he wrote Mikhail a few weeks later. "How could I fail to be-lieve that if I follow my system strictly, luck is in my hands? And I need money, for me, for you, for my wife, for writing a novel. Tens of thousands are won here easily. And besides, I came here with the idea of saving all of you and myself from disaster." Gambling addiction researchers today would call this magical thinking, an irrational, compulsive belief in the existence of a system that, once divined and rigorously adhered to, will inevitably result in success.

Shoving his winnings deep in his pockets, Dostoyevsky rushed to his room and locked the money in a large travel bag. He vowed to himself that he would leave Wiesbaden the next day, without returning to the roulette table, and he tried valiantly to keep this promise, but as day turned to dusk, the waiting became unbearable. Finally he retrieved a portion of the money and hurried back to the casino, determined to con-quer the spinning wheel one more time. Only this time, as before, came the mistakes, and with them the losses.

The next day he was back at the Kurhaus, and the day after that, and the day after that—winning and losing, over and over again, until, by the fourth day, he'd lost nearly half of what he'd won within that first hour. Fearful that he could no longer control himself, he stuffed most of the remaining five thousand francs into two envelopes: one to his brother Mikhail, instructing him to hold on to the money until he returned to Petersburg, and the other to his sister-in-law, Varvara Konstant, who was to deliver the money to Dostoyevsky's wife, Marya Dmitriyevna.

In a letter to Varvara, Dostoyevsky tried to explain why his system had suddenly failed him. Many gamblers, he said, lose their shirts because they don't know how to gamble. But he *knew* perfectly well the secret to winning: "It simply consists of restraining oneself at every moment, no matter at what phase of the game, and of not losing one's head. That's it, and by following it, it's impossible to lose." The rub, he insisted, was "whether, having learned this secret, a person is able to take advantage of it. You can be as wise as Solomon, with the most iron character and still lose control. . . . And therefore blessed are they who do not gamble and who view the roulette table with repulsion as the greatest stupidity." Alas, he was not one of these temperate souls.

Dostoyevsky was fast discovering another secret: that beneath all the shimmering beauty of the Kurhaus, the old-world elegance and refined entertainment, lay a culture of hideous exploitation and ruin. This truth was first revealed to the Russian public in 1859 by a well-known Russian journalist, Fyodor Dershau, in a scathing exposé of European casino life. Prior to Dershau's article, Russians had long associated gambling with upper-class refinement, largely because so many among the nobility were gamblers. One contemporary manual outlined how any "pleasant player" must face even the heaviest losses: with composure, dignity, calmness, and confidence. "A true gentleman, even if he loses his entire fortune, must not show emotion," says Alexei in *The Gambler*. "Money should be so far beneath the gentlemanly condition, that it is almost not worth worrying about." But Alexei, like his creator, belonged to the "plebeian, mercenary" category of gambler, the "riffraff" who could not afford to uphold such gentlemanly rules, and instead "play very filthily," getting worked up over every ruble won and lost.

Such a gambler would have felt especially out of place in European casinos, which catered to "higher, better society," as one local authority in the gambling resort of Baden-Baden put it. These casinos, with their opulent, French-inspired architecture, upheld their air of exclusivity by operating only during certain hours, maintaining strict dress codes, and offering refined entertainment and fine dining.

Dershau's article, called "From the Notes of a Gambler," showed Russians the ugly reality beneath this glamorous facade. European casinos, he said, were cold-blooded institutions, backed by a powerful administration of city governments and professionally trained croupiers whose sole mission was to take advantage of human weakness and separate players from their money. The house always won—and not because of any superior mathematical odds, but simply because the system pitted a soullessly rational machine against human players who were unable to resist natural greed and temptation. By way of illustration, the journalist told the story of a man who won a half million francs, only to lose them again a few weeks later, because he could not resist the compulsion to return to the casino in order to win even more.

Dershau took special aim at the image of casinos as places of high culture and refined entertainment. Of the casino in Bad Homburg, he wrote:

> Here in this den of social evil reigns the complete debauchery of stormy, boiling passions, and often entire fortunes are lost here in the course of a few hours. . . . But no matter how striking its luxury, how remarkable the great, lacquered gaming hall and famous terrace; no matter how brilliant the endless balls and celebrations given here; no matter how great the efforts of the local administration to ennoble the Homburg casino with blinding external brilliance, nothing can smooth over the sharply conspicuous character of a gaming den.

It was a symbol of the German casinos' depravity, Dershau noted, that players who had lost everything were routinely given just enough money so they could go somewhere else to shoot or hang themselves. One desperate young man who'd lost his entire fortune had shot himself in front of spectators crowding around the roulette table at the famous Wiesbaden Kurhaus. "This sad event did not even interrupt the gambling," Dershau reported. "The man calling out the numbers went on turning the wheel with the same cold-bloodedness with which he'd just ordered the attendants to clean off the green baize of the treacherous table onto which the brains had spurted from the dead gambler's shattered head."

Dostoyevsky likely read "From the Notes of a Gambler" when it came out in 1859; the article may even have provided him with an initial impetus for *The Gambler*, whose subtitle, *From the Notes of a Young Man*, echoes the title of Dershau's article. But he hardly needed Dershau to confirm what he himself had learned through personal experience in Wiesbaden's Kurhaus over those agonizing four days in the summer of 1863.

Repulsed as he was by this glittering den of vice, Dostoyevsky was unable to stay away. The thrill of standing on the edge of the abyss overpowered any intentions of self-discipline he may have brought to the gaming rooms. Though he insisted to himself and others that he gambled simply to earn fast money and help those who needed him, the truth was that gambling had become its own reward, a form of metaphysical delight and the illusion of spiritual transcendence. In the vast gaming hall, amid the gentle whoosh of the wooden carousel and the implacable click of the ivory ball, Dostoyevsky felt truly alive. No wonder he loved these lines from Pushkin:

> *In all, all that portends doom*
> *Is concealed in the mortal heart*
> *An inexplicable pleasure*
> *A security deposit, perhaps, on immortality.*

After his stint in Wiesbaden, hoping that Polina's company would assuage his bruised ego, Dostoyevsky rushed to Paris. But when she greeted him at her hotel room door, on the evening of August 14, 1863, he could tell from her trembling voice and tear-stained eyes that something was wrong.

"I thought you weren't going to come," she said in an agitated voice. "I wrote you a letter."

"What letter?" he responded with concern.

"So you wouldn't come."

"Why not?" he said, the fear rising in his voice.

"Because it's too late."

He hung his head. "I must know everything," he said, "let's go somewhere, and tell me or I'll die."

She suggested that they go to his hotel room. They rode in silence,

Polina never meeting his gaze. Dostoyevsky guessed what had happened: she'd found another man. When they got to his room, he fell suddenly at her feet, hugging her knees and sobbing. "I have lost you, I knew it!" he cried. Then, regaining his composure, he began to ask her about the other man. "Perhaps he is handsome, young, and glib. But you will never find a heart such as mine."

His name was Salvador, she told him, and he was a Spaniard, a medical student. Dostoyevsky pressed her for more information, urged her to change her mind. When he realized it was hopeless, he switched tactics, telling Polina how much she meant to him, begging her to remain his friend. He even suggested that they travel to Italy together as they'd planned, only now "like brother and sister." When she hesitated, he launched into one final desperate plea. "I love you to distraction," he said. "I can't tell you how much I love you, and if you knew it, you would not have made me suffer what I have suffered." But she would continue to do just that—to start with, by agreeing to continue on to Italy together, after all.

Three days later, en route to Italy, they stopped in Baden-Baden. Dostoyevsky played roulette every day, losing heavily enough that he was forced to send an urgent letter asking his wife to return a portion of the money he'd sent her through Varvara the week before. He also wrote to Mikhail, asking him to scrape together whatever he could find and send it to him right away. Meanwhile, determined to reverse his romantic fortunes, he insisted to Polina that he still had hopes that she would return his affection. "I did not say anything to this," Polina recounted in her diary, "but I knew that it was not going to happen." The next day Dostoyevsky tried to resume the conversation, but Polina refused to engage with him on the subject, "so that he could neither cherish hope nor be quite without it."

So that he could neither cherish hope nor be quite without it: the phrase captured Polina's approach to Dostoyevsky not only for the remainder of their two-month-long journey but for the next several years of their fitful love-hate relationship. From Baden-Baden they went on to Turin, then to Rome and finally Naples, where they parted ways with their romance still in limbo. Dostoyevsky briefly returned alone to Turin; then, before head-ing home, he stopped in the chic gambling resort of Bad Homburg, where several days at the tables left him penniless. When he wrote Polina to ask for money, she sent him three hundred rubles. By the time Dostoyevsky returned to Petersburg, he had nothing to show for his travels but empty pockets and the barest outline of a new novel—the story of a gambler who fritters away his life in European casinos.

IN JANUARY 1864, a ray of hope appeared on the horizon. After the sudden closing of *Time*, Dostoyevsky and his brother received permission to resurrect their banned journal and publish it under the new name of *Epoch*. Appearing in the magazine's first issue, in March of that year, was the beginning of another new work: *Notes from Underground*. Given the magazine's eleventh-hour reprieve—and his own precarious fortunes—the novelist was staking a great deal on this unusual, intensely philosophical novel. "It's absolutely essential that it be good," Fyodor told Mikhail. "I *myself* need that." He was also hoping that working on *Notes* might take his mind off recent news from the doctor that his wife hadn't long to live.

Less than a month later, on April 15, 1864, Marya Dmitriyevna passed away. After burying her with her family in Moscow, Dostoyevsky rushed back to Petersburg, to his brother—"the only person I have left," he would later tell his friend Baron Vrangel. To Dostoyevsky's horror, though, he found that Mikhail, too, was dying now, of a serious liver illness that had gone undetected for two years—brought on, Dostoyevsky was certain, by the enormous stresses of running the journal. Three months later Mikhail died, leaving Dostoyevsky not only bereft but buried under a fresh mountain of personal and professional challenges. "Suddenly I was left alone, and I was simply terrified," he told Vrangel. "My whole life had been broken in two at once. In one half, which I had crossed through, was everything I had lived for, and in the other, as yet unknown half, everything was alien, everything new, and there was not a single heart that could have replaced those two for me. I had literally nothing left to live for."

The death of Mikhail brought a host of complications, as Dostoyevsky vowed to carry on running *Epoch* himself while taking responsibility for nearly thirty thousand rubles (more than three hundred thousand dollars today) of his brother's debt—to protect his brother's posthumous reputation, and to keep Mikhail's family from falling into poverty. "His family was left literally without any means," Dostoyevsky wrote Vrangel; "they may as well have gone begging." It would have been easier to close down the journal or offer it to creditors, freeing him to focus on his own stalled writing career. Instead, Dostoyevsky made a trip to Moscow to collect a sum of ten thousand rubles that a wealthy old aunt had agreed to advance him as his share of her will, and then poured that money into keeping the journal afloat. But the censors would not permit this former political prisoner to use his own name on the journal, either as an editor or as the publisher, forcing him to publish the magazine anonymously, which of course diminished sales.

In the months that followed, Dostoyevsky's literary career was in free fall. The final installment of *Notes from Underground* had run in *Epoch* in June; though today it is considered a masterpiece of philosophical fiction, in its time it was a flop—bizarre, confounding, and, to most of his contemporaries, downright repulsive. Now his own writing—not to mention his health and spirits—took a back seat to his desperate efforts to save the magazine. Working day and night editing pieces, corresponding with authors and censors, reading proofs, and handling the accounting, he rarely managed more than five hours' sleep and was unable to find a moment's free time to publish anything of his own in the journal. "The public," he said, "did not encounter my name, and even in Petersburg, not just in the provinces, people didn't know that I was the journal's editor."

On June 9, 1865, *Epoch* formally announced it was closing, leaving Dostoyevsky with a slew of new debt and an undertow of shame over his failure to keep the journal alive. "I would gladly go into penal servitude again for just as many years," he wrote, "just so as to pay off the debts and again feel free."

He did have a few ideas for generating income. He would start up a publishing imprint to bring out his own works; he'd create a popular almanac of his miscellaneous fiction and personal reflections on contemporary events; he'd find a publisher to bring out his complete collected works. Of all these plans, however, only one came to fruition: it was around this time that Dostoyevsky attracted the interest of the publisher Fyodor Stellovsky, and their acquaintance soon led the flailing writer into the disastrous contract, signed on July 1, 1865, that would imperil his career.

"I'm alone," he told Vrangel. "I no longer have my former friends or my former forty-year-old self with me. And meanwhile, I keep thinking that I am only just preparing to live. It's funny, isn't it?"

THE INFLUX OF MONEY from Stellovsky may well have helped account for this uncharacteristic moment of optimism. But there was another reason: once again, Dostoyevsky had fallen in love. This time he was courting Anna Vasilyevna Korvin-Krukovskaya, the tall and beautiful twenty-two-year-old daughter of a retired general and landowner in the Vitebsk province on Russia's western frontier.

Dostoyevsky had become acquainted with this talented aspiring writer the year before, when she submitted two stories, "Dream" and "Mikhail," for publication in *Epoch*. The stories were submitted under a pseudonym, because Anna's conservative father "did so hate women writers," according to her sister Sofya, "and suspected every one of them of behavior that had nothing to do with literature." In December 1864, along with payment of 181 rubles for her work, Dostoyevsky sent a letter to the young woman revealing that he was charmed by the "youthful directness, sincerity, and warmth of feeling" he'd sensed in her story, and inviting her to strike up a correspondence. Anna naturally agreed, grateful for his interest in her literary career.

For Dostoyevsky, though, the motives were also personal. In those crushingly lonely months after the deaths of his wife and brother, the arrival of this young writer meant the possibility of a platonic epistolary romance that might lead to something more, much as his publishing relationship with another aspiring young female writer, Polina Suslova, led to a romantic affair.

Korvin-Krukovskaya kept her correspondence with this well-known

writer strictly confidential, but one day her father happened upon the letter in which Dostoyevsky tried to engage her interest. "Anything may be
expected from a girl who is capable of entering into correspondence with
a strange man unknown to her father and mother and receiving money
from him," he lectured his daughter. "You sell your novels now, but the
time will probably come when you will sell yourself."

With time, however—and steady persuasion from his wife—the general softened. Reluctant to see his family torn apart by the sort of ideological conflict captured brilliantly in Turgenev's recent *Fathers and
Sons*, he reconciled with his daughter, allowing her to resume her correspondence with Dostoyevsky, and even to meet him on an upcoming
family trip to visit relatives in Petersburg—under her mother's strict supervision, of course. "Remember, Liza, a great responsibility will rest
upon you," Korvin-Krukovsky told his wife. "Dostoyevsky is not a man of
our society. What do we know about him? Only that he is a journalist,
and a former convict. A fine recommendation! There's no disputing it;
you must be very, very cautious with him."

Their first meeting, in March 1865, was awkward, to say the least. The
novelist and erstwhile editor appeared at the relatives' grand drawing
room, shifting uncomfortably as Anna's mother, her sister Sofya, and two
elderly German aunts stared at him as if he were some exotic beast. Five
days later, however, Dostoyevsky paid another visit, and this time he
found Anna and Sofya alone. This encounter was "the height of success,"
Sofya would remember, admitting that she herself was developing a bit of
a crush on the older man. He continued to visit them throughout their
stay, usually in the evening, sometimes as often as three or four times a
week, enthralling everyone present with stories from his professional and
personal lives.

Toward the end of their stay, Mrs. Korvin-Krukovskaya invited Dostoyevsky to a party she was hosting for her lofty circle of Petersburg acquaintances. It was a "stately, airy, and colorless" event, Sofya recalled, with
servants in tailcoats and white gloves gravely carrying around trays of tea,
fruits, and sweets to the sepulchral guests. Dostoyevsky arrived in an ill-
fitting suit and soon grew irritated and confused, as he often did in the

company of strangers. When the hostess tried to introduce him to the other guests, he growled unintelligibly and turned his back, finally retreating to sulk in a corner alone.

One guest caught Dostoyevsky's attention, however: a distant relative of the Korvin-Krukovsky family, a suave and handsome young officer in dashing epaulets. One look at this smooth operator and Dostoyevsky hated him. When the younger man finally sat down in an armchair by Anna, leaning over to whisper in her ear, Dostoyevsky was beside himself with rage. Overhearing Anna's mother, a woman of German descent, remark that one advantage of Protestantism over the Russian Orthodox Church was that Protestants read the Gospels more often, Dostoyevsky pounced. "But were the Gospels written for *society* women?" he snarled from his corner. "It is written, 'In the beginning God created man and wife,' or again, 'The man shall leave his father and mother and cleave to his wife.' That's the way Christ understood marriage. But what would be said of it by the mamas who think of nothing but how to get their daughters off their hands in the most profitable manner?" A long, uncomfortable hush fell over the room, until finally the guests turned back to one another and started talking loudly, as if to drown out the memory of Dostoyevsky's faux pas.

Surprisingly, Dostoyevsky continued to call upon the family even after the fiasco. Etiquette required them to welcome him, but by now Anna had lost interest in him, and she began to take pleasure in contradicting and even teasing him during each visit. Sensing that she was slipping away from him, Dostoyevsky grew demanding, insisting that she tell him how she'd spent the day and with whom, and shunning any young man who seemed to have her interest. Anna started to avoid her older suitor, pretending not to notice him, or engaging another guest in conversation as he approached. On one occasion, after he'd had enough of her taunting, Dostoyevsky finally blurted: "You are an empty-headed, silly, naughty little girl; that's what you are!" On another, he dismissed the young people of the time as "dull and half-educated," more interested in revolutionary fantasies than in the monumental work of Alexander Pushkin, Dostoyevsky's favorite writer. Unafraid of provoking him, Anna responded nonchalantly that

Pushkin was considered outdated now. Enraged, Dostoyevsky snatched his hat and stormed out, declaring that it was useless to argue with a little Nihilist, and that he would never set foot in their house again. The next day, he returned as if nothing had happened.

A few days before their departure from Petersburg, in late April, the novelist arrived in a strangely amiable mood. After escorting Anna into the dimly lit drawing room, he asked her to join him on a small divan, took her hand, leaned toward her, and proposed to her.

Anna declined his offer.

DOSTOYEVSKY SPENT THE FOLLOWING MONTHS in excruciating loneliness, his mood depressed further by his penury and neglected career. Longing for a solution to this dire overall state, he turned once more to the woman he had begun describing as his "eternal mate," Polina Suslova. The two had not seen each other since 1863, but their correspondence continued, even as Polina wandered through Russia and Europe in search of intellectuals and artists and lovers to pique her interest.

Dostoyevsky had long harbored hopes to rekindle their affair, peppering his letters with subtle hints—and sometimes outright entreaties— that the two might marry. Though she rebuffed his overtures, Polina nevertheless declined to put an end to their relationship. In the spring of 1865, Dostoyevsky poured out his agony in a letter to Polina's sister, Nadezhda Suslova. "Apollinaria is a sick egoist," he told her. "In her relations with me there is absolutely no humanity. After all, she knows that I love her even now. Why does she torture me, then? Fine, don't love me, but then don't torture me either."

And yet he longed to see that same "sick egoist," so much so that, in June 1865, he sent a new appeal to the Literary Fund, explaining his straitened circumstances (the demise of *Epoch*, his poor health, his pressing debts) and asking for a loan to help him get to Europe, where he could work in peace on a promising new novel. The loan was granted, and by the end of July, Dostoyevsky was in Wiesbaden, where Polina was due to arrive en route from Zurich to Paris. He was also hoping for a return of the luck that had occasioned his fast and glorious win at Wiesbaden's Kurhaus two years earlier, conveniently forgetting the disaster that followed.

Sure enough, five days into his stay, the inevitable occurred: he lost everything, down to the very last ruble from the watch he'd pawned. Desperate, he appealed to Ivan Turgenev, then living in Baden-Baden, for a loan of a hundred thalers. The two writers were cordial, but they were hardly close friends, making the request—more than a thousand dollars today—all the more presumptuous for Dostoyevsky. Turgenev sent him fifty thalers, which he said was all he could afford at the time. Dostoyevsky would not pay back the loan until 1876; it became a long-running source of embarrassment for him, and a point of tension in the writers' increasingly acrimonious relationship.

Arriving in Wiesbaden just as the penniless Dostoyevsky was on the verge of being dragged out of the Hotel Victoria and off to the police, Polina must have seemed like a ray of hope. It is not clear what transpired between them during the several days of this reunion; Dostoyevsky had been hoping to rekindle their love, even to accompany her to Paris, but if he made such an overture we can reasonably assume she rebuffed him. After a few days she departed, leaving the writer to his lonely indigence.

Days later, he wrote Polina that "my situation has worsened unbelievably. No sooner had you left, than on the morning of the very next day I was told at the hotel that orders had been given not to serve me dinner or tea or coffee." Nor would they clean his clothes, or come when he called. "All the servants treat me with an inexpressible, very German disdain. For a German there is no higher crime than to be without money and not to pay on time." Two days later, he told her in a subsequent letter, his affairs had become "abominable to the point of nec plus ultra; it couldn't be worse." The hotel was now denying him even the dignity of a leftover stub of candle in the evening. "I'm tormented by the inaction, the indefiniteness of a waiting situation without firm hope, the loss of time, and cursed Wiesbaden, which disgusts me so much that I can't even tell you."

He needed to get out, to escape to Paris, back home to Russia—anywhere but Wiesbaden, where the urge to play roulette was matched only by his excruciating inability to win. Yet he lacked even the money for postage, let alone train fare. "Save me and deliver me from misfortune," he pleaded to his friend Baron Vrangel. "Send me a hundred thalers for a very short time." He felt confident that Vrangel, who had seen him at the lowest point of his life—his Siberian exile—would not judge him. "That is why I in fact made up my mind to confess to you this stupid and craven act of mine. Let it be between us."

HELPLESS AS HIS SELF-IMMOLATION at roulette was, it also happened to inspire one of his boldest literary gambles to date. At this latest low point, Dostoyevsky hit upon a powerful idea for a new novel: the story of a young man, living in extreme poverty after being expelled from the university, who, "after yielding to certain strange, half-baked ideas floating in the air, has resolved, out of light-mindedness and out of the instability of his ideas, to get out of his foul situation at one go. He has resolved to murder an old woman." These are the words Dostoyevsky used to pitch to Mikhail Katkov, the powerful editor of one of Russia's leading conservative literary journals, *The Russian Messenger*, the idea for what would eventually become *Crime and Punishment*.

Dostoyevsky had dealt with Katkov in the 1850s, when the editor advanced him five hundred rubles for a story he never ended up submitting; after arguing over the terms of their agreement, the two had had a falling-out. But that was then, and this was now, and Dostoyevsky was desperate; if Katkov liked the idea for his novel, he asked, might the publisher be willing to send him three hundred rubles right away in Wiesbaden, as an advance? Katkov did just that, and so began one of the most important literary partnerships of Dostoyevsky's career.

Crime and Punishment would prove a deeply personal work, a novel in which the writer laid bare his own broken soul at a time of abject misery and shame. The novel's hero, Raskolnikov, is so crushed by poverty that he steals catlike in and out of his tiny Petersburg garret, overcome by "some painful and cowardly sensation" every time he passes his landlady, to whom he owes money. In a state of fevered self-loathing and resentment, he concocts a theory about how murdering a dishonest old pawnbroker who cheats and torments her clients will somehow save humanity from the scourge of her existence, while at the same time lifting him out of his own state of disgrace. So, too, Dostoyevsky, in the midst of his self-abasement in Wiesbaden, had concocted his own plan to extract himself from his situation "at one go"—not through murder, but by staking his future on this new novel.

By the end of September, Dostoyevsky had managed to escape Wiesbaden for Russia, thanks to funds from both Baron Vrangel and one Father Yanyshev, of Wiesbaden's Russian Orthodox Church; the publishing advance from Katkov reached him only once he was back in Petersburg. That entire fall and winter, the writer dedicated himself to *Crime and Punishment*. It was grueling work, especially given the other challenges he faced that fall—not least his efforts to put his late brother Mikhail's disastrous affairs in order. Emilya Fyodorovna was a constant thorn in his side; no matter how much help and financial support Dostoyevsky offered her and her family, it was never enough for the ungrateful widow. His irresponsible stepson, Pasha, was an endless source of concern, as was Dostoyevsky's own younger brother Nikolai, who had grown seriously ill. (Though perpetually unwell, Nikolai would survive his older brother by two years.) The stress undermined the writer's own health, his epileptic attacks growing steadily more severe.

Yet he was able to focus on the task at hand: the all-important new novel, whose first section would be due at *The Russian Messenger* at the beginning of 1866. "I have to put myself in confinement without money," he told Father Yanyshev in November, "in order to win incomparably more and, most importantly, *more certainly* later." Dostoyevsky also found the time to call on Polina, his "eternal mate," though he met with the usual, unfortunate results, as she told her diary: "Today F[yodor] M[ikhailovich] was here and we argued and contradicted each other all the time. For a long time now he has been offering me his hand and his heart, and he only makes me angry doing so."

As the hard fall months stretched into dreary winter, he worked nonstop, living on kopecks and spending what little money he had to support Pasha and Emilya Fyodorovna, who took his money while blaming him for her family's misfortunes. To his sister-in-law Domnika Dostoyevskaya, the author wrote, "You and brother Andrei seem to be the only *kind relatives* I have left." Baron Vrangel had also become like family now, one of the few people to whom Dostoyevsky felt comfortable pouring out his sorrows: "I'm working like a convict," he told his friend:

> I have grown nervous, irritable; my character has been ruined. I don't know what this will lead to. I haven't been to visit anyone all winter long, haven't seen anyone or anything. . . . And that's the way things will continue until the novel is finished—if I'm not put into debtors' prison. . . . My kind friend, you at least are happy in a family, but fate has denied me that great and *only* human happiness.

In April 1866, Dostoyevsky would make yet another effort to achieve that great happiness for himself. While visiting his relatives, the Ivanovs, in Moscow, he was introduced to a "pert and lively" twenty-year-old named Marya Ivanchin-Pisareva. The young woman captured his imagination, so much so that one morning, when the family had gone to Easter matins, Dostoyevsky stayed home with her and, completely out of the blue, proposed. Taken aback by the unexpected proposal from a man more than twice her age, Marya responded by quoting a line from Pushkin's poem *Poltava*: "Petrified by the years / The heart of the old man flames up." Thinking that she might flatter the writer with the literary reference, instead she broke the older man's heart.

Spurned again, Dostoyevsky continued to dedicate his energies to *Crime and Punishment*, the one thing capable, it now seemed, of resurrecting him. The first quarter of the novel had been published in the January and February 1866 issues of *The Russian Messenger*, but Dostoyevsky still had a long way to go. "With God's help," he told Vrangel, "this novel may be a superb piece. It will produce a sensation among the public. . . . The main thing is that my literary name will be reestablished." In a May letter, he conceded: "At the present moment it is my sole hope."

Dostoyevsky had good reason to believe that *Crime and Punishment* might reverse his fortunes. His first literary gamble since *Notes from the House of the Dead* three years earlier that truly seemed to be paying off, it was different from anything ever attempted in Russian literature, and readers eagerly awaited each new installment. So irresistibly intense and graphic was this "psychological account of a crime," as Dostoyevsky described the novel in his original pitch letter to Katkov, that even readers who were appalled by the realistic description of the murder and its aftermath could not put the book down. Interest in the serialized novel was bringing *The Russian Messenger* hundreds of new subscribers each month, endearing him to Katkov and catapulting him into the front ranks of literary Russia, alongside Leo Tolstoy and Ivan Turgenev. Almost as important, *Crime and Punishment* brought Dostoyevsky a regular income of a little over four hundred rubles a month.

There was just one complication. In the maelstrom of these last frenzied months of financial hardships and fresh literary hopes, Dostoyevsky had completely forgotten about the contract he'd signed a year earlier with Fyodor Stellovsky. Only in June 1866 did he suddenly realize that the deadline for the novel he owed Stellovsky was just four months away. Reluctant to interrupt work on *Crime and Punishment*, which was proving such a boost to his career, he offered to buy off Stellovsky by paying a forfeit. But the publisher refused. Dostoyevsky then asked Stellovsky for an extension of three months. Again the publisher refused, telling the writer "straight out," according to Dostoyevsky, "that since he's convinced that I now have no time to write a novel twelve signatures [192 printed pages]* in length . . . it's more advantageous for him to refuse an extension and a forfeit, because then everything I will write afterward will be his."

This is how Dostoyevsky described the matter to his former would-be fiancée, Anna Korvin-Krukovskaya, with whom he had maintained a polite correspondence despite their rocky past. Well aware that failing either to

---

*A signature, also known as a printed sheet, was the equivalent of sixteen printed book pages.

finish *Crime and Punishment* or to produce the new novel for Stellovsky would be disastrous to his career, Dostoyevsky had no choice but to work on both novels at once. "I want to do an unprecedented and unconventional thing," he told Korvin-Krukovskaya: "write thirty signatures [480 printed pages] in four months, in two different novels, of which I'll work on one in the morning, and the other in the evening and thereby finish on time."

Yet as the weeks turned into months, amidst all the other responsibilities he was trying to manage, Dostoyevsky could not find a moment to work on the novel for Stellovsky. The thought of the publisher "worries me to the point of torture," he told a writer friend. "I even dream of him." By the beginning of October 1866, with the deadline for the Stellovsky novel less than a month away, Dostoyevsky had written not a single line of the promised work. All he had were the old notes he'd scratched down in Wiesbaden more than three years earlier—notes for the story of a wanton Russian gambler lost in a European resort town called Roulettenburg.

IN THE EARLY DAYS of her relationship with Dostoyevsky, Anna Snitkina could hardly have known much of this. But she was an attentive listener, and soon she was learning the man as well as his work. The more they worked, the more the characters in this new novel, *The Gambler*, came alive for her. Moreover, she took an active interest in the story, asking sharp questions as he dictated; she herself was "amazed by my own boldness in expressing my views about the novel." It was as if she knew the characters personally and had her own stake in the game. The character of Polina, in particular—sensuous, egotistical, cruel Polina—"aroused my contempt." On the other hand, Anna felt sympathy for the kindly Englishman, Mr. Astley, a man of prosaic practicality and common sense, values Anna herself had been raised with.

The young stenographer had a more difficult time appreciating the novel's hero, Alexei, "whose irresoluteness I could not forgive," she recalled. "Dostoyevsky was wholly on the gambler's side," she said, but she saw none of the "poetry" Dostoyevsky insisted was in him. Mercurial, impractical, and impulsive, Alexei was foreign to Anna's pragmatic world-view, and she found his behavior more than a little distasteful. Perhaps Anna's intuition, a trait that would serve her and Dostoyevsky well in years to come, was triggered by the shrouded egoism of a penniless gambler who compensates for his own feelings of inferiority by testing fate day after day.

Despite their disagreements, or perhaps because of them, Anna enjoyed their hours together in that gloomy apartment, illuminated by an imagination that took her to places that were unfamiliar yet strangely seductive. "Leaving his house still under the influence of ideas new to me," she later described, "I would miss him when I was at home, and lived only in expectation of the next day's meeting with him." She found herself spending less time with her family and stopped attending stenography lectures or visiting friends. "How empty and trivial their talk seemed to me in comparison with the fresh and original views of my favorite author!"

The feeling was mutual. Admiring Anna's efficiency, her seriousness, her ability to remain cheerful in the midst of crisis, Dostoyevsky was surprised by how self-conscious he became in her presence, how he weighed his words lest he say something to offend her. He began referring to her as *golubchik*, or "little dove." From the start, he later told her, he marveled at "the genuine warmth you showed about my interests, and your fellow-feeling for the catastrophe hanging over my head." As he teetered toward ruin, his own family could muster only "words, words, words" in response. Yet this "outsider, this young girl with whom I'm barely acquainted, immediately puts herself in my position. Without moans and groans, without exclamations and shows of indignation she undertakes to help me out—not in words, but in deeds. . . . I was so emotionally alone at that time that finding another person who genuinely felt for me was an enormous joy."

3.

A Novel Proposal

S oon enough, Dostoyevsky and Anna had the better part of a novel completed. On October 29, the last day of dictation, the writer invited his stenographer to a celebratory dinner he was planning for friends after the successful delivery of the manuscript to Stellovsky. Never having been to a proper restaurant, and unsure of her ability to carry on a conversation with Dostoyevsky's illustrious literary friends, she declined.

On October 30 she brought Dostoyevsky the transcription, giving him time to make any last-minute changes and deliver the final manuscript to Stellovsky the following day. Handing her the fifty rubles they had agreed to as payment, he shook her hand and thanked her warmly for her collaboration.

"*The Gambler* was finished," Anna triumphantly recalled. "From October 4 to 29, that is, in twenty-six days, Dostoyevsky had produced a novel of seven two-column signatures long in large format—the equivalent of ten normal signatures," or 160 pages. She felt proud to have had a hand in this extraordinary feat.

But the notoriously unscrupulous Stellovsky—still counting on the chance that Dostoyevsky would fail to deliver the new manuscript on time, thereby forfeiting his rights to anything he might write for the next nine years—was not to be defeated so easily. On October 30, when the writer went to Stellovsky's home to deliver the materials, he was told that the publisher had left suddenly for the provinces, for an unspecified length of time. When he marched over to Stellovsky's publishing office, the manager there flatly refused the manuscript, saying that he was not authorized to accept any materials.

Dostoyevsky had foreseen such a ruse. A few days earlier, he had consulted a lawyer recommended by Anna's mother; the lawyer had advised him to take his manuscript to a police officer and obtain an official notarized receipt. Only by the time he had left Stellovsky's publishing office, it was already too late to find a notary, and at the police station he was told that the officials needed to handle his matter were not present and he should return later that day. Not until ten o'clock that evening was he finally able to hand the manuscript to the police inspector, who supplied him with a receipt of delivery.

October 30, the day Anna brought her employer the final transcription of *The Gambler*, was a special day for another reason: it was Dostoyevsky's birthday. On that day, for the first time since she'd known him, Anna arrived at his apartment not in the usual drab black cotton dress she'd worn since her father's death, but in a lilac dress she saved for special occasions. Dostoyevsky marveled at the change, remarking how the color became her, how much taller and more graceful she seemed in the long silk dress. Anna "was very pleased to hear these praises."

Her mood quickly soured, however, at the entrance of Emilya Fyodorovna, the dour widow of Dostoyevsky's brother Mikhail, who had come to wish her brother-in-law a happy birthday. Dostoyevsky enthusiastically introduced Anna as the young woman who had helped him finish his novel and avert catastrophe. But the older woman responded curtly, then stood before Anna in haughty silence. Embarrassed, Dostoyevsky ushered Anna aside, inviting her to glance through some papers and books that had just come out. Anna flipped through the materials distractedly until Emilya Fyodorovna's contempt got the best of her and she prepared to leave. Dostoyevsky begged her to stay, apologizing for his sister-in-law's ungraciousness, but Anna remained firm. He saw her to the front hall, where he reminded her that she'd promised to receive him at her house very soon. "When can I come, then?" he pressed. "Tomorrow?" Anna hesitated, but at last she agreed to receive him at seven in the evening that Thursday.

In the days leading to this visit, Anna felt both sadness and fear. She missed "the merry rush to work" they had shared, along with "the joyful meetings and the lively conversations," but she was intimidated by the prospect of hosting Dostoyevsky in a social setting. "His promised visit not only gave me no joy, but on the contrary, weighed me down," she recalled. "I was aware that neither my mother nor I was capable of being a fascinating conversationalist for a man as clever and talented as he." While she "dreamed of seeing him again," at the same time she "wished he had forgotten his promise to visit us." She spent most of that Thursday making the rounds of local stores, looking for the kinds of pears and sweets she knew he liked, rehearsing in her mind any potential topics she could bring up should the conversation between them lag.

Finally, by seven thirty, after a long day of anticipation, Anna was ready . . . but Dostoyevsky failed to appear. Eight o'clock came and went. And then eight thirty. Anna was starting to wonder if he had changed his mind when, finally, he was announced. He had been looking for her address on Kostromskaya Street for a good hour, but she'd forgotten to tell him that in the evenings the gates were locked and the house could be reached only from Slonovaya or Malenkaya Bolotnaya streets. The awkwardness was dispelled with the entrance of Anna's mother, to whom Anna hastily introduced the writer. Dostoyevsky gallantly kissed Mrs. Snitkina's hand and warmly thanked her for the invitation, raving about Anna and the invaluable assistance she had provided him. He seemed a different man to Anna, more charming and charismatic than she had ever seen him.

Mrs. Snitkina left briefly to prepare the samovar, then returned to the living room, where the two were sitting in uncomfortable silence. This time it was Dostoyevsky who broke the awkward hush, regaling his hosts with story after charming story, even recounting the tale of Stellovsky's nasty trick. More than half a century later, it was not this particular story Anna would remember, but simply how happy it had made her to see Fyodor Mikhailovich and her mother getting along so well. Mama was enchanted by their illustrious guest, a natural raconteur who put everyone at ease; as the evening stretched on, it was as though the three had known one another for years.

At one point that night, Dostoyevsky mentioned that he was preparing to resume work on *Crime and Punishment* and asked Anna to stay on as his stenographer.

"I'll do it gladly," she responded, but she was concerned that Professor Olkhin, who had secured the job for her, might object. "He may have another pupil of his in mind for this new job of yours."

But Dostoyevsky told Anna that he'd grown accustomed to working with her. "Or perhaps the truth is that you don't want to work with me any longer? In that case, of course, I won't insist." Anna hastened to reassure him that Olkhin was unlikely to object but that she would consult him anyway, just to be sure.

Dostoyevsky left at eleven. Ecstatic over the evening's success, Anna rushed back to the dining room to celebrate with her mother. Ten minutes later, the maid came in to report that the cushion from Dostoyevsky's luxurious sleigh had been stolen sometime that evening. The cabdriver's despair was matched only by Anna's fear that Dostoyevsky might never again return to her neighborhood.

That emotional roller coaster of an evening—and the entire week before—left Anna flustered. Visiting her sister, Masha, the next day, she told the story so quickly and animatedly that Masha had to stop her more than once just to keep up. A slender beauty with blue eyes and magnificent hair, Masha had always intimidated Anna, and she had grown only more aloof since her recent marriage to an illustrious professor. After humoring Anna for a while, Masha told her that her crush on Dostoyevsky was surely "all for nothing." She accused Anna of having dreams of marrying the writer that could never come true, "and thank goodness they can't—if he's that ill and overloaded with family and debts!" Anna did *not* have a crush on Dostoyevsky, she shot back. She was simply "happy to chat with a clever, talented man and appreciated his constant kindness and attention to me."

Then again, Anna thought, maybe Masha *was* right: "Was I really infatuated with him? Was it possible that this was the beginning of the love I had not yet experienced in my life? What an insane dream that would be on my part! Was it possible at all?" In which case, what should she do? Invent some excuse to decline further work from him, to avoid a potential conflict between employment and a deeper relationship? Or stop seeing him or even thinking about him, so that she might "immerse myself in some other kind of activity and restore my former state of inner calm, which I'd always prized so highly?"

In the end, Anna reasoned that there would be no harm in continuing to work as Dostoyevsky's stenographer, a job for which she had worked so hard to prepare. And why should she deprive herself of those "heartfelt, interesting talks" that went along with the work?

Anna was due to meet with Dostoyevsky the following Monday, to begin work on *Crime and Punishment*. The day before, she was sitting at the piano, distracted by the tune she was playing, when she failed to hear the doorbell ring. A few moments later, she heard footsteps behind her. She turned around: it was *him*, Dostoyevsky, inside her home, an oddly timid expression on his face. She got up from the bench and went to him.

"Do you know what I've done, Anna Grigoryevna?" he said, shaking her hand firmly. "All these days I've missed you so much and all day today, ever since morning, I've been thinking about it. Should I come to see you or not? . . . On Thursday I was here, and on Sunday I turn up again!" He was always welcome in her home, she responded simply. And there they stood, looking at each other, until Dostoyevsky suddenly said: "But how cold your house is! And how cold you are yourself today!"

Noticing her dress, he asked where she was going. To Alarchin Bridge, she told him, to see her godmother. Why, that was on his way, he said, offering to take her.

At one point during their sleigh ride, there was a sharp turn in the road. Reaching out to support his passenger, the novelist put his arm firmly around her waist. "Please don't trouble yourself—I won't fall out!" she was quick to say, gently pushing his hand away.

As the sleigh whisked the two of them through the snow-covered streets of Petersburg, they chatted merrily, Anna's anxiety dissipating into the crisp November air like wisps of smoke. When they finally said good night, the writer squeezed her hand and made her promise again that she would come to his house the next day to agree on a working schedule. Whether Anna ever did speak to Professor Olkhin, we will never know. Even if she did, it seems certain that this was one professional decision she made entirely on her own.

AT THE END of *The Gambler*, which takes place a year and a half after Alexei's ill-fated love affair with Polina, he has fallen completely off the deep end. Having served as valet to a councillor named Hintze, worked as a lackey, and fallen into debtors' prison before having his freedom secured by some mysterious person, he tries to find work as a Russian language tutor, all the while gambling, hoping for that one big score that would get "all those Hintzes, all those hotel managers, all those magnificent Baden-Baden ladies . . . talking about me, telling my story, astonished at me, praising me, and bowing before my new winnings."

The sensible, down-to-earth Englishman, Mr. Astley, is finally forced to confront his dissipated friend, much as it often fell to Mikhail Dostoyevsky to tell his brother the painful truth about his gambling habit. "You've turned to wood," Mr. Astley observes. "You've not only renounced any goal whatsoever apart from winning, but . . . your dreams, your most essential desires at present don't go beyond *pair* and *impair, rouge, noir,* the twelve middle numbers, and so on, and so forth!" To which Alexei can only respond angrily: "Enough, Mr. Astley, please, please don't remind me."

Like his wayward hero, Fyodor Dostoyevsky often felt guilty over abandoning those who needed him during his jaunts to European casinos. Yet he repeatedly convinced himself that he *needed* to gamble, using the same rationalization that he now put into the mouth of Alexei: "I've driven it all out of my head for a time, even the memories—until I've radically improved my circumstances. Then . . . then you'll see, I'll rise from the dead!" If the writer often ignored the dangers of such magical thinking in his own life, in *The Gambler* at least he shows an acute understanding of the psychology of his own addiction, not to mention the potential collapse of his life should he fail to conquer his habit. For the resurrection Alexei promises Mr. Astley, of course, never happens. In the novel's final lines, we see Alexei, down to his very last gulden, contemplating whether to walk away from the roulette table or try his luck one last time. He takes the coin out of his pocket, stakes it on *manqué*, and wins. And then he gloats to the reader:

> There's what your last gulden can sometimes mean! And what if I had lost heart then, what if I hadn't dared to venture? . . .
> Tomorrow, tomorrow it will all be over.

Whether that tomorrow will bring another temporary triumph, or leave him once again destitute, remains unclear. What *is* clear by the end of the novel is that, whatever momentary ups or downs he might experience during his next go at the spinning carousel, Alexei, as a man, is finished. His self-immolation at roulette has reached the point of no return.

Dostoyevsky, on the other hand, still had the chance to redeem himself, both professionally and personally. And *The Gambler* did pay off—although in much the same way as his few good bets at the roulette table: staving off disaster while giving him a temporary rush, fleeting and dangerous. In completing *The Gambler* on time, he did save himself from Stellovsky's extortionate contract, but it did not produce another ruble of income for the writer. Nine years would pass before Stellovsky finally paid him, five years late, for including the novel in his 1870 edition of Dostoyevsky's complete collected works. Nor did the novel—not one of the writer's most inventive or artistically daring—make a real splash in literary circles. Moreover, in diverting his attention to finishing *The Gambler*, Dostoyevsky was forced to stop work on the steady serialization of *Crime and Punishment*, which *was* making a splash, leaving him now with only two short months to complete that more important novel.

Still, his mad dash to complete *The Gambler* had brought Dostoyevsky his invaluable helpmeet. And now that Anna Snitkina had agreed to continue working with him on completing *Crime and Punishment*, he was elated.

———

ON THE BRILLIANT, FROSTY MORNING of November 8, 1866, the day they were to begin their work on *Crime and Punishment*, Anna decided to walk rather than take a cab to Dostoyevsky's house and ended up arriving a half hour late. The writer, who had been waiting for her near the door, appeared in the hall as soon as he heard Anna's voice.

"So you're here at last!" he said happily, helping her with her hood and coat. Together they repaired to his study, which seemed to Anna unusually bright that day.

"How happy I am that you've come!" he said. "I was so afraid you'd forget your promise."

"Has something pleasant happened to you?" Anna asked, struck by his ebullience.

"Yes, it has, as a matter of fact. You see, last night I had the most marvelous dream."

He told her that he attributed great meaning to his dreams, having found them reliably prophetic. In this dream, he said, he was sitting in front of the special rosewood box that stood on a nearby table in his study, leafing through his manuscripts and letters, when he found among them a tiny, brilliant diamond.

"And what did you do with it?" Anna asked, uncertain where the story was headed.

"That's the pity of it—I can't remember! There were other dreams *after* that, and now I don't know what became of the diamond. But that was a good dream."

She asked how he had been keeping busy since she last saw him.

"I've been thinking up a plot for a new novel," he answered.

"You don't say! An interesting one?"

"To me, quite interesting. The thing is, though, that I can't seem to work out the ending. It pivots on the psychology of a young girl. If I were in Moscow, I'd ask my niece Sonyechka, but, as it is, I'll turn to *you* for help."

Flattered, Anna nodded eagerly and settled in to listen.

First, he described the backstory of each character. The hero was an artist with a harsh childhood who had lost his father when he was young. A seemingly incurable disease had forced him to abandon his art for ten years, but after recovering from his illness he falls in love with a woman, even though he is still married. This love torments him. In time his wife dies, followed by his sister. He is mired in poverty and debt . . .

Anna knew enough about Dostoyevsky's past to know that he must have been describing his relationship with his family and his own late wife. The hero's loneliness, his longing for a new life, his yearning for love—these, Anna knew, were Dostoyevsky's own feelings. He described his fictional artist in the same terms she had often heard him use in describing himself: a man who had grown old before his time; an artist who had a warm, tender heart but could also be gloomy and suspicious, incapable of expressing his feelings to others, frustrated by his failure to realize his ideas in artistic form.

"But, Fyodor Mikhailovich, why do you keep insulting your hero like that?" Anna asked.

"I see you don't like him either?"

"Just the opposite. I find him very likeable," she countered. "He has a splendid heart. Think of how many sorrows he has had to bear, and how he submits to them! Another man experiencing so much misery in his life would have grown hard, but your hero goes on loving people and helping them. No, you are definitely being unfair to him."

"How happy I am that you seem to understand him!" he said, beaming. He went on with his story: "And so, in that critical period of his life, the artist meets a young girl of about your age, or maybe a year or two older. Let's give her the name of Anya, so as not to have to call her 'the heroine.' It's a nice name, Anya . . ."

If this was an autobiographical novel, as now seemed certain, this Anya must have been based on Anna Korvin-Krukovskaya, whom Dostoyevsky had mentioned to Anna in their many conversations. The heroine, he explained, was gentle, wise, kind, full of life. She was also extremely tactful in her personal relationships.

"And is your heroine pretty?" Anna asked.

"Not a real beauty, perhaps, but she is very nice-looking. I love her face."

Something pinched Anna's heart, and she grew suddenly hateful toward this other Anna. "But, surely, Fyodor Mikhailovich, you are over-idealizing your 'Anya.' Can she really be all *that*?"

"She is *precisely* 'all that'! I have studied her thoroughly!"

He continued: As the hero and Anya got to know each other, he grew even more attracted to her and dreamed of marrying her. But "what could this old, sick, debt-ridden man possibly give a young, alive, exuberant girl?" he asked. "Wouldn't her love for him require a terrible sacrifice on her part? And afterwards, wouldn't she bitterly regret uniting her life with his?" The writer fixated on his characters' age disparity: "Would it be possible at all for a young girl so different in age and personality to fall in love with my artist? Wouldn't that be psychologically false? That's what I wanted to ask your opinion about, Anna Grigoryevna."

"But why would that be impossible?" she said defiantly. "If, as you say, Anya isn't merely an empty flirt and has this kind, responsive heart, why *couldn't* she fall in love with your artist? So *what* if he's poor and sick? Where's the sacrifice on her part, anyway? If she really loves him she'll be happy, too, and she'll never have to regret anything."

"And you seriously believe she could love him genuinely, and for the rest of her life?" he said, falling briefly silent. "Put yourself in her place for a moment," he finally continued, his voice trembling. "Imagine that this artist is—*me*; that I have confessed my love to you, and asked you to be my wife. Tell me, what would you answer?"

And suddenly Anna understood.

> His face revealed such deep embarrassment, such inner torment, that I understood at last that this was not a conversation about literature; and that if I gave him an evasive answer I would destroy his self-esteem and pride. I looked at his troubled face, which had become so dear to me, and said,
>
> "I would answer that I love you and will love you all my life."

Stunned by her own reaction, Anna had difficulty believing that she wasn't dreaming. An hour later, when Fyodor Mikhailovich started talking about the future, she interrupted him: "How can I make any decisions about anything now? I'm too horribly happy!"

THEY DECIDED NOT TO TELL anyone except for Anna's mother, at least until they had set a wedding date. Promising to call on Anna the next day and spend the evening at the Snitkins' home, Dostoyevsky escorted her to the door, tenderly fastening her hood for her. Just as she was about to leave, he stopped her.

"Anna Grigoryevna," he said, "now I know what became of the little diamond."

"Truly?" she asked. "So you remembered your dream?"

"Not the dream, exactly. But I've found it at last, my little jewel, and am determined to keep it all my life."

"You've made a mistake, Fyodor Mikhailovich," she laughed. "It's no diamond you've found, but just an ordinary little pebble."

"No," he said to her with great seriousness, "I'm convinced that this time I've made no mistake."

Mrs. Snitkina, on the other hand, was concerned. She liked Dostoyevsky, had been charmed by him during his recent visit. But she knew well the hardship that a marriage to this significantly older man—whose health and finances were both precarious—would entail for her daughter. Nevertheless, she knew her daughter well enough to recognize that any attempt to dissuade her would only backfire. Anna had demonstrated her self-possession all too clearly, not least through her unyielding refusal to be courted by any of the men her parents had commended to her. And so, hoping for the best, Mrs. Snitkina gave her blessing.

It must have reassured her that Dostoyevsky proved an ardent fiancé. He visited the Snitkins every afternoon, bringing treats from his favorite confectioner, and he and Anna would retreat into a quiet space where they would chat until deep into the evening. Anna enjoyed the role of bride-to-be, visiting the best Petersburg stores each day to stock up on his favorite fruits and sweets. Soon Dostoyevsky was visiting even on days when he had other professional engagements. "I ran away like a school-boy!" he boasted one day on arriving at Anna's home. "We'll have a half an hour together, anyway!" As always, though, he stayed longer. At the stroke of ten, Anna entreated him to head home before it became too dangerous to travel, but he begged her to let him stay just another ten minutes, lamenting that it would be a whole day before he'd get to see her again. She insisted, suggesting that her yardkeeper accompany him home; when Dostoyevsky declined, Anna withdrew her offer, then secretly ordered the yardkeeper to follow him home at a discreet distance.

Once a buttoned-up employee, shrouded in mourning cloth and a res-olutely professional demeanor, Anna was transformed almost overnight into a bright, vibrant woman, deeply in love. "What has become of the strict, straitlaced Anna Grigoryevna who used to come to my house to take dictation?" Dostoyevsky mused one day. "Someone must have made a substitution!"

So be it, Anna thought. She rather liked this person she was turning into; it was as though she'd summoned back the jovial, mischievous girl her classmates once knew and loved. Instead of busying herself nonstop with productive activity, now she allowed herself to relax, thinking back warmly on each day's rendezvous with her fiancé, and imagining what their next visit would have in store.

They talked about many things in those first weeks of their engage-ment. Insisting that they keep no secrets from each other, Anna was eager to satisfy her curiosity about her future husband, this man she still hardly knew. He told her stories about his tender love for his soulful mother and his coolness toward his temperamental father, and about his affection for his older brother, Mikhail, to whose family Dostoyevsky still felt finan-cially indebted after the dissolution of *Epoch*.

On the topic of his previous loves, Dostoyevsky was less illuminating. He spoke little of his unhappy marriage to Marya Dmitriyevna, whom he later described to Anna as "strange, mistrustful, and sickly-fanciful." Of Polina Suslova he said even less, despite having disclosed to Anna—within the first days of their work on *The Gambler*, in fact—that he had cheated on his dying wife with her. Anna had probably heard enough about his past already, however, and she knew the character of Polina from *The Gambler* well enough to recognize that Dostoyevsky might still harbor feelings for her real-life counterpart. Yet Anna had enough confidence in their relationship that she managed to block Polina from her thoughts, or perhaps simply to convince herself that in time she would eclipse Dostoyevsky's old flame.

And what did he tell her of his misbegotten courtship of Anna Korvin-Krukovskaya, whom she had initially mistaken for the heroine of the tale he'd spun into his marriage proposal? Less than the whole truth, judging from Anna Snitkina's account in her memoir. Dostoyevsky ostensibly told her that the courtship had ended because of their "diametrically opposed" outlooks on life—including, presumably, their views on marriage and family. Korvin-Krukovskaya had proven "too inflexible," Dostoyevsky said, to make a good wife. For her part, Anna surmised in her memoir that Korvin-Krukovskaya "lacked that willingness to compromise which is indispensable to every good marriage, particularly marriage to such a sick, irritable person as Fyodor Mikhailovich," and that she was "too committed to political party affairs to give much attention to her family."

These words shed revealing light on how Anna was beginning to reconcile her feminist ambitions with her desire to become a wife and mother. Her description of her own feelings—and her judgment of her fiancé's former paramours—suggests that she, like the Russian feminists of the 1850s, viewed the roles as not contradictory but complementary. By contrast, Anna Korvin-Krukovskaya followed the path of the later, more radical feminists; shortly after rejecting Dostoyevsky, she broke with her family, moved abroad, and took an active part in the radical French socialist revolutionary movement. To her younger sister, she explained why she could never have married the "nervous and exacting" Dostoyevsky. "He seems to be constantly grasping me—sucking me into himself. I was never myself with him," she complained. "He does not need a wife like me, not in the least. His wife needs to devote herself entirely, entirely to him. . . . And I cannot do that; I want to live myself."

Yet Anna Snitkina felt all the *more* herself around the writer—perhaps in part because their relationship promised her both domestic and intellectual fulfillment. She felt pride when Fyodor Mikhailovich praised her choice of silverware or furniture for their future home, and she enjoyed trying on stylish hats and dresses for him. She also welcomed his guidance of her literary education, and was inspired by him to read Honoré de Balzac, Victor Hugo, George Sand, Sofya Smirnova, and, of course, Alexander Pushkin. He discouraged her from "frivolous novels" and insisted that she limit her theatergoing to plays that "convey high and noble impressions to the spectators," not "empty triviality."

While she generally heeded his advice, appreciating his wish to "shield me from any corrupting influences," on occasion Anna would feel emboldened to protest. When he found her leafing through some French potboiler, he gently took the book out of her hands, reminding her that such books would soil her imagination.

"Then why do *you* read them yourself?" she asked. "Why soil your own imagination?"

"I'm hardened," he answered. "Certain books are necessary to me as material for my work. A writer must know everything and experience much."

Dostoyevsky was many things—generous, attentive, encouraging—but, as his behavior demonstrates, he could also be condescending, even patriarchal. It was a trait he inherited at least in part from his self-righteous father, who was certain of his own virtue and demanded that his family live up to his example. The writer's priggishness was surely fueled by his emotional insecurity after years of traumatic relationships with women. He probably felt safer when he was in control, when he believed that a woman was following his counsel and loving him unconditionally, as Polina Suslova and Anna Korvin-Krukovskaya had never done.

Whatever his emotional insecurities, however, Dostoyevsky believed that Anna had come into his life for a purpose. "God entrusted you to me," he told Anna early in their marriage, "so that none of the seeds and riches of your soul and heart should be lost, but on the contrary, should grow up and bloom richly and luxuriantly. He gave you to me so that I could atone for my enormous sins by presenting you to God well-developed, directed, preserved, saved from everything that is base and deadens the spirit."

He was the sinful artist, she his deliverer—a dynamic with the trappings of an unhealthy codependency—and no doubt there *were* elements of codependency throughout their early years together. From the beginning, however, they also felt a mutual love and gratitude. Dostoyevsky needed Anna to restore his dignity as a man and artist, but she also needed him, in ways she was just beginning to realize. The literary education she received in his company, however condescending at times, fostered in Anna an artistic sensibility that would make her a valuable partner in every aspect of his writing and publishing career. At the same time, he offered her an instructive window into the personality of an artist who needed "to know everything and experience much" in order to write. Dostoyevsky's intense hunger for experience could be not only self-destructive but harmful to their marriage; yet, as Anna was beginning to discover, he also relied on it as a crucial source of creativity. She may never have said so explicitly, but this trait was surely an important part of what she found both fascinating and maddening about him.

Over the course of those long, intimate conversations during the months of their engagement, though, Anna did wonder about one thing: Why hadn't he just proposed to her straightforwardly, as most men did? The reason, Dostoyevsky finally explained, was self-protective. Couching his proposal as a fictional story would have made it easier for him to avoid humiliation if he sensed she might refuse him. To which Anna made a little confession of her own: she'd been terrified as he built up to his proposal, embarrassed at first that she couldn't understand the story he was telling, then jealous when she concluded he was talking about Anna Korvin-Krukovskaya. Even now, she told him, she still had trouble believing her good fortune.

"So it follows," he gushed, "that I took you by surprise and extracted your consent by force! Now I see that the novel I told you was better than any I ever wrote—it had an instant success and produced the desired effect!"

IN THE HAPPY WELTER of their engagement, they nearly forgot about *Crime and Punishment*. Dostoyevsky had been working on the novel for well over a year now, from the summer of 1865 through 1866, and the work had appeared in steady installments in *The Russian Messenger*. He had promised Katkov the last two installments by the end of November, but the magazine was notorious for its delays, which would give him a few weeks' breathing room. Finally, near the end of November, Anna told Dostoyevsky to close his doors to visitors and work on the novel every afternoon from two to five straight, and then come over to her flat in the evening and dictate from the manuscript. Which is exactly what he now did: every evening, after chatting with Anna for an hour or so, he paced around the room as she sat and took dictation. It felt to Anna just like the days of their work on *The Gambler*—or better, in fact; rarely had the novelist been in such a cheerful frame of mind while composing, and rarely had his writing progressed so smoothly. In roughly four weeks, the last installments of *Crime and Punishment* were completed.

Over the many months of working on the book, Dostoyevsky had filled three large notebooks containing his evolving ideas. From these notes it is clear that he had added a number of elements not present in his earliest concept for the novel as he'd described it to Katkov in 1865. After the murderer, Raskolnikov, undergoes a torturous internal reckoning, trying to make sense of why he committed the crime, he finally confesses to Sonya Marmeladova, a meek young prostitute whose alcoholic father he'd met at the beginning of the novel. To his astonishment, Sonya embraces Raskolnikov, telling him that "no one, no one in the whole world, is unhappier than you are now!" This act of extraordinary compassion marks the beginning of the murderer's regeneration. Confessing to the crime, Raskolnikov is sentenced to eight years of penal servitude, and Sonya follows him to Siberia.

In exile, the murderer arrives at a fuller understanding not only of the deeper motivations of his crime but also of its dire social implications. Through a dream-allegory—in which the world has descended into an

Armageddon of armies of possessed people, destroying one another in the name of intellectual pride and ideological certainty—Raskolnikov comes to realize that his long-held theory about the social utility of murder was rooted in a profound egoism. It was the sickness of a humiliated young man, anxious to prove that he was "extraordinary," who was willing to disregard the normal boundaries of human morality in order to assert his will on the world.

Only through the sort of Christian humility and compassion embodied by Sonya could Raskolnikov ever achieve redemption. The process would be long and harrowing—so much so that it "might make the subject of a new story," Dostoyevsky suggests in the novel's final lines. And indeed he would go on to explore the themes of compassion, egoism, and redemption in each of his remaining major works. These themes would take on an increasingly sociopolitical bent, as he warned readers that the radical Russian intelligentsia—who believed their social theories were paving the way to Utopia—were in fact leading their country to hell.

But that would all come later. In the late fall of 1866, Dostoyevsky and Anna were occupied with more mundane matters—including their finances, which were still tight. Given the success of *Crime and Punishment*, the writer was hopeful that Katkov would want to publish his next novel. In the meantime, though, it was becoming clear that they would not be able to afford a wedding before the middle of February. They would also have to find a new apartment: under constant financial pressure from his brother's widow, Emilya Fyodorovna, Dostoyevsky had finally agreed to lend her family his current apartment, on the corner of Stolyarny Pereulok and Malenkaya Meshchanskaya Street, paying their rent in the bargain.

Nor was that the end of his generosity, Anna discovered one frigid November day when he appeared at her home wearing only his thin fall coat. She was about to send a servant to his home to fetch his winter overcoat when he sheepishly confessed that he'd pawned it after Emilya Fyodorovna came by that morning begging him to cover a fifty-ruble debt she'd incurred. That same day, both his stepson, Pasha, and his ailing brother, Nikolai, had also asked for money. He'd been unable to refuse his family in need, he told Anna, but she need not worry: the weather was getting warmer, and his fall jacket would tide him over until the next re-mittance from *The Russian Messenger*.

But she *was* worried—and outraged, both at the self-centeredness of Dostoyevsky's relatives and at his own imprudence in agreeing to their demands. It was a pattern that would grow more and more familiar:

> The moment Fyodor Mikhailovich got hold of any money, all his relatives—his brother, sister-in-law, stepson, and nephews—would instantly put forward their sudden but urgent needs; and out of the three or four hundred rubles received from Mos-cow for *Crime and Punishment* no more than thirty or forty would remain to Fyodor Mikhailovich by the next day.

That day, hearing her fiancé's explanation, Anna broke into sobs. But then, choking back her tears, she confronted him angrily: It might be no-ble to want to help his relatives, she shouted, but not at the risk of his health. His obligation now was to *her*, his future bride, and if he were to freeze to death she would be devastated. Dostoyevsky tried to reassure her by explaining that he was *used to* pawning his winter coat; in fact, he'd pawned and retrieved it five or six times the previous winter.

When Anna recounted this episode in *Reminiscences*, fifty years later, she likened her behavior to that of a "madwoman," describing her response as "a hysterical fit" and saying she was "ashamed" of her outburst. She failed to give herself credit for the intelligence and self-assertiveness she showed in response to Dostoyevsky's weak apology: "I made use of his remorse to exact from him a promise that this kind of thing would never happen again," then gave him eighty rubles of her own money and told him to re-trieve his coat out of pawn.

As they said good night, Anna apologized "for the scene I had made." Dostoyevsky seemed mostly relieved that it was over. "There's no cloud without a silver lining!" he responded gently, as she tied her white knitted scarf around his neck and threw a plaid cloth over his shoulders. "Now I'm really convinced of how much you love me. You couldn't have cried like that if I weren't dear to you."

That night she lay awake in bed, worrying that he might change his mind about her, or that he might have caught a chill on his way home. Early the next morning, she went straight over to Dostoyevsky's home and rang the doorbell insistently. Fedosya came to the door and invited Anna in, assuring her that Dostoyevsky had arrived home safely and in good health.

"This was the only 'stormy' evening we had during the three months of our engagement," Anna recalled half a century later.

4.

What Is to Be Done?

Anna had set out to work as amanuensis to a celebrated writer; now
she was to become his wife. This was not the way her life was meant
to unfold—not, at least, according to the values of the "emancipated girl
of the sixties," as understood by the feminist movement of the time. The
"New Woman" was expected to make her own way in the world, securing
both financial and social independence. If she did marry, it should be to
an enlightened "New Man" in a so-called fictional marriage, orchestrated
by like-minded couples in order to convince their parents that the union
was legitimate. The man would go through the motions of courtship and
a church ceremony, after which he would give his bride a permit for separate residence and then wish her well on her path to independence. If the
partners were attracted to each other, these unions might involve sexual
relations, but this was by no means required. For a man, participation in
such a fictitious marriage demonstrated his enlightenment and willingness to contribute to social progress. For his "wife," it meant freedom—to
pursue any profession she wished, perhaps even to start her own business,
like the heroine of Nikolai Chernyshevsky's immensely influential novel
What Is to Be Done?

Published in 1863, when Anna was almost seventeen, *What Is to Be
Done?* swiftly became a bible for the Russian feminists of the 1860s. First
appearing in *The Contemporary*, a leading journal of the radical intelligentsia, the novel follows Vera Pavlova, a poor girl living with her brother

and a mother who is intent on marrying her off to the owner of their tenement house. Vera is saved—from both her family's poverty and this loveless marriage—by a young medical student named Lopukhov, who marries her fictitiously and then releases her to live life as she pleases. Though conservatives condemned the novel as an endorsement of sexual promiscuity, the heroine's story was not meant to celebrate unbridled sexual license but rather a woman's freedom to choose whether to engage in sexual relations with her "husband," or to change marriage partners at will in order to satisfy her sexual needs. But even erotic fulfillment is not enough for Vera; economic independence is more important still, as Lopukhov teaches her. "Everything is based on money," he explains. "The person who has money has both power and rights. That means that as long as a woman is living at a man's expense, she's in a state of dependence." Inspired by his advice—typical of the feminists of the 1860s— Vera goes on to set up a highly successful profit-sharing dressmaking business, which soon grows into a full-fledged commune in the heart of the Russian capital. Through her role as an entrepreneur, then, Vera Pavlova becomes one of the earliest agents of women's liberation in Russian fiction, exhibiting willpower, social consciousness, and the capacity for pragmatic action—the very model of a modern, emancipated woman.

Educated readers of both sexes went mad for Chernyshevsky's novel. They read it "almost like worshippers," recalled one contemporary critic, "with the kind of piety with which we read religious books, and without the slightest trace of a smile on our lips. The influence of the novel on our society was colossal. It played a great role in Russian life, especially among the leading members of the intelligentsia who were embarking on the road to socialism." Georgi Plekhanov, the father of Russian Marxism, raved: "Who has not read and reread this famous work? Who has not been charmed by it, who has not become cleaner, better, braver, and bolder under its philanthropic influence? Who has not imitated the purity of the principal characters? . . . We all draw from it moral strength and faith in a better future." Vladimir Lenin himself would call Chernyshevsky "the greatest and most talented representative of socialism before Marx," poring over *What Is to Be Done?* "not for several days but for several weeks" in his youth, recalling it as a story "that supplies energy for a whole lifetime." Forty years later, he would borrow the title "What Is to Be Done?" for a famous political tract on Russian socialism.

The novel had a profound influence on an entire generation. The young women of the time regarded Vera Pavlova as a role model, the exemplar of emancipated womanhood. It was said that every schoolgirl in the mid-1860s knew Vera Pavlova's story almost by heart and "was considered a dunce if she was not acquainted with [her] exploits." She "symbolized the women's movement of the 1860s," a Russian literary historian wrote many years later. "In her aspirations and her enterprises were reflected the stage that the woman question had reached at the time." Under its influence, observed a writer of the time, "girls, bred in the most aristocratic families, rushed penniless to Petersburg, Moscow, and Kiev, eager to learn a profession which would free them from the domestic yoke, and perhaps someday from the possible yoke of a husband." In the fall of 1863, gentry girls returning to their homes in Petersburg after their summer retreats paid up to twenty-five rubles for a copy of the novel, composed of serial issues of *The Contemporary* bound together.

Some who were taken by Chernyshevsky's message left their husbands and children, moved to the provinces, and supported themselves through translation work and other odd jobs. Communes and business cooperatives modeled on Vera Pavlova's were established by women holding copies of Chernyshevsky's novel in their hands as they met to form their business plans. (Not a few of these cooperatives collapsed when members were unable to reconcile their differing interpretations of the novel.) *What Is to Be Done?* would become the most widely read novel in nineteenth-century Russia—and the book that defined, more than any other, the ideals of the Russian feminist movement for decades to come.

Anna Snitkina would almost certainly have read *What Is to Be Done?* or at least have been familiar with the feminist ideals it espoused. Though she left no record of her thoughts about the novel, she referred to herself proudly as "a girl of the sixties," a common term for the emancipated women of the time. Indeed, securing a self-reliant future was so important to Anna that on her first day of work with Dostoyevsky, when she left his house in a depressed mood, uncertain whether she could work for such a difficult man, she feared that "my dreams of independence were on the verge of crumbling into dust."

But how did her dreams of independence compare with those of the radical Russian feminists of the 1860s? Here is how Anna's daughter Lyubov' Dostoyevskaya later described her mother's attitude toward the radical feminist movement:

> An obedient daughter of the Orthodox Church, she looked upon free love as a mortal sin. Short hair and spectacles seemed to her very ugly. She loved pretty clothes and graceful coiffures. She tried to read Darwin [a favorite of the radical intelligentsia], but found him very wearisome; the idea of simian descent did not attract her. Her young imagination was fired only by the poems and novels of the Russian authors. She had no desire to be carried off by a student; she preferred to quit her parental home on her husband's arm, with the blessing of her father and mother. In all the new movement towards emancipation, my mother chose only what was really good in it—work, and the independence it offers to all who take to it seriously.

While Lyubov' harbored a clear antipathy toward the radical intelligentsia (and the revolution they'd stoked), her analysis is largely on target: Anna Snitkina may have been *in* the feminist movement, but she was not entirely *of* it.

In an important sense, Anna wanted what all Russian feminists wanted: the freedom to choose her own path in life. Like Chernyshevsky's Vera Pavlova, who was determined to make her way in the world, Anna took the bold step of becoming a stenographer rather than following in her sister's footsteps and marrying a man who would provide for her. Like Vera, who refused to enter into a marriage of convenience orchestrated by her mother, Anna had rejected her mother's matchmaking efforts, and the counsel of family and friends, to marry the man she loved—in her case, an ill, financially unstable writer twenty-five years her senior. It was the first of many such risks she would take in the coming years, risks that place her squarely in league with other daring nineteenth-century Russian feminists.

Anna shared with these feminists intelligence, ambition, and sheer force of will, all necessary qualities for progressive women challenging the status quo in a deeply traditional society that had spent centuries under autocratic rule. Though barely out of her teens, Anna had demonstrated her independent streak first at the Mariinskaya Gymnasium, and then by becoming one of Olkhin's top stenography students, even as most of her classmates simply dropped out.

Had Anna never met Fyodor Dostoyevsky, she might have channeled these extraordinary personal qualities into any number of successful callings—although it's highly unlikely that she could ever have become a revolutionary, the path many "female Nihilists" of her generation eventually followed. Anna shared the radical feminists' dedication to social justice, but where they called for the dismantling of the Russian autocracy, she favored moderation and compromise. In part, this was a matter of upbringing: Anna had enjoyed a relatively stable and happy childhood, whereas many of the day's most radical feminists had been shaped by their oppressive family environments. Vera Zasulich, who was born five years after Anna and would famously attempt to assassinate the governor of Petersburg in 1878, recalled her unhappy childhood: "No one ever held me, kissed me or sat me on his knee; no one called me pet names. The servants abused me." Vera Figner, whose father "punished us cruelly and unmercifully," projected hatred of her own father onto Tsar Alexander II, whom she helped assassinate in 1881. Many of these young women had watched helplessly as their mothers failed to defend their children against a father's tyranny: Figner's mother had so feared her husband that she would not even hold her children or play with them. No wonder Figner and other radical feminists developed a hatred of patriarchy, and often completely severed ties from their families, friends, and traditional society in favor of wholehearted commitment to revolution.

Not so Anna, who remained close with her own family throughout her lifetime, grateful for her parents' benevolence, even as she carved out

a progressive path of her own. Having been raised by a loving and generous father and a strong, enterprising mother, she associated family with
solace and support, and she inherited from her mother the belief that a
woman could be personally and professionally fulfilled even within a traditional marriage.

Like Nikolai Chernyshevsky and his fellow radicals of the era, who
had little interest in the emotional dimensions of family life, the "female
Nihilists" disavowed traditional romance, considering it a throwback to
the unenlightened past. Anna, by contrast, never rejected traditional romance outright; nor would she have considered fictitious marriage an
option. Although she chose her own spouse, she would have found it difficult to go through with the marriage to Dostoyevsky if her mother had
refused to give her blessing. Her mother "did not attempt to dissuade me
(as others later did)," Anna recalled, "and I was grateful to her for that."

WHILE HER MORE RADICAL CONTEMPORARIES were devouring the
works of Chernyshevsky, Darwin, and the German philosopher Ludwig
Feuerbach, Anna preferred to spend her time in the more spiritually and
emotionally nuanced worlds of the classical Russian writers she'd grown up
with: authors such as Alexander Pushkin and the poet Vasily Zhukovsky,
who created on the page full-blooded people with authentic human experience.

Primary among them, of course, was Dostoyevsky, whose work plumbed
psychological depths Chernyshevsky's novel never touched. And the incomplete but prophetic work he began almost fifteen years before *What Is to Be
Done?*, Anna's beloved *Netochka Nezvanova*, offered a very different vision
of what it meant to be a woman in nineteenth-century Russia.

The "uninvited nobody" of *Netochka Nezvanova* is a sensitive and
strong-willed orphan girl who rises above her peripatetic life of poverty,
relational dysfunction, and even personal pathology to become a fully
empowered woman and artist—a singer with a uniquely powerful voice
of her own. It opens with two-year-old Netochka living in poverty with
her widowed mother, who is married to an alcoholic musician of mid-

dling talent named Efimov. Netochka finds herself caught between her mother and her increasingly megalomaniacal stepfather, though she eventually comes to share his fanciful belief that he is an unrecognized genius whose wife stands in the way of his success. When Efimov runs off in a fit of madness, Netochka winds up in the family of wealthy Prince X, where she forms a passionate, almost romantic attachment to Prince X's proud and domineering daughter, Katya. Resentful of this interloper, Katya responds to Netochka's affection by playing sadistic psychological games with her. Finally, as a teenager, Netochka is shipped off to live with Katya's meek elder half sister, Alexandra Mikhailovna, and her oppressive husband, Pyotr Alexandrovich.

A shrewd observer, Netochka spends her days brooding over the couple's enigmatic relationship. "I watched, I noticed, I divined certain things," she says, "and from the beginning a vague suspicion arose in me that some mystery lay at the bottom of it all." At the age of sixteen, while secretly prowling around the family's library—a room she'd been strictly forbidden to enter—she happens upon a letter, tucked away in a novel, to Alexandra Mikhailovna from a former lover, a man far beneath her socially with whom she'd carried on a longtime platonic affair while married to Pyotr Alexandrovich. The author of the letter pours out his pain at having to end their relationship after it became public knowledge. Although Pyotr ultimately forgives his wife for the lapse, he cruelly plays on her guilt, turning her life into "long and hopeless suffering, martyrdom, sacrifice endured meekly, abjectly and fruitlessly. It seemed to me," Netochka writes, "that the one for whom the sacrifice was made scorned and derided it. I saw a criminal pardoning the sins of the righteous, and my heart was torn." The discovery throws Netochka into an existential maelstrom:

> I was shocked and frightened. In the midst of a simple life of dreams, on which I had lived for three years, reality had caught me by surprise. I was frightened to think that I was holding a great mystery in my hands, and that this mystery was now linked with my whole existence.

One reason Netochka is so scandalized by this letter, of course, is that it demonstrates how social prejudice—and marriage to a sanctimonious egoist—had robbed Alexandra Mikhailovna of the chance to be loved by a man who respects her. But there's another reason the letter is "a revelation, the unlocking of a secret" for her: "I knew the person to whom it was written"—someone, Netochka now understands, with a secret personal life of her own. This must have struck the young orphan—and by extension, a reader like Anna Snitkina—as an unusual sign of independence for a woman trapped in a loveless marriage. "I knew that I had done wrong to read the letter," Netochka confesses, "but the excitement was overwhelming! . . . The letter aroused so much within me. I had, truly, guessed the future."

The surviving text ends shortly after this, in the kind of melodramatic scene for which Dostoyevsky was famous: Pyotr Alexandrovich discovers Netochka with the letter, which he has clearly known about for some time, and proceeds to unleash upon both her and his wife a tirade so furious that Alexandra Mikhailovna collapses, and Netochka herself is terrified. Shaken, Netochka nevertheless defends herself against her accuser and, in a bold act of self-assertion, rebukes Pyotr Alexandrovich for his cruel treatment of his wife.

When Dostoyevsky's work on the novel was cut short by his arrest in 1849, it left the heroine's arc incomplete and many questions unanswered. Yet it's clear from the sections that were published, from his correspondence, and even from the subtitle he had intended for the final work, *The Story of a Woman*, that his ambition for this book was even greater than was recognized at the time. Not yet thirty years old when it was published, Dostoyevsky viewed *Netochka Nezvanova* as his first big novel, but also as a major literary contribution to the debate over women's rights, more than a decade before the "woman question" came to dominate the Russian cultural scene.

Dostoyevsky's portrayal of a woman's journey to liberation was different from that of Chernyshevsky's Vera Pavlova. Vera is presented every step of the way with a clear set of choices, always managing to make the right (meaning, for Chernyshevsky, rational) decision, the one that will continue her upward march toward enlightenment and autonomy. Not so Netochka, whose journey to self-actualization is neither linear nor upward, requiring her to trudge relentlessly through dark valleys of harsh revelation, family dysfunction, and inner conflict. From her own family's tiny garret to Prince X's luxuriant home, to the troubled home of Alexandra Mikhailovna and Pyotr Alexandrovich, Netochka is confronted repeatedly with challenges every bit as psychological as they are social. *Netochka Nezvanova* is one of the first works in Russian literature to center, and take seriously, a woman's complex inner life.

Dostoyevsky's unfinished novel also revealed an insight into human pathology that would one day become a hallmark of his great novels. Particularly notable was his portrait of Netochka's unhealthy relationship with her stepfather, a bond that verged on incestuous codependency: "I had only one pleasure, which was dreaming and thinking about him," she writes. "I had only one true desire, which was to do anything that might please him. . . . Little by little I felt I was rising above him, that I could dominate him a little and that he needed me."

Dostoyevsky also captured the alienation felt by a young woman facing an uncertain future. "How should I, an outsider, enter uninvited into this life?" Netochka laments, after finding the secret letter from Alexandra Mikhailovna's lover: "I felt like a person who is leaving for good a home and a hitherto peaceful and unruffled life, setting out on some long and unknown journey, who looks around for the last time, thoughtfully bidding farewell to the past, feeling sick at heart and full of misgivings about the harsh and hostile future that perhaps is waiting on the road."

BY THE TIME *What Is to Be Done?* was published in 1863, of course, *Netochka Nezvanova* had long since faded from the spotlight. Yet for Anna Snitkina it was Netochka's story, not Vera Pavlova's, that remained the archetypal story of female emancipation, the literary touchstone for her own identity as a woman. The parallels between Netochka and Anna are unmistakable: their worship of art and artists, their passion for reading ("I was destined," Netochka says, "to live through that future by getting to know it first in books"); most notably, Netochka's "compassionate *motherly* feeling" toward her dissolute stepfather, a "half-crazy man" who "seemed to me so pitiful, so humiliated," yet who "aroused my fantasy," would find an eerie echo in Anna's compassion for her own husband, another troubled addict whose genius aroused her fantasy. It was as though Anna's relationship with Dostoyevsky had begun, in mysterious and complex ways, long before they had ever even met.

Anna admitted as much during her late-evening conversations with her fiancé in the weeks after their engagement, which gave her a chance to learn more about him while also revealing secrets of her own. On one such occasion, she admitted that Dostoyevsky had long been a household name in the Snitkin family, and that as a teenage girl she had fallen in love with both his characters and their creator himself. She had been "quite a daydreamer," she said, and the characters in novels "were always real people to me." To illustrate, she detailed what she liked and disliked about each of the main characters in another of his novels, *The Insulted and Injured*. "You see," she told Fyodor Mikhailovich, "I can still remember the names of your characters!"

"*I* don't remember them," he responded, admitting that he had "only a vague recollection" of the novel.

"But you can't have forgotten!" she said, recounting the plot back to him. He promised to reread it.

"By the way," she continued, "do you remember you once asked me if I'd ever been in love? 'Never with a real person,' I said, 'but when I was fifteen I fell in love with the hero of a novel.' When you asked me which novel, I changed the subject. I didn't want you to think I was just flattering you to get the job. And I wanted to be completely independent." The novel in question was *Notes from the House of the Dead*, for whose autobiographical narrator she felt great pity and compassion. "Those were my feelings when I came to work for you. I wanted to help you terribly, to somehow lighten the existence of the man whose work I so adored. I thanked God that Olkhin had chosen me and no one else to work for you."

Her mention of *Notes from the House of the Dead* seemed to upset Dostoyevsky, however, so Anna tried to lighten the mood by changing the subject. "You know, it was fate," she said, "that predestined me to be your wife." And by way of proof she revealed the nickname her family had given her at sixteen.

"Please," she insisted, "you call me 'Netochka' too."

"No!" Dostoyevsky answered firmly. "My Netochka had to bear a lot of sorrow in her life, and I want you to be happy. I would rather call you Anya—that's the way I fell in love with you."

5

Crossing the Threshold

The wedding ceremony took place on the fifteenth of February, 1867, in the brilliantly illuminated, vast-domed hall of Petersburg's Troitse-Izmailovsky Cathedral. Dostoyevsky had specifically chosen the date, thirteen years to the day after his release from prison. "Freedom, a new life, resurrection from the dead . . . What a glorious moment!" exclaims his autobiographical narrator in *Notes from the House of the Dead*, published seven years earlier. For Dostoyevsky, the wedding marked a radical break from the hell of his past several years, and he considered his marriage to Anna, whom he called his "future everything," a "resurrection into a new life."

His bride's response was more muted. "For half the wedding ceremony," Anna recalled, "I was in a kind of fog." She crossed herself mechanically and responded perfunctorily to the priest's questions in a barely audible voice. From the blur of that event she would remember above all her beaming husband's face—the face of a man who seemed to have found happiness for the first time in his life, and for which she was the cause.

Soon after their return to the Snitkins' home, champagne started flowing, and countless familiar and unfamiliar faces filed in and out of the apartment to congratulate the married couple. Her mother's tenants, having learned of Anna's marriage to the well-known author, came by and sprinkled her with hops, symbolically ushering in a rich and abundant life. Guests who had attended the ceremony remarked how the pale, serious girl they'd seen at the cathedral had been replaced by a rosy-cheeked, radiant bride.

A few days after the wedding, the newlyweds joined Anna's sister, Masha, and her husband for a lively dinner. After the rest of the guests had left, Anna and the writer stayed on, swilling champagne as they shared stories of the whirlwind weeks of their courtship and engagement. Suddenly Dostoyevsky broke off midsentence and tried to lift himself from the couch, only to slump suddenly toward Anna. His face pale and distorted to the point of unrecognizability, he let out a terrible scream, almost a howl, as he toppled to the floor.

Masha screamed, then jumped up and ran out of the room, sobbing frantically. Her husband ran after her. But Anna, remaining squarely where she was, grabbed the writer by the shoulders and pushed him forcefully back up onto the couch. By this point he had lost consciousness and began to slide back off it, almost lifeless. Pushing away a nearby table— lamp and all—so that it wouldn't obstruct his fall, she crouched on the floor where Fyodor lay, holding his head in her lap as he convulsed. With her brother-in-law and his maid trying to calm Masha, Anna was left all alone to care for her new husband. A few minutes later, his convulsions subsided and he regained consciousness, although he remained disoriented for a time and unable to speak coherently. For every word he attempted to utter, another one came out.

When Masha and her husband returned, the three of them lifted Dostoyevsky back onto the couch—whereupon he suffered another attack, this one more intense than the last. Once again Masha panicked, and as her husband tried to calm her, Anna remained alone with Fyodor— this time for two terrifying hours—peering into his wild, staring eyes as groans and screams distorted his face.

"What a dreadful night I spent," Anna later wrote of that evening, the first time she had witnessed her husband in the throes of epilepsy. "It was then that I realized . . . the full horror of Fyodor Mikhailovich's disease. I was almost convinced that my darling, beloved husband was losing his mind—and what terror that thought inspired in me!" To an acquaintance, she would remark, "To be conscious that he is in agony and there's nothing you can do to help him—this was the sort of suffering with which I, evidently, was supposed to pay for the happiness of our intimacy."

There would be other costs, as well, as became increasingly evident to Anna in the weeks after the wedding. To begin with, she was overwhelmed by the endless stream of visiting guests, most of whom were acquaintances of her husband's. In Anna's own "patriarchal and hospitable family," as she described it, guests would come over only on Saturdays and holidays, but never like this, unbidden, and in throngs that seemed to mill throughout the house every single day. At first, Anna managed to find some enjoyment in the company of Dostoyevsky's literary friends—the poet Apollon Maikov, for instance, or the philosopher Nikolai Strakhov. "The literary world was an unknown entity to me until then," she said, "and I was fascinated by it." But even that pleasure was short-lived, for as soon as the writer noticed that his younger friends—closer in age to Anna—were bored, he would whisper to her: "Anna, darling, you can see they're bored, take them away, amuse them." And, of course, she would. This soon became less a privilege than a chore.

No longer was there any time for reading or for stenography, which she was still determined to master. Most painful of all, the ceaseless parade of company left Anna with almost no time alone with her husband, something she had so cherished during their engagement period. No sooner would she steal a minute with him in his study than someone would interrupt them or call her away on some urgent housekeeping matter. By the end of the day, they were both so exhausted that she fell sound asleep immediately, as Dostoyevsky lay next to her, book in hand. They had been married only a short while, and yet to Anna it felt as if they were already cooling, if not even growing apart.

Perhaps in time, she thought, she would adjust to this new rhythm of life, would learn to manage her time more efficiently, so that she could be with her husband and do a few of the things she loved while also overseeing the household. But it soon became clear that she faced another challenge: her husband's hostile relatives. From their skeptical looks, their cutting remarks, and their frequent, undisguised efforts to unnerve her, she could tell they didn't like her. Was it her youth they resented—or her erstwhile profession as a mere stenographer? She didn't know. But before long she was able to piece it together: their antagonism was largely about money, pure and simple.

Emilya Fyodorovna had been opposed to the marriage from the beginning, as it represented a serious threat to the income stream she'd been enjoying for years. Having held Dostoyevsky responsible for the failure of *Epoch*, she continued to blame him for her family's financial ruin long after the magazine's dissolution, and her persistent demands kept her brother-in-law on the verge of penury. She made a point of communicating her contempt for him to her entire extended family, often in the slyest, most backhanded ways, soliciting not only pity but also allies in her cause of shaming Dostoyevsky into continued support for the family. "My primordial enemy," he once said about Emilya Fyodorovna. "(I don't know for what.)" Once she recognized the marriage as a fait accompli, she changed tactics, offering her "superior" homemaking skills to the inexperienced Anna, and making a point of subtly reminding Dostoyevsky that his late wife, Marya Dmitriyevna, had been a better homemaker than his bride.

The writer's stepson, Pasha, was crueler still, trying everything he could to scuttle the marriage. Initially, Anna welcomed the news that he would continue living with them in Dostoyevsky's apartment after the wedding, believing that the presence of another young person—Pasha was nineteen, just two years younger than she—would liven things up a bit, and that he might even help her navigate her way around the family home. But Pasha, she quickly discovered, had a very different agenda.

Initially, he scored points with Dostoyevsky against Anna by playing the victim card, begging for pity as a persecuted orphan whose place in the family was being usurped by this newcomer. When that grew stale, he became conniving and ruthless. He would steal food from the pantry or drink up all the cream just before a meal, a time calculated to annoy Dostoyevsky, and then blame the aggravation on Anna's poor home management skills: "Well, papa, such things didn't happen when *I* was in charge of the housekeeping!" Other times he would feign tenderness toward Anna in Dostoyevsky's presence, telling his "papa" what a good influence on his moral development she was—but then turn around as soon as his stepfather left the room and malign Anna to her face, often bringing her to tears. Every once in a while, he would simply walk straight into Dostoyevsky's study, interrupt his stepfather at work, and file a direct complaint against the new mistress of the house.

At first, Anna tried to commiserate with the young man. She recognized that he'd grown used to viewing Dostoyevsky as beholden to his family, having lived with him ever since the writer took him in at the age of eight. But it was more complicated than that. With his finely tuned manipulative instincts, Pasha must have sensed that his stepfather harbored a guilty conscience with respect to his late mother, and while the boy probably never knew its source (Dostoyevsky's secret affair with Polina), he certainly viewed the writer's psychological vulnerability as an opportunity. And now, with Anna's sudden appearance threatening his comfortable way of life, he had more reason than ever to do so.

Anna had no idea how to deal with Pasha's machinations, which fell well outside the bounds of anything she'd ever encountered. At first she hoped that Pasha would tire of his hostility, but that never happened. Anna shielded her husband from his stepson's subterfuge, as well as her own distress, so effectively that Dostoyevsky never registered the extent of his wife's suffering. On the few occasions when Pasha marched in to complain about Anna's treatment of him, the exasperated writer would respond by reprimanding not Pasha but Anna: "Anyechka," he would say, "that's enough fighting around with Pasha. Don't hurt his feelings—he's a good boy!" When she asked how exactly she'd hurt Pasha's feelings, Dostoyevsky just groused that it made him sick to listen to all this nonsense, and he wished Anna could be more indulgent.

Anna was "outraged" by her husband's failure to support her. "He, 'the great master of the heart,' failed to see how difficult my life was and kept foisting his boring relatives on me and defending Pasha, who was so hostile to me." In darker moments, she even contemplated leaving him. "Although I loved him ardently," she wrote, "my pride would not have allowed me to remain with him if I believed that he had stopped loving me."

But she was convinced that he was an unwitting pawn in the hands of his scheming relatives.

Years later Anna would regret not being more assertive with Pasha, as "a girl of the sixties" would have been expected to be. "But let's not forget," she wrote:

> even though I was already past twenty, I was a complete child in the worldly sense. I had spent my few years of life in a kind, harmonious family where there were no complications and no struggles. For this reason, Pasha's insolent behavior astonished, insulted, and wounded me, but I was at first incapable of doing anything to prevent it.

Anna was caught between a rock and a hard place. She must have known that, by failing to stand up to Pasha, she was not only taking undeserved abuse but failing to live up to her feminist ideals. But unlike Pasha, who had little regard for others, Anna was concerned about her husband's well-being and aware that emotional stress made his terrifying epileptic attacks more intense and frequent. "Pasha was already complaining constantly about *me*," she recalled, "so that if I started complaining about him, what would my darling husband's life have turned into? It was my desire, after all, to preserve his peace of mind, even though that made things difficult."

Anna's abasement in these early months was a nadir of her relationship with Dostoyevsky, a clear contrast to both her youthful feminist ideals and the position of power she would eventually come to wield in the writer's life. Readers today might recognize in the newlyweds' dynamic the classic signs of martyr syndrome, typical in marriages between prominent people and their adoring spouses. In *Reminiscences*, Anna had enough distance to identify this unhealthy dynamic in these early months of her marriage. "I loved Fyodor Mikhailovich without limit," she wrote, but

> my love was entirely cerebral, it was an idea existing in my head. It was more like adoration and reverence for a man of such

talent and such noble qualities. The dream of becoming his life's companion, of sharing his labors and lightening his existence, of giving him happiness—this was what took hold of my imagination.

In time, Anna would achieve each of these goals—sharing Dostoyevsky's work, easing his burdens, and making him happy—and she would do so without the humiliation or the relinquishment of her own power that were characteristic of this earlier period in their marriage. In the moment, however, she had not yet developed a successful strategy for countering the onslaught of abuse from her in-laws—or her own husband's failure to arrest it.

Eventually, things came to a head. One evening, when Dostoyevsky was out, Pasha marched up to Anna and announced that his stepfather had made a "colossal mistake" in marrying her, that she was a "terrible housekeeper," and that she was spending too much of "the funds intended for all of us." Anna ran to her room and threw herself onto the bed, distraught. When Dostoyevsky returned later that evening, Anna was prepared to hide the truth, as she had for weeks, but she finally summoned the courage to tell him everything: "how hard my life was, how I was being insulted in his house," how hurtful it was that he favored his relatives' needs over hers. "I told him how mortified I was and how I was suffering." The more he tried to console her, the more her tears flowed.

Dostoyevsky gazed at her in astonishment. In denial or willful ignorance of his stepson's behavior, he chided Anna for not having been more honest with him, for not having come to him sooner. He even wondered aloud if the problem was that she hadn't sufficiently asserted her own authority, thus encouraging Pasha's impertinence. Dostoyevsky was capable of astounding insensitivity to his wife's travails, and he often demonstrated this same inability to read people and situations in other aspects of his life—most notably in his gambling sprees and business dealings. But his failure to come to his wife's aid when she most needed him put their young marriage at risk, leading us to wonder how this writer, who captured human failings and their consequences so vividly in his art, could so callously disregard the needs of the person closest to him in real life.

As Anna explained what a burden the constant entertaining had become, Dostoyevsky allowed that he'd noticed the flood of visitors but said he was sure they came only because Anna was such a welcoming host and everyone had such a good time at their house. Come to think of it, he'd assumed that Anna found the guests interesting, especially those who were around her age; why else was she so gracious and engaging with them? He was just glad that the matter was behind them now, he said, before reassuring Anna of his love, expressing amazement that she could ever have doubted it.

He had been missing their old talks, too, he admitted, and had been longing to spend more time alone with her. As a matter of fact, he'd been thinking of traveling to Moscow to meet with Mikhail Katkov, the editor of *The Russian Messenger*, in the hopes of selling his next book. Why didn't Anna come with him? The city had more than enough cultural attractions to keep her entertained while he was with Katkov, and he'd been eager to introduce her to his sister Vera Mikhailovna Ivanova and her family. "How about it, Anyechka, will you come?" Anna needed no convincing; the trip would mean a reprieve from the hardships of recent weeks, and it would give her a chance to introduce her new husband to her younger brother, Ivan, who was studying agriculture in Moscow.

When Pasha and Emilya Fyodorovna learned of the upcoming trip, they made no attempt to interfere. They assumed Dostoyevsky was going to Moscow to obtain more money, as their coffers were getting low.

UNFORTUNATELY FOR ANNA, the family welcome was no friendlier in Moscow than in Petersburg. The Ivanovs were predisposed to dislike her, disappointed that their favorite uncle had chosen to marry this young stenographer instead of another beloved relative, an aunt on their father's side they wanted Dostoyevsky to marry after her husband was gone. They could just picture this interloper, too—an edgy, arrogant Nihilist, no doubt, severe and bespectacled. Indeed, Anna recalled, when she appeared at their door and "they saw a young woman, hardly more than a girl and, what's more, one who practically trembled before them, they were astonished and couldn't take their eyes off me." Still, there was more wonder in their gaze than warmth.

Anna was also something of an exotic attraction on her visit to Moscow's Petrovskoye-Razumovskoye Agricultural Academy. Her brother, Ivan, a handsome, pink-cheeked seventeen-year-old boy with curly blond hair and a buoyant, childlike personality to match, was the youngest student at the academy, and well liked by everyone. When Ivan's friends heard that Anna would be visiting, they scrambled to get a look at the wife of the well-known author. Looking on as Ivan and his classmates argued over whether Dostoyevsky had slandered their generation in his latest work, *Crime and Punishment*, or if he was in sympathy with it, Anna, "of course, came to my husband's defense." The novel's poverty-stricken student-turned-murderer, Raskolnikov, was clearly a stand-in for the young Russian Nihilists of their day, whom Dostoyevsky felt had been so poisoned by Western ideas that they would murder for the sake of an abstract theory. The character of Raskolnikov, then, evoked a much larger cultural debate in nineteenth-century Russia, between two groups known as the Slavophiles and the Westernizers.

The Westernizers celebrated Peter the Great's modernization of Russia at the beginning of the eighteenth century and looked to European values and institutions as models for their own socially and politically lagging country. Critic Vissarion Belinsky succinctly summed up the Westernizers' credo in his famous 1847 letter to writer Nikolai Gogol, declaring that Russia's "salvation lies not in mysticism, or in ascetism, or in pietism, but in the progress of civilization, education, and humanitarian values," which, for Belinsky, all came from the West.

The Slavophiles fundamentally disagreed, arguing that Russia's unique historical development, and geographical location between Europe and the East, had fostered a distinct set of national principles. Peter the Great's attempt to superimpose Western ideals and political forms onto Russia had been a colossal mistake. Central to the Russian character, maintained the Slavophiles, was the Orthodox Christianity that had come from Greece, whereas Western culture and religion were infected by Roman ideas of rationality, egoism, legality, and empire. Western societies, moreover, were founded on violence and therefore required the rule of law to govern relations among people. Such ideas, the Slavophiles argued, were foreign to Russia, which had preserved the spirit of Christian brotherhood through its centuries-old institutions of peasant communities. Russia's future salvation, then, lay in a return to the patriarchal values and customs of pre-Petrine Russia, with the peasant commune serving as the country's ideal social form. "A commune," wrote the Slavophile thinker Konstantin Aksakov, "is a union of the people who have renounced their egoism, their individuality, and who express their common accord; this is an act of love, a noble Christian act."

In 1852, a Slavophile philosopher named Ivan Kireyevsky published an extremely influential article, "On the Nature of European Culture and Its Relation to the Culture of Russia," in which he laid out the full gamut of dichotomies that distinguished Russia from the West. The West, he argued, privileged reason and argument; Russia, feeling and faith. The West suffered from the precariousness of individualism, whereas Russians enjoyed the solidity of family ties. The West privileged luxury and artificiality; Russia, simplicity and moral fortitude. The Western psyche was fraught with inner anxiety and an overly intellectual conception of virtue, whereas Russians enjoyed an inner tranquility combined with a healthy mistrust of the self that led one to strive toward moral self-perfection. Kireyevsky's dichotomies were simplistic and self-congratulatory, to be sure, but in the words of one Slavic scholar, "they helped nineteenth-century Russian art to define its mission."

Dostoyevsky was deeply influenced by Slavophile ideas. "We have at last become convinced that we, too, are a distinct nationality, original in the highest degree," he wrote in *Time*, "and that our task is to create our own new form, a native one that belongs to us, taken from our soil, taken from our national spirit and our national principles." Beginning in the early 1860s, he became a leading proponent of the cultural ethos known as *pochvennichestvo*, which called for educated Russians to return to the traditions of their native soil (*pochva* means "soil"), having been split off from the majority of their fellow Russians since Peter the Great's Westernization campaign. (Raskolnikov's name derives from the word *raskol*, or "split.") The social institutions of the Russian peasantry, Dostoyevsky said, provided "more solid and moral foundations" for the solution of Russia's social problems "than . . . all the dreams of Saint-Simon [a French socialist theorist] and his school."

Like many Slavophile thinkers, Dostoyevsky was politically conservative, a supporter of the Russian autocracy. He considered that institution an expression of the age-old familial relationship that had always existed between the tsar and his people, who revered their monarch as the earthly embodiment of God. "The ancient truth," Dostoyevsky wrote, "which from time immemorial has penetrated into the soul of the Russian people: that their Tsar is also their father, . . . and that the relation of the Russian people to their Tsar-Father is lovingly free and without fear." No wonder Dostoyevsky reacted so sensitively to any perceived slight of his homeland: to criticize the state or its leaders was, for him, to insult the soul of Russia herself.

To a contemporary American audience, artistic principle and nationalism might seem like odd, if not disturbing, bedfellows. But in order to judge Dostoyevsky fairly for his time, we must recognize that his nationalist views had emerged out of a long tradition of Slavophile thought, as well as a passionate, well-informed engagement with the social and cultural issues of his own day. In time, the views Dostoyevsky held would take on increasingly jingoistic overtones—a trend in vogue throughout Europe in the nineteenth century, where thinkers often proclaimed that God had destined their land to create a new world order and lead the other nations to a glorious future. But in the 1860s nationalism like his had not yet crossed that line.

The students discussing *Crime and Punishment* in Ivan Snitkin's dorm room would have understood this cultural context; they would have known that what they were debating was not only a matter of literary interpretation but one of the pressing cultural questions of their day:

What is Russia's relationship to the West? Where should the social and political models for her future come from? Dostoyevsky would explore these questions throughout the rest of his career, debating them openly in his journalistic writing and placing them at the core of his novels, dramatizing them in all their philosophical and psychological complexity. One of the writer's significant contributions to Russian literature is the way he managed to transform contemporary debates about Russian national identity into timeless meditations on the human quest for meaning and truth.

To the disappointment of the young guests, the author himself was not there to weigh in on their debate, as he was off meeting with Katkov about the new novel. Yet he returned in time to meet Anna's brother later that same day, and the older man took an immediate liking to his young brother-in-law. He came to love Ivan like a son himself, and considered it his duty to protect the impressionable young man from the Nihilist tendencies surrounding him. Anna was overjoyed that the two most important men in her life had at last met. Her brother, after all, was the one who had given her the dictation practice she needed to master stenography, which in turn led her to Dostoyevsky.

But the real reason for their visit to the Russian capital, Anna well knew, was the all-important advance the writer was hoping to secure from Katkov. For months, readers of *The Russian Messenger* had been riveted by *Crime and Punishment*, the last sections of which had recently appeared in the February 1867 issue. Alas, this success did not mean any more income for them: Katkov had already paid Dostoyevsky in full (just over five thousand rubles) for the serialization of that novel, and no one had yet offered to publish it in a stand-alone edition. Still, the novel had created enough of a sensation that the writer felt confident that he had some leverage in soliciting a new book deal from Katkov. And the stakes were high: Dostoyevsky viewed selling the new project as crucial, both professionally and personally, as it would give the couple some needed breathing room as they navigated their new life together.

And yet, as he stood before the regal, gray-bearded Mikhail Katkov in the headquarters of *The Russian Messenger*, animatedly laying out the reasons the journal should invest in him again, the writer had only an inkling of what he was asking them to invest in. This was a pattern with him: asking publishers for an advance before he had fleshed out a new idea in the slightest. It would be months before Dostoyevsky's notebooks and correspondence began to include references to this new work-in-progress, later to be called *The Idiot*.

The initial idea revolved around a character pejoratively nicknamed "the idiot" by his own mother, who abandons him in his youth and then cruelly maligns him as an idler to all who will listen, even though he has actually come to support his entire ungrateful family. Eventually the disillusioned boy compensates for his inferiority complex by growing into a man of limitless pride and violent passions, before finally transcending his tragic past—under the purifying influence of love—and performing a noble feat for which he is destined.

In the arduous months to follow, both the character of "the idiot" and the book named for him would undergo so many transformations—each a cause of creative agony for the writer—that by the time it began appearing in print in 1868, only a trace of Dostoyevsky's original concept remained. The character, first envisioned as a proud, violent tramp who undergoes a spiritual conversion, would be transformed into an already transfigured, Christlike figure, "an absolutely beautiful human being" who attempts to bring about the moral regeneration of his fallen country.

But as he was making his case to Katkov, Dostoyevsky knew none of this. All he knew was that he needed a publishing deal—and he got one. In exchange for a thousand-ruble installment of the advance, the writer would set to work right away on the new novel, which was slated to begin serial publication in 1868.

Hearing this, Anna was relieved. For it meant they could now start planning for their future. The Dostoyevskys intended to put the thousand rubles—along with three or four hundred the writer hoped to receive for an article about his former mentor, the late critic Vissarion Belinsky—toward a three-month honeymoon in Europe. There, free at last of financial pressures and meddling relatives, they could enjoy each other's company, while Dostoyevsky finished the article on Belinsky and settled down to work on his new novel. They knew that his relatives would be furious about the trip, which would cost money they felt they were entitled to, so Anna and her husband decided not to reveal their intentions until their plans were firmly in place.

AS SOON AS THEY RETURNED to Petersburg, Anna's old torments—the nonstop hosting duties, the taunts from Pasha—resumed almost immediately, making their extended honeymoon plans seem all the wiser. Still, the Dostoyevskys kept their plans to themselves as long as they could. One evening, at dinner, the family was discussing Emilya Fyodorovna's suggestion that they start looking for a summer vacation rental. She knew of an excellent house near Pavlovsk with a large garden and many rooms.

"Anna Grigoryevna will be happier in the company of young people. And I—well, so be it!—I'll make the sacrifice and take over the housekeeping, which isn't going too well for our dear hostess in any case."

"Only there isn't any point in our looking for a summer house," responded Dostoyevsky, abandoning the plan to maintain their secrecy. "Anya and I are going abroad."

At first the relatives took this as a joke, before realizing that he was serious. In the awkward silence that followed, the writer retreated to his study, while Anna and Pasha stayed in the dining room and the other guests congregated in the living room.

"I see perfectly well that this is some trick of yours, Anna Grigoryevna!" Pasha began in any angry voice.

"*What* trick?"

"Oh, you don't un-der-*stand* me?" he sniped. "Why, this absurd trip abroad, *that's* what! But you are very much mistaken in your calculations. If I *permitted* your trip to Moscow, it was only because *papa* had to go there to get money. But a trip abroad—that's a whim of yours, Anna Grigoryevna, and I won't allow it under any circumstances."

Anna did not know how to respond to his impudence. "But perhaps you'll have mercy on us?" she finally said, sighing in bitter irony.

"Don't count on it! After all, this whim of yours is going to cost money, and the money isn't for you alone, you know, it's for the whole family—our money is held in common."

Later, Dostoyevsky's relatives filed into his study—one by one, like petitioners—to tell him that they were opposed to the trip. The last to appear was Pasha, who demanded that if *papa* was going through with this absurd idea, he should at least leave them money in advance. Pasha would speak to Emilya Fyodorovna and her children and let his stepfather know the next day just how much would be required.

Anna's mind was reeling. Of the thousand-ruble advance Dostoyevsky had just received from Katkov, he had already planned to set five hundred aside for his relatives and the couple's living expenses before their departure, leaving only five hundred for the trip. That would be just enough for them to get by comfortably for a month, at which point Dostoyevsky could start work on the Belinsky article, which might fetch another three or four hundred rubles if they were lucky.

The next morning, just as Anna had feared, Emilya Fyodorovna announced that she and her family would need, beyond the five hundred, an additional two hundred for Pasha, whom she'd agreed to look after in Dostoyevsky's absence. The writer tried to get her to agree to three hundred total, but when she refused, he simply gave in. That same day, as fate would have it, a young woman appeared with several court orders for Dostoyevsky to pay off half of a previously incurred thousand-ruble debt, or his furniture would be attached. Between his own debts and those of his relatives, Dostoyevsky now owed seventeen hundred rubles, with just a thousand in his possession.

That evening, he confirmed what Anna had feared: he was canceling the trip. "Fate is against us, my darling Anyechka," he said, in a state of complete denial. "If only you knew, my darling, how badly I feel that this cannot happen now! How I've dreamed of this trip, how necessary I felt it was for both of us!"

Perhaps Dostoyevsky was still blind to how controlling his relatives were, even after Anna pointed it out to him. But the histrionic tone of his words—at least as Anna recalled them in her memoir—suggests that he may simply have found himself too weak to stand up to the family. Either way, his deference to his family's demands was putting his young marriage at risk. "If we were to save our love," she later recalled, "we needed to be alone together, if only for two or three months, and I had to calm down from all the agitations and unpleasantries I'd suffered. Only then would the two of us come together for the rest of our lives." And now that opportunity was slipping away.

Then she had an idea.

Her dowry—clothes, a piano, a few little tables, some other furniture—this could all be pawned, couldn't it? Surely that would raise the funds they needed for their trip. The prospect of losing such precious items pained her, and she worried what her mother would say. More than once, in the months after the wedding, Mrs. Snitkina had expressed her concern that "the good habits I was brought up with would vanish thanks to our Russian style of living with its disorderly hospitality." With so many guests milling about in the Dostoyevsky home—dinner parties and champagne and games and endless conversations, day after day, night after night—Anna feared she was falling prey to the worst elements of Slavic sloth. And her mother had also chided Anna "for my inability to make Pasha treat me with respect."

So it's no wonder Anna "feared my mother's displeasure"—especially as some of her dowry had been bought with her mother's very own money. "What if Mama accuses my husband of excessive favoritism toward his own family and doubts his love for me?" she thought. "How she'll suffer, who always put her children's happiness above her own."

Anna passed a sleepless night. At five a.m. the bells for morning mass rang, and she dressed quickly before going to pray in the Church of the Ascension across the street from their house. After praying fervently, she left the service and went directly to her mother's house. The sight of her daughter at this early hour, eyes red from weeping, alarmed Mrs. Snitkina. But Anna wasted no time in telling her mother everything: that the trip to Europe was off, that she'd now have to spend the summer with the extended Dostoyevsky family, that their love was hanging in the balance.

Mrs. Snitkina understood at once. "What else is to be done when your happiness is at stake?" she said. "You and Fyodor Mikhailovich are so different from each other that if you don't become close now, as married people should, then you never will. You must leave as soon as possible, before the holidays, before new complications come up."

It was the last thing Anna expected to hear from her mother, but exactly what she needed. As surprised as she was relieved, she rushed home and arrived before Fyodor Mikhailovich had awoken. As Anna was getting his coffee ready, Pasha strode into the dining room. Where had she been, he wanted know, and what had she been doing? "Are you still dreaming of those European spas?" he asked.

"But you know perfectly well we're not going abroad," she responded.

"What did I tell you? Now maybe you've learned that I know how to get my way, and I *don't* allow any European trips!"

Anna was outraged by the boy's brazenness, but she was anxious to avoid a blowup. If she wanted to persuade her husband, she would have to stay calm.

Approaching her husband on such a delicate subject at home was impossible, as someone might overhear them—most likely Pasha himself, a conniving eavesdropper. When Dostoyevsky emerged and told Anna he had to go out to the apothecary, she saw her opportunity and offered to come along. On the way, she suggested that they stop in at the Church of the Ascension to pray, hoping it might soften his mood. By the time they left the chapel, Anna was in an unusually buoyant mood. "How happy I am, Anya, that you're taking it so well," her husband said, knowing how much the trip had meant to her.

"But it can still take place," she blurted out, "*if* you agree to the plan I'm going to propose to you." Trying to maintain her calm and resolve, she explained her plan to sell her dowry. Just as she'd feared, he rejected it immediately, categorically refusing to let her sacrifice her own possessions. They argued for a time, she "begging him to let me have at least two or three months of a calm and happy life," and he refusing to give an inch.

Finally, as they wandered into a deserted part of the city, along the Moika embankment, Anna "burst into such violent sobbing that poor Fyodor Mikhailovich was at last taken aback." Which must have been exactly what she intended: she needed him to hear the violence of her frustration, to understand what might happen if he didn't agree to her plan. With a kind of composed ferocity, she choked out how hard these weeks had been for her, and begged him to give them the few months of calm they needed. For under the present conditions, she made clear, "we not only would never become friends, as we used to dream, but would perhaps separate forever. I implored him to save our love, our happiness."

It worked. Sensing the depth of his wife's suffering for the first time, and witnessing her passionate resolve, Dostoyevsky relented and agreed to everything.

Had Anna simply accepted her husband's concession to his family, it might have meant the beginning of the end of their marriage. Instead, she used her keen insight into her husband's psychology and took decisive action at a pivotal moment. This willingness to risk everything, and often to force her husband's hand, would be crucial both to the survival of their marriage and to their later business undertakings together. Anna's enterprising nature gave her the ability to recognize a critical opportunity and seize it at exactly the right moment. And Dostoyevsky knew enough to *listen* to her in such moments and to follow her lead. By drawing on her wisdom and inner strength, Anna helped Dostoyevsky find his own.

This was an essential part of the dynamic that made their relationship work. As soon as she entered Dostoyevsky's life, Anna had shown the judgment and perseverance necessary to support him as he salvaged his career. When he delivered his meekly roundabout marriage proposal, she sensed that he had as much at stake as she did, and she boldly accepted. In doing so, she affirmed his worth as a man in a way that none of his previous loves had done; this, in turn, allowed him to conquer his self-defeating depression for a time and emboldened him to begin a new chapter in his life. Now, with their futures once more in jeopardy, Anna confronted him directly and convinced him of what they needed to do.

This dynamic between them could lead to subtle (and at times *not*-so-subtle) power struggles. Early in their marriage, in order to preserve Dostoyevsky's peace of mind and sometimes her own, Anna was often the one to stand down in moments of strife—except in those critical instances when she sensed that surrender could in fact mean the end of their relationship. On such occasions, and then more regularly as their marriage went along, it was Dostoyevsky who was forced to submit.

No matter the shifts in their balance of power over time, though, their love for each other was deep and intense. Like so many of Dostoyevsky's characters, Anna and her husband often seemed most emotionally in sync when facing a crisis. He needed to teeter on the edge of destruction in order to tap into his deepest emotional and creative instincts, while she was most resourceful in moments of extreme urgency or when helping the writer channel his frenetic creative energy.

Given such dynamics, it is hardly surprising that in the years of their marriage they would know only a few brief stretches of the sort of calm Anna had grown up with. Their shared life was as emotionally turbulent as it was creatively fruitful. And, while Anna often reminisced about her "quiet, measured, and serene" upbringing, it's unlikely that she could have been fully satisfied by a more peaceful life. She always retained the excitable character that had first distinguished her at the Mariinskaya Gymnasium—"one of those fiery natures," as her schoolmate Marya Stoyunina remembered. Like Netochka Nezvanova, Anna was drawn to, indeed energized by, the intensity and struggle of life with a man like Dostoyevsky.

Not long after their agreement on the Moika embankment, an appraiser came to estimate the value of Anna's pawned furniture. On the evening of the same day, at a large family dinner, the couple announced that, in two days, they were leaving for their trip, after all.

"Permit me, *papa*, to make an observation," began Pasha, thrown off by the news.

"No observations!" Dostoyevsky exploded, before turning to address the whole group. "All of you will receive the amount you have stipulated and not one kopeck more."

After dinner, Dostoyevsky's family filed angrily into his study to receive a portion of their allowance, plus IOUs for the remainder, to be disbursed by Anna's mother in early May after she received the money from the pawnbroker. Anna even persuaded her husband to give Pasha some extra money for a summer coat, hoping it might appease the bitter young man. It didn't work: as they parted, he assured Anna that her treachery would not go unpunished. When they returned, he warned, they would "measure swords and see whose side victory will be on."

But Anna was too elated about their upcoming trip to care. On the bright, sunny afternoon of April 14, 1867, she and her husband boarded a train to Germany to begin a three-month honeymoon.

It would be four years before they returned.

*The casino at Baden-Baden, where Anna (inset) confronted
her husband's demons herself in 1867.*

II

THE RECKONING

6.

A New Beginning

E xhausted from their travel preparations, and wanting nothing more than to decompress, Anna settled in for a restful journey by rail. She later regretted sleeping through most of Prussia, including the historic city of Königsberg, which she had been eager to see. By morning they had passed through Weichsel and Elbing and other little towns, most of them lined with charming stone houses crowned by great crisscrossing beams and trellised with overgrown ivy and grapevines. The farther south they went beyond the Baltic Sea, the prettier the scenery became. Every detail caught her eye: the fir- and pine-covered mountains rising in the distance; the elderberry hedgerows and wild cherries in full bloom; the three-storied houses of Berlin, with their shingled roofs.

All of it was new, all of it fascinating. Along the way they debarked to spend the night in one such town. There, Anna recalled, they encountered greedy hotel owners who charged exorbitant rates and never answered their bell, not to mention peddlers who foisted their wares on the couple at seemingly every stop. All in all, however, it seemed to Anna like the start of a perfect European honeymoon. And, with Katkov's recent advance and some additional funds from Mrs. Snitkina in hand, for once the couple felt financially stable.

At one stop along the way Anna bought herself a little notebook she would use to write down observations, a seemingly small decision for which posterity must thank her. That notebook would become the secret diary she kept during the first year of her marriage. Not only a treasure trove of biographical and historical detail about this period in her husband's life, the diary is itself a shining example of nineteenth-century personal travelogue—all the more valuable as it was never intended for publication, which lends it an uncommon intimacy.

The weather in Dresden when they arrived, with the exception of a few cool, drizzly days, was warm and splendid—an ideal backdrop to what was shaping up to be a true respite from their earlier troubles in Petersburg. "There was nobody standing between my husband and me," Anna recalled. "I had the opportunity to fully enjoy his company." Contributing to this growing closeness was her discovery, shortly after arriving in Dresden, that she was pregnant. The news delighted both Anna and her husband, who was attentive and solicitous toward her, and she dreamed in her diary of how the new arrival would further deepen their love. "We are supremely happy together," Anna wrote.

If Anna and her husband felt any pangs of insecurity over the financial implications of their additional mouth to feed, she left no record of it in her diary. The two passed their days strolling together through Dresden's massive Grosser Garten, ambling through the enormous park to the Ostra-Allee or sipping coffee on the Brülsche Terrasse, with its charming grove of pollarded lime trees. At night they enjoyed long, leisurely meals at the Helbig, a restaurant on the bank of the Elbe, where they gazed out at old men fishing in the river, while back on the bank women drank beer and knitted in the fresh air. Anna would never forget those daily visits to Dresden's many museums, her favorite being the famed Zwinger gallery. She would remember, too, clear evenings at the outdoor Café Reale, as the setting sun marked out the little homes and castles nestled in the mountains surrounding Dresden. The Elbe was so striking in such moments that even Dostoyevsky's usual complaints were quieted.

Yet not every moment was so peaceful. Being so far from home couldn't keep Dostoyevsky from worrying about their financial situation, anxious that some creditor might discover his whereabouts. Even their location was a source of low-grade aggravation for him: unlike wide-eyed Anna, traveling abroad for the very first time, he had seen it all before—this "land of holy wonders," as the poet Alexei Khomyakov once called Europe—and he was not impressed. Over the course of three trips through Europe earlier in the decade, Dostoyevsky had nurtured a growing antipathy toward the very lands—England, France, and Germany in particular—that the Westernizers back home felt Russians should emulate.

In articles published in *Time* and *Epoch*, in his fiction, and in *Winter Notes on Summer Impressions*, Dostoyevsky's scathingly ironic travelogue about his 1862 sojourn through Europe, the writer made his skepticism toward Europe clear. "How they struggle to convince themselves that they are content and completely happy," he had once mused about the self-satisfied people of Paris. In fact, he argued, it was Russia that actually had much to teach the rest of the world, understanding as she did deeper spiritual truths entirely foreign to the materialistic West.

And yet, if only out of sheer necessity, here he was, back in Europe. It felt to him as if his life were going in circles. "The question occurred to me of why I was in Dresden, precisely in Dresden, and not somewhere in another place, and for what precisely had it been worth dropping everything in one place and moving to another," he groused later that summer in a letter to Apollon Maikov. "The answer was clear (health, debts, and so on), but what was also bad was that I sensed very clearly that no matter where I live now, it turns out to be *all the same*, in Dresden or anywhere, anywhere abroad, everywhere a loner."

Work, too, was much on his mind. He had yet to take any notes for *The Idiot*, though ideas were at least beginning to percolate about this book that he would have to start writing no later than the fall in order to get the first installments to *The Russian Messenger* on time. He was also trying to write his article on Belinsky, which increasingly felt like a noose around his neck. Belinsky had been a strong influence on Dostoyevsky in his youth, but the man's liberal ideas no longer resonated with him. He was a fool to have taken on the article in the first place, Dostoyevsky told Maikov, and now wished only to "scrape away" liberal ideas like Belinsky's, which he considered "cursed dregs, ingrown, and retrograde." He now recoiled at the educated society championed by the critic, dismissing them privately as "a heap of everyone that has renounced Russia, not understanding her and becoming Frenchified." And Belinsky himself: "wasn't he really a conscious enemy of the fatherland, wasn't he really retrograde?" No wonder, then, that Dostoyevsky so resisted the assignment—or that his hostility toward Russian liberals and Westernizers became such a dominant element in his fiction in this period, first in *The Idiot* and then in *The Possessed*.

Anna, meanwhile, was taking it all in: the museums, the sweet-smelling bakeries and charming cafés, the bridge over the beautiful Elbe, and, above all, the men and women of this foreign world so new to her. An ardent people-watcher, she entertained herself for hours simply sitting in a café or strolling the narrow Dresden streets. Unlike her husband, she had been looking forward to spending time in Germany: Like so many Russians of the time, she had nurtured grandiose images of this most progressive of European countries, a favorite destination of Russian tourists and intellectuals alike. She had grown up with a picture of beautiful Frankfurt am Main on the wall of her family's Petersburg apartment, and had even taken classes taught in German at the Mariinskaya Gymnasium.

Yet now, to her growing dismay, Anna was finding this "land of holy miracles" to be less a place of profound spiritual insight than a capital of material gratification. To the cash-poor newlyweds, the locals appeared to know the cost of everything but the value of nothing: "Oh, these Germans," Anna wrote, "who won't let you enjoy a single sight without paying for it!" She also found them rather obtuse, a common stereotype some Russians of the time perpetuated about their neighbor to the West. "Germans really are too stupid," Anna remarked of a waiter who couldn't figure out what she wanted—a repeated frustration that may have overlooked the limitations of her German conversational skills.

And then there was their hunt for accommodations. The Dostoyevskys visited several buildings with placards reading FURNISHED ROOMS TO RENT, Anna recounted, but "when you go inside to look, there's nothing ready." At last they found an apartment on Johannesstrasse, in the Altstadt, with its quaint four-story buildings with tall gabled roofs lining narrow cobblestone streets. The landlady, a tall, thin Swiss woman by the name of Zimmerman, struck them as kind and trustworthy, if a bit tedious.

But by this point, they were tired of searching, and this apartment would have to do.

Something else, too, bothered Anna: "I think there must be something in my appearance that annoys the Germans, because all the women stare at me so hard." One weapon Anna wielded against this intrusive German gaze, her diary suggests, was to do some serious staring of her own. She read her subjects like characters in a novel, spinning entire plots around their actions and expressions. One disabled German girl she observed on a number of occasions Anna began referring to as "my invalid," piecing together in her mind the girl's complicated family story on the basis of the various people with whom Anna saw her interacting. Nor was she the only invalid Anna saw: While strolling around town, she encountered many other men and women with twisted limbs and mangled faces, casualties of the previous year's Austro-Prussian War. But she did not fully understand what she was looking at, being unaware of the details of recent European history and never having witnessed such sights in her sheltered life.

Anna was capable of seeing beauty, too, of course—in faces and in art. Two faces, in particular, stirred her: those of Raphael's Sistine Madonna and Murillo's Mary with Christ Child. The couple would gaze at these works for an hour at a time, and Anna often returned to the Zwinger on her own when her husband was working. "Never has any picture before made such an impression on me," she wrote of Raphael's *Sistine Madonna*. "What beauty, what innocence, what sorrow are in that divine countenance, what humility and suffering in those eyes."

What was it that so moved Anna in the soft, suffering beauty of that exquisite face? Perhaps, with her new family's fortunes still so uncertain, she was thinking of the looming burden that lay ahead. She loved Dostoyevsky; of this she was certain. And the obligation she'd taken on by marrying this man continued to provide her with a deep sense of purpose, even happiness. Yet mingled with these feelings were pangs of sorrow, as well as a clear awareness that she, too, was a woman whose destiny would now be forever entwined with an extraordinarily challenging calling. She made frequent visits to Dresden's Russian Orthodox church, where she prayed passionately for her husband, for their future child, and only then for herself.

Even as she was meditating on those artistic images of spiritual beauty and strength, Dostoyevsky had begun to gaze at *her* in amazement, ascribing to her a kind of spiritual light. "He called me an exquisite creature, sent from heaven above," Anna wrote, "and said he loved me passionately. God grant it may continue." As she had already begun to understand back in Russia, however, while it often entailed a pas de deux of domination or submission, with Dostoyevsky love was rarely a partnership of compassionate equals. And even as he came to appreciate his young wife's beneficence, he began putting that virtue to the test.

After ten days in Dresden, Dostoyevsky started picking fights with Anna. Between the wedding, the family squabbles, and the journey to Dresden, it had been far too long since he had done any serious work, and he was growing restless. Finally, he asked Anna to allow him to take a short trip to Bad Homburg, a gambling resort some 280 miles away.

"When I think of him going away and leaving me here alone, cold shivers run down my spine," wrote Anna, particularly anxious over how she would handle her frequent bouts of morning sickness without him. "I can't imagine what I'll do. Just sit around in the depths of melancholy in these three rooms, with no Fedya." And yet, seeing how his isolation from family and colleagues was beginning to wear on him, Anna characteristically shifted attention from her concerns to his. "Since the thought of this trip fills his mind to the exclusion of everything else, why not let him indulge in it? He'd never get rid of it any other way." Convincing herself that a quick fling at roulette would improve his mood, Anna gave in.

Did she actually believe these arguments or was she just rationalizing to herself, as the spouses of addicts often do? Anna left us no direct answer to this question, but her diaries from Dresden suggest that at first she viewed her husband's gambling as a temporary diversion sure to rejuvenate him while causing little financial distress. Some recent scholars have criticized Anna for this, suggesting that, by refusing to restrain Dostoyevsky more forcefully at this critical moment, she was actually enabling him.

There may be some truth to this judgment, but it fails to account for the cultural context that influenced Anna's approach to her husband. By giving in to Dostoyevsky's request to gamble, Anna was following the Russian customs of the time, whereby a wife was expected to accept a husband's gambling habit without complaint. Only if such a habit became excessive might she intervene to restrain it, if only to minimize the financial damage it caused. If a woman dared to do more than that, she might quickly become a social pariah, as other strong-willed women of the time discovered. Karolina Pavlova, for example, was a prominent poet born to a wealthy aristocratic family, but she married a minor writer who gambled away her vast fortune, sometimes at the rate of ten to fifteen thousand rubles an evening. For a few years Pavlova looked the other way, but when she realized that her husband had secretly mortgaged her own property to support his gambling habit, she initiated proceedings against him. He was arrested, jailed, and eventually sentenced to a ten-month exile—although he was convicted not because he had robbed his wife's coffers but because authorities had found various censored books in his library during the search. As for Pavlova herself, for her bold act of self-assertion, she was rewarded with social censure and abandonment by even her closest friends, who never forgave her for ruining her husband's reputation.

If Anna Dostoyevskaya was not more forceful in refusing Dostoyevsky's gambling request in Dresden, then it was at least in part because she had few positive female role models to guide her. Moreover, as time would tell, Anna's decisions may have demonstrated a deeper sort of wisdom and psychological insight into her husband than she has been given credit for.

On May 4, the day he was scheduled to leave, both Anna and Dostoyevsky were anxious about this first extended separation of their marriage. They paced up and down the platform as they waited for the warning bell, then missed it when it finally rang, leaving him just enough time to jump into the third-class wagon—without even saying good-bye—before the doors slammed shut behind him. Standing on the platform, Anna smiled up at him through the thick glass carriage window, watching him take a seat in the crowded carriage next to a very old man. Dostoyevsky smiled back at her, placing his hand over his heart—signifying love, Anna knew—and holding up four fingers, one for each day he would be gone, to remind her how soon he'd be back. When he saw tears in her eyes, he shook his finger side to side, scolding her gently. But as she ran alongside the slow, screeching train, she broke into a sob.

Pulling her veil over tear-stained eyes to evade the intrusive gaze of German onlookers, Anna ambled back to their apartment on Johannesstrasse, taking the long way to distract herself. She stopped at the post office, where the postmaster—by now familiar with this Russian couple, who came nearly every day—handed over a letter addressed to her husband. Anna looked at the envelope, stunned. It was from Polina Suslova.

Anna had reason to be alarmed. Still prone to doubts about this man to whom she had joined her life, she had been secretly reading his letters for weeks. And with good reason: Dostoyevsky had been corresponding with Polina Suslova, whom Anna had heard about early in their relationship, and she could not help but deduce that something was happening between them. "It's not good, I know, to read one's husband's letters behind his back," she confessed to her diary, "but I couldn't help it." A week before, she had discovered another letter from Polina, this one sent just a few weeks prior. "After I had read it, I felt cold all over, and shivered," she recalled. "I was so afraid the old feelings were going to revive and swamp his love for me."

Careful not to betray her agitation to the postmaster, Anna calmly left the post office, then marched briskly back to their apartment, where she grabbed a knife and meticulously opened the envelope so that she would be able to close it again later without a trace—a procedure she'd mastered in recent weeks.

The letter itself has been lost, unfortunately, but Anna's reaction to it hasn't. "It was a very stupid, clumsy letter," she recorded that day in her diary, "and speaks poorly about the intelligence of the writer. I'm quite sure she is furious about this event [Dostoyevsky's marriage to Anna] and that's how her feelings of insult are expressed." In her diary she notes that the envelope was postmarked from Dresden, though scholars have since confirmed that Polina was in Moscow at that time, and in all likelihood she had simply sent the letter through an acquaintance who happened to be visiting Dresden.

Anna read the letter again. The sender "calls me Brylkina (very stupid and not at all clever)"—Brylkina being a rather unattractive name that sounds similar to, or could even have been taken by Anna as a misspelling of, an unflattering Russian word meaning something like "the rebellious girl." In this Anna was mistaken: Polina was referring not to her but to a female friend who actually *was* named Brylkina, a woman Dostoyevsky had met in Petersburg shortly before his departure to Germany, a fact the writer had mentioned to Polina in a letter sent on April 23. But Anna knew nothing of this April 23 letter—a good thing, for it would have only strengthened her worst fears, suggesting that, for all his passionate declarations, Dostoyevsky may still not have been fully committed to her.

In that long and detailed letter, sent from Dresden, Dostoyevsky gives Polina a thorough recap of his recent business affairs—but also takes her into confidence about his marriage. It is clear in the letter that Dostoyevsky had not seen Polina in many months, perhaps even a few years, for he catches her up on everything that has happened to him during this time. But it is equally evident that he still had feelings for his former lover—so much so that he takes pains to outline the circumstances of his relationship with Anna in a tone that might be called businesslike, even defensive. "My stenographer, Anna Grigoryevna Snitkina," Dostoyevsky writes,

> is a young and rather attractive girl, twenty years old, from a good family, who had finished her gymnasium studies superbly, with an extraordinarily kind and clear character. Our work went wonderfully well. The novel *The Gambler* (now already published) was finished October 28, in twenty-four days.* Toward the end of the novel I noticed that my stenographer loved me sincerely, although she had never said so much as a word to

---

*Actually, the novel was finished on October 29, according to *Reminiscences*.

me about that, and I liked her more and more. Since I've been terribly lonely and distressed with life since my brother's death, I proposed to her. She agreed, and here we are, married. The difference in ages is horrible (20 and 44),* but I'm becoming more and more convinced that she will be happy. She has a heart, and she knows how to love.

It was Polina's response to this letter that Anna held in her hand in this moment.

At a loss for what to do, she walked over to a mirror and closely studied her face, now breaking out in little red blotches, always a sign of great agitation for her. Then she sat down to open the little box where her husband kept his correspondence, removed all the letters within, and reread them one by one. After completing this grim task, she went outside into the fresh air and found a stationery shop, where she bought a small quantity of sealing wax to restore the opened envelope to its original look.

DOSTOYEVSKY'S EXPRESS TRAIN arrived in Leipzig at five thirty in the evening. Exhausted, nerves well frayed by now, he spent five hours awaiting his connecting train in the station's enormous waiting room, buffeted by the smells of smoke and beer, getting up from time to time to eat or drink or pace around the station. He fell to thinking—about his debts, about his chances of winning big, about his love for Anna and his "weak-willed, muddled" decision to take this trip in the first place. Suddenly he couldn't fathom why he'd abandoned an "angel so pure, clear, quiet, gentle, beautiful, innocent, and who believes in me." As soon as he arrived in Bad Homburg, he poured his feelings into a letter to Anna: "How could I have left you? Why am I going? Where am I going? . . . What I'm doing is stupidity, stupidity, and more important, nastiness and weakness, but there is a slight chance here."

---

*Dostoyevsky was forty-five when he wrote this letter.

Stupidity, nastiness, and weakness: he had fallen prey to such vices before, and in the very same city. It was just four years ago, in October 1863, that he had stopped in Bad Homburg after his monthslong rendez-vous with Polina, the one that soured after he learned that she'd fallen in love with a handsome young Spaniard. The roulette wheel had treated him no less cruelly than Polina herself, leaving him flat broke. Now, al-most four years later, he was returning to the same casino as a newly mar-ried man, to try his fortunes once more.

By the time he arrived in Bad Homburg, the writer's nerves were so frayed that he could hardly stand upright. He hastened from the train station to the Hotel Victoria, a cosmopolitan haven popular with travel-ing dignitaries and statesmen. In his letter that day, he told Anna he would spend only two days before returning to Dresden, three at most.

Not that Dostoyevsky wasted any time mingling with the cosmopoli-tan crowd, which made him feel completely out of place. In truth, every-thing about Bad Homburg—a gambler's paradise nestled within the quiet rural seat of a Hessian noble family's estate, amid mineral springs and beautiful natural surroundings—drove Dostoyevsky mad. Its elegant trappings, he felt, belied a darker reality: that this "little escape" was actually an enormously profitable business built on stoking the gambling habits of moneyed men, who brought their families for a week of spa treatments and shopping even as they themselves slunk off to the casino.

By wrapping gambling into an attractive family resort experience, the owner of the spa, French businessman François Blanc, had managed to transform a once frowned-upon activity into chic entertainment of the highest order, while growing extremely wealthy in the bargain. By the time of Dostoyevsky's first trip there, in 1863, the casino was receiving a thousand visitors a day—a success that would spur Blanc to create the fa-mous casino at Monte Carlo, earning him the moniker "the Magician of Homburg and Monte Carlo." The highly sophisticated facade of Blanc's casinos, its spirit of aristocratic gentility and refinement, left Dostoyevsky suspicious and envious in equal measure.

On that Friday morning, though, no such high-minded objections stopped Dostoyevsky from walking three hundred meters or so along the

bright cobblestone Louisenstrasse, past the expensive shops and hotels—
the Englischer Hof, the Russischer Hof, the Hôtel de France—all the way
to the casino, known as the Kurhaus. It was a long, marble, two-story neoclassical building, with well-heeled men in top hats walking arm in arm
with ladies toting parasols.

Inside, visitors breezed through the ballrooms: the men in their cutaways and striped pants, the ladies in dark, frilly velvet, their skirts as
many as seven or eight feet in circumference. It was not uncommon for
one such garment to bump rudely into the next, particularly during the
weekend, when the casino was jammed with German tourists; on those
nights, Dostoyevsky told Anna, the "crowding, closeness, pushing, rude-
ness" became almost unbearable. But on this Friday morning the casino
was relatively quiet. Dostoyevsky strode past casual visitors in the café and
headed straight to the familiar gaming hall, a cavernous room with golden
chandeliers dangling from an intricately frescoed ceiling suspended above
the billiard and roulette tables. Most of the hard-boiled gamblers were
already gathered, sweating under their shirts and chemisettes. And now
here he was, too, standing with anticipation amid the sparkling gold and
silver coins laid out across the tables, under the glare of the hundreds
of gaslights from the chandeliers. In such moments, he was focused—
monomaniacally so. This capacity for obsession had always alarmed his
late brother Mikhail. Years before, after receiving Dostoyevsky's letter
from Wiesbaden, Mikhail observed that the tone of his brother's letters changed dramatically as soon as he arrived in the gambling town.
"About your travels, about your impressions, you no longer write a single
word." Perhaps Dostoyevsky was thinking of his brother's admonition
during this latest trip to Bad Homburg, when he permitted himself a rare
stroll one day in the park, later writing to Anna that "the place here is
charming. . . . It would be nice to stay a while here if it weren't for the
damned roulette."

But, of course, the damned roulette was all that mattered now. And
so, as soon as those sweetly alluring words, *"Faites vos jeux!"*—"Place your
bets!"—came thundering from the lips of one of the six croupiers dressed
in black, sitting imperiously around his table, Dostoyevsky gave himself

over completely to the game. By midday he had lost sixteen German imperials, leaving only twelve plus a few thalers. After breaking for lunch, however, he returned "with the intention of being impossibly prudent"—that is, of following his fail-safe system to a T—and promptly won back all sixteen imperials and an additional hundred guldens to boot. Certain by this point that he could win three hundred, for they were "already in my hands," he took a risk and lost it all.

It went on like this, for hours, until Dostoyevsky realized something crucial: he did not have what it took to make money in this way. Watching a German player bet calmly, and then collect his thousand guldens as if it were all in a day's work, he became convinced that he was just not "built like that," that he was too much the volatile Russian to maintain a winning streak at roulette. "If one is prudent, that is, if one is as though made of marble, cold, and *inhumanly* cautious," he told Anna, "then definitely, *without any doubt*, one can win *as much as one wishes*." The only problem, he reasoned, was that one needed to play for a long time to make that happen, and to be wealthy enough to ride out the downturns. From his jealous, ethnocentric perspective, this meant being coldhearted like the Germans, as Dostoyevsky often described them.

That day Dostoyevsky was relearning a lesson he had understood three years earlier, when he created the underground man of *Notes from Underground*: human beings are fundamentally irrational and life utterly unpredictable. Any system, whether for the purpose of conquering the roulette wheel or creating the perfect society, was bound to fail. It was this insight that fueled Dostoyevsky's distrust of the radical intelligentsia of his time, who believed that humankind could rationally engineer the ideal society and in this way create universal happiness on earth. If Europe had indeed led the world to the pinnacle of human achievement, Dostoyevsky wryly wondered in *Notes from Underground*, would that not then spell the end of all human striving? While the radicals bowed before the God of Progress, Dostoyevsky and his underground man would go on defying them, if only to prove they were free to do so, that they were not pawns in someone else's "rational design."

And yet there he stood, in a hotbed of Western materialist excess, transfixed by the spinning wheel. He knew rationally, of course, that this way of making money was absurd, that his system was a mirage, and yet he could not seem to escape. He could not have seen himself as an addict, exactly; more than a century would pass before gambling was classified in such terms. He may have viewed himself as simply an honorable man trying against all odds to provide for his family and friends. But he also knew, surely, that he was desperate.

He gambled ten hours a day, every day, interrupting his play only for a brief meal or to check for a letter from Anna at the post office. In the evenings he headed back to the Hotel Victoria, along glamorous Louisenstrasse, sparing no thought for the natural beauty just beyond the town's border or for anyplace other than the casino. The two days bled into that possible third, then into four, five, and six. His letters to Anna grew frantic, filled with loneliness and self-loathing:

> Without any exaggeration, Anya: I find this all so disgusting, so horrible, that I would gladly flee, and when in addition I recall you, my whole being just dies to see you. Oh, Anya, I need you, I've sensed that. When I recall your serene smile, that joyous warmth that floods the heart in your presence, I am irresistibly drawn to you. You usually see me, Anya, gloomy, sullen, and fretful: that's only from the outside; that's the way I've always been, broken and wrecked by fate; inside it's something else, though. Believe me, believe me!

It became a common refrain of his letters from Bad Homburg: *Believe me.* "My longing to see you greatly hindered me from successfully ending this damned gambling and coming to you, since I was not spiritually free," he wrote, with tortured logic. He strove to reassure her that "this is even all for the best: I'll be rid of that cursed thought, the monomania, about gambling. Now again, just as the year before last (before *Crime and Punishment*), I'll triumph through work."

Even the losses he incurred in those few disastrous days could not seem to dissuade him from his absurd faith that some rational system could still save him. "About twenty times now, on approaching the gambling table, I've made an experiment," he told Anna. "If you play coolly, *calmly*, and with calculation, there's *no chance of losing*. I swear to you, there's not even a chance!" With just four more days, he insisted, "I would be certain to win back everything. . . . But of course I'm not going to gamble!"

Yet he continued to gamble, and to lose, begging Anna for money in letter after letter. He was forced to pawn his watch, but then won enough to redeem it; soon he had to pawn it again, this time forever. He begged his wife to trust that this was all part of a divine plan: "The future is simply a riddle," he wrote. "But God will save us somehow. Never in my whole life have I calculated longer than six months, just like anyone who lives on his own labor, practically day labor, and it alone." And he had a plan of his own: Immediately upon his return to Dresden, he would write Katkov and ask for another five hundred rubles. A few days later, he decided to ask for a thousand instead.

He also insisted to Anna that this latest binge was stirring his creative juices—and clearly it was sparking his ambition as well. In his letters he declared his goal of making his next novel, *The Idiot*, his greatest work yet: "Try to understand, Anya: it has to be magnificent, it has to be even better than C[rime] and Punish[ment]. Then reading Russia will be mine; then the booksellers will be mine as well." He was counting on *The Idiot* to be a smashing success, and not just for the sake of his career, but for Anna: He wanted to make her proud, he told her, to prove to her that he was no scoundrel after all, but a worthy husband and future father. He needed her to believe in him.

He also needed her help, which is one reason the fervent declarations of these letters do not ring entirely true. Dostoyevsky let Anna know that his hotel bill was growing, and he doubted he'd have enough to last until his return to Dresden—complaints that she was sure to recognize as tacit requests for money. His pathetic letters from Bad Homburg offer a first-hand glimpse of Dostoyevsky manipulating his wife into accepting, even supporting, his gambling. At some points in the letters he sounds like a child speaking to his mother, at other points like a confessor addressing a priest. "It was as if I was risen from the dead," he wrote, upon receiving a letter from Anna after a daylong wait that he said had torn him apart. "I had never, never before been so worried and so afraid as yesterday. . . . No, Anya, one must love strongly in order to feel that way!" He reproached himself for not taking her with him, as her presence might have done him good, but at the same time wanted his wife nowhere near this den of vice. Through it all, one thought tormented him: "Your judgment alone is terrifying to me! Can you, will you now respect me? And what is love without respect? After all, because of this our whole marriage has been shaken. O my friend, don't blame me permanently."

Yet, for whatever reason, Anna never reproached him for his gambling. "At least I know that there is a being who loves me for my whole life," he told her. "You are a kind, radiant, saintly soul." Perhaps it would have been better, he sometimes mused, if Anna actually had scolded him during such episodes instead of pardoning him, for her boundless kindness only intensified his guilt. But in the end he recognized that in Anna he had a rare source of unconditional support—a prospect that was both uplifting and terrifying. He nurtured the idea that Anna had awakened in him "countless new thoughts and feelings and impulses," through which he "has become a better man."

Moreover, Anna's faith in him reinforced a lesson that was to be embodied in so many of the downtrodden characters in his fiction, from the feckless copy clerk Makar Devushkin in *Poor Folk*, to the fiery Nastasya Filippovna Barashkova in *The Idiot*, to the lecherous old Fyodor Karamazov in *The Brothers Karamazov*: that every human being, no matter how far they may have fallen socially or morally, is worthy of redemption. In those agonizing days in Bad Homburg, Dostoyevsky was desperate to preserve a modicum of dignity and self-respect for himself. In helping him do just that, Anna was offering him what he considered one of the most important gifts any human being can give another.

ON THE DAY she received her husband's first letter from Bad Homburg—written before his gambling binge had begun—she was "overjoyed" by his innocent report of the journey. "Words cannot express how happy it made me . . . I read it a second and then a third time, and secretly kissed it. How wonderfully can my Fedya write—it's just like talking to him." As the drama of his gambling mania unfolded in the days that followed, she became increasingly distraught. "If only Fedya would come back," Anna lamented, "for my suffering is greater than I can bear." She was "oppressed by the thought that making money by roulette isn't such a good idea," but squelched her instincts, immediately adding, "It is better not to analyze thoughts like that."

She took pains to distract herself, roaming the streets of Dresden, wandering daily into her favorite cafés and museums, then checking at the train station every evening to see if Fedya had returned. She engaged in long conversations with their landlady, Madame Zimmerman, and wrote letters home to her friends and family—including one especially difficult letter to her mother, begging her to secretly pawn Anna's fur coat and send the proceeds right away. She even took day trips to historical sites, including the nearby town of Pillnitz, home of the summer residence of the Saxon kings. Gazing up at the forested hillside, Anna glimpsed the ruins of an old fortress against the dark blue sky, with footpaths leading to the remains of a small Gothic tower. "So gorgeous was it that I would gladly have sat here, if possible, till the evening, if only Fedya had been with me."

On a whim, she decided to follow the winding path up the steep mountain—the highest she'd ever climbed, it soon became clear. The higher she went, the grander the panorama below: the view extended several miles, taking in mountains, vineyards, and little villages, with the town of Pirna visible in the distance. Suddenly a thunderstorm struck; the bright spring day turned threatening, with thin gray sheets of heavy rain in the distance and great thick clouds stacking themselves into dreadful apparitions, darker and darker by the minute. Thunder cracked and echoed right through the woods and back through the mountains, lightning streaking across the sky. Anna had never seen anything like it, at such close range; it was a terrifying sight but a glorious one, too. "Somehow, I was not afraid here," she wrote in her diary:

If death were coming my way, so be it; it would just be my fate;
if it didn't find me now, under the trees, it would come for me
some other time, as Destiny has in store for me. The sight was
truly marvelous, and took me right out of myself. I trembled,
but not from fear so much as being carried away with awe before the inexorable powers of nature.

We have no record of another instance where Anna engages in such
metaphysical reflection or speaks in such explicit, almost Dostoyevskian
language about the implacable forces of life. Even as Fate was toying with
her husband in Bad Homburg, it was exerting its mysterious power over
Anna in the German countryside. And on that afternoon she experienced
a kind of epiphany: from this point on, she would no longer allow herself
to view the world through old paradigms. No, she would blaze a path of
her own, out in the open, unprotected from life's surprises and terrors.

BY THE END of his spree in Bad Homburg, Dostoyevsky had lost everything he'd brought with him, having failed miserably to make the money
they needed to tide them over. On Monday, May 15, after being gone
nearly a week longer than promised, he finally returned. He seemed "a
little bit different," Anna noted as she met him at the train station, though
perhaps that was just "the dust of the journey." When they reached their
apartment, a maid served them tea, and Dostoyevsky wasted little time
asking if any letter had come for him. Anna handed him Polina's letter,
observing him closely as he seemed to feign confusion. "Did he really not
guess who it was from," she wondered, "or was he only pretending?"

He opened the envelope and, after glancing at the signature, began to
read. She studied his face as his fingers held what must have been a "precious piece of writing." He lingered for a long time over the first page, as
if not understanding something, and when he finished, his face began to
flush. Anna thought she saw his hands trembling. She sat there as calmly
as possible, pretending to know nothing about the letter's contents, even
asking him what "Sonyechka" (Dostoyevsky's niece, Sofya Ivanova) was

writing to him about. "It's not *from* Sonyechka," he responded, a bitter smile now playing around his mouth. She had never seen him smile in quite that way; it seemed to contain a note of true dejection, though she couldn't be sure. Then he grew flustered, so much so that he was unable to comprehend anything Anna said. This bolstered her suspicion that there was something untoward going on, yet she resolved not to ask any questions. Not yet.

With this episode, a slow-seeping poison—the fear of betrayal—had crept into their relationship. Seized with sporadic misgivings about her decision to marry Dostoyevsky, Anna made a point of continuing to read all of her husband's correspondence on the sly. But she stopped short of confronting him directly about the letters from Polina. Why? For one thing, she was afraid of upsetting him, knowing how quickly his agitation could trigger an epileptic seizure: "I am so afraid of his temper leading up to a fit." But she also believed that she could put an end to his bad behavior, and any potential infidelity in particular, through the power of her love. "There is only one thing that can possibly save him," she told her diary, "and that is a good relationship between the two of us." Of course, such a statement might be dismissed as the naive rationalization of a young woman unable to assert her will in a marriage to a volatile and controlling man. But Anna would reiterate this belief throughout her life. Even in old age, she declared that her husband "looked on me as a rock on which he felt he could lean, or rather rest."

Yet Anna herself would not rest. Rather than rely on her belief in the healing power of her love alone, she took action: she initiated her own secret correspondence with Polina Suslova. It was an unusually canny decision from a young woman who, though disinclined toward drama, was unafraid of confrontation when the situation demanded. With the survival of her marriage at stake, Anna began a protracted battle to save it in her own quiet, meticulous way—by managing the crisis shrewdly from behind the scenes.

While we know about this correspondence from Anna's diary, she reveals nothing about what was discussed in her letters with Polina, and none of them have survived. But it's clear that she was taking a profound risk in conducting the correspondence under her husband's nose, especially when it eventually became clear that he was on to her. But Anna refused to back down, even after he "advised" her during a heated exchange that she had "better not dare interfere" in his personal affairs. To which Anna responded that she "could do quite well without his advice," and kept up her clandestine correspondence with her husband's former lover.

In the weeks after his return from Bad Homburg, Anna was increasingly bold about challenging Dostoyevsky on matters she considered important—especially when it came to her husband's lapses into misogyny. She scolded him for his frequent attacks against Nihilist women, for instance, telling him that while she herself was no Nihilist, "I don't like to hear a woman being disparaged." At another point, Dostoyevsky jeered that most of the emancipated women of Anna's generation lacked the character to follow through on long-term goals. "Take such a simple thing as, say, stamp collecting," he told her. A man who takes up such a hobby, he argued, would surely keep it up for years, even a lifetime. "But a woman? She'll burn with desire to collect stamps," buy an expensive album and pester her family and friends for stamps, only to lose interest and let the album collect dust. Anna responded by dragging her husband "into the first stationery store we came across" and buying—"with my own money—a cheap stamp album." She maintained her collection steadily for the next forty-nine years, long after her husband's death.

The newlyweds found themselves arguing almost every day—about nothing, about everything. With money still a nagging concern, Anna rightly sensed that much of the tension between them was rooted in their financial problems and Dostoyevsky's insecurity over his ability to provide for them. If not for their miserable circumstances, she told her diary, "we could be the happiest of couples." They checked the post office daily, in vain, to see whether Katkov had answered Dostoyevsky's request for additional funds. On one such day, the novelist, morose and itching for a fight, chastised Anna for moving the furniture around in their apartment just to defy him. Only later did he reveal what had actually prompted his accusation: "Even if I don't have money now, I *will* one day," he bristled, "and nobody needs to despise me for not having it."

His words stung Anna. "Money means nothing in the world to me," she seethed in her diary, "and even if it did, and I'd wanted to be rich, I could have been rich long ago by marrying T . . . who had proposed to me." It wasn't money that had led her to choose Dostoyevsky, she insisted, "but his mind and soul that I loved."

Soon afterward they made up, as always. Only this time Anna was seized by an impish desire to further the conversation. Not only did her husband have no right to accuse her of mercenary motives, but *his* love wasn't exactly pure, was it? Didn't he have a few secrets of his own?

"I'm going to write a pretty strong letter," Anna said.

"To whom?" he asked, bewildered.

"To a certain person I know who has hurt me very much. I am not prepared to put up with insults, especially when they are underserved."

"It is horrible to repay evil with evil," he lectured, "and forgiveness is the nobler part."

"Ah, but that's not my way of thinking," she responded slyly.

He leaned over and kissed her repeatedly. Finally, mustering a roguish playfulness, he said, "You *are* vindictive, aren't you?"

"Maybe I am," she responded, "but not with you."

He gave her a quizzical look. Jokingly calling her "authoress" and "literary woman," he pressed her again about what she was planning to write.

"A letter," she responded plainly.

"May I ask to whom?"

"No."

"Oh, come on!"

"I'm not going to tell you."

It was late. Dostoyevsky advised Anna to go to bed, even though he was still burning with curiosity. Anna was fairly certain he knew whom she was referring to, which was just as she wanted it, though she would complain in her diary, "How often, I wonder, do I need to keep being so secretive about my activities? . . . I hate it, but what else can I do?" Yet she was confident that this privacy was essential to protecting her marriage. One senses that a part of her even enjoyed keeping the secret—that it was her way of maintaining some modicum of control within a relationship otherwise marked by a troubling imbalance of power. She craved the control that her knowledge of Fedya's dirty little secret gave her, even gloating on occasion that her husband "positively eats out of my hand!"

BEYOND THIS SLENDER MEASURE OF CONTROL, however, Anna craved connection with others; she yearned for a community of her own. One day she summoned the courage to call on Dr. Julius Zeibig, vice president of the Royal Stenographic Institute of Dresden, citing a letter of recommendation Professor Olkhin had provided her before she left Russia. Beyond his value as a professional connection, Anna thought that Zeibig might help by recommending sites of interest in the area, or even arranging for the Dostoyevskys to have special access to museums.

When they finally met, Zeibig invited Anna to the next assembly of the Stenographic Institute. There he introduced Anna to his colleagues, pointing out that she had come all the way from Russia with a letter from a well-known specialist in their field. But when the president extended greetings to Anna, in front of everyone, she became so flustered that she was unable to manage even a word in response and simply bowed. After the conclusion of business, however, she found herself at a long table drinking beer and chatting with the members of the society, who introduced themselves to Anna, and she regained her confidence. She started chatting away with them in her self-assured if fractured German, feeling "as if I were at home." By the time members of the society started drinking to her health and offering her berries and pastries, Anna knew she had found a professional group she could call her own. Before Zeibig escorted her home, she made a brief, heartfelt speech in German thanking the group for their cordial reception and inviting them to come to Petersburg, promising to arrange a welcome as gracious as the one they had given her.

To Anna the evening was a "triumph," both personal and professional. And apparently the feeling was mutual, for two days later a story appeared in the German newspaper *National Zeitung*, describing the warm reception that Dresden's Stenographic Institute had given to "a Russian lady . . .

who has studied the Gabelsberger System and uses this system frequently in Petersburg."

Dostoyevsky was less impressed. Far from being proud of this "Russian lady" in the national news who happened to be his wife, he greeted Anna's social triumph with hostility, chiding her for allowing herself to be "recruited into the ranks of her admirers." When Zeibig's colleagues invited Anna and her husband to future social gatherings, she felt obliged to decline. Once, when she and her husband were approached on the street by a friendly member of the group, Dostoyevsky made it perfectly clear that he wanted nothing to do with this or any other member of the Stenographic Institute.

With that, Anna's hopes for a professional community of her own went up in smoke. Her husband's familiar jealousy had reached an extreme pitch in Dresden, and she resolved "to be more careful, so as to avoid any complications like that in the future."

Given their behavior, it would be natural to view Anna's relationship with Dostoyevsky as an unhealthy codependency between a volatile artist and submissive peacekeeper. It is a familiar pattern, historically, in relationships between artists and their spouses. Anna herself sometimes portrayed their relationship in such terms: "I simply cannot bear quarreling," she admitted in her diary. "I would rather give in every time to keep the peace." But the dynamic between them was not so simple, and to paint Anna's behavior purely in terms of pathology underestimates her capacity for rational assessment and self-preservation.

In this first year of her marriage, Anna was developing her own subtle, if unspoken, calculus for how best to manage her relationship with her brilliant but self-involved, often abusive husband. She made her own judgments on how to navigate his attempts at oppression: allowing Dostoyevsky to travel alone to Bad Homburg but refusing to let his secret correspondence with Polina go unanswered; giving up on the Stenographic Society but persisting with her stamp collection; protecting his peace of mind so as not to put a strain on their marriage while still quietly enjoying the autonomous space she preserved for herself.

Nevertheless, like a character in her husband's fiction, Anna was also discovering that rational decisions about how a wife should behave had little to do with what she could ultimately expect of herself. She made up her mind "never to cry without a real reason," and yet found this to be an impossible goal. She did her best "to appear in good spirits," knowing how her husband admired her composure, and yet could not abide his chauvinist insults without righteous anger. She may have known rationally that "making money by roulette isn't quite right," and wished that her husband "would get this miserable idea of winning at the tables out of his head," but habitually put such thoughts out of her mind, and often allowed herself to get excited upon learning of one of his big wins.

Nor could she hide from herself the truth that sometimes "my suffering is greater than I can bear." The loneliness of their life abroad weighed on her, as did the challenge of being married to such an "interesting and enigmatic" man as her husband, whom she was still trying "to get to know and unriddle." If she had previously "thanked God that Olkhin had chosen me" to work for Dostoyevsky, she was increasingly convinced that whatever "Destiny has in store for me" might be more trying than she had anticipated.

This surrender to the vagaries of life has eerie echoes in the stories of Dostoyevsky's own tragic heroines. In *Crime and Punishment*, Sonya Marmeladova, the unfortunate daughter of a poverty-stricken alcoholic, accepts her fate as a prostitute and submits to her life of suffering; later she urges the murderer Raskolnikov to do the same as the only path to redemption. *The Idiot*'s Nastasya Filippovna, one of Dostoyevsky's most tragic female characters, is taken in at the age of sixteen as the concubine of a wealthy landowner after losing her father in a fire. Her history of abuse by men will turn her into a reckless fatalist who enjoys courting disaster and using her beauty and intelligence to torment the men who desire her.

Though neither a prostitute nor a femme fatale herself, Anna Dostoyevskaya shared with these tragic heroines a depth and complexity and a willingness to accept the challenges of fate. Through her marriage to Dostoyevsky, she was discovering firsthand that people are contradictory, love is mysterious, and destiny can be a darker and more powerful force than she, the Snitkin family's good daughter, had ever had occasion to reckon with. As her diary makes clear, this straitlaced young woman was even attracted to some of the more dangerous aspects of Dostoyevsky's life, for all the suffering his excesses might cause her. It seemed to her that "a whole new world had risen in my mind," and within it she was discovering her own unique sort of power.

Polina Suslova had felt something similar in her affair with Dostoyevsky, as had Anna Korvin-Krukovskaya, whose wooing of Dostoyevsky was partly an act of rebellion against a strict father who could not bear the thought of his daughter marrying a former political prisoner. But Polina had toyed with Dostoyevsky's heart for the sheer sadistic pleasure of it, and Korvin-Krukovskaya had ultimately refused to accept his neediness and controlling nature. Anna Dostoyevskaya, on the other hand, neither toyed with him nor rejected him. She was simply trying to build a sustainable life with him.

BY EARLY JULY, the couple had finally received one piece of good news: Mikhail Katkov agreed to send Dostoyevsky another five hundred rubles right away. It was only half of what the writer had asked for, but it was enough—just—to get them back on their feet. "My spirits were greatly revived," Anna wrote. Dostoyevsky was a different story. With the first installments of *The Idiot* due in a matter of months and his Belinsky article stalled, he was convinced that he needed a change of environment to recharge his creative batteries. And so the couple planned to move to Switzerland for a few months. On their way, Dostoyevsky suggested that they stop in Baden-Baden, a gambling resort he knew from his travels with Polina four years earlier.

Clearly, his itch for roulette had not been satisfied by his disastrous trip to Bad Homburg, and one has to wonder whether his idea of decamping for Switzerland wasn't just an excuse to stop by Baden-Baden. He would play for two or three weeks at most, he assured Anna, giving him time to win enough to free them from their financial difficulties. He still believed he had a fail-safe system for winning, if only he had enough time in one place to put it into practice.

Anna, normally far more levelheaded and practical than her husband, now fell under the influence of his magical thinking. "He spoke so persuasively," she recalled, "that he convinced me, too." She "willingly agreed" to stop in Baden-Baden, recalling that "it was all the same to me where we lived, so long as I didn't have to part with my husband."

As the horse-drawn carriage pulled away from their apartment on Johannesstrasse, Anna gazed out at the cobblestone streets of Dresden, at the attractive little German homes with their well-manicured lawns. "Good-bye now, Dresden," she wrote in her diary, "most likely we will never see you again!" Despite the tension of their weeks in the city, she was determined to look fondly on this first stage of their honeymoon. "How happy we have been here, together," she mused. "I don't really count our little differences one bit, as I know Fedya loves me and the cause of it all is just his irritable volcanic nature; even with that I love him beyond words."

She had not forgotten about the letters from Polina; the possibility that Dostoyevsky was still engaged in an affair continued to plague Anna, even as she carried on her own behind-the-scenes correspondence with her husband's erstwhile lover. But Anna would soon discover another mistress about to come between her and her husband—a rival far more formidable than Polina Suslova.

7

The "Gambler Wife"

The horses clomped along the narrow poplar- and chestnut-lined cobblestone streets of Baden-Baden. Rocking gently inside the carriage beside her husband, Anna looked excitedly out the window, bemused by the sight of a boy and girl riding a donkey right in the middle of the street.

Soon the cab stopped in front of a stone building fronted by a garden; a sign above the entrance read CHEVALIER D'OR. A smartly dressed teenage boy soon brought them upstairs to a modest, attractive room with two beds, and the Dostoyevskys ordered tea while maids tidied up the room.

The town—"indisputably the most glamorous and well-frequented watering hole in Germany," according to the popular *Reichard's* travel guide—had an unmistakable charm. Baden-Baden had become the preferred European playground of the Russian aristocracy, including its imperial family, not to mention the peerages of artists and writers—all of whom came not just for the gambling but for the mineral baths, the clean air, and the famed beauty of the Black Forest itself.

Dostoyevsky himself had been here twice before, once for a short stay in 1862, as part of the European tour described in *Winter Notes on Summer Impressions*, and again with Polina Suslova in September 1863, for three days of romantic torment and heavy gambling losses. Something, though, had compelled him to return to this place full of such traumatic memories. Perhaps he was subconsciously retracing with Anna the steps he'd once taken with Polina, hoping to get it right this time, to put a proper punctuation mark on this part of his life. Or perhaps the trip was his way of reliving an exhilarating period in his life, a time when nothing was set in stone and everything was possible—in love or roulette. Whichever it was, he wasted little time in getting down to the task at hand.

Waking earlier than usual on the rainy Friday after their arrival, he took fifteen ducats and a few thalers and headed straight to the town's casino. Anna, who wasn't feeling well, stayed behind, sewing hooks on her dresses, mending her coat, and sorting out clothes. When her nausea became overwhelming, she turned off the lights and lay in bed without moving. Three hours later, Dostoyevsky returned. He had lost everything he'd brought with him.

They still had fifty ducats, or a little over two hundred dollars today—enough to carry them for a short while, Anna calculated. She suggested they place their remaining cash in a leather purse she'd recently purchased, and Dostoyevsky liked the idea. It was a good arrangement: he would be the gambler, Anna his banker. As shrewd a move as this may have been, it is unclear how much control this safeguard actually gave her. After all, when she had wished to sell her modest dowry months earlier, in order to pay for their trip to Europe, she felt obligated to first ask her husband's permission.

Such murkiness about who should control the purse strings in the Dostoyevskys' marriage reflected a deeper confusion in Russian society at the time. By the mid-nineteenth century, married women had gained nominal rights to control their own property and some legal protection of their assets. They were allowed to retain possession of their dowry and any property they inherited, and even to keep this property in the event of divorce. Yet in the highly patriarchal Russian society of the time, one historian notes, such "legal norms were accorded little intrinsic value by either state officials or society generally, and in any case appear often to have been poorly known [and] unevenly enforced." Which meant that, despite these reforms, men could effectively do as they wished with their wives' property—a particularly dangerous prospect for a woman whose husband happened to be a gambling addict.

In an effort to economize, the Dostoyevskys moved to an apartment on Gernsbacher Strasse above a blacksmith's shop. When the writer returned from the Kurhaus later that day, Anna opened her eyes in the darkened room where she'd been napping. One look at his face told her what had happened. "I got up and implored him not to despair, telling him I would let him have more money. He begged me to give him another five ducats, which I immediately did, and he thanked me as if I had bestowed on him Heaven knows what."

By eight o'clock, however, he had not returned. Soon it was nine. Then ten. And still no Fedya. Fearful thoughts began flitting through Anna's imagination. "He's had a seizure in the rooms and was unable to tell anybody where he lived," she thought. "Maybe he's dying this very instant, and I won't be able to say my final good-bye." At eleven he finally came home, agitated and distracted. For the past three hours, he said, he had felt an intense longing to come back to her, but he'd been on such a winning streak that "he hadn't dared to leave the tables, despite his longing for me, in the hope of winning still more. I comforted him and assured him there was nothing to worry about, that nothing had happened to me while he had been away, and that all that mattered was that he calm down and not be agitated. But she remained self-possessed enough to note in her diary that his pain also constituted a burden for her:

> He would spare me none of his self-reproaches, calling himself stupidly weak, saying that he was not worthy of me, that he was a swine and I was an angel, and a lot of other foolish things of this sort. It was all I could do to calm him down, and to try and distract him. . . . Poor Fedya, how I do pity him!

It went on like this for days. Each morning, upon being awoken by the banging of metal from the blacksmith's shop below, Dostoyevsky was off to the casino. As Anna sat in her room for hours, hungry and anxious, her husband blew what money he had and then tried to win it back.

Trips to the pawnbroker became daily affairs. There was not a thing of value the Dostoyevskys owned, nor an item of clothing they possessed, save a few undergarments, that was not pawned at some point during their stay in Baden-Baden. On one occasion, Dostoyevsky pawned Anna's wedding ring, and within hours he had gambled away the money he'd received for it. He managed to redeem the ring later in the day, but Anna knew it was only a matter of time before he lost it again, and she was right.

At length it became clear that she couldn't trust Dostoyevsky to go to the pawnbroker alone, either. There was no telling how he might go wrong without supervision: he could make a bad deal, or pawn more than he should, or lie to her outright and go to the Kurhaus instead. Finally she warned him that if he didn't give his word of honor that he would come straight home after securing a loan from the pawnbroker, she would insist on going with him. "What do you mean, go with me?" he snapped. "How can you stop me going to the tables if I want to?"

It was a good question. How *could* she stop him? He was like a frenetic child in this casino town. "There is no doubt that Fedya needs to be protected, not only from others, but from himself, because he has no will power at all," Anna told her diary. "He promises, he gives his word of honor, and then immediately does the opposite." She worried about who would provide for their future child, due early in the new year, if they should lose everything. To keep herself ready for any future work opportunity that might come her way, Anna kept up her daily stenography practice, while also working on her French translation skills. "I am very concerned about the child's future," she confessed to her diary. "I must work, and work, and work, so that the little one can have somebody to depend on."

In the meantime, she resolved to do whatever it took to keep her husband away from the gaming halls—or, failing that, to accompany him, in order to serve as a restraining influence. And that is exactly what she started to do. Daily—or so it seemed—they made the trek from their apartment to the casino, down promenades lined with sparkling jewelry shops and fine restaurants, passing well-heeled men in top hats and women whose hats and veils were dotted with colored ribbons and brilliant sparks of gold. "There they are, all decked out," Anna would think, "while I must wear, day in, day out, my shabby old black frock which is terribly hot for me, and far from pretty."

Soon they reached Baden-Baden's celebrated Kurhaus, a two-story building of pale red sandstone, its eight striking columns standing with patrician solidity against the backdrop of the Black Forest Mountains. Open from May to October, the casino housed around fifteen gaming tables total in separate halls, where gamblers could play roulette, poker, and blackjack from mid-afternoon until early the following morning. As one contemporary guide to Baden-Baden noted, the "bright and shining" casino attracted "elegant spa guests" from all over Europe.

Anna followed Dostoyevsky into the Kurhaus restaurant or reading room, or the large, ornate hall where balls and musical performances took place, or sometimes directly into one of the building's two impressive gaming halls. Dostoyevsky favored the Red Hall, a space modeled on Versailles, with a thirty-foot ceiling with golden chandeliers. Hundreds of gaslights illuminated the green baize of the roulette tables and the red carpet below, and golden-framed mirrors reflected the phantasmagoria of reds and greens, silvers and golds, that lent the space its grandeur.

The people she saw here came from all over the continent and abroad. There were moneyed aristocrats and industrialists, artists and writers—even fellow Russian novelists like Ivan Turgenev and Ivan Goncharov, who were both in Baden-Baden that summer. Turgenev, who had been living in Baden-Baden since 1862, had spent many hours gambling in the Kurhaus himself. In the opening of his novel *Smoke*, he described the casino: "In the gaming rooms the same well-known figures crowded round the green tables with the same dull, avaricious expression, partly puzzled, partly embittered, but fundamentally predatory, which gambling fever imparts to even the most aristocratic features." Later in the novel, a female character reacts to seeing the casino for the first time:

> The sight of a roulette wheel and dignified-looking croupiers, whom, had she met them elsewhere, she probably would have taken for ministers, the sight of their swift rakes, the little piles of silver and gold on the green cloth, the old women gambling and the cocottes in all their finery, brought Kapitolina Markovna to a state resembling dumbfounded frenzy. She had com-

pletely forgotten that she should be utterly disgusted and merely looked on, looked on intently, occasionally shuddering at the sound of each new exclamation. The whirring of the ivory ball in the depths of the roulette wheel entered every fiber of her being, and only when she was back in the fresh air did she find enough strength to heave a deep sigh and call gambling an immoral invention of the aristocracy.

Anna Dostoyevskaya reacted to the Kurhaus with a similar mixture of fascination and moral disgust. She admired the elegance of the place, especially the reading room and the attractive outdoor patio where the couple often enjoyed concerts, and she was fascinated by how different players approached the game of roulette. (She "could not help noticing," for instance, "the curious fact" that one Russian lady staked "three times in a row on zero and won.") She envied the well-dressed, wealthy guests, was annoyed by pushy players who crowded around the tables, and was dispirited by the locals who tried their luck on Sunday, "only to lose all the money they make during the week." Returning to her diary, she wrote, "What a pity!"

This, then, was the place where her husband did the terrible thing he did: carrying on a private life, completely inaccessible to Anna, in which he repeatedly lost every ruble they had. If she could not stop him, she would at least join him as he gambled, though more as a bystander than as a participant. And yet, to her great dismay, the place soon became like a second home to them. It was one thing to read about her husband's gambling in his manic letters from Bad Homburg; it was another to see and experience it almost daily with her own eyes.

She stood next to him as he played, holding their leather money pouch and doling out to him just enough to appease him in a given moment, while keeping the rest safely in her possession. Though Dostoyevsky was reluctant to allow her into the gaming halls, and often chided her for coming there, he also believed that Anna's presence might improve his luck. One hot July afternoon, she watched him stake on *passe* (the numbers 19 through 36) and win; then put a heap of silver on red and lose;

then place six gold pieces on the last twelve and win three ducats and some silver. She told him she was bored and begged him to quit the table—although "my main reason for going," she admitted in her diary, "was to preserve our winnings."

On another occasion, wandering into the gaming hall alone from the reading room where she'd been waiting for Dostoyevsky, she watched him quietly from a distance. Holding a heap of silver in his hands, he gazed monomaniacally at the table and carousel before him. He must have been winning, Anna concluded, which meant it was time to get him out of there before he lost it all. She walked up to him and tapped him on the arm, but his eyes were fixed on the slowing carousel. When he finally turned around, Anna was aghast: "He looked dreadful, all flushed in the face, and with bloodshot eyes, like a drunken man." He snapped at her for interrupting his play. Dostoyevsky had forbidden her to enter the hall without his permission, considering the gaming halls a place of dangerous temptation for a proper young woman. At first Anna claimed she'd been trying to escape a gentleman who was pestering her, but when Dostoyevsky marched into the reading room to confront the scoundrel, she changed her story, suggesting that maybe the fellow had just been trying to ask her about the day's news. She kept parrying his questions until he finally lost interest and moved on.

They had lighter moments, too, but even those could be soured by her husband's penchant for psychological games. One afternoon, as Anna "lay on the sofa, looking at the wall and thinking, my favorite activity these days," Dostoyevsky walked through the door, his face pale and gloomy. She braced herself for the worst, but then his sullen expression gave way to a sly smile.

"Well, I've won a little," he said, holding up a purse.

"A *little?*" she said, counting his winnings: forty-six new gold pieces, or just under six thousand dollars today—some three months' income for the cash-strapped couple. "Why, it's a whole purse full of gold!" She knew to forgive him for these manipulative ploys, so like the games his own fictional characters play, happy to grab whatever fleeting moments of happiness she could. Fedya whipped a bouquet of flowers out from behind his back, and an errand boy appeared with a basket of berries and apricots; Anna threw her arms around her husband's neck and kissed him. For a few hours, the dark cloud hanging over them dissipated in a flurry of food, wine, and flowing conversation. "It really did seem," she wrote, "as if we could hope our worst times were over." Later that day Dostoyevsky suffered another loss. And within a few weeks almost all of the forty-six new gold pieces were gone.

BY THE THIRD WEEK IN JULY, their situation had become dire. "Oh God, how all this tortures me!" lamented Anna in her diary. "All my clothes and all my decent possessions will have to go now, for how can I possibly imagine he'll win?" And yet, the minute he came to her pleading for forgiveness as well as more money, she simply urged him not to be upset and handed over ten of their last fifty francs. He returned a few hours later, having lost everything. They had forty francs to their name now, or just under two hundred dollars.

One notable feature of Anna's running account of Dostoyevsky's gambling exploits is that she focuses not on his uncontrolled behavior but simply on whether he would win back the lost money. There are cultural reasons for this. In nineteenth-century Russia, few looked upon compulsive gambling as an addiction in the same light as, say, excessive alcohol consumption. Russian fiction of the time portrayed gambling either as an admirable exercise in audacious risk, or as the result of a personal character flaw, almost never as an unhealthy compulsion or true illness. In her contemporaneous diary, Anna makes no reference to gambling as an illness beyond her husband's control. By the second decade of the twentieth century, however, Freud and others had introduced a more nuanced understanding of psychology into Russian public discourse, and in her memoirs Anna acknowledged Dostoyevsky's gambling as not "a simple weakness of will but . . . a disease for which there was no cure."

In the moment, however, all she could do was hold out the hope that "my presence during his play would provide a certain restraining influence." And with every passing day her faith was dwindling. "My God, when shall we be able to extricate ourselves from this accursed swamp that we've sunk into?" she wrote. "We'll never get away, and we'll probably go on playing here through eternity, playing, and playing, and playing, and waiting for the great win that never comes."

They kept sinking, good money following bad. Increasingly, Anna was seized by uncontrollable fits of sobbing, partly brought on by her morning sickness. One day, Dostoyevsky had the audacity to tell her that her crying was getting on his nerves. "I call that disgusting egotism!" exclaimed Anna in her secret diary. She was also bothered by the way he kept supporting his ungrateful relatives when her own extended family was also in need:

> I can see that he definitely does not want to bother himself about my family. He worries dreadfully when Emilya Fyodorovna . . . is short of money, or if [his nephew] works too hard, or Pasha can't have everything he wants; but he doesn't care a rap what sort of worries we have to endure, and never even notices our deprivations. He regards me, his wife, as his property, and considers it only natural that I should have to suffer all kinds of need and unpleasantness.

Anna had devoted herself to her husband, who seemed to have no idea that "he ought to try to ensure a peaceful life for his wife, that she shouldn't have to constantly worry about where the next meal will come from. How horrible and unjust it all is!" In the same diary entry, though, she turned her anger on herself "for harboring such horrid thoughts against my own dear, darling husband. I am definitely a disgusting creature." Anna's diary is full of moments like this, where she is morally perceptive enough to recognize her husband's selfish behavior, only to have that very insight trigger an avalanche of self-loathing.

Even when she managed to stave off such "horrid thoughts" about herself and her husband, Dostoyevsky's family had a way of interfering in their lives—as Anna was reminded when her mother wrote to say how hurt she was to have learned of Anna's pregnancy not from her daughter herself but from Pasha, Anna's unscrupulous nineteen-year-old stepson. The letter was a serious blow to Anna, who had kept the news about her pregnancy quiet out of fear that her mother would have insisted they return to Petersburg if she'd known Anna was expecting. If that should happen, Anna observed,

> our former difficult life would begin all over again, and our love was not yet deep-rooted enough to sustain the ordeal. Pasha would have found some way to come between us, while I wouldn't have been able to withstand his attacks, not without adequate support from Fyodor Mikhailovich. It would have ended with me going with my child back to my mother.

And now, amid this disturbing train of thought, to discover that Pasha had gone and told Mama about her pregnancy: it was confirmation of everything Anna feared, an act of betrayal as despicable as any he'd yet committed. At first she suspected her husband must have told Pasha. But Fedya had not said a word about her pregnancy to anybody, he assured her, nor written to either Pasha or Emilya Fyodorovna for weeks. Pasha must have simply assumed it, they reasoned, or somehow figured it out by piecing various details together, a sleuthing skill honed over many years of manipulating others for his own benefit.

Anna wrote her mother a long letter begging for forgiveness and explaining exactly why she had not told her about the pregnancy. She concluded with a full disclosure of their sorry financial state, which she knew was even worse than Mrs. Snitkina could have suspected, and then asked for more money. "I simply hated having to write her like that," Anna confessed to her diary. She knew her mother had financial problems of her own—brought on in no small part, in fact, by the monthly interest she was still paying on Anna's and Dostoyevsky's pawned dowry items. "Sweet, darling Mama, how she loves us and longs for us to prosper, but all the time she seems to get nothing from us but complaints and requests for money."

Pained by their wretched situation, Anna longed for Russia. With the

melodies of old Slavic songs flitting through her mind, she told Dostoyevsky that one day she planned to publish her own collection of poems
under the title "Slav Night Poems of a Russian Lady on Her Travels,"
which she would dedicate to the "accursed race of Baden-Baden." Yet even
as she yearned for home, Anna feared what might happen if they did return: "I would dearly love to see my own people again, and yet I'm terrified to think of going back to Russia. I am so afraid that Fedya might stop
loving me. It's as if I'm still unsure of his love." Thinking of both Dostoyevsky's family and Polina Suslova, she added, "I am constantly seized
with a terrible fear that somebody will come along and usurp the place I
now hold in his heart." She began to wonder whether anybody had ever
managed to hold his affection for very long: "It seems to me that this man
has never loved anybody. . . . He's too preoccupied by other thoughts and
ideas to become too attached to anything earthly." No matter how much
she wanted to go home, she was convinced they would need to stay away—
for at least a while longer.

A MONTH INTO THEIR STAY in Baden-Baden, Dostoyevsky's destructive mania was unstoppable. Life there was torture for Anna, an affront to
the values she had grown up with. Her family, her country, her financial
stability, even the husband she thought she knew—everything she valued
in the world was slowly being stripped from her. Fedya seemed capable of
gambling their last kopeck away, and as far as she was concerned he could
have it: "I don't care, he doesn't listen to one word I say," she told her diary.
"I'm sick of being tortured, I've had enough of the way he treats me, and
I'll just throw the money at his feet and leave him and go off alone, because I can't continue on like this any longer."

And yet she stayed, kept searching for something solid to hold on to
amidst it all. The "grizzling heat, squalling children all around us, the
smithy's unbearable hammering"—it all echoed the roiling uncertainty
inside her. To relieve her nerves, she took grueling but cathartic hikes to
the top of Mercury Mountain, losing herself in the panoramic view of the
Black Forest and the little towns clustered along the Rhine. Climbing

onto the stone ledge of the New Castle on the edge of town, she gazed out over Baden-Baden, her eye lighting on the "pernicious place that contains the roulette tables," where she knew that her husband, at that very moment, was in the process of ruining them.

When it came time to pay the landlady, they had no money at all, but Dostoyevsky assured Anna that he had a plan: he would pawn some of their remaining items for fourteen guldens. It wasn't much, but it was enough to keep the landlady at bay for a time. Only rather than bringing the money directly home, as Anna had expected, he stopped at the Kurhaus and lost half of it.

"That was idiotic," she snapped at him upon his return, for once unable to contain herself, angry not just at the loss but at her husband's maddening "fantasy that he was going to get rich from roulette." Cornered, he made a pathetic attempt to blame *her*: "Why didn't you tell me the money was to be used for rent?" he fumed. "You should've reminded me, and now I've gone and gambled it all away!" Dostoyevsky, of course, knew full well what the money was for. "It really is terrible of him trying to project his own guilt onto others," Anna noted.

A few days later, things between them finally came to a head. Anna received a letter from her mother reporting that she was likely to lose their pawned furniture, as she'd been able to pay only three months' interest on it. When Anna shared the news with Dostoyevsky, he mumbled something about her mother's "damned furniture." For Anna, this insult "was the last straw." Opening her diary, she unleashed weeks of pent-up resentment: "The whole time I'm at his side, I never worry him with a single question, and let him say anything he wants to me, and all this because of the tenderness I feel toward him." When his gambling "fever is at its worst, I'm always the first to console him in his losses, and offer him my things to pawn without hesitation, knowing they'll be lost. Never in my life have I reproached him with all the money he's lost." And yet now he had the audacity to accuse *her* of being "harsh" toward him. "That's all the thanks I get for never grumbling at him," she wrote, wondering now whether her patience and forbearance had been worth it in the end. After all, his first wife, Marya Dmitriyevna, "never hesitated to call him a rogue and a rascal and a criminal, and to her he was like an obedient dog."

It was an acute insight into an aspect of Dostoyevsky's personality that later biographers and psychologists would often note: his tendency toward masochistic self-laceration, which had long impelled him to seek out relationships with emotionally unavailable or even abusive women who conquered his heart not through compassion but through domination. Now, in this moment of desperation, Anna herself assumed a new, more aggressive approach toward her husband. "If he thinks I am his slave, there to obey his every whim, he makes a great mistake," she told her diary. "It's time he abandoned this delusion of his."

And so, audaciously and in secret, Anna herself went to gamble.

Two days after their fight, she had another letter from her mother, this one containing a bank note of 150 rubles. It was fifty less than she was expecting, but still something—around sixteen hundred dollars today, enough to recoup a portion of Dostoyevsky's recent losses, pay the landlady, and retrieve some of their belongings from the pawnbroker. But Anna had other plans for the money: "For the first time in my life," she told her diary, "I felt fully justified in going to the roulette rooms and trying to win a bit." She had been contemplating such a move for some time, "but could never carry out my plan, as Fedya was always in the way. But today I made up my mind."

The reasons for Anna's decision were complex. Certainly their financial straits were one motivation: If she won, she might straighten out their finances, and maybe even pay for that trip up the Rhine she'd been dreaming about. And her decision was no sudden impulse. For weeks she had been studying other roulette players and gaining confidence in her own judgment about how to play the game. This is why the thing that upset her most about her husband's playing, even more than his losses, was the fact that he "cannot bring himself to stop playing at the right time, and to take my advice." It was "almost as if he were ashamed of following my advice, seeing as he always did the exact opposite of what I said. Evidently, he wanted to show that I had no influence over him." At the same time, she told Dostoyevsky outright, his "very idea of winning a fortune through roulette was utterly ridiculous," a statement clearly intended to wound, if not emasculate, him.

Now she was about to embark on the ultimate power play, marching into this largely male enclave to undertake a high-stakes move that, if it worked, would put her on equal footing with her husband, seizing control of their finances, and arguably besting him on his home turf. As reckless as Anna's decision may have seemed, given their financial circumstances, it was in fact an extension of the same daring, defiance, and belief in personal autonomy that she'd long displayed in other aspects of her life. And, as often in moments of strife with Dostoyevsky, it involved not direct confrontation but a subtler, wilier sort of face-off, quietly entering his world to assert her will.

Donning the dressy hat she'd bought in Dresden—simple rough white straw, with roses around the brim and over the right ear, and two loops of velvet ribbon—she took nine guldens and change from the money her mother had sent and walked briskly through the backstreets to the Kurhaus. It was an unusually hot summer Tuesday, and the casino was still sparsely populated, making it easy for Anna to find a place at one of the roulette tables. A thin crowd of elegantly clad women and smartly dressed men hovered nearby, sipping wine and puffing on richly pungent papirosas. Anna does not specify whether this was the Red Hall, where Dostoyevsky spent most of his time, or the secondary room, but either way she could have had no doubt that she might run into him at any moment.

She staked a thaler on the first twelve numbers and won two. Then she bet on the last twelve, and won another two. That put her up by four thalers. Then she lost three times in a row, only to win back two thalers, then another four, then lose two, then win five. She was up by seven, now eight, or one hundred ten dollars in today's money. It was a terrific roll, she knew—just the time for her to quit the table, as she'd so often advised Dostoyevsky to do after a winning streak.

And yet, at that moment, "my strength of mind seemed to desert me." She was unable to pull herself away; "something seemed to tempt me to stake on the center numbers, which never won." The lady next to her was doing the same, "obviously annoyed at my making the same bets as she did. I even thought I heard her make a remark about it." But Anna kept on doing it anyway, pressing up against the woman so closely that the flower in her hat became entangled in the lady's veil. Then she stopped paying attention to the lady altogether, began making her own decisions, all her attention concentrated on that green baize table, the spinning carousel, the whirring ivory ball. She began losing, one spin after another—until, just as inexplicably, she started winning again. Then she lost, then won again. . . . When she found the presence of mind to count up her coins, she discovered that she was up by nineteen thalers, or two hundred seventy dollars. It was money the Dostoyevskys could have used, certainly; along with the money from her mother, it would have been enough to pay off many of their most pressing debts, not least their back rent.

"I'd like Fedya to come in now, so that I could show him," she thought with defiance, as she placed another bet.

Sure enough, at that very instant, there he was, standing in the doorway. "I could've easily crept out without his seeing me, but was horrified at the whiteness of his face"—a dead giveaway that he'd just suffered another loss. At the sight of him, her defiance gave way to concern and she rushed up to him, without even noticing that she'd lost her latest bet.

When Dostoyevsky saw her, he was furious—that she would come alone, at her age, in her condition, to such a place. He grabbed her hand now to escort her right out of the casino, lecturing her sternly on how she should have quit the table immediately after winning, or she was bound to lose everything she'd won.

"I've noticed things like that happen to you, too," she responded bitterly, her defiance returning. Besides, she added, "it wasn't such a tragedy losing a few five-gulden pieces, seeing as I had just had some money sent from Petersburg." Unlike her husband, she had managed to leave the tables with only one thaler less than she'd come with.

In truth, Anna later admitted to her diary, she "felt horrible about not leaving the gaming hall" while she was ahead, when she would have had enough to "be able to send a little present to my poor, darling Mama." More pointedly, she reflected, if she had quit sooner she could have shown her husband the nineteen thalers she'd won. "That is so like Fedya," she told her diary, "he couldn't come while I was winning, but had to make his appearance just at the moment when I lost because of him."

THE DOSTOYEVSKYS CROSSED a Rubicon in their relationship that day. It was as if some terrible new bond had formed between them, these two gamblers living in the same flat. For Anna, it had a hint of nihilism; she referred to her and her husband as "a demented couple" destined to "go on playing, and losing everything." Dostoyevsky, for his part, started teasing Anna that she was his "gambler wife," taking some malicious pleasure in reminding her how lucky she was that he'd appeared in the nick of time to save his "lost wife."

Anna Dostoyevskaya, a gambler? How could she have taken up an activity so foreign and even repulsive to her? An activity she'd tried so hard to prevent her husband from engaging in, and one that violated her own most deeply held values?

Clearly, Anna was no addict. She had never gambled before, and by all accounts she never would again. The incident at Baden-Baden was clearly a desperate measure, a provocation—and perhaps, in some ways, a lesson. Still, her flirtation with roulette was more than a passing whim; it was the culmination of a crisis months in the making. In the weeks beforehand, she had been prone to uncontrollable emotional outbursts. She blamed this on her pregnancy, which she felt had "undermined my will power and made me capricious and obstinate." But in less self-critical moments, she knew that Dostoyevsky's compulsive gambling was just as responsible for her harried state, wearing her down until she gave in to the impulse. "We are poor, poor people, both of us, and all because of this accursed roulette," she admitted, before adding that, under such circumstances, "it isn't worth controlling myself."

One can hardly imagine the pert young woman who showed up at Dostoyevsky's apartment in October 1866 uttering such a statement. The bleak abandon of such sentiments reveals just how low she had sunk since then—enough that she was prepared to don a new persona that would once have been abhorrent to her. Her defenses down, her reserves of self-control depleted by the delirium of the past weeks, she was open to possibilities of selfhood that she previously never would have considered. Nothing was sacred. Everything was on the table. At times, Anna appears to have felt that her existence had been reduced to an animal struggle for survival. "All our energy these days," she wrote in desperation, "seems to be focused on eating and drinking!"

In that gaming hall, which looked and felt like an elaborate temple, roulette seemed to offer Anna a chance at some kind of transcendence. A lifelong Orthodox Christian whose faith formed a core part of her identity, Anna had already proven herself receptive to other forms of spiritual life. While watching that approaching thunderstorm from the mountainside near Pillnitz, for example, she had felt a temptation to court destiny. So, too, in this moment of rupture, she was intensely attracted to another kind of dark epiphany—the religion of the roulette table, where homage is paid to the gods of chance and fate is anything but certain.

If Anna Snitkina was raised in an environment of Christianity, community, and clear moral guidance, the newlywed Anna Dostoyevskaya had spent the early months of her marriage in a far more decadent world. Her flirtation with gambling allowed her, for a moment, to escape the daily pressures that were crushing her, but it also gave her a chance to understand her husband's harrowing experience directly. Though gambling was the stuff of daily conversation—and tension—between them, she had never experienced firsthand the feelings Dostoyevsky must have felt while playing roulette, nor come this close to understanding the thrill he derived from that spinning carousel. Gambling, then, was Anna's way of both defying her husband and joining him in his cloister of vice, in much the way children of inmates sometimes pursue lives of crime as an unconscious strategy for deepening their connection to a parent who has been emotionally or physically absent.

Anna had defied her husband by becoming him. It was at once an act of rebellion and an act of love.

8.

Turgenev

I van Turgenev was the last person Dostoyevsky wanted to see in Baden-Baden. But there was no way around it, especially after Ivan Goncharov mentioned that Turgenev had spotted Dostoyevsky in the gaming hall but resisted the temptation to interrupt him at the table. To Dostoyevsky, who still owed Turgenev the fifty thalers he'd borrowed in Wiesbaden in 1865, this was unpleasant news. Beyond the shame over a debt he still couldn't repay, though, Dostoyevsky had deeper reasons for wishing to avoid Turgenev.

The two had known each other since the 1840s, when they had met as fledgling writers in a circle organized by Vissarion Belinsky, who recognized them both as major new talents. They were friends at first, with Dostoyevsky playing the fervent admirer to his slightly older, more polished colleague. Even back then, though, the irritable, perennially strapped writer had felt lacking around Turgenev. Yet the wide acclaim for *Poor Folk* had so inflated Dostoyevsky's ego that he drove away many of his fellow writers, Turgenev included. The older writer now composed a satirical verse calling his upstart friend "a pimple on the nose of Russian literature," an insult that put an abrupt end to their friendship. Only after Dostoyevsky's return from Siberian exile a decade later did the two men, softened by experience, finally renew their relationship. What brought them together was the fierce public quarrel over Turgenev's 1862 novel

Fathers and Sons, which Dostoyevsky defended from attacks by the radical intelligentsia.

Dostoyevsky genuinely admired Turgenev's talent, openly praising it to others and even inviting Turgenev to contribute a story to *Epoch*. Yet he could not help disapproving of the writer's pessimistic worldview, telling his brother Mikhail that "Phantoms," the story they commissioned, "exhibits *lack of faith* due to impotence." Russia needed its authors not just to provide criticism, Dostoyevsky believed, but to offer a positive ideal to live by, an enduring vision of spiritual beauty in a broken world. And that was something Turgenev seemed incapable of offering. "He is an atheist through and through," Dostoyevsky said:

> But my God, deism gave us Christ, that is, such a lofty notion of man that it cannot be comprehended without reverence, and one cannot help believing that this ideal is everlasting! And what have they, the Turgenevs, Herzens, Utins [Nikolai Utin was a Russian revolutionary], and Chernyshevskys, presented us with? Instead of the loftiest divine beauty, which they spit on, they are all so disgustingly selfish, so shamelessly irritable, flippantly proud, that it's simply impossible to understand what they're hoping for and who will follow them.

Turgenev confirmed Dostoyevsky's fears with his novel *Smoke*, published a few months before the couple arrived in Germany. Written and largely set in Baden-Baden, where the writer had retired several years earlier to lick his wounds after the public uproar over *Fathers and Sons*, this new novel was a savage attack on court circles, the chattering intelligentsia, and anyone else—progressives and conservatives alike—who believed that Russia had some special mission in the world. Turgenev conveyed this message through the lengthy speeches of a character named Sozont Ivanich Potugin, who declares that "in the course of ten whole centuries old Russia has produced nothing of its own, in government, the judicial system, science, art, or even crafts." He marvels at London's

Crystal Palace, hailing it as an "exhibition of everything which human inventiveness has achieved—an encyclopedia of humanity, so to speak," while sniping that Russia and everything she'd created "could go to blazes and not disturb a single nail or a single pin."

Smoke was hardly the first work of Russian literature to criticize Russia or extol the virtues of European culture. It was just the latest salvo in the perennial debate between the Westernizers, who believed that their country's future development should be based on Western social and political models, and the Slavophiles, who believed in Russia's unique historical destiny and native genius. Turgenev's embarrassment over his country's social, economic, and political backwardness compared with Europe drew on a strain of thought dating back to the famous *Philosophical Letters* published in 1836 by the philosopher Pyotr Chaadayev. "We have given nothing to the world," Chaadayev declared in the influential tract. "We have not added a single idea to the mass of human ideas; we have contributed nothing to the progress of the human spirit; and we have disfigured everything we have touched of that progress." The sentiments of Turgenev's Potugin tracked Chaadayev so closely that it's hard to imagine that Turgenev wasn't thinking of the philosopher while composing his novel.

Then again, Turgenev needed no prompting to be ashamed of his country. From a young age, the urbane, wealthy landowner had nurtured a visceral hatred of the Russian autocracy, as well as the institution of serfdom, whose backwardness and cruelty he'd witnessed firsthand. He had little patience for the Slavophiles' idealized view of the Russian past, and he admired the democratic ideals of contemporary Europe, however imperfectly realized. His classmates at Petersburg University nicknamed him "the American" for his Westernist sympathies.

The publication of *Smoke* fueled a public firestorm even more virulent than *Fathers and Sons* had, turning Turgenev's few remaining literary friends into fierce critics. Whatever their politics, almost nobody liked the novel. In a letter to Turgenev, one critic advised him that most readers were "frightened by a novel inviting them to believe that all of the Russian aristocracy, and indeed all of Russian life, is an abomination." The members of Moscow's exclusive, high-society English Club even considered issuing a collective letter denouncing Turgenev and terminating his membership.

Of all the inflamed responses to *Smoke*, among the fiercest came from Dostoyevsky, whose outlook had grown increasingly nationalist since his return from Siberia—while Turgenev, ensconced in his beloved Europe, had moved in the opposite direction.

"One can't listen to such criticism of Russia from a Russian turncoat who could have been useful," Dostoyevsky wrote to Maikov after reading *Smoke*. He dismissed Turgenev as one of "those trashy little liberals and progressives" who "find their greatest pleasure and satisfaction in criticizing Russia." *Smoke* happened to appear a year after an assassination attempt on the life of Tsar Alexander II, the "Tsar-Liberator" whom Dostoyevsky credited with restoring his own freedom, and Turgenev's antipatriotic novel struck a painful personal nerve. Dostoyevsky admitted to Maikov that he "disliked the man personally," right down to "the aristocratically farcical embrace of his with which he starts to kiss you only to offer you his cheek."

Bristle as he might at the prospect of calling on Turgenev, Dostoyevsky knew he had little choice; if he didn't, he would seem to be avoiding a colleague in order to duck a long-standing debt. And so, on the scorching afternoon of June 28, he finally summoned the nerve to walk to Turgenev's charming two-story house on Schillerstrasse, near the little Oos River.

The meeting began cordially enough, with the two writers maintaining an outward decorum as they chatted about the contemporary Russian novel, atheism, and Nihilism, while also acknowledging the deep ideological split in their country. As soon as they started discussing their personal beliefs, however, things went downhill. The problems began when Turgenev declared himself a proud atheist—a statement that may well have been calculated to rattle Dostoyevsky, whose strong Christian faith was well known in Russian literary circles. Turgenev went on to proclaim that Russians "ought to crawl before the Germans, that there is one path common to everyone and unavoidable—civilization, and that all attempts at Slavophilism and independence are swinishness and stupidity." In fact, he continued, he was just then writing a long article against the Slavophiles.

Listening to all this with barely controlled anger, Dostoyevsky suggested that his host should order a telescope from Paris.

"What for?" Turgenev asked.

"Russia is far from here," replied Dostoyevsky. "It seems like you're having a hard time understanding us from so far away." Then, disingenuously posturing as a commiserating fellow author, he plunged the dagger where he knew it would hurt: "But I really didn't expect that all this criticism of you and the failure of *Smoke* would irritate you so much; honest to God, it *isn't worth it*, forget about it all."

"But I'm not at all irritated," said Turgenev, turning red but trying to maintain his composure. "What do you mean?"

Having produced the desired effect, Dostoyevsky changed the subject. Then, preparing to leave, he stopped, turned around, and proceeded to unleash on Turgenev three months' worth of resentment toward the Germans: "Do you know what rogues and swindlers one comes across here?" he said. "Really, the common people here are much worse and more dishonest than ours. . . . You go on talking about civilization; and what has civilization done for them?; what can they boast of so very much before us?"

As Dostoyevsky raved on, Turgenev turned pale ("I'm not exaggerating a bit!" he told Maikov) before responding: "In talking like that you offend me *personally*. You should know that I have settled in here permanently, that I consider myself a German, not a Russian, and I'm proud of that!"

More shocked than he let on, Dostoyevsky shot back sarcastically: "Although I have read *Smoke* and have been speaking with you now for a whole hour, I couldn't have expected that you would say that. Please forgive me for having offended you."

With that, the two enemies parted "quite politely," according to Dostoyevsky, though he vowed to himself that he "would never again set foot in Turgenev's home," whether in Baden-Baden or in Russia. For the remaining seven weeks of his stay in Baden-Baden, Dostoyevsky ran into Turgenev just once in the gaming hall, and though their eyes briefly met, they exchanged not a word. More than a decade would pass before they spoke again.

This tense meeting between two of the foremost Russian writers of their day left a mark on the nation's literary history. Even today, it is still cited as a classic example of the Westernizer-Slavophile debate raging throughout the nineteenth century. And it would have a direct influence on Dostoyevsky's future work—as in *The Possessed*, where he conjured a scathing caricature of Turgenev in the figure of the writer Semyon Karmazinov. In *The Idiot*, which Dostoyevsky was just then contemplating, he would continue his campaign against Turgenev and his ilk by portraying a uniquely Russian ideal of spiritual beauty and morality that he considered materialist European culture incapable of matching. The meeting with Turgenev confirmed for Dostoyevsky that his mission as a Russian writer must be to stand against "all those Turgenevs, Herzens, Utins, and Chernyshevskys" who chose Europe over their own land, and to inspire in his countrymen an uplifting vision of their national greatness.

DOSTOYEVSKY HAD BEEN THINKING about these issues for a long time, of course, ever since his return from Siberian prison camp. In 1862 he took an extensive trip through Europe, where he encountered firsthand the fruits of European "progress" he'd been reading and hearing about for years, chronicling his impressions the following year in the satirical travelogue *Winter Notes on Summer Impressions*, first published in *Epoch*. No locale was spared, but he saved his harshest attacks for France, knowing how large the country loomed in the Russian imagination. (French had been the language of the Russian aristocracy ever since Peter the Great had Westernized Russia two centuries earlier.)

Beneath their glittering exterior and confidence in their own virtue, Dostoyevsky viewed the French as a people who had squandered their lives in the accumulation of money and the acquisition of things. They were so keen to "convince themselves that they are content and completely happy," and had such a great psychological investment in their own cultural superiority, that any expression of self-doubt would be devastating. The French, he suggested, must convince themselves that everything has been "resolved, signed, and sealed," that "everything shines with virtue."

Otherwise, "they might think that the ideal had not been attained, that in Paris there is still no perfect earthly paradise, that there might be something more to desire."

As for the well-known French revolutionary slogan, *liberté, égalité, fraternité*—words that had become a battle cry for both Western liberalism and Russian socialism—it seemed the height of hypocrisy to Dostoyevsky. "What liberty?" the writer demanded. "Equal liberty for everyone to do anything he wants to within the limits of the law. When may you do anything you want to? When you have millions. Does liberty give each person a million? No. The person without a million is not the one who does anything he wants but the one with whom they do anything they want." This being the case, France had not attained anything resembling true equality, either—a point so self-evident that Dostoyevsky did not bother to expound upon it.

He reserved his heaviest fire for the final term. *Fraternité*, the shibboleth that had most captured the imagination of the radical intelligentsia back home, was also in his view "the chief stumbling block for the West." Western man might speak of brotherhood as "the great motivating force of mankind," Dostoyevsky argued, yet true brotherhood cannot be mandated from above but must be "found in nature." And "in the French nature—to be sure, in the Western nature in general—it has not shown up; what has shown up is a principle of individuality, a principle of isolation, or urgent self-preservation, self-interest, and self-determination." In Dostoyevsky's view, "it is not the separate personality, not the *I*, that must plead for the right to its own equality and equal value with *everyone else*, but rather this *everyone else* . . . must recognize his equal value." And the individual must sacrifice himself to society, not by demanding his rights but by giving them up unconditionally. "The Western personality is not used to such a turn of affairs: it demands with the use of force, it demands its rights; it wants to *be separate*—and so brotherhood does not come." It would take "thousands of years," in his view, for the Western personality to achieve such a state of authentic and spontaneous brotherhood.

Europe may have failed to achieve the ideal of *fraternité*, but there was one place where true brotherhood *could* be "found in nature," and of course that place was Russia. "One does not find in Russian man the sharp-edged, closed-off, stubborn quality of the European," Dostoyevsky had written in *Time* years before. "[The Russian] sympathizes with everything human, independently of all differences of nationality, blood, and soil. He finds and instantly acknowledges everything reasonable in whatever is, from any point of view, universally human." He offered the work of his literary hero, Alexander Pushkin, as proof that Russia had synthesized the fruits of European civilization into a "Russian ideal" of universal reconciliation. This was why, as Dostoyevsky had written elsewhere, "Europe and its task will be completed by Russia."

Exactly how that would be accomplished, the writer had not yet defined. The subject would come into sharper focus a decade later, when he argued in his *Diary of a Writer* columns that Russia was destined to spread Christian goodness throughout the world by establishing a Pan-Slavic Christian empire. Yet Dostoyevsky's tendency toward messianic nationalism was already in full view. In 1867, the year of his meeting with Turgenev, he wrote: "Our people are infinitely higher, more noble, more honest, more naïve, more capable, and full of a different, very lofty Christian idea, which Europe with her sickly Catholicism and stupidly contradictory Lutherism, does not even understand."

For more than a century and a half, such simplistic, even fanatical nationalism, coming from one of literature's most profound minds, has baffled and bothered readers. Some scholars have called Dostoyevsky a nativist, others an imperialist, and certainly both elements marked his thinking in the 1860s and '70s. But his brand of nationalism must be distinguished from the more violent strains of nativism that were just then beginning to crop up in Russia, Europe, and the United States. Russia's isolation from Roman Catholic and Enlightenment influences had enabled it to preserve the ideal of Christian love, he felt, and positioned the country to become a leader among nations by modeling for the world what true freedom, equality, and brotherhood—rooted in the principles of selfless Christian love—might actually look like.

No matter how extreme his Russian patriotism, however, it's important to note that Dostoyevsky never condoned violence for any reason, especially not in the service of any ideal of social justice. His character Ivan Karamazov would encapsulate the writer's personal credo, renouncing the "higher harmony" promised by the Utopian Socialists if that harmony should cost the tears of even a single child. Much of the work of his later career was motivated by his horror at the social revolutionaries of his day as they skated down a slippery moral slope toward justifying murder and terror for the greater good. His novels consistently exposed darker, egoistic motives behind such "rational murders"—as in the actions of Raskolnikov in *Crime and Punishment* and Verkhovensky and his secret revolutionaries in *The Possessed*.

Yet ideas tend to take on a life of their own, and Dostoyevsky is responsible for a fervent, messianic nationalism that later generations would adopt in service of bloodier goals, making him an unintentional forefather of some of the more violent expressions of Russian nationalism in the twentieth and twenty-first centuries.

DOSTOYEVSKY'S RESENTMENT OF TURGENEV was not just a result of his intense patriotism, however. He was also struggling under a serious inferiority complex triggered by his difficult financial circumstances, shame over his inability to support his young wife and future child, and the humiliating circumstances of his exile. "My future seems very depressing," he wrote Maikov, "and worst of all is the question of what will happen to the people who depend on me for help." He also missed Russia. They had been gone for four months—already a month longer than they'd planned, and there was no telling when they might return. "To go the way I have, without knowing and without foreseeing when I'll return, is very bad and distressing." The longer he was away, the stronger his nationalism grew; it became a kind of coping mechanism against the vagaries and daily insults of his increasingly rootless existence abroad.

And what did Anna make of all this? "I know this conversation with Turgenev has excited Fedya beyond words, and that he always gets beside himself when people repudiate their fatherland," she wrote in her diary on the day Dostoyevsky told her about their meeting. She also knew what it meant for him to have to grovel before Turgenev. Like her husband, she recoiled at the spectacle of this pampered Russia-hating writer, who'd never had to suffer for his art, now criticizing his motherland from his privileged enclave in Baden-Baden. "I would have thought no Russian writer on earth would want to repudiate his country and least of all declare himself a German!" Anna wrote. Russia "has supported him and done its utmost to encourage his talent. And now he abandons it and says that if Russia were to go under, the world would not be worse for it. Of all the appalling things for a Russian to say!" To Anna, who was trying desperately to live a decent life and remain a faithful Russian citizen abroad, the meeting with Turgenev was a painful reminder of how much she longed to be home, even as that dream remained elusive.

Some scholars have dismissed Anna's expressions of patriotism as mere echoes of her husband's positions. And there's no doubt that his ideas influenced Anna, who after all was still just shy of twenty-one years old. But Anna's own behavior, before and during their years of exile, proves that she was forming her own personal attitudes toward the big cultural questions of her day. During their stay in Baden-Baden, her first face-to-face encounter with the Continent that had given birth to the progressive ideas of her formative years, Anna found herself rethinking her relationship to the "land of holy wonders" and the values it stood for. To Anna, the most urgent question was not *What is Russia's mission?* but *What is my own mission, as partner to a Russian writer?* It was a question that would occupy her for the rest of their stay in Europe—and one she would answer, in time, not in words but in deeds.

After her brief spate at the roulette table, Anna settled back into her old daily routine, trying to manage her husband's gambling addiction until he had won back enough money for them to leave Baden-Baden. She had never imagined that they would stay at any of their honeymoon destinations for more than a couple of days, but they had been here nearly two months now, "as if condemned by the Devil himself to stay chained to one place." It would feel like eternal damnation if they didn't get away, but with what money? "Our circumstances at the moment are so appalling that they could scarcely be worse," Anna told her diary. "Who in the world is there to help us? Where is the benefactor ready to free us from our miserable position?"

The couple weighed their options. Dostoyevsky thought of appealing to Maikov, asking him to find money somehow, but never did; he tried to call on Goncharov to borrow money, but the latter never seemed to be at his hotel. Turning to Turgenev was out of the question. And Dostoyevsky hadn't written a word in Baden-Baden, his creative energy overwhelmed by his gambling mania. But he was still generating new story ideas, and he needed to find a new outlet for them. He thought briefly of contacting the writer Ivan Aksakov, with whom he'd discussed a collaboration the year before, but that was an uncertain prospect and would take too long to explore. He was tempted to approach another journal, to offer them a new novel by January in exchange for an immediate advance. But that was pie in the sky, Anna told him; there was no way he could come up with a new work that quickly, especially since he still owed Katkov the first installments of *The Idiot*, and they could not risk disappointing the endlessly patient editor yet again.

Together, they weighed and discarded one plan after another. Anna knew that staying in Baden-Baden would be the end of them, but they could afford neither Paris nor Rome. Finally they decided to move to Geneva, a town with a decent climate and—at least as important—no casinos. Perhaps here Dostoyevsky might shake this destructive fever of his, and free himself to sit down and write his novel.

Not every day was she able to summon that kind of enthusiasm. On the very day of their departure Fedya was back at the roulette table, losing fifty francs they needed for train fare plus twenty more he received from pawning a ring. Anna was forced to pawn her earrings to cover their fare. And even then—an hour and a half before departure—he couldn't resist one last fling, returning to the Kurhaus with twenty francs and losing it all. When he returned to his wife, head bowed in shame, she told him that, instead of being hysterical, he should instead help her by fastening the trunks and paying the landlady.

No one was there to see them off, a fitting end to their grim stay in Baden-Baden. Drenched in perspiration from lugging their own bags down the stairs, the Dostoyevskys slunk into a carriage and headed to the train station. "I was overjoyed that at last we were leaving this accursed town," Anna confessed, "and do not expect ever to return. I will even forbid my children ever to come here, so much have I endured in this place."

Three months into their honeymoon, they were beginning a new journey to yet another foreign town, with no money, no friends, and no serious professional prospects, save a few scattered rough drafts of her husband's new novel, *The Idiot*.

And a child growing inside her.

9.

Life and Fate

Anna peered out the window as the train whipped through the tortuous Rhine Valley, its craggy riverbanks overgrown with late-summer greenery, tiny Swiss houses framed by thick-forested mountains in the distance. The farther south they traveled, the more imposing the mountains became, their rocky peaks rising above the clouds. At last, a hilly metropolis came into view, nestled among pristine forests at the far end of Lake Geneva.

In the town of Geneva itself, steam-driven trolleys huffed and clattered their way everywhere, as ladies and gentlemen promenaded in their finery past expensive stores laden with sparkling jewelry, chocolates of every shape and size, and the latest European household goods. The Dostoyevskys sensed something different here; where so many European capitals were filled with hungry masses and bourgeois superciliousness, this city possessed a quiet, seductive charm. It felt like a place of respite. The crisp fall air was a relief after the scorching summer heat of Baden-Baden. Even the *bises*, the sudden gusts of winds carrying the scent of the lake, seemed to invite trust in the town's soothing powers, although they did tend to exacerbate Dostoyevsky's attacks.

On the day they arrived, they went looking for an apartment. When the rooms in the hilly center of town proved too expensive, they strolled across the bridge to a less expensive section, off the rue du Mont Blanc, where they found a charming and spacious second-floor apartment with a view of the bridge and the island of Jean-Jacques Rousseau. Anna took an immediate liking to the building's landladies, who welcomed them with a warmth the Dostoyevskys had not experienced since their stay with Madame Zimmerman in Dresden. It was more expensive than they could afford, true, but Anna knew that physical comfort was important to her husband, and with a child coming they would need the space. After paying for a month in advance, they had all of eighteen francs left; they were expecting fifty rubles more from Anna's mother, and another 150 as a loan from Maikov, but even that would carry them for only a limited time on a shoestring budget. Yet they were used to making do, pawning their belongings when things got desperate. After what they had just been through in Baden-Baden, they were determined to embrace Geneva as a blessing.

For the first time since Dresden, the couple was able to establish a daily routine. Dostoyevsky typically worked at night and awoke each day after eleven, by which time Anna had been up for hours. After breakfast they took a walk, as advised by Anna's doctors, and upon returning, Dostoyevsky got right to work. Around three in the afternoon they would go to an affordable restaurant for lunch; then, as Anna rested, her husband would spend a few hours at a café on the rue du Mont Blanc, poring over European and Russian newspapers. In the evenings they would take a long walk, window-shopping for jewelry Dostoyevsky couldn't afford. Finally, they came home and returned to work—the writer had started dictating *The Idiot* to Anna—or read books in French together.

They dreamed about their future family, too. If the new child were a boy, they would name him Misha, after Dostoyevsky's late brother, Mikhail; a girl would be named Sonya, after his niece and also after Sonya Marmeladova, the prostitute to whom the young murderer Raskolnikov confesses in *Crime and Punishment*. Anna admired her husband's solicitousness during her pregnancy; he was becoming more and more dependent on her, she noticed with some pleasure, and their love appeared to have strengthened under the pressure of their hardships. She was certain that "when the child is here his love will be even greater."

Fedya was of a similar mind. "Anya, we have grown so much together that a knife couldn't cut us apart," he told her. "Soon there will be Sonya, there will be two angels, and I can imagine how you will be with her, how good it will be." The more he got to know his young wife, the more she surprised him with new facets of her personality. In a letter to Maikov, he described Anna as "a young, kind, and wonderful creature" who "has turned out to be stronger and deeper than I knew her to be and imagined, and in many cases she has simply been a guardian angel for me." He marveled at her ability to comfort him, even as he was making her life miserable: "Anna Grigoryevna pawned *everything* of hers, her last things (. . . how she tried to comfort me, how she languished in thrice-cursed Baden-Baden, in our two rooms over a blacksmith shop)," all because he was powerless "to resist the temptation of winning." Yet he recognized that "none of that justifies me in the least," and as Anna's "defender and protector," he knew he was wrong to risk bringing her to "ruination" along with him.

Dostoyevsky's letter to Maikov exhibited a degree of self-awareness that often eluded him outside the confines of his art. Showing a genuine understanding of the terrible position in which he'd put his wife, he took responsibility for his bad behavior without the self-indulgent histrionics that frequently accompanied his confessions to Anna herself. Still, his portrait of their relationship overlooked an inexorable shift in the dynamic between them. While he may have considered himself Anna's "defender and protector," by now it was clear that she was perfectly capable of taking care of both herself and her husband. Dostoyevsky did confess to a concern that, given his age and "morbid personality," he might lack the "energy and capacity to respond" to "the child and the twenty-year-old in her." Yet Anna never complained of any lack of energy or ardor on her husband's part; she showed no concern over the difference in their ages, as it was precisely his fascinating life experience that she found attractive. "It was his mind and soul that I loved," she told her diary.

EQUAL TO THE COUPLE'S SHARED LONGING for Russia was their growing distaste for Europe, which only deepened in September as a host of luminaries gathered in Geneva for the first international Peace Congress. The inaugural event of a recently formed group of social activists, radicals, and revolutionaries known as the League of Peace and Freedom, the congress was meeting to lay out a vision for social reform designed to lead to world peace. The attendees included Russian revolutionary thinkers such as the socialist writer Alexander Herzen and Mikhail Bakunin, a prominent anarchist then living in exile in Europe.

At first, Anna was excited to be in Geneva for such a momentous occasion. "On the final day of the congress," she jotted down in her diary, "there will be an outing on the lake and a dinner paid for personally by Victor Hugo. I would like to see all that." Hugo would bow out at the last minute for health reasons, but thousands of others attended, and tens of thousands across Europe signed a petition supporting the group's goals; the result was a new breath of life for dreams of liberty that dated back to the European revolutions of 1848. For many, the days-long affair symbolized the end of the benighted barbarism that had once ruled Europe.

Dostoyevsky, on the other hand, was repulsed by the very idea of the congress.

Out of morbid curiosity, he invited Anna to join him to see a speech by Bakunin. He had heard his brand of socialist rhetoric before, of course, having once belonged to a band of young revolutionaries himself. "They began with the fact that for the achievement of peace on earth the Christian faith has to be exterminated," Dostoyevsky complained in a letter to a relative:

> large states destroyed and made small ones; all the capital be done away with, so that everything be in common. . . . All this without the slightest proof, all of it memorized twenty years ago, and that's just how it has remained. And most importantly, fire and sword—and after everything has been annihilated, then, in their opinion, there will in fact be peace.

Peace through destruction: this was the socialists' utopian formula, a vision of liberty driven by an ethos of violence. Since his days in the Petrashevsky Circle he had turned full circle, rejecting any vision of social progress that involved the cost of a single human life.

Like her husband, Anna sensed the contradiction between what was being preached at the Peace Congress and who was preaching it. One speaker barked out hackneyed slogan after slogan; another made a ten-point proclamation against war in a tone that struck her as downright bellicose. When an Italian speaker issued repeated shouts of "Down with papacy!" the president of the congress tried to force the speaker off the stage. But the crowd cheered him on, and as their cries grew even louder, he gesticulated so violently that he knocked a glass of water onto someone's head. One woman sitting next to Anna turned to her to ask whether they should fear for their safety. No, Anna assured her, it was a peaceful gathering—although privately she wondered why this peace congress seemed so much more like a war rally.

She had heard her husband disparage the socialists and revolutionaries before, but now, witnessing them herself for the first time, she, too, sensed that their motives were not true justice and universal harmony but something more sinister. Beneath the patina of their oratory she detected an angry egoism, just as the glamorous European way of life increasingly seemed to hide a fundamental arrogance. "What's this stupid congress for?" she wrote. "People don't have anything to do, so they gather at various congresses, at which only loud phrases are spoken, and nothing comes of it. True, I regretted that we wasted energy there."

Many of the attendees agreed with her, and the congress was widely criticized at the time for its anarchistic and revolutionary overtones. Yet many others considered it a success, and when the League reconvened in Brussels after the Franco-Prussian War, its attendees would lay the philosophical groundwork for what eventually became the United Nations. Anna's exasperation at her family's straitened circumstances doubtless colored her response to the proceedings, as did her husband's hostility toward the project; with virtually no friends in Geneva to talk with, they were like an echo chamber venting their frustrations at each other.

AFTER A DAY OF THE RAUCOUS NONSENSE of the congress, Anna wanted to spend a peaceful evening with her husband. As they stopped at the post office, Dostoyevsky reached into his pocket and accidentally pulled out a small, crinkled piece of paper on which something was written in pencil. Anna reached for the note, asking him what it was, but he wouldn't release it. Growling at her, he seized Anna's arm, but she refused to let go. Eventually the paper tore, and as the pieces fell to the ground, Dostoyevsky upbraided Anna for what she'd done. She responded by calling him a fool, turning on her heels, and walking home alone.

She had reason to be suspicious, after discovering her husband's correspondence with Polina in Dresden a few months before. And yet, characteristically, Anna was quick to blame herself for her rash behavior. "I'm a terribly rotten person!" she told her diary. "I'm full of irritation, suspicion and envy; it now seemed to me that it was a new note, and significantly, that it was a note from a certain individual [i.e., Polina], with whom I don't want Fedya to renew relations for anything in the world."

But this wasn't a piece of mail; it was a scrap of paper, a message that seemed to have been passed by hand. Polina, there in Geneva? It was unthinkable.

As soon as her husband was out of sight, Anna returned to pick up the torn shreds of paper, then rushed home, a parade of grim scenarios flitting through her mind. Maybe Polina *had* come to Geneva, she thought, and Fedya had been seeing her secretly. "After all, he'd betrayed [his first wife], and who's to say he's not betraying me, too?" She "had to know with certainty" whether he was seeing his erstwhile mistress. But then, within moments, she was scolding herself for even harboring such thoughts. "Yet what can I do if my character is like that, that I can't be at peace, if I love Fedya so much that I'm jealous? God forgive me for such a low deed, that I'm spying on my husband, toward whom I really shouldn't have any mistrust."

At home, she pieced the letter together. She could make out an address—*rue de Rive, Messrs. Blanchard dessous [basement]*—in what looked like Polina's familiar handwriting. Anna was overcome by a dire train of thought: Maybe he was with his lover that very moment. If not, why should he have tried to hide such a note? She started sobbing furiously. "I bit my hands, squeezed my neck ... I was afraid I was going to go out of my mind." She was haunted by the prospect that Polina had returned for Dostoyevsky not because she loved him but "only to spite me, knowing that it would be painful for me. . . . And now they both think that he can deceive me, just as he once deceived Marya Dmitriyevna." Tomorrow, she decided, she would go to the address and confront Polina directly. "And then I would have to leave him."

When he got home a few hours later, Dostoyevsky asked Anna what was going on, but she responded curtly and turned away. He was as angry as she was: Why had she pounced on him that way at the post office? What was she so afraid of? The scrap of paper was just a note from a pawnbroker, he said, passing on the address of another pawnbroker. Anna must have wanted to believe him, but she couldn't; instead she went alone to another room, where she dashed off a letter to her brother, Ivan, asking him to check whether Polina was still in Moscow.

Before the night was over, the couple made their peace, with Dostoyevsky chalking up the incident to the irritations of the Peace Congress the day before. The idea didn't seem entirely far-fetched to Anna; their time at the congress, where there "was a lot more fighting" than agreeing, "and all the orators proclaimed not peace, but war," may well have roused some latent antagonism within them, just it had in the crowds. Still, the skirmish had disturbed the tranquility Geneva seemed to promise. Anna slept badly, waking up in the middle of the night thinking, "Is it possible that tomorrow . . . all of my happiness will be destroyed?"

The following day, as Dostoyevsky worked at home, Anna sneaked off to the rue de Rive to track down the mysterious address. What she found was neither Polina's place nor the pawnbroker's but a basement apartment that was home to one Monsieur Blanchard and his wife, a large, imposing dressmaker whom Anna sensed she'd better not upset with too many prying questions. Had she misread the address on the pieced-together scraps of paper? Or did the Blanchards know more than they were letting on? Anna remained suspicious, convinced that she might run into her husband and Polina any second. After lunch, when Dostoyevsky retired for a nap, Anna returned to the rue de Rive to speak to the concierge, but she was nowhere to be found. "I would've given her a half franc to thoroughly find out everything."

Anna never would receive any answers to these questions that plagued her. Whatever was happening between her husband and Polina would remain an unsolved mystery for her, as it has remained for us. And nowhere in her diary would she mention Polina again—with one notable exception.

A few weeks later, in October 1867, the Dostoyevskys stopped in at the post office, where there was a letter waiting for Anna. Dostoyevsky demanded to know who it was from: just as she had feared that her husband was maintaining an illicit correspondence with Polina, he remained aghast at the idea that his wife and mistress were exchanging letters behind *his* back. (Given his own experience with such a love triangle, is it any wonder that Dostoyevsky became a master at portraying strange and complicated affairs in his novels?) In fact the letter was an innocent note from her friend Marya Stoyunina, updating Anna on recent news from Petersburg and congratulating her on the upcoming birth of her child. But Stoyunina's handwriting happened to resemble Polina's, and if that was enough to make Fedya suspicious, Anna was not about to set his mind at ease. He peppered her with questions, and when he discovered that the letter was sent postage due, he flew into a rage. It was bad enough that Polina was writing to his wife; that this secret correspondence was also costing them money pushed him over the top. The whole walk home he berated Anna, who walked several paces away, quietly reading the letter to herself. Finally, unable to take his antics any longer, she told him it was just a letter from Stoyunina.

"To hell with her," he growled, "she just cost us ninety centimes."

"If you're so worried about money," Anna fired back, "I'll go and sell something and give you the money!"

And that was it: the last we hear of Polina. It was a weirdly abrupt dénouement for an obsession that had nearly torn their marriage apart. There's no evidence that Dostoyevsky ever saw Polina again; their last confirmed encounter was in November of 1865, nearly a full year before Dostoyevsky met Anna, and most scholars agree that the affair petered out after his marriage. After years of love and quarrels and reconciliations, Polina had finally told him outright—with none of her usual hedging— that she was no longer in love with him. "She and Dostoyevsky made their farewells," writes scholar Marc Slonim, "knowing only too well that their paths would never cross again."

By the fall of 1867, even his correspondence with Polina had ended—as, it would seem, had Anna's. Perhaps she was finally convinced that it was over between her husband and his former mistress. Or perhaps she had simply resolved to make it so, by keeping his attention focused on his family and his work.

ANNA'S OWN ATTENTION was increasingly directed to her difficult pregnancy. By the end of 1867, her diary entries dwindle to a few cursory lines, then end altogether. If anything, her love for Dostoyevsky seems to have grown stronger by the end of the crisis over Polina. More than once, in those early months of their marriage, she had contemplated leaving him. Yet she resolved to salvage their love, drawing on her faith—in him, and in the strength of their bond—to carry her through.

Dostoyevsky, meanwhile, was in need of faith to keep him from plunging into despair over his new novel, which was now badly stalled. Their finances remained in shambles. He had already received three advances from Katkov, and he knew that "I absolutely cannot ask Katkov for anything *now*," not until he'd delivered the first installments of *The Idiot*. He was also banking on the idea that the serialized novel would be strong enough to attract a contract for a stand-alone book edition. "This has to be a very good novel. It can't be any other way; it's a sine qua non."

Yet all he had to show for the past four months was a lackluster article about Vissarion Belinsky and some rough sketches for *The Idiot*. Worse yet, when he finally sent the Belinsky article off to Maikov, asking him to deliver it to the editor of the almanac where it was to be published, the essay mysteriously disappeared, along with the payment Dostoyevsky was counting on. Now their hopes of financial recovery would hang entirely on *The Idiot*, whose first installment was due to Katkov in January 1868, just a few short months away.

As late as October 1867, Dostoyevsky was still making and unmaking the novel's outline. The story line kept changing, and the characters remained unclear in his imagination. The very idea behind the novel—to portray "an absolutely beautiful human being"—was now in question. In moments of despair, he wondered whether such a type existed at all. And even if it did, would anyone in Russia or Europe be open to his message of selfless Christian compassion? The answer, he decided, was no—which only made him want to write the book all the more.

When he'd first mentioned the idea for the novel to Katkov during their meeting in Moscow in the spring of 1867, Dostoyevsky had had only an inkling of what it would be about. Now that he was clear in his intention, he was daunted by the enormous creative challenge. "I don't think there can be anything harder than that, especially in our time," he told Maikov. "Only my desperate situation compelled me to take on this under-developed idea. I took a risk, as at roulette: 'Maybe it will develop under my pen!' That's unforgivable."

Unforgivable, perhaps, but this kind of creative high-wire act was as necessary to Dostoyevsky's process as roulette. Just as he needed to feel that voluptuous vertigo of watching the roulette wheel spin, he needed to feel the danger inherent in artistic creation—the danger of staking every-thing on an idea without knowing if it can be achieved. This is one reason Dostoyevsky so often took advances long before the idea for a novel had ripened. He was driven not just by financial need but by a craving for creative risk.

The Idiot needed to be so many things. It had to be a hit with the read-ing public, of course, so that it would fetch a lucrative contract for a sepa-rate book edition. But Dostoyevsky's more powerful motivation was to convince Russians—by now thoroughly corrupted by Western ideas—that true social progress would come not from the revolutionary visions of the Geneva Peace Congress but only through his cherished Christian ideals of humility and kindness, as embodied by the Russian people. It was a position he had been arguing for years—in the pages of *Time* and *Epoch*, in *Winter Notes on Summer Impressions*, and in his novels. Now, as he worked late into the night, pacing nervously, twitching and muttering to himself, Anna grew concerned that the process was affecting his health. She wanted to support him but was at a loss for how to do so. "My God, how I hope with my entire soul that his novel comes off," she wrote in her diary. "That's my most genuine desire. I constantly pray about that."

She had another reason to be concerned: his gambling compulsion was returning. Dostoyevsky started talking about going to Saxon les Bains, a chic gambling resort nestled in the Swiss Alps about five hours away by train. "He definitely has the intention of going there," Anna confided to her diary. "What a strange man. It would seem that fate has punished him roundly, and showed him many times that he can't get rich from roulette. No, this man is incurable, he is still convinced all the same—and I'm sure he will always be convinced—that he will definitely become rich, will definitely win."

By early November, Dostoyevsky's creative agony had become too much for either of them to bear, and she gave in. "To distract him from his gloomy thoughts, I suggested the idea of making a trip to Saxon les Bains to try his luck at roulette once more." Overjoyed at her blessing, Dostoyevsky left for the resort at once.

As soon as he arrived, he went straight to the casino. Later that day, he sent off a letter describing the torments of those first few hours, while chastising Anna for letting him go in the first place. "Oh, darling, you shouldn't even allow me to get at the roulette wheel," he wrote. "As soon as I touch it, my heart stops, and my arms and legs tremble and go cold." And he made her a promise: "I'm giving myself my honest and *great* word that tonight, from 8 to 11, I'll play . . . in the most prudent fashion, I swear to you."

The next day, she received a letter that opened with all-too-familiar words: "Anya, darling, my dear, I have lost everything, everything, everything!" Unlike his letters from Bad Homburg, however, there was no attempt to convince her that this time he'd stick to his system and come home with winnings. Instead he conceded that "the novel alone will save us." He even presented his losses as a godsend, reminding Anna how a surge of creativity after his ill-fated gambling spree in Wiesbaden in 1865 had led directly to the writing of *Crime and Punishment*. "It would be difficult to be in greater perdition, but work pulled me through. I'll set to work with love and hope and you'll see what happens in two years." No matter how he tried to justify his behavior, though, he knew it was unforgivable. All he could do was assure Anna that "the time will come when I will be worthy of you and no longer rob you like a nasty, vile thief!" To earn back her respect, he promised, "I'll never, never gamble again."

She had heard it all before: the promises, the self-condemnation, the desperate pleas for respect. What was new this time was that Dostoyevsky seemed to understand that gambling had become necessary to his creative process. Among all his claims in this letter from Saxon les Bains, Anna was astute enough to recognize that this, at least, was plausible. And yet, having stood near the same abyss herself in Baden-Baden, having reckoned with its dizzying darkness, she was able to view his ravings from a calm distance. "I didn't especially grieve" over his failure at the tables, she told her diary. "I took it philosophically, stoically, because I had expected it and had grown used to the thought that everything would be lost."

Equally familiar to her were the grandiose promises often triggered by a gambling disaster. "My friend, don't be sad that I have ruined you," he insisted. "Don't worry about our future. I'll make everything, everything right!" But she no longer paid much attention to such promises or the complicated plans that followed, which she found as incomprehensible as they were fanciful. The one thing she did take seriously was his art. Which is why she was overjoyed that, as soon as he returned to Geneva, her husband settled down to his writing with a focus Anna had not seen in months. In twenty-three days, he finished about ninety-three pages of *The Idiot* for the January issue of *The Russian Messenger*. Anna's gamble in encouraging him to go to Saxon les Bains had paid off. What was more, as the novel's first sections took shape, they both began to believe that this might be the book to save them financially.

The Idiot is the story of Prince Myshkin, a young man in his mid-twenties from an impoverished old noble family, who returns as a stranger to his native Russia after a four-year treatment for epilepsy in Switzerland. He brings with him nothing but a small tote containing the entirety of his worldly possessions, and the conviction that he will be able to redeem his fallen social status through acts of Christian goodness. There is indeed something irresistibly childlike about Myshkin (whose name derives from *myshka*, or "mouse"), a quality that both disarms and discomfits everyone he encounters. At the home of his distant relatives, the Epanchins, Myshkin meets the haughty, spoiled, and dreamy Aglaya Epanchina, who finds the prince's innocent goodness beguiling; he also spies a portrait of the beautiful, fiery Nastaya Filippovna Barashkova, who has been seduced and later abandoned by the wealthy landowner who'd taken her in.

Drawn to both women—Aglaya as a budding romantic interest, Nastasya as the object of his Christian compassion—the prince finds himself unable to choose between two very different kinds of love. He is drawn into a triangle that includes the ruthless and violently jealous Parfyon Rogozhin, who is passionately in love with Nastasya and will stop at nothing to possess her. Though Rogozhin is fond of Myshkin, he nevertheless attempts to murder the prince, until the young man is saved at the last minute by a severe epileptic attack that shocks and horrifies Rogozhin.

Here, then, was a real plot: a bizarre love story replete with murderous rage and intense psychological drama, two of the elements that had made *Crime and Punishment* such a success. The writing, it seemed, was going well at last.

THIS WAS REASSURING, as the couple were increasingly preoccupied by their baby's approaching due date. Worried about Anna's condition and his own peace of mind, Dostoyevsky invited Anna's mother to come and stay with them in Geneva after the new year. (Mrs. Snitkina had hoped to be present at the birth, but fell ill and arrived in Geneva only at the beginning of May.) In the meantime, the Dostoyevskys chose a midwife, one Madame Barraud, to assist with the delivery. The expectant father took great joy in caring for his pregnant wife, practicing the walk to Madame Barraud's home every day to make sure he knew it when the time came. In December they moved to a larger, two-room apartment on the rue du Mont Blanc, next door to an English church. "Anna Grigoryevna has been waiting with reverence, loves our future guest with all her heart, has been bearing up cheerfully and bravely," wrote Dostoyevsky to Maikov. "But recently her nerves have been on edge and she has been visited by gloomy thoughts: She's afraid of dying."

The weather turned stormy in late January, and within just a few weeks Dostoyevsky suffered two seizures. The second of these, on the night of February 20, left him dazed, severely weakened, and barely able to stand. An hour after she finally persuaded him to go to bed, Anna felt a pain in her abdomen, which grew stronger every hour. Labor had begun. She endured the pains on her own as long as she could, afraid to wake up her husband. Finally, after three hours, she got up and tiptoed into his room, tapping him lightly on the shoulder as he slept.

"What's the matter, Anyechka?" he mumbled.

"I think it's started. I'm suffering terribly."

"I'm so sorry for you, dear," he said tenderly, then fell immediately back to sleep.

Realizing he was too weak to make the walk to the midwife without risking another attack, Anna tried to bear it on her own for as long as possible, yearning for Mama, for Ivan, for anyone who could help her, as "my only guardian and defender, my husband, was himself in a helpless state." She prayed feverishly through the night, as the storms raged outside, the wind and rain rattling the windows. The next morning, she finally awoke Dostoyevsky. When he realized that she'd been in agony all night long, he immediately threw on some clothes and rushed out the door to fetch Madame Barraud.

The midwife's servant came to the door and told Dostoyevsky that her mistress had just returned from a visit and did not wish to be awoken. At his wits' end, the novelist declared that if she didn't wake her mistress at once he would smash the glass door altogether. Madame Barraud promptly appeared, and together they went to see Anna. Chastising the expectant mother, the midwife insisted that Anna's labor had been hindered by her carelessness and said that she would come back in seven or eight hours to check her progress.

Eight hours later, the midwife still had not come; when Dostoyevsky went to fetch her again, she was out dining with friends. The frightened servant gave him the address, and Dostoyevsky tracked her down, insisting that Madame Barraud come with him to check on Anna's condition. Curtly explaining that Anna's labor was in her view progressing badly, and that the delivery was unlikely before late evening, Madame Barraud promised to come later, and then turned back to her friends. At nine in the evening, when she still hadn't shown, Dostoyevsky went to fetch her a third time, interrupting her friends at their game of lotto to declare that if she didn't come this instant he'd fire her on the spot and find another midwife. The threat worked. Apologizing to her friends, she left the party and went with Dostoyevsky to see Anna, grousing when she arrived: *"Oh, ces russes, ces russes!"* "Oh, these Russians, these Russians!"

Trying to make amends, Dostoyevsky prepared Madame Barraud a fine supper consisting of hors d'oeuvres, sweets, and wines. This pleased Anna immensely, giving her overwrought husband something to keep him occupied during her labor. "His face showed such torment," she later recalled of those harrowing hours, "such desperation!" Hearing him sob, she began to fear that she might actually be at risk of dying, and the thought terrified her: What would happen to *him* if she died? "It was not so much myself I pitied as my poor husband, for whom my death might prove catastrophic," she would remember. "It was then that I realized what burning hopes and expectations he had for me and our future child. The sudden crushing of those hopes, in light of Fyodor Mikhailovich's impulsive and unrestrained nature, might be the end of him."

Madame Barraud warned Anna that focusing on her husband instead of herself was retarding the course of labor, and the midwife eventually banned him from the delivery room altogether—which only made Anna worry about what might be happening to him outside the locked door. As her labor pains intensified, she lost consciousness repeatedly, and when she came to, under the gaze of the strange nurse, Anna often had no idea where she was or what was happening. In her intervals of lucidity, she asked the midwife or nurse to check on her husband.

At about five in the morning of February 22, Anna's shrieking ceased. Dostoyevsky, who had been kneeling outside her door crossing himself, was alarmed to hear an unfamiliar cry. When he heard it a second time, he realized that a baby had been born—his baby, *their* baby. Beside himself with joy, he jumped up, shoved open the hooked door, and threw himself down beside Anna's bed, kissing her hands. "We were both so happy that our dream was fulfilled," Anna recalled, "that a new being was in the world, our first-born!"

The midwife brought them the baby, cleaned and wrapped in a cloth, and congratulated them on the birth of their daughter. Dostoyevsky made the sign of the cross over Sonya, kissed her tiny, wrinkled face, and said, "Anya, look, what a beauty we have!" Anna rejoiced in her little girl and also in her husband's tender face, transported by happiness as she had never seen before.

For the next several weeks, the Dostoyevskys' home was suffused with joy. They reveled in parenthood; Anna was charmed by her husband's tenderness toward little Sonya, and he wrote ecstatic letters home about the joys of fatherhood. To Anna's delight, he was present for every bath; he loved to wrap the baby in her little piqué blanket, carrying her around the apartment, rocking her in his arms. The minute he heard Sonya's cries, he interrupted his work to check on her. Anna watched him sit at their daughter's crib for hours, talking and singing to her in a ludicrous voice. Whenever he went out, he showered Anna with questions upon returning: "How's Sonya? Did she sleep well? Did she eat?"

As spring came to Geneva, the happy exhaustion of Sonya's first weeks settled into a steady glow that filled the entire household. Still, anxiety was never far away. Their expenses increased with the baby's arrival, and Dostoyevsky still had previous debts to settle before he could reclaim their pawned items. To make matters worse, they were thrown out of their apartment after complaints about the baby's crying, and the move would bring additional costs. *The Russian Messenger* was late on its payment, which the couple badly needed, but Dostoyevsky couldn't pester Katkov for any more money until he'd sent the promised second installment of *The Idiot*—and, once again, he was stalled.

To recharge his creative juices, the writer made another trip to Saxon les Bains. This time, he lost everything within half an hour of arriving. "Well, what can I say to you now, my heavenly angel whom I so torment," he wrote Anna immediately. "Forgive me, Anya, I have poisoned your life!" Later that evening, however, feeling a familiar surge of inspiration, he assured Anna that "if this vile and base incident had not now occurred, this waste of 220 francs, then perhaps neither would there have been the amazing, superb idea that has now occurred to me and that will serve as *our* ultimate *overall salvation*!" He would write Katkov, he said, explaining that the arrival of his daughter had slowed him down, making him late on delivery of the last installment; that he needed to move to somewhere with a better climate to finish the novel, but the book would be finished by the fall; and that if it was good enough, the income from a separate book edition would allow Dostoyevsky to pay off his creditors and finally return to Russia. If only Katkov could send another three hundred rubles now, that would be enough to get them through these next months. "*The main thing* is the success of my novel!" he told Anna. "If the novel is a success, then everything is saved." As far as we know, Dostoyevsky never actually wrote this letter—Anna may have dissuaded him from it—but he returned to Geneva with renewed energy and plunged back into his work.

The spring weather remained beautiful and warm, and the family took long strolls at the doctor's suggestion through the luxuriant Jardin des Anglais, where little Sonya slept soundly in her carriage for hours. In early May, however, a *bise* sprang up on one such outing, and the baby caught a chill.

When they returned home that evening, Sonya started coughing, and her temperature was high. They went immediately to the best children's doctor in Geneva, who assured them it was nothing serious. Relieved, they went home. The doctor checked up on the patient regularly for the next several days, trying to calm the worried parents, reassuring them that, despite her coughing and fever, she was on her way to recovery. Then, three hours after the doctor left on the morning of May 12, Anna and her husband found Sonya lying in her crib, still and pale. She was not breathing. She had died a few hours earlier.

The trauma left them stone-cold with agony.

For the next two days, the couple did not leave each other's side. They visited one government office after another, seeking permission to bury their daughter. On the day of the funeral they dressed Sonya in her little white satin dress, and together they gently placed her body in the coffin. A few days later they took the coffin to the Russian church for the funeral service, and then to the cemetery at Plainpalais, an oasis in the midst of the bustling Swiss city. There, amid the chirping birds and bright sunshine, they buried Sonya in the children's section, a quiet corner on the edge of the cemetery. They visited every day for the rest of their stay in Geneva, leaving flowers for their daughter and crying over what they had lost.

Dostoyevsky blamed his daughter's death not just on Geneva's changeable climate but on the arrogance of the Swiss doctor and the utter incompetence of their baby nurse. He had always disliked the Swiss, Anna knew, "but the coldness and heartlessness shown by many of them during the time of our most acute grief"—such as their neighbors, who sent their maid to ask the grieving couple not to cry so loudly—"only exacerbated this dislike."

But if the Dostoyevskys could no longer remain in Geneva, which constantly reminded them of their loss, neither could they afford to leave Switzerland altogether. So they decided to move to the town of Vevey, on the opposite shore of Lake Geneva. As they settled in for the four-hour steamer ride across the lake, Anna peered into her husband's face, which had thinned and hollowed in the weeks since Sonya's death, and listened in anguish as he poured out a lifetime of pent-up sadness. "For the first time in my life with him," Anna recalled, "I heard him cry out bitterly against the fate that had persecuted him all his life." He recounted the details of his lonely youth after the death of his beloved mother, the gibes of literary friends who had turned against him, and the profound suffering of his prison years. He spoke at length, too, of his greatest dream of all—to have a family of his own—which had never happened with his first wife. And now, when "this great, this only human happiness—having a child of your own" had finally come to him, fate had snatched it away.

Anna tried to comfort him, begged him to accept their shared tragedy, but he could not, not yet. "There are moments that are unbearable," wrote Dostoyevsky to Maikov. "I'll never forget it and never stop feeling unhappy. . . . Even if there's another child, I don't understand how I'll love it, where I'll find the love; I need Sonya. I can't acknowledge that she's gone."

Alas, the move to Vevey failed to provide the comfort they needed.

"In all the fourteen years of our married life," Anna wrote, "I cannot recall a summer more wretched than the one my husband and I spent in Vevey in 1868. Life seemed to have stopped for us." During walks near the lake, they found their eyes glancing across to the town where their little girl was now buried. Every child they encountered was a painful reminder of their loss. Even a trip together to the mountains, where they could be alone, was little help. Thanks to constant prayer and her mother's steady consolation, Anna at least managed to assuage her sadness little by little. But not her husband. The curtain of grief drawn in front of him simply would not lift.

A few months later, in early September 1868, Anna wrote to Dostoyevsky's younger brother Nikolai of their "terrible grief": "How happy we were in those three months when Sonya was still alive; it was such a full life that we needed nothing more. What a dear, quiet girl my Sonya was. She recognized us, laughed at us and loved it terribly when Fedya sang to her." And then, characteristically, Anna shifted her focus away from herself and toward her husband. "Poor Fedya, he is in such anguish you wouldn't believe, and only consoles himself with the thought that there will be another."

DOSTOYEVSKY SCHOLARS HAVE OBSERVED that the writer never portrayed a woman like Anna in his fiction, preferring instead the type of femme fatale embodied by his mistress Polina Suslova. Yet as he constructed the story of *The Idiot* around the theme of transcendent compassion, it was surely because the "absolutely beautiful human being" at the novel's center was inspired by Anna herself. "I cannot live without you, Anya," he told her while kissing her good night late one evening in Geneva. "It was for those like you that Christ came. I say this not because I love you, but because I know you." Buffeted by their daily struggle for survival, the torment of Dostoyevsky's cycles of creativity and self-sabotage, and now the death of their daughter, Anna had stood by her husband's side through the darkest days of their marriage, loving him with an intensity and a selflessness that seemed to him almost Christlike.

10.

The Possessed

Dostoyevsky had no choice but to force himself to write, for summer was turning to fall, and the first pages of *The Idiot* were due at the start of the new year. "How unpleasant and disgusting it [is] to write," he told his niece. Even as he struggled to portray his "absolutely beautiful human being," he was seized by doubts over whether his hero's story was a fair reflection of the ugly realities of life—realities the writer himself had endured so painfully in recent months. "At every moment (inwardly) he asks himself the question: 'Am I right or are they right?'" Dostoyevsky jotted in his notes for the novel. Worse yet, he had no clear sense, from a purely artistic standpoint, whether the book was any good. Like quixotic Prince Myshkin himself, however, Dostoyevsky would push forward with the work, which by now had become not just a necessary commercial gamble but a deeply personal moral statement. "Everything, my entire fate, depends on the success of the novel!" he told Maikov.

As he planned each installment, the novel's plot continued to evolve in his imagination, albeit in unpredictable directions. After recovering from the fit that saved him from Rogozhin's knife, Myshkin asks for Aglaya Epanchina's hand. Mistrustful of the intentions of this strange, awkward man, the Epanchins arrange a gathering of distinguished guests to see how the prince performs in polite society. Not surprisingly, he fares poorly, launching into a passionate lecture on the superiority of the Russian spirit and the potential for universal harmony on earth—a harangue so intense that it triggers another epileptic fit.

The book was starting to move, then, in unexpectedly tragic directions. Which was no more than a reflection of their life itself. By fall it had become clear to the Dostoyevskys that they needed to make an immediate change in their circumstances, or depression might finish them both. In September they abandoned Vevey and moved two hundred miles southeast to Milan, gathering alpine wildflowers as they traveled the Simplon Pass and descended to the Italian side in a charming cabriolet. The soothing mountain breeze did them good, as did the sight of the Lombardy peasants, who reminded them of Russian peasants back home.

Yet beneath the calming rhythms of Italian life, fresh storms continued to brew. Autumn in Milan that year was cold and rainy, mirroring the couple's desolation. "Anna Grigoryevna is patient but misses Russia, and we both cry about Sonya," Dostoyevsky wrote to Maikov in October. In a moment of compassion toward Anna, he continued: "I can see that she's miserable, and although we love each other nearly more than a year and a half ago, it's nonetheless distressing to me that she is living with me in such a sad monastery." Yet returning to Russia was not yet an option; until he had the money to settle his debts, that would only mean "winding up in debtors' prison upon arriving."

Deprived of the long walks they enjoyed, and unable to find Russian newspapers or books in the reading rooms, the couple soon grew weary of life in Milan. After two months they moved on to Florence for the winter, hoping for a happier place for Dostoyevsky to finish the novel. Yet even there the writing continued to torment him. He kept wondering whether the novel was any good, but he hadn't yet learned to trust his wife's opinion. "My only reader is Anna Grigoryevna," he told Maikov. "She even likes it very much; but after all, she can't judge *about my things*." Just recently the writer had praised Anna's personal qualities in another letter to Maikov, but he hadn't learned to afford that same respect to her literary judgment or to involve her more explicitly in the creative process.

Plagued with doubts, he began to question whether he was capable of realizing his vision for the work. The more *The Idiot* seemed to come into focus for Dostoyevsky, the more he remained "bitterly convinced that never before in my literary life have I had a single poetic idea better and richer than the one that has now become clear to me." Yet time was not on his side: "I have to rush as hard as I can, work without rereading, ride the post horses hard and, in the final analysis, I still won't be done in time." And yet rush he did, striving to conjure the Prince Myshkin of his imagination.

After Myshkin comes to, following his seizure at the Epanchins' social gathering, he has a change of heart and decides to propose to Nastasya Filippovna. The older woman is moved by the proposal—the prince is the first man she's ever encountered who has not tried to possess or use her for his personal gain—but she is unable to believe in her own goodness and fears that she will only ruin the guileless Myshkin. And so, when she happens to see Rogozhin on her way to the church where she and Myshkin are to marry, she runs off with him. Yet her love will prove insufficient for this brutally passionate man, whose attempts to dominate her culminate in jealous rage and murder. In a bizarrely haunting final scene, Rogozhin and Myshkin, his former rival, keep midnight vigil over the murdered woman's body. Having failed miserably to regenerate a fallen world, the shattered Prince Myshkin is sent back to Switzerland to be cured once again.

Dostoyevsky was dissatisfied with the finished pages he sent off to Katkov. But he hoped that the story's thunderous climax and haunting finale would attract major offers for a stand-alone book publication.

The offers never came.

Far from the triumph Dostoyevsky had promised Anna, *The Idiot* landed with a thud. Readers and critics alike found its themes confusing, its writing frenzied and uneven. But "the chief criticism" among Russian readers, Maikov warned in late 1868, as Dostoyevsky was still hurrying to finish, "is in the fantasticality of the characters."

Not that he needed readers to tell him the book had failed. He saw it all too clearly himself: His hero, who was meant to rehabilitate the fallen Nastasya Filippovna, conquer the evil Rogozhin with the power of goodness, and induce humility in arrogant Aglaya, achieves none of the above.

Rather, his angelic "Prince Christ," as the writer called Myshkin in his notes, wreaks inadvertent havoc on everything and everyone he touches, his goodness vanquished by the ugly realities of his time.

Dostoyevsky's great fear—that he might never bring his prince's idealized image to credible life—had been confirmed. And yet *The Idiot* does offer memorable if distorted glimpses of his ideal of moral perfection, in moments like the ecstatic aura Myshkin experiences just before an epileptic seizure, a moment of "the highest degree of harmony [and] beauty" that arouses in him "a hitherto unheard-of and unknown feeling of fullness, measure, reconciliation, and an ecstatic, prayerful merging with the highest synthesis of life." Dostoyevsky had long been transfixed by the power of such ecstatic visions, having experienced them himself more than once in his eventful life—just before an attack, at the moment the tsar rescued him from death, even in his rare moments of victory at roulette. In the months following Sonya's death, he grew obsessed with these fantastical visions, as if he might will them to change his real life.

AND THAT REAL LIFE came with bills to pay. Up to this point, the writer had been receiving 150 rubles per sixteen-page signature for *The Idiot*, for a total of seven thousand rubles (just over eighty thousand dollars today), three thousand of which had already been advanced to him. And part of the remaining four thousand would go toward interest Anna's mother owed on items Anna had pawned in Petersburg to finance their trip. Meanwhile, Dostoyevsky continued to bleed money to Pasha and Emilya Fyodorovna and her family whenever they asked—an ongoing insult to Anna, who had sacrificed so much yet still often felt herself a supplicant to her husband.

The hoped-for single-volume edition of *The Idiot* was nowhere on the horizon; the writer's sole source of income, his monthly stipend from *The Russian Messenger*, had come to an end; by his own calculation, the number of pages he'd furnished the magazine left him in debt to Katkov by a thousand rubles. By March 1869, the couple was once again so financially desperate that Anna pawned her underwear. If not for the two francs Dostoyevsky managed to borrow from a stranger, they might well have perished for good.

"It's not for me in my position to sit idly," he'd written Maikov just a few months earlier. Nor would he—thanks to his wife, who was often the one to come up with practical solutions to their seemingly insurmountable problems. Recognizing that her husband and his work were languishing without direct contact with Russian life and literature, she now suggested a move to Prague, a place filled with Russian émigrés. Everything about the city, Anna knew, would appeal to Dostoyevsky, who had been invited to the Slavic Congress there in 1867 and still regretted missing it. But the dream was short-lived: after a ten-day journey by steamship up the river Moldau, they quickly discovered that housing was far too expensive for them. Instead they decided to return to Dresden, a city with which they were at least familiar.

From Johannesstrasse to Victoriastrasse, their life, it seemed to them both, was going in circles. The excitement of Anna's first wide-eyed glimpse of Dresden was long gone; now the German town was merely a makeshift home, a way station where they would bide their time until they were able to return to Russia.

The couple bore their lot nobly, even managing to find humor in their dire circumstances. Together they composed limericks on the subject of their poverty, and Dostoyevsky enjoyed likening himself to Dickens's cheerfully insolvent Mr. Micawber and Anna to his long-suffering yet good-natured wife. Anna did resemble Mrs. Micawber somewhat, pawning their belongings to keep them afloat while working overtime to find the silver linings in their cloudy skies. Yet Anna's voice in these exercises could be frank, even confrontational, as demonstrated in one previously untranslated poem from 1868—a bracing assessment of her husband and his poor business decisions. At the time, Dostoyevsky had promised Katkov the first chapters of a new work by a deadline he knew he could not meet, having already committed another tale to the neo-Slavophile journal *Dawn* by the same date. Anna makes her views on the matter clear:

For two years we've been living in poverty.
The only clean thing we have is our conscience.
And we wait for money from Katkov
*for an unsuccessful novel.**
Have you any decency, my friend?
You undertook a tale for Dawn,
you took money from Katkov,
promised to send him a work.
Your last money
you blew at roulette,
and now you don't have
a three-kopeck piece, you numbskull.

"People living in such complete solitude and isolation might, in the final analysis, either come to hate each other or else draw close together for the rest of their lives," she reflected many years later. "Fortunately, it was the latter which happened to us."

Their spirits were lifted in no small measure by the news that Anna was pregnant again. They moved into three furnished rooms in the English quarter on Victoriastrasse, joined by Anna's mother, who came to help with the new baby. Dostoyevsky was as solicitous toward her as he'd been during her first pregnancy. He even went so far as to hide from her the volume of Leo Tolstoy's new *War and Peace* where Prince Andrei Bolkonsky's wife, Liza, dies during childbirth, fearing that the scene would be too upsetting to his wife. As Anna searched everywhere for the missing volume, her husband simply apologized for losing it and assured her it would turn up eventually. Which it did several months later, after the successful birth, on September 14, 1869, of their daughter Lyubov' Dostoyevskaya, who would go by "Lyuba."

"Oh, why are you not married and why don't you have a baby, dear Nikolai Nikolayevich!" Dostoyevsky gushed to his colleague Nikolai Stra-

---

*Here Anna is referring to *The Idiot*.

khov a few months later. "I swear to you that this makes up 3/4 of life's happiness, and I doubt that the rest of it even makes up one fourth."

IN THE LATE FALL OF 1869, after the failure of *The Idiot*, Dostoyevsky started pouring his energies into another work close to his heart, a new novel called *The Life of a Great Sinner*, about the spiritual journey of a tormented young Russian man who doubts the existence of God. Dostoyevsky envisioned it as a novel on the scale of *War and Peace*, and to complete the second of its five stories, set in a monastery, the writer resolved that he must finally return to Russia, to breathe his native air and feel the pulse of daily life; otherwise, "I'll lose touch with the *living stream of life* in Russia," he told Maikov, "not with the idea, but its flesh—and that has such an influence on artistic work!" Yet he and Anna both knew that this homecoming could not happen without the funds needed to cover both the costs of travel and the debts he had left behind. And the longer they stayed away from Russia, the greater the toll on both the couple's morale and Dostoyevsky's work—their sole source of income.

It pained them, too, that they were absent from Russia just as it was in the throes of a social and political crisis—a crisis they learned about only through Dostoyevsky's daily visits to the Dresden reading rooms. German newspapers were just then reporting on a widespread network of conspiratorial revolutionary organizations cropping up throughout Russia. Predicting that all this underground agitation might spark serious "political disturbances" of some sort, Dostoyevsky feared that it might occur at Moscow's Petrovskoye-Razumovskoye Agricultural Academy, a hotbed of revolutionary activity where Anna's younger brother was still a student. Afraid that Ivan might get caught up in the unrest, he suggested to Anna's mother that she persuade her son to come stay with them in Dresden for a while.

Dostoyevsky's instincts were right. A few weeks after Ivan arrived in late October 1869, a classmate of his by the name of Ivanov was murdered in a park at the order of one Sergei Nechayev, the head of a revolutionary terrorist organization. Anna and her husband listened as Ivan shared

stories about life at the academy and his fond impressions of Ivanov—
stories that proved as creatively stimulating to Dostoyevsky as they were
disconcerting to them both.

What happened at the Agricultural Academy became for Dostoyevsky
a microcosm of the moral crisis tearing Russia apart: idealistic young men
and women, intoxicated by their socialist ideas, had proven capable of murder. For years he had been warning readers of the dangers underlying such
utopian movements—of the hidden egoism at each follower's core—and
now those warnings had borne fruit.

In the wake of the news, Dostoyevsky tore himself away from *The Life
of a Great Sinner* to focus on a new novel based on the Nechayev affair.
This story would become the vehicle he used to present his views about
the apocalyptic forces brewing in his homeland. And yet, even as the
writer embarked on his new portrait of corruption, violence, and Western
materialism at home, he and his wife wanted nothing more than to return
there. Mother Russia and her desecration by revolutionary ideology would
become an increasing target for Dostoyevsky's creative energies, his fanatical passion intensifying in proportion to his absence.

Russia was in crisis; the Dostoyevskys were in crisis. Perhaps this explains why the writer was so powerfully drawn to Pushkin's poem "The
Demons," which captured the spiritual condition of his country so perfectly that he would make it the lead epigraph to this new novel, which he
called *The Possessed*. (The Russian title, *Besy*, means "Demons.")

> *Strike me dead, the track has vanished,*
> *Well, what now? We've lost the way.*
> *Demons have bewildered our horses,*
> *Led us in the wilds astray.*

Through his work, Dostoyevsky would respond to this impasse by
transforming Russia's present turmoil into a messianic vision of the healing powers of the Russian spirit. Once possessed by the idea of the Big
Win that would save his family, he was now compelled by an equally
grandiose ideal—what he sometimes called the "Russian Idea"—that

would save humanity. It was a message that seemed all the more urgent in the summer of 1870, as French and German troops lined up along their shared border, prepared to slaughter one another in what would be known as the Franco-Prussian War. This, then, was where the vaunted "progress" of the West had led: to the brink of self-annihilation. Nor, Dostoyevsky observed, was it just the masses who seethed with gleeful hatred. The professors and artists seemed just as ready to kill, confirming his sense that the West was a morally lost cause, and only Russia could redeem civilization.

Before there could be redemption, however, it was imperative to expose the severity of the illness, and that sort of illumination is what the writer set out to provide in *The Possessed*, still considered one of the world's great political novels. Taking place over the course of a month in a sleepy provincial town not far from the Russian capital, the novel recounts the tale of a secret society of revolutionaries who infiltrate the town, spreading terror and chaos as the first steps toward inciting what they hoped would be a nationwide insurrection. The group's leader, Pyotr Verkhovensky, has returned to his hometown after an extended absence, intent on commandeering a printing press for the dissemination of seditious materials. In order to create a bond of bloodshed among the members of his secret society while solidifying his own power, Verkhovensky plans the murder of one of the group's defecting members, Ivan Shatov, an erstwhile socialist turned conservative Slavophile.

A master manipulator, Verkhovensky uses the vanity and faux liberalism of the townsfolk for his own purposes—for instance, convincing the governor's wife, a self-proclaimed liberal, to organize a benefit for indigent governesses. This carnivalesque catastrophe of an event ends with all the participants making fools of themselves, fires being set around the town, and the feckless governor reduced to nervous collapse. With the town in disarray, the stage is set for the murder of Shatov, who is lured to a remote district and shot in the head, his body disposed of in a pond. This will be but one of five murders that follow from the events of that chaotic night, along with two suicides and two untimely deaths, giving *The Possessed* the highest death toll of any Dostoyevsky work.

Into this basic plot the writer wove many of his treasured spiritual and philosophical ideas, including the animating concept of *The Life of a Great Sinner*: that his countrymen would find redemption only by casting off the Western thinking that had spawned a generation of revolutionaries and returning to the spiritual wisdom of the Russian people. "And note, dear friend," Dostoyevsky wrote to Maikov in the fall of 1870, "whoever loses his people and his national roots loses both his paternal faith and God. Well, if you want to know, that's exactly what the theme of my novel is." The character who most clearly expresses this idea is the murder victim, Ivan Shatov, to whom the author gives a number of his own physical and autobiographical details.

But the novel's real hero—or rather, antihero—is the demonic, charismatic, irresistibly mysterious Nikolai Stavrogin, a character Dostoyevsky added to the work's design only after a sizable portion of the book was already written. A Byronic figure, Stavrogin has grown weary of the revolutionary ideas he once preached. Where other characters still view him as a "sun," in reality Stavrogin is a burned-out star, a black hole that draws others into his all-enveloping orbit, even as he himself has surrendered to nihilist despair. "Nikolai Stavrogin is a gloomy individual, too, a villain, too," Dostoyevsky told Maikov. "But now he appears to me as a tragic figure. . . . In my opinion he is both a Russian and human type. I have taken him from my heart."

Many have assumed, with no evidence, that Dostoyevsky was using his character to lay bare some horrific crime on his own conscience (Stavrogin confesses to raping a young girl, then looking on as the guilt-stricken child hanged herself). What is far more clear is that the author used the character to explore aspects of his own psychological journey. Once aflame with revolutionary idealism, Stavrogin has long since devolved into disillusionment, much as Dostoyevsky had before rediscovering his faith in native Russian values. (Stavrogin's life, by contrast, ends in suicide.) Still, the figure of Stavrogin lends *The Possessed* a distinctly confessional quality. It also takes a nasty little episode of political intrigue and murder and elevates it into a profound meditation on the contours of the revolutionary mind.

Into this dark maelstrom the writer injects one bright, human moment: the moving birth of Ivan Shatov's son by his estranged wife, Marie, who has returned to him after years of separation. Drawn directly from Dostoyevsky's own experience of the birth of his daughter Sonya, the scene is replete with autobiographical details: the author's helplessness, his wife's attempts to talk sense into her babbling husband, his frantic search for a midwife, and finally the father's intense joy at the appearance of the fragile new life:

> Shatov spoke in an incoherent, stupid, and ecstatic way. Something seemed to be tottering in his head and welling up from his soul apart from his own will.
>
> "There were two and now there's a third human being, a new spirit, finished and complete, unlike the handiwork of man; a new thought and a new love . . . it's positively frightening. . . . And there's nothing grander in the world."
>
> "Marie," he cried as he held the child in his arms, "all the old madness, shame, and deadness is over, isn't it? Let us work hard and begin a new life, the three of us, yes, yes . . ."

A few hours later Shatov will be brutally murdered, victim of the revolutionary madness he had once espoused.

WHILE DOSTOYEVSKY POURED OUT his pain through his art, Anna was expressing her own love of country by creating a Russian home right in the middle of Dresden. As much like her own pragmatic mother as she was unlike most of Dostoyevsky's fictional heroes, Anna sought to bring a new equilibrium to their chaotic existence. Certainly it helped to have under one roof—albeit a cramped, German one—the four "people most beloved and precious in the world to me—my husband, my child, my mother, and brother." And now her brother, Ivan, was filling her husband's creative imagination with stories about the very tumult from which he had been so eager to protect the young man.

More than just a witness to history, then, Anna was becoming a participant in historical events—following, in a way, the example of the legendary Decembrist wives. A half century earlier, these women had joined their exiled husbands in Siberia, settled in the vicinity of the prison camps, and built entire towns that stand to this day. While the Decembrist wives had traveled far east, into the Russian heartland, Anna had gone west to Europe, to the birthplace of the feminist ideas she grew up with and the revolutionary ones she and her husband now feared. In her European exile she was forging a path uniquely her own, one defined by neither the feminist nor the traditional narratives of her past, but rather by a creative synthesis of the two, a kind of radical traditionalism.

Anna saw how her husband was becoming increasingly known among the Russians in Dresden as a fellow patriot who might lend his voice to their Pan-Slavic efforts. She chuckled to see how his devotees brought him flowers and books and pampered their little Lyuba with toys and presents. Toward the end of 1870, the Russian community assembled at the home of a well-known Orthodox priest and asked Dostoyevsky to draft a letter to the German chancellor on the occasion of Russia's decision to assert her rights to maintain a naval fleet on the Black Sea. The writer used the letter as an opportunity to express his fervent nationalism, praying "to God for the happiness of our beloved Motherland and that He may long preserve her from affliction."

Affliction, however, was precisely what the motherland was experiencing, making their absence all the more painful. "Living abroad seemed like a prison in which I was trapped and from which I could never free myself," Anna wrote in her memoir. "I was convinced that fate had condemned me to remain forever in an alien land." Anna had sought for months to shield her husband from her unhappiness, holding back tears and complaints in his presence, occupying herself with long hikes, pouring her feelings into her diary, in order to grant Dostoyevsky complete peace of mind. And, until now, it had mostly worked. But she spent much of 1870 unwell—even after Lyuba had been weaned, the twin pressures of motherhood and penury were taking their toll—and no matter how hard she worked to keep a comfortable home for her family abroad, she was reminded daily that this home was never more than makeshift.

And now here she was, pregnant again.

According to the doctors, Anna's protracted illness, accompanied by nervousness and exhaustion, was due to a combination of depression and something they classified as "severe exhaustion of the blood," the result of commencing a new pregnancy while still nursing Lyuba. But Anna regarded their diagnosis as hogwash, and she refused to take the iron they prescribed.

Dostoyevsky, meanwhile, was going out of his mind with worry. He was convinced that Anna's real ailment was the same malady that was afflicting him: homesickness. "Anna Grigoryevna has even fallen ill from missing Russia, and that torments me," he wrote to his niece. "Anna just pines. As usual, she's been helping me rewrite until recently; but there's no way her inner longing, her homesickness can be chased away."

Prepared now to accept even destitution as the cost of homecoming, Anna needed Russia for her soul, just as Dostoyevsky needed it for his art. Without Russia, she feared, he would die professionally, while she might well die literally. Their longtime fear of debtors' prison in Russia was finally outweighed by the even greater fear of an open-ended exile in Europe. Dostoyevsky had been in prison before and would gladly have traded this current hell. At least then he had been among his own people. "If only you knew what deep revulsion, to the point of hatred, Europe has stirred up in me against her in these four years!" he confessed in a letter to Maikov.

Anna was of the same mind. At long last, she wanted out.

11.

The Final Spin

In early 1871, a ray of hope appeared from an unexpected quarter: Fyodor Stellovsky. After the insults and indignities of 1866, Anna and her husband would have been perfectly happy never to hear the man's name again. But a recent advertisement announcing a new edition of *Crime and Punishment* to be published by Stellovsky had prompted Dostoyevsky to ask Apollon Maikov to collect the nearly thousand rubles due to him according to their original contract, or else pay the writer a forfeit of three thousand rubles for breaking the contract. Surely Stellovsky would not risk forfeiting his contract, or courting a lawsuit, over a thousand rubles. Between this and a thousand the writer was expecting from *The Russian Messenger* for the first installments of *The Possessed*, the Dostoyevskys felt sure they could survive a few more months, while making arrangements to return to Russia before Anna's due date in early August.

Except that Dostoyevsky had missed a serious loophole in the contract with Stellovsky, as Maikov explained in reply. For the all-important clause on which the couple was hanging their hopes stipulated no specific date by which Stellovsky must pay the writer for a new edition. And when Maikov approached Stellovsky's agent to ask for the payment, the wily publisher pleaded poverty, insisting that he lacked the cash to settle the debt. It would have to wait.

Furious and distraught, Dostoyevsky instructed Maikov to use the broad power of attorney he'd given him months earlier to bring immediate suit against Stellovsky. The writer was certain that he would win this suit—precisely the sort of misplaced confidence that overcame him at the roulette wheel. Sure enough, it quickly became clear that Stellovsky had no intention of paying up, at least anytime soon. It would be four years, in fact, before the author saw another ruble from Stellovsky.

Without the hoped-for windfall, their plans to return to Russia were once again in question. Unbeknownst to Dostoyevsky, however, Maikov had continued to work behind the scenes on his behalf, taking the initiative of asking the Literary Fund to lend the writer four hundred rubles to help him get back to Russia. When his query met with success, the jubilant Maikov wired Dostoyevsky to summon him back to Petersburg immediately and collect his loan.

Thrilled by the telegram, Dostoyevsky rushed home to tell Anna. As they talked it over, though, something about the news started to seem . . . not quite right. Had it even come from Maikov? After all, he'd never mentioned any plans to approach the Literary Fund on his friend's behalf—and when Dostoyevsky wrote back for an explanation, he got no response. Strengthening their suspicion, Maikov's telegram was sent on April Fool's Day. Was this a prank? If so, it was devised by someone familiar enough with their affairs to invent exactly the kind of windfall they needed. "At first," Anna recalled, they took it "as somebody's joke or as the cunning scheme of one of his creditors or perhaps even Stellovsky himself to get Fyodor Mikhailovich to Petersburg," whereupon the publisher would threaten Dostoyevsky with debtors' prison as a way to duck his own thousand-ruble debt on *Crime and Punishment*. It wasn't until Maikov finally responded to a frantic letter that the Dostoyevskys accepted that the offer was real after all.

Still, after playing out the worst-case scenarios in their minds, the prospect of Dostoyevsky returning to Petersburg suddenly terrified the couple. If he should return to Petersburg now, the creditors could have him clapped in chains the minute he set foot in the capital. Anna would be left alone in this freezing, damp German town she had grown to detest, giving birth without her husband. She remembered all too well the spring of '68, when the Swiss doctor's sloppy diagnosis had ended in death for their little Sonya. She could not fathom going through something like that without him. And, even if they should manage to find the money for her to return after him, it would be far too risky for her to make the nearly seventy-hour trip alone without her husband or a nanny to accompany her. Anna and the baby would have to remain in Dresden for another year, a scenario unacceptable to them both. "Why, all of Stellovsky and all my affairs aren't worth that!" Dostoyevsky told Maikov.

When they left, it would have to be together.

LIKE A CAGED BEAST, the writer prowled about their Dresden apartment, day and night, as he worked to complete *The Possessed*, which was causing him greater creative torment than anything he had yet written—more than even *The Idiot*. For months he kept tearing up passages and revising, covering great heaps of paper with so many scribbled notes that he soon lost track of the system he'd devised for checking what he wrote. If only he were able to compose without haste, he complained to Strakhov, "the way the Tolstoys, Turgenevs, and Goncharovs write." But he had no such luxury: he had to complete this book, and fast. The generous Katkov was expecting a fresh installment soon, and the writer could not afford to let their good genie down.

One reason for his rush to publication was the novel's topicality—its urgent relevance to events back home in Russia. Another was the fact that there was a major new competitor on the literary horizon. Leo Tolstoy's first novel, *War and Peace*, had been appearing for the past few years in the pages of *The Russian Messenger* to enormous acclaim. Dostoyevsky, on the other hand, had not had a hit since *Crime and Punishment*, and he knew perfectly well that he needed to reestablish his literary stature through this new book. "I have tackled a rich idea," he enthused to Maikov, "one of those ideas that have an undoubted resonance among the public. Like *Crime and Punishment*, but even closer to reality, more vital, and having direct relevance for the most important contemporary issues."

Yet he had the worst time gaining traction on the book. Epileptic at-

tacks waylaid him for weeks at a time now, and he was increasingly para-
lyzed by the fear that Europe was destroying his talent while making it
impossible for him to support his growing family. "I'm afraid," he admitted to Maikov, "like a frightened mouse. The idea enticed me, and I've
come to love it awfully much, but will I be able to manage it? won't I fuck
up the whole novel?—that's the problem!"

Anna was painfully aware that her husband had pinned his commercial hopes on *The Idiot* in the same way, but she was not about to lose faith
in him at such a critical moment. Still, she realized she had to do something to jump-start his work on *The Possessed*. And suddenly her increasingly sharp survivor's instinct kicked in. "In order to soothe his anxiety
and dispel the somber thoughts which prevented him from concentrating
on his work," she recalled, "I resorted to the device which always amused
and distracted him."

One day in mid-April she found an opportunity to bring the conversation around to one of Dostoyevsky's favorite topics—roulette—and asked if
he might want to try his luck once more at the tables in Wiesbaden. "He'd
won a few times, after all," Anna coaxed him, "why not hope that this time
luck would be on his side?" It was just the sort of argument, she knew, that
her husband had so often used to rationalize a gambling binge—and which
she'd often found herself powerless to counter—but now she was seizing it
for her own purposes. She even allowed him to take along one hundred
twenty thalers, a full third of their remaining savings. Only she would not
join him, as she had in Baden-Baden; this time he would have to face the
tables alone. "Of course, I did not believe for a moment that he would win,"
Anna recalled many years later:

> and I very much regretted the hundred thalers which would
> have to be sacrificed. But I knew from my experience of his pre-
> vious visits to the roulette table that after going through some
> intense emotions and satisfying his craving for risks, for gam-
> bling, he would return assuaged. And . . . he would settle down
> to his novel with new energy and make up for all the lost time
> and work in two or three weeks.

It was an enormous gamble, but the sacrifice was, Anna knew, essential. Where an outside observer might have considered her gambit reckless for a couple in their situation, it was in fact an extension of Anna's talent for calculated risk. A few years earlier, she had engaged in her own gambling adventure out of an instinctive need to confront her husband's demons on his own turf. Now she followed another intuition: that the only way to save her husband, and their family, was to thrust him right back into the inferno of his gambling addiction. That same fire had nearly ruined them before, of course, but she also accepted her husband's belief that gambling fueled his creative spirit—which in turn was essential to their financial survival.

From the beginning, this volatile combination—of persistence, ambition, and daring on Anna's part, and a cycle of self-destruction and mad productivity on Dostoyevsky's—had been a central dynamic of their relationship. It was what gave a twenty-year-old stenography student the courage to show up in Dostoyevsky's life in the first place, and to rescue him from the brink of professional and personal collapse. And this powerful alchemy of personality traits on both of their parts is what allowed the structure of their marriage, and their joint professional undertaking, to grow through the decades.

Reluctant to tell Anna's mother what was happening, Dostoyevsky suggested that she explain that he was simply going to Frankfurt on business for a few days. If he should lose all his money—as Anna knew he would—they agreed that he would let her know by telegram, at which point she would immediately send him thirty thalers for the fare home. In case her mother came across their correspondence, they worked out a code: *"Schreiben Sie mir"* ("Write me") would mean "Send me the money."

DOSTOYEVSKY LEFT FOR WIESBADEN in the middle of April, as the roads were still thawing. The promise of renewal was in the sweetly scented air, tempering the memory of winter's recent fury. After checking into the Taunus Hotel, he wasted little time in making the familiar trek past the luxurious hotels and the English-style spa grounds, straight to the beautiful Kurhaus.

As soon as he crossed through the dark vestibule into the casino's main gaming hall, amid the glow of candlelight and the familiar chattering of polyglot voices, Dostoyevsky felt right at home. In an instant, all the languor and depression of the past weeks melted away.

What happened during his first few days of gambling is a mystery. What we do know is that, around midday on Thursday, April 15, Dostoyevsky stood at the roulette table and started naming his bets with a rapid intensity. He bet, and lost. He bet again, and lost. An hour flew by. And then it was gone—the hour, and the money.

He had lost everything, every last thaler he had brought with him.

A few hours later he found himself at the post office. He had just enough to send Anna a telegram, which he dictated to the man behind the counter. In his frantic state he managed to enunciate at least one phrase in clear German:

"*Schreiben Sie mir.*"

The next day, shortly after noon, he received a letter from Anna—without the thirty thalers he was expecting. He went back to the hotel and wrote her what he later considered to be a "vile and cruel letter," upbraiding her for failing to send the promised money. He returned to the post office again at two thirty. Still no money. He came back a third time at four thirty, and the postman handed him a letter from Anna with thirty thalers.

"When did it come?" Dostoyevsky grumbled.

"Around two o'clock," the man responded.

"Why did you not give it to me when I was here after two?" Dostoyevsky wanted to ask. Instead he turned and left the post office. Minutes later, he was back in the gaming hall.

"Now, Anya," Dostoyevsky wrote her the next day, "I swear to you that I didn't intend to gamble!" Still . . . what if he were to try his luck for just a few minutes? Staking just five of those thirty thalers, not the whole sum?

He should have known better. After reading Anna's alarming letter, in which she told him to hurry home, he'd grown terrified about what might happen to her if he lost everything. And he had had a series of distressing dreams: one of his father, a horrible dream of a kind he'd experienced only twice before, each time foretelling some disaster that had come true; then, just three days ago, a dream that Anna had turned gray. Given all these foreboding signs, he had decided that he must not gamble away these last thirty thalers.

When he returned to the casino, he told himself, it was only to watch the action.

Standing by the table, his eyes fixed on the seductive wheel, he started making imaginary bets in his head. "Would I guess right or not? What do you think, Anya?" he wrote. "I guessed right about ten times in a row; I even guessed zero." Had he been playing, that guess would have gained him a payout of thirty-five times his bet.

The fever grew hotter. His instincts seemed infallible.

Only now he found himself speaking aloud the bets he'd been making in his head, placing actual bets on the table. "Anya, Anya," he implored her to remember as he told the story, "I'm not a scoundrel, just a passionate gambler." In five minutes, he won eighteen thalers.

He was ready to rush out of the hall triumphant, telling himself that he'd leave on the last train that night, bringing home some winnings. Yet his feet did not move. "At that point, Anya, I lost control of myself." He kept betting—and making mistakes. He kept losing, but he could not stop. In five minutes, the eighteen thalers he'd won disappeared. Then the thirty Anna had sent. By nine thirty, everything was gone.

He rushed out of the hall "like a madman" and went searching for a priest.

Racing frantically through the labyrinthine backstreets of Wiesbaden, looking for the "Lord's shepherd," he spied the onion dome of what he took to be a Russian Orthodox church. He ran toward it, only to discover that it was no Russian church at all but rather a synagogue. He stopped in his tracks, petrified. Turning on his heel, he raced back to the hotel and started writing to his wife: "Anya, please, for the sake of Lyuba, for the sake of our future child, don't worry, don't be upset, and read this letter through to the end, carefully. . . . Calm down, angel, and listen, read to the end. Please don't go to pieces."

But he was going to pieces himself, and delivered the terrible news in one fell swoop: "My priceless one, my eternal friend, my heavenly angel, you realize, of course, that I lost everything, the whole thirty thalers you sent me." And then he told her the story, right up through the frantic search for a priest that had led him to a synagogue.

As a woman who knew her husband intimately—and who was accustomed to poring over every word he wrote—Anna would have been able to read between the lines of his letter. She knew how seriously he took dreams and omens, knew of his many visits to fortune-tellers, clairvoyants, and savants, understood how he had placed his faith in that old woman who'd once told his future with beans. His letter made it clear: Dostoyevsky had been trying to seek penitence from a god he had always wanted to believe in, when he was tricked by some dark force. His gambling mania was now turning him—had perhaps *already* turned him—away from Orthodox Christianity, the native religion of the Russian people. And it had rendered him an apostate—a Jew, in fact, an embodiment of the coldly rational materialism that Dostoyevsky had come to associate with European culture. All the suffering of his past four years would have amounted to nothing, in his mind, if in the end he lost his Russian soul, succumbed to deadening Western values.

Much as Raskolnikov, in the depths of his guilt-ridden despair, felt the urge to confess his crime to Sonya rather than a clergyman, Dostoyevsky realized in his darkest hour that what he in fact needed was not a church but his own all-forgiving confessor, the one person who accepted him without judgment. Which might explain the unusual promise he made in the first postscript to his letter: "I *won't go see* a priest, not for anything, not in any case," he told Anna. "He is one of the witnesses of the old, the past, the former, the vanished! It will be painful for me even to meet him!" The only confessor he needed now was the person who had stood by his side through the scourge of his terrible addiction all these years, an illness that nearly ruined them but also bound them so tightly that, as Dostoyevsky had once put it, "a knife couldn't cut us apart."

But this incident had shown him something else: that his gambling was putting Anna's life at risk. It was an act of the basest moral turpitude, just the sort of sadomasochistic choice toward which he had long gravitated, but no longer. "I know that you'll die if I lose again!" he exclaimed. "I'm not at all a madman. After all, I know that [if that should happen] I'm done for." The chilling thought of how his behavior had affected her, and what her death would mean for *him*, was enough to awaken him to truths he had long ignored. "Anya, believe that our resurrection has arrived," he insisted, "and believe that beginning today I'll achieve my goal— I'll give you happiness." In a third and final postscript, he thanked his wife for her immeasurable patience and devotion and made her a promise: "I'll remember this my whole life and bless you every time, my angel. No, now I'm yours, yours inseparably, entirely yours."

Through the last ten years of their lives together, until his death in 1881, Dostoyevsky would keep this promise. Nothing would come between them again—no more secret mistress, no roulette, no illicit passions of any kind. "His fantasy of winning," Anna reflected a quarter century after his death, "was a kind of obsession or disease from which he recovered suddenly and forever."

AN ADDICTION as merciless as Dostoyevsky's, conquered? How did it happen?

Scholars have sometimes explained the end of the writer's gambling addiction by noting that there was no public gambling in Russia, or that the Prussian government shut down the German casinos in 1872, depriving Dostoyevsky of any opportunity to gamble during his frequent trips to the country in the 1870s. Yet legal gambling existed in European countries other than Germany; if he'd been determined to do so, Dostoyevsky could easily have found opportunities to head back to the tables. There is simply no evidence that the thought ever crossed his mind.

Nor was the writer's repatriation to Russia an adequate explanation for the banishment of his addiction. For one thing, the psychological and biological factors that researchers believe fed Dostoyevsky's addiction—

anxiety, poverty, and epilepsy—did not disappear upon his return to Russia. On the contrary, at least in the short term, his poverty and attendant anxiety only intensified as the couple struggled to build their life from scratch, and with a new child to boot. Was it the cultural environment of Russia herself, then, that cured him? One Slavic scholar, William J. Leatherbarrow, seems to think so, concluding from his reading of *The Gambler* that:

> the semiotic system with which Dostoevsky surrounds the act of gambling in his novel implicates that act deeply in his vision of European cultural collapse. Is it not, therefore, only to be expected that he should feel no need to gamble when in his native Russia and that such a form of demonic possession should overwhelm him during years of desperate exile in the wilderness of Western Europe?

Given Dostoyevsky's hypersensitivity to physical and cultural stimuli, this argument must be given its due. Yet it doesn't account for the fact that the conditions he deplored in European culture did not change significantly during the 1870s, when he returned to Germany for several long forays without ever, as far as we know, being lured back to the casinos.

No, any explanation of the end of Dostoyevsky's gambling must take into consideration the one factor that goes almost entirely unmentioned in the vast body of scholarly theory about his addiction: the lessons he had internalized from his marriage to his young wife.

Dostoyevsky may have given Anna an education in life, but it was she who brought him back from the brink. "You alone are my savior," he told her in that frantic letter. She rescued him from bouts of despair, salvaged his career, and saved his life on more than one occasion, cupping his head in her hands during his epileptic seizures, taking care to place her body between him and the floor to protect him from injury. As he acknowledged, "you have pawned everything of yours for me in these four years and roamed after me, homesick for your native land," losing their beloved child and jeopardizing her own health along the way.

It was Anna who gave Dostoyevsky permission to end his crazed quest for acceptance, to let go of the roulette table—the last of his mistresses, that psychological security blanket he had clung to against the day when Anna's love might suddenly dry up. The steadiness of that love was altogether new in his life, and this more than anything emboldened him to undertake the risk of being fully vulnerable before another human being. "No, now I'm yours, yours inseparably, entirely yours," he wrote her from Wiesbaden, and he was.

For much of his life, Dostoyevsky had experienced love as a matter of either domination or submission. Anna helped him to rewrite that script into a new narrative that was more like a kind of profound interdependence. It would take months, even years, for this new understanding to change his behavior—and their relationship would never entirely shed its volatile power dynamic—but the germ of the fresh narrative emerged clearly, as if in a flash, on the evening he fled that Wiesbaden casino.

Their marriage on the cusp of a new phase, Anna and Dostoyevsky would soon learn to recalibrate the feverish rhythms of their first five years together. To be sure, the personal characteristics that had brought them together—her fortitude, compassion, and tolerance for risk, and his intense creative hunger, bouts of depression, and attraction to extreme behavior—remained at play. But Anna would soon begin to channel her personal energies into managing a business while raising a family, even as Dostoyevsky discovered fresh sources of artistic inspiration in the joys and tribulations of the new life they would build together against the backdrop of a darkening political landscape.

THAT WAS ALL TO COME, THOUGH. First, Anna had to get her husband back to Dresden, and then get their family out of Germany altogether. Pawning a few more items, she sent him thirty more thalers for train fare, and then waited four days for him to return. "I have in store about three days of unbearable torment, psychic, of course," he wrote her the day after his gambling fiasco, adding: "I realize how distressing pawning things is for you, but soon, soon it will all end forever, and we'll be renewed. . . .

Just to get to Russia soon! An end to our time in these cursed foreign lands and these fantasies [of winning]! Oh, with what hatred I recall this time."

Once again they had to work around Anna's mother, who was sure to suspect something when Dostoyevsky failed to return on the day he'd promised. Anna agreed to tell her that he had suffered another seizure and that he'd decided to rest for another two or three days before returning, rather than risk another attack. Two days later, he wrote to assure Anna that even if he wasn't home by midnight on Tuesday, "then, *please*, I implore you, don't despair and don't imagine that I've lost again. *That won't and can't happen.*" But he instructed her to have some dinner ready for him, and implored her, "if you're completely a Christian, darling Anya, don't forget to prepare *a pack of cigarettes* for my arrival."

Dostoyevsky returned to Dresden on April 20, calm and in good spirits, and settled right back down to writing *The Possessed*. When he wasn't working, he and Anna made plans for their move back to Russia and the impending birth of their child, due in July. He sent a note to Katkov, relaying all the details of his recent losses, before begging the editor to speed up the remittance of the thousand rubles he had promised. Katkov agreed to send the money by the end of June, before their departure. The couple had hoped to have three to four thousand rubles in hand to cover the trip and the expenses they would incur upon arriving in Russia, but they resolved to make the journey anyway on Katkov's thousand. The money arrived in the last days of June, and they wasted no time in winding down their affairs in Dresden: redeeming their things from pawn, settling their many debts, and packing for the trip.

Two days before their departure, Dostoyevsky called Anna into his study, showed her several thick packets of oversized paper, and asked her to burn them. She looked at the bundles of papers in front of her—some of them bound with string, others loose, all of them covered in his inky scrawl. Each bundle contained years of toil and sacrifice. Here were early drafts of *The Idiot*, his novella *The Eternal Husband*, and an early variant of *The Possessed*. Anna had been at his side through the years of creative agony and joy that had produced this mountain of work. She understood the significance of what he was asking her to do, and it gave her pause. "I felt so badly about destroying the manuscripts that I began imploring him to let me take them along." But he insisted.

Dostoyevsky's fears were not irrational. As a former political prisoner still under the surveillance of the secret police, he knew he would be searched at the border and his papers confiscated. They were about to embark on an almost seventy-hour journey, with Anna over thirty weeks pregnant and no nurse to help them, and an extended delay at the border might force Anna into a hasty, unsanitary birth en route, putting both her and the newborn's life at risk. And so, without further argument, Anna picked up the pile of papers, and she and her husband tossed them into the fire. Thus perished the early drafts of three of Dostoyevsky's major novels, lost forever to future generations of readers and scholars.

Only, in his haste, Dostoyevsky had overlooked the notebooks to those same novels—notebooks Anna quickly gave to her mother and brother for safekeeping, instructing them to bring them along when they returned to Russia a few months later. It was a split-second decision that would not only protect her family's interests but preserve for future generations an invaluable body of material illuminating the creative process behind some of her husband's most important novels. It was one of many such crucial, culture-shaping decisions she would make in the years to come.

On July 5 they traveled from Dresden to Berlin, then boarded a train for Russia. Feeling unwell, Anna huddled under warm blankets and asked Fedya to keep baby Lyuba entertained and distracted during the long journey while she slept. The doting father obliged, hopping off the train with Lyuba at stops along the way to play games on the platform, buying her milk and food, all the while keeping an eye on Anna, who seemed to be resting comfortably during the journey but whose health might take a turn for the worse at any moment.

After forty-four hours of exhausting travel, they finally arrived at the border station in Verzhbolovo, and passed through the German patrol without difficulty. Still, when they had to get off the train and face the Russian patrols—who proved no less officious or obnoxious than German officials—the couple were gripped with fear. Other passengers were searched only briefly, but the Dostoyevskys were detained outright, their bags and suitcases ransacked, as a cluster of officials began crowding around the table and peering closely at the books and slim packet of manuscripts they had confiscated. Exhausted, and petrified about missing their connection, they could do nothing but wait.

As passengers scurried in and out of the busy customs hall, officials unzipped the couple's bags, rooting around among their most personal possessions. Then, out of nowhere, Lyuba started shrieking at the top of her little lungs, "Mama, give me a roll!" Unable to stand the noise another moment, the patrols shoved the books and manuscripts across the table, clamped the bags shut, and hustled the annoying family out of the room.

Boarding the train in a state of shock, the Dostoyevskys fell into their seats and the train shoved off, the giant wheels laboring slowly over the iron rails and then picking up speed as the train station and Germany faded into the distance behind them. Twenty-four hours of grueling travel lay before them, and many challenges awaited the family at home. With a child on the way, roughly sixty rubles left to their name, and the threat of debtors' prison looming, the challenge of rebuilding a life for themselves in Russia would be anything but easy.

But none of that was on Anna's mind as the train whirred through the Russian steppe:

> Our consciousness of the fact that we were riding on Russian soil, that all around us were our own people, Russian people, was so comforting that it made us forget all about the troubles of our journey. My husband and I were joyful and happy and kept asking one another if it was really true that we were in Russia at long last. That was how wondrous our realization of our long-cherished dream seemed to us.

Anna with the couple's two surviving children, Fedya (left) and Lyuba. When Dostoyevsky was away—to Bad Ems for his health, to Moscow for his triumphant Pushkin address— she looked after them, and the business, while worrying over his welfare.

III

THE PAYOFF

12.

The Publisher

In her memoirs, Anna thanked fate for the trying first four years of her marriage. In that time, she reflected, "I had developed from a timid, bashful girl into a woman of decisive character, no longer frightened by the struggle with life's misfortunes." Her female friends observed in her a greater flintiness and reserve around men, and reproached her for not paying attention to her physical appearance, for not dressing well, for not doing her hair fashionably. "Even though I agreed with them," Anna wrote, "I did not want to change." With her signature combination of ambition, steely pragmatism, and risk tolerance, Anna ignored the criticisms of friends and remained focused on what she knew was right and necessary. If her first blush of love for Dostoyevsky had been, in her own words, "more like an adoration and reverence," that love had by now morphed into a kind of active force, one that would not only speed the writer's ascent into the front ranks of Russian literature but also launch Anna herself onto a significant and lasting career path of her own.

No sooner had a newspaper announced Dostoyevsky's return than the couple was forced to contend with creditors appearing almost daily at their apartment. Yet through shrewd negotiations, sweet talk, and outright threats—all without the knowledge of her Fedya, who had proven far too gullible to trust with such matters—Anna managed to send these men on their way. She made it known to all of Petersburg that an impenetrable barrier now stood between her husband and those who would fleece him. To one such character, a shady German merchant who had done business many years earlier with Dostoyevsky's brother Mikhail, Anna promised to write up the whole story of his groundless threats and publish it in a Petersburg newspaper. "Let everybody see what the honest Germans are capable of!" she told him indignantly. The merchant backed down and accepted Anna's terms, never to pester the Dostoyevskys again. Anna was discovering her own power as a negotiator.

She would deal no less firmly with Pasha, whose profound selfishness had reached new depths. During their European exile, he had sold off to a secondhand bookseller the entire library Dostoyevsky had left with him—and then had the nerve to blame the couple for failing to send him money on time from Europe. And yet, even after all that, his importunate demands for money continued.

"Well, how's *papa*, how's he feeling?" Pasha asked Anna a few weeks after the couple's return, an insincere sweetness coloring his voice. "I have to talk to him—I need forty rubles desperately."

"But you know that Katkov hasn't sent anything yet and that we have no money at all," responded Anna. "I pawned my brooch today for twenty-five rubles." She showed him the receipt.

"So what! Pawn something else."

"But everything I *have* is pawned already," she said, marshaling every ounce of strength to restrain herself from clobbering the insolent young man.

"Well, there's something I simply must purchase," he persisted.

"Buy it after we get some money."

"I *can't*. I can't put it off."

"But I have no money!" Anna said, making it clear this conversation was over.

It was evident to Pasha that he was dealing with a different Anna from the one he'd known before, but the sly young man was convinced he had one trick left up his sleeve: complaining about Anna to *papa*. To his shock and disappointment, however, his old tactics no longer worked. "I have turned over the entire household management to my wife," Dostoyevsky told Pasha one day after the young man marched into his stepfather's study to file a complaint against Anna. "So however she decides, that's the way it will be."

As infuriating as Pasha was, to Anna he was no more than a nuisance. Her waking thoughts were occupied by far more pressing concerns, namely how to build a future for her family. As her husband strove to reestablish his literary connections, Anna worked fourteen hours a day—not only as a wife and mother, but also as a stenographer, secretary, and financial manager—all the while seeking outside work to supplement the family's meager income. Adding to these burdens was a host of misfortunes that confronted Anna within a year of their return to Russia: a life-threatening operation three-year-old Lyuba was forced to undergo for a broken wrist-bone that a previous doctor had set incorrectly; her agonizing separation from her one-year-old son, Fyodor, called Fedya, who remained in the care of a nurse at a summer home they rented in the spa town of Staraya Russa; the absence of Anna's mother, who was suffering from an incapacitating foot injury; the news that her brother's wife was in confinement and her pregnancy not going well; her sister Masha's sudden death from malaria, which Anna wasn't informed of until weeks after it happened. To top it all off, she herself took ill with a serious throat infection that nearly killed her.

"Troubles don't come singly," went a Russian proverb she quoted in her memoirs to describe this period, adding: "That is when you see plainly that a merciful God in sending us ordeals grants us the strength to endure them!"

And endure them she would.

THE POSSESSED WAS PUBLISHED serially in *The Russian Messenger* between 1871 and 1872, and it caused a public firestorm. The novel gained Dostoyevsky a host of new enemies in the literary world, while solidifying his dubious reputation as "a cruel talent," as one influential contemporary critic, Nikolai Mikhailovsky, later called the author in a famous article. It shocked and titillated its Russian readers, this tale of political murder laced with sexual depravity, social dysfunction, and spiritual sickness—not to mention its account of the molestation of a twelve-year-old girl, a passage so uncomfortable that Katkov refused to publish the section in *The Russian Messenger*.

The novel also infuriated the radical intelligentsia, who saw in Dostoyevsky's scathingly satirical portrait of the Russian revolutionary movement a direct attack on them. Nor were they misreading; the writer had made good on his promise to Maikov that in this novel he'd make clear his "opinions down to the last word." More conservative readers—a minority among the literary public—appreciated what they saw as the novel's political message: that the revolutionaries were in many cases immoral destroyers and egoists masquerading as social crusaders. Still, even these admiring readers agreed with literary critics that *The Possessed* was overburdened by too many plot lines, overwritten characters, and an overall portrait of contemporary Russia that was more caricature than social realism.

Anna kept a studied distance from these ideological and critical debates, focusing instead on a more pressing consideration: with the novel now complete, the family's sole source of income had dried up, and they were back to living almost hand to mouth. With nothing of Dostoyevsky's to transcribe for the moment, Anna decided to contribute to the family income by taking up outside employment as a stenographer, for which she received a letter of recommendation from her former teacher, Professor Olkhin. At first she applied for a temporary stenographer post at a conference to take place in the western provinces, but her husband could not bear the thought of his wife traveling such a distance alone. "So ended my effort to earn some money by stenography," Anna recalled.

Not easily deterred, she cast about for other opportunities to earn extra money. Early in 1873, after she and Dostoyevsky unsuccessfully tried to interest various publishers in a separate edition of *The Possessed*, they finally got a bite—but after all the negative criticism the book had received, the best offer they received was for a mere five hundred rubles, to be paid in installments over two years. The offer was too paltry to consider, but it gave them an idea: years earlier, during their European travels, the couple had tossed around the idea of starting their own press and publishing Dostoyevsky's works themselves. It was an idea the writer had pondered on and off since the 1840s; he'd even mentioned the idea to his brother Mikhail, though to no avail. It had remained an unreachable dream—but with Anna at his side, anything seemed possible.

For a couple in their financial circumstances, the prospect could hardly have seemed more far-fetched. Dostoyevsky himself was incapable of running such a business, so the management would fall to Anna, who was both inexperienced in business and burdened by other family responsibilities. And for a twenty-six-year-old woman to wade into such dangerous waters struck Dostoyevsky's family and friends as downright foolhardy. Certain that such a risky undertaking would only sink the family deeper into debt, they tried to talk the couple out of it.

Anna herself understood the risks, which were indeed enormous. "In those days," she recalled, "no writer published his own works, and even if such a bold fellow did appear, he would inevitably pay for his daring by taking a loss." Up to that point, the Russian book business consisted of printing shops that typically bought the rights to an author's work and then printed and distributed the books throughout Russia, with nearly all the profit going to the publisher and very little to the author. Nor were gender politics on the couple's side. In the history of the notoriously cutthroat Russian book business, there had been only one translation and publication company successfully owned and run by women. Founded in 1863 by Marya Trubnikova and Nadezhda Stasova, two of the pioneering early feminists of the 1850s, the Women's Publishing Cooperative employed as many as thirty-six women and brought out textbooks, children's books, and translations of European classics such as Hans Christian Andersen's fairy tales and Darwin's *On the Origin of Species*. The Women's Publishing Cooperative was still in business as Anna was mulling the prospect of starting her own firm (it would close six years later, in 1879), and the names Trubnikova and Stasova were well known in the publishing world. By this time Anna very likely knew of them, especially since she and her husband had become friendly with one of their close colleagues, Anna Filosofova, the third member of the original feminist triumvirate. In February 1873, in fact, around the time Anna was launching her publishing venture, the Dostoyevskys received an invitation from Filosofova to a gathering of friends who sympathized with her successful efforts to organize higher-education courses for women.

Despite this direct link between Anna and the early feminists, it is doubtful how much she could have learned from Trubnikova and Stasova's particular business model, as they had the advantage of being able to rely on each other, as well as a team of employees. Anna, by contrast, would be embarking on this venture with an impetuous, impractical man as both her only business partner and her sole author—and one whose commercial track record was uneven at best.

But Anna had long since proven herself a shrewd manager of Dostoyevsky, the author and the man. Together they had overcome professional and personal challenges that would have ended many a lesser marriage. Dostoyevsky was facing an almost hopeless impasse when they met, but Anna had helped him stave off disaster through her intelligence, work ethic, and emotional support. Her friends and family may have doubted the couple's prospects for business success, but Anna and her husband had reason to believe that they were equal to the task.

Anna went about researching the publishing industry with her usual methodical thoroughness and nerve. She arranged to wander into bookstores posing as a curious customer, and would press the shopkeepers for information about the sales of specific books, how the store worked with publishers, even what discounts they received. At one print shop, where she was ordering business cards for her husband, Anna chatted up the owner, who explained that most books were published "on a cash basis," meaning the store had to pay outright for stock on receipt. (If an author had a proven track record, a printer might extend a six-month credit, charging interest on the unpaid balance after six months.) Paper suppliers would offer similar terms, she learned from this same unsuspecting store owner, who went on to give Anna a rough estimate of the total cost of paper, printing, and binding for publishing a book.

With what she learned, Anna sketched out the beginnings of a plan. A limited edition of thirty-five hundred copies of *The Possessed*, printed in large, elegant type on satiny white paper, would cost roughly four thousand rubles. At the usual sale price of three rubles fifty kopecks per copy, that would mean gross profits of 12,250 rubles, or nearly $200,000 today. After deducting the roughly 30 percent bookseller discount for bulk orders, as well as other expenses, the Dostoyevskys stood to net well over four thousand rubles—a handsome sum, especially when compared with that measly five-hundred-ruble offer.

After several months of such reconnaissance missions, Anna concluded that, whatever the risks, owning their own publishing enterprise was too lucrative a prospect to pass up. She ordered paper from one of Petersburg's best manufacturers, who gave it to her on credit. She then arranged for the printing and had the books bound. And so, on January 22, 1873, a day that Anna would proudly remember as the start of her career as a publisher, an advertisement appeared in the Petersburg newspaper *The Voice* announcing the independent publication, in a single volume, of Fyodor Dostoyevsky's *The Possessed*.

By ten o'clock that morning, a messenger from the bookshop of M. V. Popov showed up at the Dostoyevskys' publishing "headquarters"—their modestly furnished four-bedroom apartment on Serpukhovskaya Street—to place an order for ten copies. Anna brought the books into the vestibule and announced the price: thirty-five rubles, with a 20 percent bookseller discount.

"Why so little? Can't you make it thirty percent?" he pressed.

"Impossible," she said.

"Then twenty-five percent, at least?"

"Really, no—impossible," Anna responded, confidence belying her inward fear at the thought of losing her very first customer.

After a few moments of hesitation, the buyer accepted Anna's terms and handed her the cash. Elated, she was overtaken by a surge of generosity and gave the man thirty kopecks for his cab fare.

There were more rings at the door before the morning was out. Buyers came from all over Petersburg, and some from out of town as well, in each case negotiating fiercely with Anna, who gave as good as she got. Around noon that day, an elegantly dressed salesman arrived from a prominent Petersburg bookseller—a shop where Dostoyevsky himself often bought books, and to which he'd proudly brought a freshly bound copy of *The Possessed* just the day before. The salesman imperiously announced he would be taking two hundred copies of the novel on consignment, at a 50 percent discount, just as the writer had purportedly promised the day before.

Anna refused. The publishing company might be in her husband's name, she explained, but it was she who made the sales decisions.

"But then can I talk to Fyodor Mikhailovich himself?" the salesman pressed, obviously hanging his hopes on Dostoyevsky's more pliant nature.

"Fyodor Mikhailovich worked all night, and I will not wake him up before two o'clock," she responded. At which point the salesman asked her to let him take the two hundred copies with him back to his store and pay Dostoyevsky directly at a later time. Again Anna flatly refused, proceeding to explain her entire discount structure. The salesman turned around and walked out.

Within an hour, a messenger from the same bookstore—this one in more modest attire and far more deferential—appeared, asking to pay cash for fifty copies of *The Possessed* at a 30 percent discount, just as Anna had stipulated to his boss an hour before.

Overjoyed at her morning's success, she wanted to share her triumphs with her husband, but she would have to wait until he came out of his room. She knew not to speak of important business matters in the morning, when Dostoyevsky, still under the influence of his nightmares, would often emerge in an irritable mood. So that morning she gave him time to drink his two cups of scalding-hot coffee in the dining room, retreat to his study, and greet the children before following him in. Sending the children back to the nursery, she sat down at her usual place by his writing desk.

"Well, Anyechka, how's our business going?" he asked teasingly.

"Marvelously," she said.

"You've managed, perhaps, to sell a book?" he continued with a wry smile.

"Not *a* book, but a hundred and fifteen," she responded, abandoning her jocular tone and sitting up straight in the chair.

"You don't say!" he said, assuming that Anna was just having a good joke with him. "Congratulations, then."

"But I'm telling you the truth," she responded, vexed. "Why don't you believe me?" She removed from her pocket a piece of a paper with her notes about sales numbers, along with a wad of three hundred rubles in banknotes.

Dostoyevsky stared at the money, dumbfounded. This was no joke, after all. His Anyechka had indeed been selling his books.

"Our publishing business began brilliantly," she recalled. Before the end of the year, they had cleared three thousand copies of *The Possessed*. Over the next couple of years they would sell out the remaining five hundred copies, netting the couple, just as Anna had calculated, a profit of four thousand rubles—just under fifty-five thousand dollars today—which was enough to pay off some of their most urgent debts. "I felt a rare sense of triumph," Anna wrote. "I was happy about the money, of course, but mainly because I had found myself an interesting business." And, in a hint of how much she thrived on exceeding the low expectations of others, she took special pleasure in the fact that her enterprise "had done so well despite the warnings of my literary advisors."

A few swindlers managed to take advantage of her inexperience, but, ever a quick study, Anna learned from her mistakes. She also wasn't above having a little fun with it all. The novel's Russian title, *Demons*, delighted certain book buyers: "I came for the demons," they would say, or "Let me have a dozen demons." (The couple's superstitious old nanny was less amused: with so many strangers coming to their home asking for demons, she was convinced that Mrs. Dostoyevskaya was breeding the powers of darkness in their apartment.)

THUS BEGAN ANNA'S CAREER as Russia's first solo woman publisher, a career that would in time wrest Dostoyevsky out of debt and continue to provide for their family for almost the next four decades. Beyond these benefits, the business model Anna devised, which was unique in Russia at the time, had liberated her husband, a working creative who had been forced for decades to depend on an exploitative system for his livelihood. Now he was able to earn far more than he ever had from his novels, through a business that the Dostoyevskys controlled themselves.

Though no businessman himself, Dostoyevsky was starting to recognize the extent of his wife's practical talents. "I rely on your help in everything," he wrote Anna in the summer of 1875. He had already signed a document granting her control over the copyrights to all of his works, as well as a solid passport, a document authorizing Anna to receive money orders at banks and conduct her own business affairs—something that Russian wives were not allowed to do without their husband's express permission until 1914.

He also began granting Anna a degree of involvement in his creative work that he had never considered giving to anyone else. He trusted her literary judgment implicitly: When she advised him to change the color of a character's hair or dress, he listened. If she could visualize a scene he'd created, Dostoyevsky was certain that his readers would, too; if not, he knew something was amiss. Several years later, as he was dictating the scene in *The Brothers Karamazov* in which Alyosha Karamazov returns from the funeral of the little boy Ilyusha, he saw Anna wiping away tears with one hand even as she wrote with the other. He walked over and kissed her on the forehead without saying a word, his eyes beaming with gratitude.

He was amazed by Anna's intuitive grasp of his work—"such understanding, such feeling, such intuition," Dostoyevsky later told a friend, "that you'd be hard pressed to find in any critic. I tell her often: Why don't you, little mother, take up literature, write a novel." Anna did try her hand at fiction, composing two untitled stories and a few plays, all of which have recently been discovered among her archives. These works, composed after her husband's death, display Anna's social sensibility as well as the sly sense of humor once noticed by her gymnasium classmates. The play *Recommendation* deals with a poor girl named Dunyasha, housemaid of a woman called Anna Grigoryevna Fyodorovskaya, who is the widow of a famous writer. When Dunyasha is given notice, she asks her employer for a recommendation but is refused. She then takes advantage of Anna Grigoryevna's absence for a few days by placing a fake ad in the local newspaper: "Mrs. Fyodorovskaya is recommending her maid for work." Several would-be employers show up at the Fyodorovskys' home to interview Dunyasha, though one by one they all turn her down after realizing she doesn't know how to sew, iron, or nurse children. The play ends with the return of Anna Grigoryevna, who not only follows through with her intention of firing Dunyasha but threatens her with retribution for her trickery.

The real-life Anna Grigoryevna also penned a one-act play called *Marmeladov's Confession*, an adaptation of the tavern meeting between Raskolnikov and the alcoholic ex-clerk Marmeladov in *Crime and Punishment*. Judging from a note on the title page of the manuscript, Anna received the censor's approval to stage the play in 1910. But there is no record that the play was ever performed, or of Anna's intention to publish any of her plays or stories. Her real contribution to fiction would be in service of her husband's work.

She was teaching him to write better, too. Self-conscious about his prolix style, Dostoyevsky found artistic inspiration in the directness of Anna's letters. From Bad Ems he wrote her: "I admire your letters and read them with enjoyment and say to myself every day: 'What a clever woman my wife is.' I write eight pages, for instance, and won't manage to say everything, while you have everything said wonderfully in four pages—everything that's necessary, in a business-like way; intelligently, nothing extra, with the sense to realize what exactly needs definitely to be said, and with subtlety of *feeling*."

Sometimes he would steal plots outright from his wife. When Anna shared a story about an old lady she had met on her way back from the typographer's office, Dostoyevsky made it the basis of his short story "Century," one of his personal favorites. The humorous poetry the couple had composed together to counter the doldrums of their European travels also found its way directly into Dostoyevsky's novels, in the form of Captain Lebyadkina's absurd verse in *The Possessed*, or the gymnasium students' incoherent epigrams in *The Brothers Karamazov*. Anna received no credit for these "borrowings," but there's no evidence that this bothered her. She kept her eye on the long game, knowing that his creative borrowings were the family's financial gain.

For Dostoyevsky, the psychological benefits of Anna's publishing success were every bit as important as the financial rewards. At last he was able to free himself from the humiliating ranks of what he considered the "literary proletariat," ending his subservience to the whims of powerful editors and publishers to seize the kind of independence experienced by wealthier aristocratic contemporaries like Tolstoy and Turgenev. Financial security also gave him the privilege of speaking his mind more freely on social issues. Only now the object of his ire was no longer the state, as in his youth, but rather the radical intelligentsia and revolutionaries who were determined to destroy it.

It is little wonder, then, that when Prince Vladimir Meshchersky, the archconservative publisher of the reactionary journal *The Citizen*, offered Dostoyevsky the position of editor, the writer gladly accepted. The position brought many advantages. The journal, which was well funded by the government, offered him a decent annual salary of three thousand rubles. The job also gave him the opportunity to launch a column he would call "Diary of a Writer," a small-scale version of a more ambitious project he had been mulling for years: a self-contained personal almanac of contemporary life, in which Dostoyevsky would hold forth, in essays, stories, and sketches, on contemporary social and political issues. Nothing quite like it had ever been attempted in Russian literature before. This column for *The Citizen* would serve as a dry run for that project, while his role as editor would give Dostoyevsky a platform to broaden his own readership while promoting the work of like-minded thinkers. That his own ideological position was more or less in concert with that of the government also meant that he would receive minimal resistance from the censors.

Not surprisingly, his work at *The Citizen* would earn Dostoyevsky a fresh batch of literary enemies—progressive Russian voices unable to forgive this onetime political prisoner, who once had exhibited enough courage to face execution for his radical ideals, yet now aligned himself with the notoriously archconservative journal. And Dostoyevsky's health took a toll right along with his reputation. During the summer of 1873, his family moved to a new apartment in Petersburg in order to be closer to the journal's publishing headquarters. There, hunched over manuscripts in the overheated, dusty office, the writer developed shortness of breath and a nasty cough—the first stages, Anna believed, of the emphysema that eventually killed him.

Ideological disagreements with Meshchersky arose almost immediately. Dostoyevsky quickly grew frustrated with both journal politics and the poorly written articles he was given to edit. He fired off rude letters to the worst offenders, handing them over to Anna to be mailed. After glancing at the letters, however, she wisely decided to hold them back, often telling him a few days later that she'd "forgotten" to send them—by which point his anger gave way to gratitude to Anna for saving him from certain heartache. More than a dozen of these unmailed letters survive in Anna's archives; had they been sent, Dostoyevsky's brief and troubled career at *The Citizen* would likely have come to an end even sooner than it did.

The final straw came when Meshchersky began advocating for the construction of special university dormitories for the purpose of maintaining government surveillance over the students. For Dostoyevsky, who knew all too well the humiliations of government surveillance—and who still sympathized in his heart with the idealistic aims of the younger generation, if not their methods—that went one step too far. In March 1874, he tendered his resignation.

Dispirited, he cast about for his next creative project. Anna, meanwhile, continued with her publishing work, following her success with *The Possessed* with the first stand-alone publication of *The Idiot* in 1874. That novel, which Dostoyevsky had once promised her would become a blockbuster, now *did* become a commercial success, thanks in no small part to the business acumen of Anna, who shrewdly marketed it to a wide reading public. The proofs were sent to the Dostoyevskys on holiday in Staraya Russa, but once the work was ready for publication, Anna returned to Petersburg alone and managed to sell every copy she'd intended. While in Petersburg, she also settled her accounts with the printer and negotiated new deals with large-scale distributors to sell additional books on consignment.

ONE APRIL MORNING IN 1874, at around noon, the maid handed Anna a visiting card bearing the name Nikolai Alexeyevich Nekrasov. Knowing that Dostoyevsky was already dressed and would appear shortly, Anna asked the maid to show the visitor to the drawing room, then brought the card to her husband. Like every educated Russian at that time, Anna knew the name Nekrasov. The greatest of the so-called civic poets, Nekrasov was also the brilliantly successful publisher of the influential journal *The Contemporary*, which had published the works of the young Turgenev and Tolstoy, as well as those of Vissarion Belinsky, and the radical writers Nikolai Chernyshevsky and Nikolai Dobrolyubov. As Anna knew, Dostoyevsky also owed his start to Nekrasov, who had brought the manuscript of *Poor Folk* to Belinsky's attention. Belinsky's ecstatic response to the novel not only got Dostoyevsky published but immediately helped to establish his reputation as a major new talent.

In the intervening years, however, their relations had been marked by growing ideological differences (Nekrasov remained a passionate liberal as Dostoyevsky grew ever more conservative), resulting in a series of ad hominem attacks on both sides. On the very day Dostoyevsky met Anna, in October 1866, he had referred to Nekrasov as an unscrupulous businessman and a notorious "cardsharper, a terrible gambler, a person who keeps talking about the sufferings of humanity while he himself drives around in horse-drawn carriages." Now, suddenly, this sometime friend—who hadn't spoken face-to-face with Dostoyevsky in nearly a decade—was at their apartment.

As curious as she was suspicious, Anna stood behind the door to the study where Nekrasov and Dostoyevsky were speaking. Now the publisher of the progressive journal *Fatherland Notes*, he was there to make a business proposition: Would Dostoyevsky contribute a novel for the next year? Nekrasov would pay two hundred fifty rubles per sixteen-page signature, a hundred more than Dostoyevsky had been receiving from *The Russian Messenger*.

As she listened carefully to their conversation, Anna's mind went into full gear. Nekrasov, she guessed, must have taken one look at their modest living quarters and concluded that Dostoyevsky would be only too happy to accept such an offer. And it *was* a good offer, even better after Nekrasov agreed to an advance of two thousand. They could certainly use the money, now that her husband had given up his job at *The Citizen*, and this opportunity would let him get back to his creative work, which he missed. It was a bird in the hand, and with a highly respected journal, no less. Yes, Anna thought, he should accept the offer.

To her dismay, though, Dostoyevsky hesitated.

"I cannot give you an affirmative answer, Nikolai Alexeyevich, for two reasons," she heard him say. The first reason was that he needed to discuss the matter with his longtime publisher Mikhail Katkov, to whom he had a tacit obligation to offer his work first. "The second question," he said, "is how my wife will react to your offer. She is at home, and I'll ask her right now."

Nekrasov had not expected this: a writer relying on his wife for such an important professional decision. Leaving him alone in the study, Dostoyevsky went to look for Anna, who had already sneaked back into her room. As soon as he appeared, she blurted: "What is there to ask about? Say yes, Fedya, say yes, right away."

"Say yes to what?" he asked in amazement.

"Oh, my Lord! To Nekrasov's offer, of course."

"And how do you know about Nekrasov's offer?"

"Because I overheard the whole conversation—I was standing at the door."

"So you were eavesdropping? Aren't you ashamed of yourself, Anyechka?" he asked wryly.

"Not in the least!" she responded. "After all, you don't have any secrets from me—and you certainly would have told me all about it anyway. So what's the big deal about my listening in? It's nobody else's business, after all, but ours."

It was the same logic that led Anna to read her husband's correspondence on the sly, and to write to Polina Suslova behind his back. Clearly, she was willing to use any resources at her disposal, including subterfuge, to protect her marriage, and now their joint publishing business. Dostoyevsky had often admonished Anna for interfering with his affairs, but he knew his gambler wife well enough by now to recognize that her audacity had also been responsible for saving him—and them—on more than one occasion. And so, returning to the study, he announced to

Nekrasov, "I've talked it over with my wife, and she is very pleased that my novel will be published in *Fatherland Notes*."

"I would never have imagined that you were under your wife's heel," said Nekrasov, relieved but still confused.

"What is there to be surprised at?" Dostoyevsky responded plainly. "She and I live together very harmoniously, I confide all my affairs in her and have faith in her intelligence and business sense. How then could I not ask her advice in a matter so important to us both?"

To Nekrasov, this was a baffling arrangement. While in his work Russia's great civic poet had waxed eloquent on the sufferings of "fallen women," as prostitutes were known, like many prominent literary men of his time he was incapable of extending that sympathy to a woman rising in power. In his poem "My Disillusionment," Nekrasov had lampooned the prominent poet Karolina Pavlova for choosing a literary career over a domestic life of pickling and jelly-making. Most of the educated public would have laughed along with him—further evidence of what a pioneering role Anna was forging for herself.

THROUGHOUT THE SUMMER OF 1874 Dostoyevsky worked furiously on *The Adolescent*, the novel he had promised Nekrasov, while taking an extended cure in Bad Ems for his worsening emphysema. Writing Anna long, rambling letters about his crushing loneliness and incurable writer's block, he griped in his usual hyperbolic fashion that his epilepsy had wiped out his imagination for good. Anna responded lovingly but firmly: "I beg you not to rush to begin work, better to let some time pass, the plan will reveal itself; rushing will only interfere," and then reminded him how he'd been "tormented for a long time over the plan" for *The Idiot* and *The Possessed* before those novels came together. "Hurrying can spoil the whole affair," she warned. "You'll have to redo the plan, and that will interfere with the artistry. Forgive me, my dear, that I am giving you advice, but I am doing it out of pure heart and as your biggest admirer who would be very disappointed if the novel wasn't a success."

Of course, she was also advising him as his publisher, for she knew that her most important author needed to be managed with great delicacy. Having watched him for years, she had come to accept these bouts of self-defeating depression as a part of his process—just as gambling had once been, to quote one Dostoyevsky scholar, "the storm which cleared the creative sky." She assured him of her love, reminded him that he'd been in this emotional state many times before, and told him that time and patience—never Dostoyevsky's strong suits—were nonetheless his surest allies. In other words, Anna was commending to her husband the principles she followed in her own life, recognizing that he needed to go through creative upheaval before he could emerge and produce great writing.

During his months away, his longing for Anna was acute. "I kiss all of you (do you understand?) in my imagination," he wrote on June 16. "Yes, Anya, in the misery of my solitude all I need was this agony, having to live without you and to be tormented. I have seductive dreams of you; do you dream of me?" And then he exhorted her "not to be prudish when reading this." Anna *was* often too prudish for his tastes, a shortcoming he complained about. That summer, however, her usually businesslike letters were sometimes punctuated by rare outpourings of passion. "My dear, dear, a thousand times dear Fedichka, I also miss you very, very much," she wrote in one letter. "I am dreaming very much about your return and am glad that now you've only got less than three weeks to heal. I reread your letters often and regret that there isn't a third page. Every night without fail at around one a.m. I awake from a dream, in which I see you, and lie for a half hour imagining you."

That is about as explicit as Anna would ever get in her letters to him— at least those that have survived. Whether due to her proper upbringing, or an instinct that the world might someday read her letters, or her fear of overstimulating Dostoyevsky, her correspondence with him is marked by a certain restraint that she never quite allowed herself to shed in writing.

She had little time for such considerations, anyway, for tensions between Dostoyevsky and Nekrasov arose almost immediately. It was a devil's bargain, this arrangement with Nekrasov's progressive journal, a deal the writer had made largely out of financial need. And now they were at loggerheads over certain passages in *The Adolescent* that Nekrasov found too critical of the radicals. "Even if we have to ask for alms, I won't compromise in [my political] orientation by so much as a line!" Dostoyevsky wrote Anna. This was no mere colorful metaphor—they had existed hand to mouth before, and might be forced to do so again—but Anna was no longer fazed by any of it. Rather than trying to change his mind on a point of principle, she would focus her efforts, as she always had, on creating the conditions that would allow Dostoyevsky to be Dostoyevsky, while at the same time protecting her family's interests.

By August, the core concept for *The Adolescent* had emerged. "The whole idea of the novel is to show that disorder is now universal; it's everywhere, in society, in its affairs, in the dominant ideas (in fact there aren't any dominant ideas), in the convictions (likewise none), in the disintegration of the basis of the family." The theme so intrigued him that he even considered *Disorder* as a title.

Dostoyevsky would explore this premise through the charismatic and mysterious character of Versilov, the landowner father whose illegitimate son, Arkady Dolgoruky, is the adolescent of the title. Many years earlier, Versilov had seduced a young peasant woman on his estate, Sofya Andreyevna, the wife of Versilov's old gardener, Makar Dolgoruky, before offering the cuckolded husband some money as compensation, and then taking Sofya abroad with him. There Sofya bore Versilov a son, Arkady, and a daughter, Liza, at which point the dissolute father abandoned his wife and daughter, sent Arkady to a boarding school, and himself continued on with his aimless travels.

When the novel opens, Arkady, having completed his schooling, has come to Petersburg in search of a position and in pursuit of his "idea": his ambition to become as wealthy as the real-life financier James Mayer de Rothschild, a grandiose goal clearly intended to compensate for deep insecurity over his illegitimacy and poverty. While in Petersburg, he forms a close and complicated relationship with his father, Versilov, whom he hardly knows yet has idealized in his imagination, as well as his mother, Sofya, a virtual stranger to him. In a story that combines elements of both the picaresque and the bildungsroman, Arkady sets out on a tour of discovery and bitter disillusionment through a broad slice of contemporary Russian life, giving the author an opportunity to comment on the full range of a society in moral disarray.

Throughout that fall and winter Dostoyevsky worked steadily on *The Adolescent*. Anna continued to worry about the family's finances, taking down dictation when she was able. She wondered what the family would do if Dostoyevsky should have a falling-out with Nekrasov—especially if there was any chance that they would have to return his two-thousand-ruble advance, part of which had already been spent. And then they would have to figure out how to live until her husband found a new source of income. *The Russian Messenger* was his only other obvious option for serial publication, but Katkov was piqued that Dostoyevsky had published *The Adolescent* in Nekrasov's competing journal. Worse yet, Katkov was at that very moment swamped by a slew of new work—including Leo Tolstoy's new novel, *Anna Karenina*. Katkov would not be able to publish anything of Dostoyevsky's for at least a year and a half.

Mulling their prospects, Anna determined that the only responsible decision was to reduce the family's living expenses. Their "ever-modest living quarters alone costs seven or eight hundred rubles a year, and a full thousand including firewood," she recalled, and they were spending three thousand a year plus interest on previously unpaid debts. To reduce expenses, they would need to spend the winter of 1874–75 in Staraya Russa, where the cost of living was far lower than in Petersburg. If Dostoyevsky was in need of creative rejuvenation, he could make a few trips to Petersburg alone, a far less expensive proposition than moving the whole family back and forth. Anna presented him with the financial case for remaining in Staraya Russa for the winter, arguing that he should spend the upcoming winter finishing *The Adolescent* and preparing for his new planned venture, an expansion of his "Diary of a Writer" column into a full-length monthly periodical. Dostoyevsky described *Diary of a Writer* as "a diary in the literal sense of the word—an account of impressions actually experienced each month, an account of what has been seen, heard, and read. Of course, it may include short or long stories, but mainly it will concern actual events." Anna painted a tempting portrait of the long, tranquil winter they'd spend together as a family in the heart of provincial Russia. Dostoyevsky agreed; Anna would recall that winter as one of her "most beautiful memories."

They settled into a routine. After lunch, Dostoyevsky would ask Anna to come to his study, and between two and three in the afternoon he would dictate what he'd written the night before, their work often punctuated by laughter and jokes and charming stories unrelated to their work. The children were healthy—they didn't need to call the doctor once the whole winter—and Dostoyevsky's breathing had improved, his nerves calm. He had not had a seizure in months.

Anna never ceased thinking about business opportunities for the family. With *The Possessed* and *The Idiot* still "having great success," she decided to reach back again into Dostoyevsky's past to republish the work that had brought her to tears as a teenage girl: his semiautobiographical prison novel, *Notes from the House of the Dead*, which had long been out of print, yet booksellers were asking for it. For this purpose she made a two-week trip to Petersburg in December 1874, to try to interest several booksellers whose orders could help make the printing costs viable. Dostoyevsky's letters to her were filled with their usual mixture of acute longing, impractical instructions, and insistent orders, as well as expressions of doubt that one bookseller who sold the Dostoyevskys' editions on commission would be interested in *Notes*. "I have a premonition that they won't take many copies," he wrote. He was wrong: Anna persuaded the bookseller to order seven hundred copies of *Notes*, covering both the cost of the printing and part of the paper, with enough left over to bring some of the money home with her.

AND SHE WAS PREGNANT AGAIN.

The family stayed on in Staraya Russa through May 1875, with Dostoyevsky taking full advantage of Anna's stenography skills during her confinement for a long, uninterrupted stretch of work on *The Adolescent*. He returned to Bad Ems that summer, again hating every minute of it, his yearning for his wife and family almost incapacitating. At one point Anna heard a rumor that her husband had fallen gravely ill in the spa town, and she was so concerned that she nearly boarded a train across the country; he wired her a few days later, laying the rumors to rest. But the terror of those few days waiting for his telegram stayed with her. "My dear, here's when you understand how much you love a person and how dear he is to you," she wrote him. "Just think, my dear and priceless Fedichka, what could have come of this? I could've had a miscarriage yesterday and paid with my life and left you and my poor kids alone. It's terrifying to think about that." She then insisted, only half in jest, that their passion for each other was responsible for this state of affairs. "My dear angel," she told him, "you and I are the most rotten of people; we had to go and become so attached to one another. Things would have been better and calmer if we'd been indifferent and left everything to the will of God."

But leaving things in God's hands was never Anna's way. "God takes care of those who take care of themselves" says the ancient proverb, and it was wisdom Anna lived by. While they were no longer begging for alms, the Dostoyevskys were not flush, bringing in no more than around two thousand rubles a year, and, with the coming addition to their family they had to account for every ruble they spent. No wonder Anna grew frustrated when her husband came home from one business trip carrying not his full payment from *Fatherland Notes* but a gift of a dozen expensive, utterly unnecessary chemises from the best shop in Moscow.

With a new baby on the way and the final installments of *The Adolescent* due soon, the couple buckled down for the final stretch of work. Dostoyevsky wrote late into the night, and Anna transcribed, when she was able, during the day.

On August 10, 1875, Anna gave birth to a boy, Alexei, bringing joy and happy exhaustion to their home. It was a remarkably painless delivery, free of the terrors and physical agony she had experienced in previous deliveries—a sure sign, she felt, that there was something special about this child. But the name, chosen by Dostoyevsky himself, also happened to be that of the autobiographical hero of *The Gambler*, whose life was anything but blessed. And, as time would tell, this real-life Alexei, doted on by his parents and beloved by his two older siblings, would suffer a fate far more tragic than any befalling his literary namesake. But that would all come later; for now, in the middle of a particularly glorious summer, life seemed to be smiling on the Dostoyevskys and their growing family.

By September, the last installments of *The Adolescent* were complete. Dostoyevsky had jettisoned his earlier idea of calling the book *Disorder*, but he stayed true to the concept of a novel that used Arkady's journey to illustrate Russian society in a state of disarray. "I'm nothing but a wretched adolescent who every minute keeps losing the sense of what's good and what's bad," Arkady laments to Versilov, after the older man encourages him to disrespect his mother and nominal father, Makar Dolgoruky. "If you'd only hinted to me then what the right course was, I'd have rushed to follow it. But, instead, you just made me angry." Arkady *is* an angry young man—the novel's title is sometimes loosely translated as *A Raw Youth*—and his journey is underscored by bitter disappointment in the father he once idealized, a father whose generation laid the groundwork for this morally adrift society.

Arkady's quest to become as wealthy as Rothschild is thwarted as he finds himself increasingly enmeshed in others' lives. He encounters, for instance, a group of radical revolutionaries who preach a brand of populist socialism that involves the assassination of the tsar and his family. From there, the hero becomes embroiled in a series of financial and romantic intrigues, including an entanglement with Katerina Akhmakova, the proud and beautiful wife of a dying general. Arkady maintains a passionate love-hate relationship with Katerina; he also holds power over her because of a letter he has in his possession that, if discovered, could cause Katerina to be cut out of her wealthy father's will.

On his journey to self-discovery, Arkady also meets the young Sergei Sokolsky, an inveterate gambler who has been having an affair with Arkady's sister, Liza. Through his involvement with Sokolsky, Arkady is exposed to the seedier sides of Petersburg life—not least, its illegal gambling salons—and gets hooked on roulette himself. He eventually wins an enormous sum, only to be drawn into an imbroglio that ends with his being accused of robbery and then thrown out of the gaming room. In these scenes—obviously drawn from personal experience—Dostoyevsky seems to be transmuting his own gambling misfortunes into a broader social commentary, about a world in which young people like Arkady are reduced to pursuing mirages of financial conquest rather than deeper spiritual meaning.

At two crucial moments, however, the hero comes into contact with individuals who embody the humility and compassion that Dostoyevsky valued so highly. One of those brief encounters is with his long-suffering mother, Sofya. Despite her traumatic past, this character, modeled on Dostoyevsky's own mother, has retained a profound soulfulness and a capacity to console her wounded son. The second encounter is with Makar Dolgoruky. In the years since his humiliation, Makar has taken up a life of holy pilgrimage; he speaks to Arkady in the soothing, lyrical style of a wizened old Russian peasant, inspiring the boy with his faith in life's mysterious goodness.

These two moments are among the best scenes in the novel, offering the reader a temporary lyrical uplift in a book otherwise dominated by an atmosphere of confusion and collapse. Dostoyevsky succeeded—perhaps too well—in capturing the chaos of his times, and many readers found the book itself disordered and fragmented. Turgenev referred to the novel as "this chaos," and another contemporary, Mikhail Saltykov-Shchedrin, called it "a mad novel." While *The Adolescent* contained many of the predominant themes of Dostoyevsky's other works—the search for God; the corrupting influence of money; the allure of sexual perversity; the dangers of European rationalism and the illusion of social progress—the story lacked the intense psychological drama or dramatic episodes that had kept readers spellbound in his most successful work.

THE MANUSCRIPT WAS far from perfect, but it would have to do, since Nekrasov was expecting it any day now. On September 15, the family of five left for Petersburg, where the author was to deliver the last installments of *The Adolescent* and collect the remainder of his advance, which had by now become necessary to them. The weather was warm and glorious on that late-summer day, as the gentry-style caravan escorted the

Dostoyevskys to the steamboat dock on Lake Ilmen, amid the bright tinkle of carriage bells and children's delighted screams. The lake itself was the color of turquoise and smooth as glass, reminding Anna of the Swiss lakes from her travels nearly a decade earlier. Arriving in Novgorod at three in the afternoon, they unloaded the luggage from the steamboat, and the family was then transported to the train station.

Later that evening, when it was time to depart, Anna went to fetch what she thought was her husband's travel trunk from storage, but, on a second look, she noticed that it wasn't his. She glanced around. There was no other black trunk in the vicinity. She grew concerned. Of all the trunks that might be lost, this one was the most unfortunate: inside it was not just her husband's overcoat and underwear, but the manuscript for *The Adolescent*. Worse, the trunk contained the notebooks for the novel, without which Dostoyevsky would be helpless. Two months of intensive labor would be lost, and he would have to reconstruct his work from scratch.

Anna blamed herself, both as his wife and his business manager, for such carelessness. As she stood leaning against a counter in the baggage room, tears streaming down her cheeks, a thought flashed through her mind. Without telling her husband, she immediately hired a cab to rush her back to the dock. It was eight in the evening now, and they were racing through the shadier part of town, where she saw people creeping out of tiny streets in between large, gray warehouses. Tramps ran after them, shouting. The frightened cabbie urged the horse on so hard that it broke into a gallop. Upon reaching the dock, Anna jumped out of the carriage, stormed up the ramp to the steamship office, and banged her fists on a dark window.

"Guard, open up—open up right away!" she shouted. "Open up, grandpa, this minute! A big black travel trunk was left here, and I've come to get it!"

"It's here," a sleepy voice replied.

She asked the guard to carry the trunk to the cab, promising to tip him.

He didn't respond. She called to the cabbie to help, but he also refused, afraid his rig might be stolen.

And so, without a moment's hesitation, Anna ordered the guard to open the door, which he did, and "I grabbed the trunk by its handle and dragged it, stopping at every step. To make matters worse, the ramp was a long one. But I managed to lug it to the cab." At which point the cabbie jumped out and hoisted the hundred-forty-pound trunk in between the seat and the coach box, and Anna climbed on top of it and sat down, "resolved not to give it up even if hoodlums should attack." Amazed, the cabbie struck his horse and started down the street, as figures emerged and started shouting at them from behind.

As they approached the railroad station, Anna caught sight of her visibly distraught husband. She told him the whole story—what they'd almost lost, what she had done to save them.

"My God!" he exclaimed. "Only think what danger you put yourself into! After all, when those rogues who followed you saw that the cabbie was driving a woman, they might have attacked you, robbed you, maimed you, killed you!" His response spoke volumes about their roles within the family: "Just think what would have happened to us, to me and the children," he moaned, warning her fecklessly: "Oh, Anya, Anya! Your rashness will lead you to no good!"

In this, he was, of course, mistaken. It was Anna's rashness that rescued his manuscript, averting disaster for his career and their entire family, just as her extraordinary daring, her tenacity and determination, had saved them many times before. Whether out of lingering chauvinism or a dogged need to view his wife primarily as amanuensis rather than manager, the writer seemed incapable of shaking his idealized image of Anna as "simple and angelic," as he'd recently described her in a letter. He needed to see her as someone requiring his protection and guidance, despite all the evidence to the contrary. But there's no sign that Anna minded this; she knew who she was and what she needed to do. All that mattered to her, on this late-summer evening, was that *The Adolescent* had been saved.

13.

A Test

They were full partners now, Anna and Fyodor Dostoyevsky, both professionally and personally. Beyond participating in his creative work as his stenographer, first reader, and editor, she also controlled all other aspects of their publishing enterprise: negotiating with paper suppliers, typesetters, printers, and booksellers, and handling almost all of their business correspondence. It was an enormous amount of work, a rare portfolio of responsibilities for any single individual to manage entirely on her own. As one recent historian of publishing in Russia has pointed out, "The editorial work involved in book publication, especially fiction, would, as a rule, be divided between the author or translator and the proofreader. . . . The publisher was responsible for the book but, as such, did not take part in the process of preparing it for publication." Anna, by contrast, was responsible for the entire process. The couple had retrofitted some of the rooms in their apartment to accommodate their publishing operation, but there is no record that they ever rented a separate office for this purpose. With finances tight, Anna had long since learned to make do on the bare minimum, in business as in their private life.

Dostoyevsky, almost in spite of himself, was discovering that his "gambler wife," as he had once teasingly called Anna, was proving just as bold at gambling as an entrepreneur as he had been at the roulette tables—and far more adept. Moreover, her own penchant for risk was balanced by the sort of strategic pragmatism and discipline her husband lacked. As a result, where his gambles often led to torment and penury, hers were fostering the most stable period in Dostoyevsky's career.

In January 1876, the first issue of *Diary of a Writer* was snatched up by thousands of readers familiar with the writer's earlier column of the same name in *The Citizen*. With Anna handling the business side of the publication, the author could dedicate all of his time to writing, and he used the platform to hone a conservative message of increasing intensity. For the next two years, Dostoyevsky would use the pages of the *Diary* to express the stridently nationalist worldview that would dominate his thinking in the last years of his life. As he had for years, he hailed the Russian people as the world's bastion of truth and morality, and he lambasted Westernizers and the radical Russian intellectuals who followed them as corrupt and disconnected from the values of their own people. He argued that only Russia, by presiding over a Pan-Slavic empire following the principles of Orthodox Christianity, could save a spiritually bankrupt modern civilization. And, in a disturbing display of intolerance, he laced these arguments with some of the most virulently anti-Semitic ideas he would ever express— repeatedly impugning Jews as the embodiment of Europe's empty materialism and cold rationalism. (The word "yid" appears regularly now not only in Dostoyevsky's private correspondence but in his novels.)

How this lifetime advocate of universal love could embrace such clearly noxious ideas is one of the greater contradictions of Dostoyevsky's art and thought—a painful blot on his reputation that scholars have debated for well over a century and a half. American scholar Joseph Frank has summed up Dostoyevsky's xenophobia, calling him "unquestionably anti-Semitic, just as he was anti-French, anti-German, anti-English and, particularly, anti-Polish—indeed, anti-everybody who was not Russian." Another scholar, Gary Saul Morson, has identified a number of "morally reprehensible" anti-Semitic motifs in Dostoyevsky's work.

It is possible to find roots of Dostoyevsky's intolerance in his religious upbringing, where his emotionally abusive father enforced his Orthodox Christian principles with an iron fist. And the writer's spirit may have been hardened in those few fateful moments when, as a Petrashevskyite, he stood prepared to die before being saved by the hand of the very same tsar who had condemned him to death in the first place. Whatever the reason, Dostoyevsky seemed incapable, even after all these years of a healing relationship with Anna, of shaking his deep-seated impulse to view compassion and domination as somehow inextricably linked.

How did Anna respond to Dostoyevsky's extreme and often contradictory ideas? We have little to go on beyond her consistent expression of her high regard for her husband's genius. We have no record that she ever demonstrated any compunction over his rhetoric or the beliefs underlying his language. This suggests that she either tacitly agreed with them, or had a strong ability to compartmentalize her personal beliefs from her responsibility to build the publishing business, provide for the family, and give her husband the peace of mind needed to continue producing his work. There was a core irony to their arrangement, with Anna playing the part of the very sort of capitalist her husband so derided, yoking them to the image of the "materialistic" Jews, even as she worked to promote his message that such "foreign" values as ambition and enterprise were abhorrent.

Though he himself never commented on that irony, by this point Dostoyevsky clearly understood what he owed to Anna's business acumen. In his correspondence with family and friends, he issued repeated passionate tributes to her hard work and commitment, often acknowledging that her efforts came at great cost to her. "Anna Grigoryevna helps me," he wrote to his brother Andrei in March 1876, "but her health is so worn out (especially by nursing the baby) that I have begun to be seriously afraid for her," while in his letters to Anna herself, the writer offered his usual blend of panegyrics laced with guilt-ridden litanies of his own shortcomings.

It was still evolving, that fluid power dynamic that had always been at work in their relationship. Where early on Dostoyevsky had presented himself as Anna's mature, worldly escort, offering to return her "to God, well-developed, directed, preserved, saved from everything that is base and deadens the spirit," by this point he recognized that Anna, with her own iron will, was capable of being *his* faithful guide through life's inferno. Dostoyevsky needed Anna, perhaps more than she needed him; it was a fact he understood, and it frightened and thrilled him in equal measure.

"My Darling Anya," he had written her from Bad Ems in July 1876, "I know that everything is in your power alone and [passage deleted by Anna], but I so highly value and trust in your mind and character that I know only [passage crossed out], . . . but, Anya, I believe in your enormous intellect [several words crossed out]." Then, two days later, in an echo of the pathetic letters he'd once sent from the sites of his gambling sprees, he wrote: "I'm so in love with you, Anya, that I don't even have any other thought except for you. . . . You're my mistress and lady, you're my queen, and it's happiness for me to obey you. . . . Anka, my idol, my sweet honest [passage crossed out], don't forget me. And that you're my idol, my god—indeed, it is so." Finally, in a sudden shift from a mode of supplication to one of dominance, he told her that "I adore every atom of your body and of your soul and I love all of you, all, because it's *mine, mine!*" Even now, after all they had been through, Dostoyevsky was apparently unable to get over the fact that this exceptional woman in whose presence he could give free rein to his every impulse, whether as artist or lover, was in fact his wife. The more she freed him to be fully himself, pathologies and all, the more he idolized Anna, needed to know that she was his alone.

This mixture of neediness and narcissism on Dostoyevsky's part, and forbearance and persistence on Anna's, had always been present in their relationship. Years earlier, when she was still insecure and unsettled, she had absorbed his abuse, cowering before his manic lurches from depressive self-laceration to explosive egoism. Now confident in her roles as wife, mother, and successful businesswoman, Anna had assumed far greater control in the relationship. Yet she still recognized her husband's volatility as an essential aspect of his creative personality, and seemed to relish the fact that she could be so many things to this complicated man: his muse and manager, his lover and wife, his first reader and biggest fan. Only now she deftly played each of these various roles from a position of strength, and with increasing confidence in the stability of their bond.

Elsewhere in his letter from Bad Ems, Dostoyevsky wrote: "My angel, all I do here is dream of you, after this year of giving birth, nursing, and working on the *Diary*, at last recovering your health in Staraya Russa. Oh, my darling, my heart aches for you; I've been recalling everything here, how you fretted, how you worked—and for what reward?" For Anna, it seems clear, the work was its own reward. Happiest when productive, she enjoyed the challenge of building a successful business. In her archives is a letter she wrote to her brother-in-law Andrei Dostoyevsky in March 1876, in which she describes the deep satisfaction she derived from her work on the publication of *Diary of a Writer*. After recounting her early success of acquiring fifteen hundred annual subscribers and selling out nearly six thousand copies, Anna continued: "But, not remaining satisfied with that, the *Diary* is circulating in Petersburg and Moscow, and I am distributing it in the provinces and sending it to booksellers I know in Kiev, Odessa, Kharkov, and Kazan. I receive good news from there. . . . Although it's a terrible amount of effort . . . I don't mind working, as long as there are good results, which based on our start we can hope for." Purposeful work, no matter how grueling, was for Anna deeply satisfying—an expression, one might say, of her unique form of spirituality.

And things were indeed going well for the Dostoyevskys. The writer was gaining a wider readership than ever, while steadily paying off outstanding debts. Adding to the family's sense of well-being, Dostoyevsky had gone months without an epileptic seizure, while their children, Alyosha, Fedya, and Lyuba, had fully recovered from their winter illnesses.

ALL OF THIS BOOSTED Anna's already high spirits, and in "this most placid of moods" she was prompted to try something rather mischievous and unexpected. It started innocently enough, in the spring of 1876, when a new novel called *Strength of Character*, by Sofya Smirnova, was just then coming out in *Fatherland Notes*. Dostoyevsky was friendly with Smirnova and had a high regard for her talent; one day, he asked Anna to fetch him the latest copy of the journal, so that he could read the new installment of Smirnova's novel. Settling down with it herself after putting the children to bed, Anna was instantly struck by one passage in particular. One of Smirnova's characters, a scoundrel who means to wreck the hero's marriage, sends an anonymous letter in which he tells the hero that his wife is having a secret affair with a gorgeous, dark-eyed lover, who after many nocturnal visits has conquered her heart for good. "And if perchance you do not believe me," the fictional letter ends, "then have a look at the locket hanging around your wife's neck and see whose face she carries next to her heart in that locket."

This passage gave Anna a prankish idea. For the rest of the evening, she set to work with pen and paper, transforming the fictional letter into a real one she would send to her own husband. She mapped out the ruse as methodically as one of her business ventures, changing a few words every two or three lines, and going through several sheets of paper before getting the handwriting just right, so that Dostoyevsky would not recognize her hand. With gleeful cunning, she put the letter in their mailbox the next morning. That evening, unable to restrain her curiosity, she marched into his study after checking on the children in the nursery, sat down in her usual chair next to the writing desk, and waited in silence, studying his every expression and movement as he paced morosely around the room with heavy steps. She even began to feel sorry for him, though *not* so sorry that she would end his mounting torment just yet.

"Why are you so gloomy, Fedya?" she asked finally.

Staring at her furiously, he circled her a few times and then stopped opposite her. "Do you wear a locket?" he asked in a choked voice.

"As a matter of fact, I do," she said.

"Show it to me!" he insisted.

"What for?" responded Anna. "You've already seen it many times." Of course he had: Dostoyevsky himself had bought the delicate piece for her in Venice.

"Let—me—see—that lock-et!" he howled.

Her prank had succeeded perfectly, maybe *too* perfectly. Ensnared in the game she had launched, she couldn't back out; nor, if she was honest, did she want to, for it was all so intriguing. Unfastening the collar of her dress, she was still reaching to remove the Venetian locket before he advanced on her, ripping the chain from her with a vicious downward yank.

At once furious with him and sorry for what she had reduced him to, she watched as his trembling hands fumbled with the spring, unable to open it.

Her joke, she realized now, had gone too far. In the gentlest possible voice, she offered to open the locket herself. But he refused, fumbling with the locket until he finally managed to pry it open. He stared at its contents, speechless: a portrait of him on one side, their daughter Lyuba on the other.

"Well, what did you find?" asked Anna, as Dostoyevsky peered at the portraits. "Fedya, my foolish one, how could you believe an anonymous letter?"

"And how do you know about an anonymous letter?" he asked, turning on her.

Because, she told him, it was she who'd sent it. To prove it, she hurried to the desk where the issue of *Fatherland Notes* was kept, reminding him about Smirnova's novel. She even showed him the sheets of paper she'd used to practice her handwriting. "My goodness, you read it yesterday yourself. I thought you'd guess at once," she said, meekly adding, "All I wanted to do was have a little joke."

"What kind of a joke is *that*?" he demanded. "Why, I've been in torment this last half hour!"

"But who could've known you'd be such an Othello and go climbing the wall without stopping to think it over?"

"In cases like this, people don't stop to think! It's obvious you've never felt real love and real jealousy," he shot back. "And just think—even if I hadn't discovered my own portrait, a grain of doubt of your faithfulness would have stuck with me, and I would have tormented myself with it all my life. I beg of you, don't ever joke about such things—I can't answer for myself when I'm in a fury!"

Yet this fury, for all of Anna's repeated apologies and tear-filled expressions of regret, may have been exactly what she was hoping to provoke. "I myself was infinitely happy that my absurd prank had ended so well," she admitted years later. She was "truly sorry for making my husband suffer," having been reminded of "what a frenzied, almost irresponsible state my dear husband was capable of reaching in those moments of jealous suspicion." After years of protecting him from stress, then, why did she do it? Maybe, as she would later write, she just wanted to "have a good laugh together." But she also admitted to being motivated by the "flicker of another thought: that my husband might take the letter seriously. And in that case I was curious about how he would react to an anonymous letter—would he show it to me or throw it into the wastebasket?" In other words, she was simply testing him. Even in this most placid period in their life, when things were going well and Anna had no reason to doubt his love, she was nevertheless pricked by insecurity. Perhaps the ghost of her husband's dalliance with Polina Suslova still haunted her; perhaps it was just that he was being inattentive to her, as a few of his letters from Bad Ems suggest. Or perhaps it is just human nature to wonder about one's spouse, to feel deep down that tiny sting of uncertainty, no matter how strong a marriage is.

Anna had always exhibited a mischievous streak, all the way back to her days at the Mariinskaya, where she was known to be a clever prankster. Yet what may have begun for her as a chummy literary prank on her husband had unexpectedly morphed into something darker, reflecting a complicated psychology reminiscent of many of Dostoyevsky's own fictional characters, to say nothing of the writer himself. It was a clumsy act of rebellion, but then, the more successful she became, the more Anna was unable to resist the all-too-human urge to do the *wrong* thing. It was a chance to prick the comfortable, well-ordered world she had worked so hard to build—a world full of that very German bourgeois self-satisfaction that she and her husband had always disliked. Well on her way to building her family's own metaphorical Crystal Palace, for a moment she seemed to follow another urge—a compulsion embodied by Dostoyevsky's underground man, who gleefully confesses, "Whether it is good or bad, sometimes it is very pleasant to smash things, too."

Anna's strange act of rebellion also recalled the complex inner workings of her husband's infernal women, from Polina in *The Gambler* to Grushenka in *The Brothers Karamazov*—yearnings and complexities not unfamiliar to Anna herself. After all, this was the same woman who had felt a seductive frisson of impending disaster as she confronted that thunderstorm in the hills near Dresden, and who four years later had sent her husband back to the roulette tables with their last money. Now, in a much more settled period in their lives, she was indulging in a moment of wildness—just as she had by secretly entering Baden-Baden's Kurhaus, in an attempt to best her husband symbolically on his home turf. It was another moment when Anna's sheer audacity and slyness, not to mention her complex psychology, were on full display. These traits, along with her fortitude, patience, and empathy, were surely part of what Dostoyevsky had always found attractive about her, just as they were essential to the long-term success of their partnership.

Anna vowed never again to play on her husband's jealousy. But she wasn't quite done with him yet, as evidenced by the provocative postscript to a letter she sent to Fyodor during his cure in Bad Ems a few months later, in July 1876. "My dear: Whom did I meet in the last day? Him!!! Guess who and be jealous! Details in the next letter." It was enough to plunge Dostoyevsky back into paroxysms of terror: "I'm afraid, really afraid," he told her. "You write that you love me and miss me, but after all, you wrote that before your encounter with him, before the postscript.... I repeat: everything is in your power.... I fall to my knees before you and kiss both your feet endlessly. I imagine that all the time and enjoy it. Anka, my god, don't treat me badly."

Such frenzied, despondent professions of love are vintage Dostoyevsky. They bring to mind Alexei's tortured confessions to Polina in *The Gambler*, in which the character plunges from narcissistic grandiosity to self-abasement and back within a single breath. "To be enslaved to you is a pleasure," Alexei told Polina. "There is a pleasure in the ultimate degree of humiliation and insignificance! . . . Remember, two days ago on the Schlangenberg you challenged me, and I whispered: say the word and I'll jump into this abyss. If you had said the word then, I would have jumped."

But Polina never did make Alexei jump, and Anna stopped tormenting her husband. In her next letter, as promised, she revealed the identity of that mysterious *he*: her former fiancé, whom she'd run into at the shopping arcade. He had come by to visit her thereafter, she told her husband, and Anna—sensing that the man was still in love with her—somewhat gloatingly showed off to him "the full extent of our [publishing] operation." Then, in a not entirely sincere gesture of concern, she advised her former beau to get married, whereupon he shook his head and asked her to please not lecture him on such matters. He left, and that was it.

As far as Anna was concerned, then, things were settled—not only with her former fiancé but with her husband as well. With this last little stunt, she seems to have scratched her itch to play psychological games with him. Dostoyevsky couched his disapproval in his usual showers of abject devotion: "I kiss you ceaselessly and my love for you grows with every passing day," he wrote from Bad Ems. "Don't imagine that it's jealousy making my love grow and that to torment a person with jealousy in such a case is sometimes useful."

To Anna, however, those little tests *were* useful, and not a little perversely enjoyable, too. Her games had given her a chance to learn things about herself, her power, and perhaps most important, the power of their love. "The fact that you're jealous is very dear to me," she told him. "He's jealous, it means he loves me. Right?"

BY 1877, *Diary of a Writer* was coming out at a steady clip, with a solid base of least seven thousand subscribers. Although no exact figures seem to have survived, we know that their income from the publication was enough to cover the family's annual living expenses of around 3,500 rubles. The typically frugal Anna even felt comfortable accepting her husband's gift of a custom-made fox coat from one of Moscow's high-end fur shops, an indulgence that may have cost as much as five hundred rubles. Thanks to Dostoyevsky's genius for self-promotion and Anna's as a publisher, the magazine was both a commercial and a critical success. And yet, Anna recalled, "the burdens of putting out a monthly journal were growing . . . namely, mailing out the issues, keeping records of subscribers' accounts, correspondence with readers, and so forth." At the same time she was trying to manage her family as well—a heroic juggling act that both awed Dostoyevsky and filled him with a sense of guilt. "You yourself don't suspect your own capabilities," he told her:

> You're managing not only an entire home, not only my affairs, but you're leading all of us, capricious and troublesome as we are, beginning with me right down to Lyosha [their one-year-old son, Alyosha]. . . . You don't sleep at night, running the book sales and the headquarters of *Diary of a Writer*. Make you a queen and give you an entire kingdom, and I swear to you, you'll rule it like no one else—so much intelligence, common sense, heart, and efficiency you've got.

The Dostoyevskys' winter and spring in Staraya Russa, with its quiet backstreets, charming parks, and crisp northern air, had been a welcome respite for Anna and her family, as was their summer with Anna's brother, Ivan, and his family at his estate in 1877. But as soon as they returned to Petersburg that August to begin work on the double summer issue of the *Diary*, their petty troubles began all over again: the bustle of city life, the daily cares, the nonstop visits from friends and colleagues. One visitor, an eccentric English fortune-teller named Mrs. Fields, both intrigued and distressed the Dostoyevskys one evening with two prophesies: that the novelist would achieve great fame, but that the family would face tragedy in the near future. As a believer in dreams and visions, Dostoyevsky took this prophesy more to heart than he admitted, which might explain why in the coming months he became increasingly obsessed with thoughts of mortality.

In December 1877, the writer began a notebook entry with the words "Memento—for the rest of my life," and went on to outline several projects he wished to undertake before he died. One of them, which would become his crowning achievement, *The Brothers Karamazov*, began to occupy so much of his mental energy that he announced to his *Diary* subscribers that he would be discontinuing the periodical for a while to focus on his creative work. Anna's office mailbox was flooded with letters expressing disappointment over the decision.

The death of Dostoyevsky's colleague and former publisher Nikolai Nekrasov in December 1877 only intensified Dostoyevsky's ruminations about mortality. Standing at Anna's side over Nekrasov's gravesite, amid the cold hush of the cemetery, the writer said, "When I die, Anya, bury me here or wherever, but mind, don't bury me in the writers' section of the Volkov Cemetery. I don't want to lie among my enemies—I suffered enough from them while I was alive!" Trying to lighten the mood, she assured him that he would have the last laugh, for *his* funeral would be as grand an affair as ever there was for a Russian artist. She would see to it that he was buried next to the poet Vasily Zhukovsky, whose work he adored, and that the Nevsky choir would sing beautifully during a mass presided over by at least one bishop, maybe two. "And you know what," she kept on musing out loud: "I'll arrange things so that not only a huge crowd of young people will follow your coffin, but all Petersburg—sixty thousand people—eighty thousand. And there will be three times more wreaths. See what a brilliant funeral I'm promising you? But only on one condition—that you live many, many years more, many, many years! Or else I'll be too miserable!"

But the family tragedy their English guest had foreseen a few months earlier would not be Dostoyevsky's. That story would begin to unfold, unexpectedly, early on May 16, 1878, as Alyosha was playing and laughing with his nurse. Suddenly, the two-year-old's beautiful oval face began to twitch. It was only a slight spasm, and the nurse took it for the kind of cramp children often get when they're teething, but Anna wasn't so sure. She called their regular children's doctor, who came at once, but he just wrote out a prescription and assured the Dostoyevskys that the spasms would soon pass. Despite his reassurances, Anna decided to visit Professor Uspensky, a well-known specialist in nervous diseases; he prescribed a sedative and promised he would come by as soon as he was able. He sent Anna home with a container of oxygen to help the little boy breathe in the meantime.

When she got home she found Alyosha completely unconscious, his small body convulsing periodically in more pronounced spasms than before. It was a strange kind of seizure; he was not in pain, she could tell, and wasn't crying out or groaning, but his spasms were unlike anything Anna had ever seen. Arriving at last, Professor Uspensky gently placed Alyosha onto the red felt-upholstered couch and examined him. "Don't cry, don't worry, it will be over soon," he reassured Anna, who was now kneeling next to Dostoyevsky by the couch. Uspensky then kneeled with him, and whispered something into Dostoyevsky's ear, but when Anna asked him what the doctor had said, her husband signaled for her not to speak. An hour later, when Alyosha's convulsions subsided and the little boy began to sleep, Anna was relieved, hopeful that this was the beginning of his recovery. But then, all at once, the child's breathing stopped and he was dead. What Professor Uspensky had whispered to Dostoyevsky, Anna later learned, was that Alyosha's death rattle had already begun.

Darkness fell upon the household. Anna Filosofova rushed over as soon as she heard the news, later describing the total sense of isolation, prostration, and helplessness of the entire family. Dostoyevsky spent the entire night on his knees weeping over his son's lifeless body, while Anna, grief-stricken and unable to focus on anything at all, made fumbling attempts to support him. The next day they took a carriage to Petersburg's Great Okhta Cemetery, the little coffin tucked in between Anna and her husband, the whole family weeping in cold silence. It was a radiant May day with the flowers in full bloom, the birds singing on the leafy branches of the old trees, as Alyosha was laid to rest next to Anna's father.

After a short service, where the litanies of the priest and melodies of the small choir were at one with the placid surroundings, the family slowly made its way to the burial ground. Tears ran down Dostoyevsky's cheeks as he supported his wife, whose own eyes remained fixed on the little coffin as it gradually disappeared beneath the earth. Exactly ten years before—that very week, in fact—on an equally glorious spring day in Geneva, Anna had watched the coffin carrying her three-month-old daughter Sonya lowered into the ground.

IMMEDIATELY AFTER THE FUNERAL, the Dostoyevskys returned to Staraya Russa. Anna managed to distract herself by focusing on her husband, whose grief was intensified by guilt over the fact that Alyosha had died of epilepsy, the terrible disease inherited from his father. Though Dostoyevsky remained outwardly calm and stoic, Anna knew that he was suppressing a profound sorrow, which she feared might have a fatal impact on his already shaky health.

In hopes of dispelling Dostoyevsky's depressive mood, she asked his friend, the philosopher Vladimir Solovyov, to accompany her husband on a long-dreamed-of trip to the Optina Pustyn Monastery. Many Russian writers before him had made this pilgrimage, finding solace among its humble and enlightened monks, and Anna was hoping the same might happen for her husband. In mid-June she sent him off—first to Moscow, where he would meet briefly with Katkov to finalize arrangements for *The Russian Messenger* to publish his new novel, *The Brothers Karamazov*, and then on to the monastery, where he would consult with the legendary confessor Father Ambrosius.

Remaining in Staraya Russa with Fedya and Lyuba, Anna was forced to bear her heartbreak alone. "This summer is the most melancholy I've ever spent," she wrote to Dostoyevsky's brother Nikolai, in July, when her husband was still away. "One keeps remembering our poor, dear Lyosha, and it is so sad, so painful, that he is already gone. I cannot wait for the fall on the off chance that during my running about I won't feel our loss so strongly."

Dostoyevsky returned from his trip later that month much more at peace, it seemed to Anna. He relayed to her the blessings Father Ambrosius had asked the writer to communicate to her, in words that would be immortalized in the chapter called "A Woman of Faith" from the first part of *The Brothers Karamazov*. In that chapter, a grieving peasant mother who has lost her son travels a great distance to a monastery to meet the famous monk Father Zosima, a character modeled on Father Ambrosius. The monk comforts the grieving woman:

> "And I will remember your little child in my prayers for the repose of the dead. What was his name?"
>
> "Alexei, dear father."

"A lovely name! After Alexei, the man of God?"

"Of God, dear father, of God. Alexei, the man of God."

"A great saint! I'll remember, mother, I'll remember, and I'll remember your sorrow in my prayers, and I'll remember your husband, too. Only it is a sin for you to desert him. Go to your husband and take care of him. Your little boy will look down and see that you've abandoned his father, and will weep for both of you: why, then, do you trouble his blessedness? He's alive, surely he's alive, for the soul lives forever, and though he's not at home, he is invisibly near you."

In real life, of course, it was the grieving father, not the mother, who'd sought spiritual comfort at a monastery. In reversing the roles of mother and father, Dostoyevsky seems to be expressing a lingering guilt that he had abandoned his wife in her grief; while his own sorrow may have rendered him unable to give her the support she needed, he managed at least to acknowledge and honor her suffering through his art.

In *Reminiscences*, Anna recounted how Alyosha's death affected her:

> I so lost my bearing, mourned and cried so much that I was unrecognizable. My customary cheerfulness vanished together with my normal flow of energy, which gave way to apathy. I grew indifferent to everything: the management of the household, our business affairs, and even my own children; and I gave myself over utterly to my memories of the last three years.

In the months after Alyosha's death, then, Anna wanted nothing more than to be present with her grief, an understandable reaction to the trauma she had just experienced. And yet she did not allow herself even this; instead, she followed the counsel of the fictional Father Zosima, returning to her husband, her family, and her work.

Upon returning to Petersburg in the fall of 1878, Anna sprang back into action. She arranged for the family to move from their former apartment, where they could no longer bear to live, to a new one, at No. 5

Kuznechny Lane. The stenographer in Anna needed to keep copying and transcribing, even as the publisher arranged for Dostoyevsky's work to reach the world. As his wife, she also knew how important it was to monitor her husband's emotional state, so essential to his creativity. Happily, the trip to Optina Pustyn Monastery had given Dostoyevsky precisely the spiritual rejuvenation he needed to resume work on *The Brothers Karamazov* once he returned to Petersburg. By December, the writer had completed not only the plan but 160 pages of the novel itself, enough for publication of the first installment in the January 1879 edition of *The Russian Messenger*.

THE NOVEL'S SUBJECT, parricide, was one that had long troubled and fascinated Dostoyevsky. For years he had been unable to get out of his mind the fellow convict he had met in Siberian prison camp who served a ten-year sentence for murdering his father before it was discovered that he was innocent. This gross miscarriage of justice, and the "deeply tragic story" of "the destruction of a still-young life by such a horrible accusation," would haunt Dostoyevsky for the next twenty years. In *The Brothers Karamazov* he brought it to life through the tale of the raging conflict between the old, lecherous Fyodor Karamazov and his eldest son, Dmitry, a passionate and explosive former army officer. At the beginning of the novel, Dmitry has returned to his provincial hometown to claim an inheritance he believes due him after the death of his mother, Fyodor's first wife. But the dissolute father refuses to pay up, preferring to use his son's inheritance to support his own debauched lifestyle. The resulting feud is further complicated by the fact that father and son lust after the same woman, the beautiful femme fatale Grushenka, for whom Dmitry has abandoned his fiancée, and to whom Fyodor is offering three thousand rubles if she will sleep with him.

Unlike Dostoyevsky's previous novels, which tended to focus on one main hero, *The Brothers Karamazov* was more about family and community than a single individual. It contained three major protagonists: the eldest, Dmitry Karamazov; the coldly cerebral, tortured middle brother,

Ivan; and the pious and humble youngest brother, Alyosha, a monk. At the novel's beginning, Alyosha is still in the monastery, under the tutelage of the famed elder Father Zosima. Dmitry is the son of Fyodor's first wife, while Ivan and Alyosha are the product of his second marriage; each of his children, after the death of their respective mothers, was abandoned by their father and sent away to live with a relative. There is also the bastard half brother, Smerdyakov, whom Fyodor had fathered with the mute village idiot, Stinking Lizaveta, in an act many considered to be rape. Smerdyakov, whose name derives from the Russian verb *smerdyet'*, "to stink," and who now serves as Fyodor's cook, is cloyingly servile, yet smoldering with resentment over his illegitimacy and lowly status.

In part one, the father, Dmitry, Ivan, and Alyosha meet at the monastery, where Alyosha hopes his beloved Father Zosima will be able to reconcile the dispute between his father and older brother. Only, in typical Dostoyevskian fashion, this moment of hoped-for reconciliation ends in outright scandal, with Fyodor acting the blasphemous buffoon before Zosima and his monks, Dmitry intimating that his father does not deserve to live, and Alyosha walking away in embarrassed shock over his family's unseemly behavior, his Christian faith having been tested to the limit.

The Brothers Karamazov explores the fundamental question that had long obsessed Dostoyevsky: how to achieve universal harmony in a society that has lost its spiritual moorings and its faith in God. It does so by using the conflict between Dmitry and his father as the dramatic backbone, while employing a number of subplots to survey a wide swath of contemporary Russian life, in much the same way Dostoyevsky's great rival, Leo Tolstoy, had done in his recent *Anna Karenina*. In this, the artistic pinnacle of Dostoyevsky's career—a novel that has rightly been placed alongside *The Divine Comedy*, *King Lear*, and *Faust* as one of the most profound artistic explorations of man's search for meaning—the author drew on the full range of his literary talent and technique, from frenzied monologues, to scandalous crowd scenes, to the contrapuntal play of roiling family drama with peaceful and contemplative monastery scenes.

The Brothers Karamazov offered readers Dostoyevsky's fullest account of the troubled state of their society, as well as perhaps his clearest positive vision of what social and spiritual reconciliation might actually look like. This would be nothing like the sort of society the radicals were pushing for, nor like the cold ratiocinations of modern scientific thinkers who rejected God and left no room for the inexplicable or spiritual dimensions of life—the very sort of thinking Ivan Karamazov is trapped in. Nor, of course, would the ideal society of the future be found in worship of the flesh-gods of money and sensual pleasure, embodied by Fyodor Karamazov and Dmitry before his transformation. Rather, Dostoyevsky's vision involved the simple lessons of spiritual courage and profound Christian faith modeled by Father Zosima, who passes them in turn to his protégé, Alyosha Karamazov.

In the novel's very first sentence, the author provocatively proclaims Alyosha Karamazov as the work's real hero. While he introduces Alyosha as a "strange man, even an odd one," Dostoyevsky also maintains that he "bears within himself the heart of the whole, while the other people of his epoch have all for some reason been torn away from it for a time by some kind of flooding wind." Amid the swirling chaos all around him, the strangely humble Alyosha Karamazov, with his deep commitment to his Christian faith and earnest struggles to live a life of active love, indeed represented for his creator the spiritual rock that would anchor a Russian society now flying off the rails and headed toward certain disaster.

Right away, readers were hooked—not so much by Dostoyevsky's message, which many found a bit quaint and even reactionary, but by the undeniable power of the story itself, with its philosophical and psychological undercurrents. Even those who adamantly rejected Dostoyevsky's social views eagerly awaited each new installment in *The Russian Messenger* to find out how this intense family drama would unfold.

Anna was thrilled with the book as well, though for very different reasons. Her husband, she knew, was now writing at the top of his form, communicating with great artistic force the deepest stirrings of his soul and yearnings for his people. The droves of appreciative letters he now received daily further confirmed for Anna the value of her efforts. So moved was she by these expressions of gratitude that she later included in

Reminiscences the text of a letter Dostoyevsky sent to a friend, describing how touched he was by the outpouring of love from the public. "These are authentic Russians," he added, "not people with the distorted outlook of the Petersburg intelligentsia, but with the genuine and right outlook of the Russian man, of whom there have proved to be incomparably more here in our country than I supposed two years ago."

Anna could clearly see, then, that her work mattered—not just to Dostoyevsky but to all of Russia. Through her successful publication of her husband's *Diary of a Writer*, as well as her assistance in getting *The Brothers Karamazov* down on paper, she was fulfilling her lifelong mission: supporting her husband's fiction career editorially, while disseminating his personal voice to the people who she believed needed it most. No matter how contradictory and often wrongheaded his ideas now seem, Anna viewed his message as one of reconciliation and resilience, a necessary inspiration for a Russian people in the throes of social and spiritual chaos and searching for a positive ideal to live by. And in those trying months following the death of her son, it was a message that Anna herself must have welcomed.

14.

At the Prophet's Side

I t was by now a familiar sight in Petersburg literary circles: thirty-four-year-old Anna Dostoyevskaya escorting her emphysemic husband up the stairs to a reading at the Municipal Credit Society or the Nobility Assembly Hall, stopping every few steps to lean on her arm as he caught his breath between spasms of violent coughing. She was carrying the book he would read from that evening, along with his cough medicines, an extra handkerchief, and a plaid scarf to wrap around his throat before they went back out into the cold air. Seeing her loaded down this way, Dostoyevsky would jokingly call her his "faithful armor-bearer."

One evening, as the couple arrived at the ballroom of the Nobility Assembly Hall, where the other speakers were already assembled in the readers' room, the men arose to greet Dostoyevsky and kiss his wife's hand, as was the custom. One of the guests, however—the distinguished novelist Dmitry Grigorovich, a longtime friend and former classmate of Dostoyevsky's—lingered a bit too long over Anna's proffered hand. Sitting down with Anna, Dostoyevsky glared at her furiously and said, "Go to him!"

"Who is 'him'?" she replied, surprised.

"You don't *understand*?"

"No, I do not. To whom am I supposed to go?" she said, laughing.

"To the one who kissed your hand *passionately* just now!"

Since nearly every man in the room had kissed her hand, Anna had no idea who the guilty party was. Fearing a domestic scene, she said quietly: "All right, Fyodor Mikhailovich, I see you're out of sorts and don't want to talk to me. So I'd better go into the hall and find my seat: Good-bye!" And she left.

Five minutes later, a host approached to tell Anna that her husband was asking for her. She went immediately to the readers' room.

"You couldn't restrain yourself?" Dostoyevsky griped, as antagonistic as before. "You came to have another look at him?"

"Oh, yes, of course," she laughed, trying to shrug off her annoyance, "and also at you. Do you need anything?"

"No, I don't."

"But didn't you call for me?"

"Nothing of the sort! Don't go imagining things!"

"Well then, if you didn't call for me, good-bye, I'm leaving." And she did.

At the first intermission, an usher approached Anna with an insistent summons from her husband. She hurried into the readers' room and saw his embarrassed face as he said in a barely audible voice, "Forgive me, An-yechka, and give me your hand for luck: I'm going on stage now to read!"

Scenes of this sort recurred at almost every literary evening. Dosto-yevsky would invariably send someone from the readers' room to find out where Anna was sitting and whom she was talking to, or crack open the auditorium door himself to look for her in the audience. The first thing he would do upon approaching the podium would be to scan the crowd in search of his wife, who unfailingly would be in her usual seat, along the right-hand wall, a few steps from the first row; to help him find her, she would conspicuously wipe her brow with a large white handkerchief or rise partially from her seat. Only once he'd spotted his wife would Dosto-yevsky begin his reading.

Event managers and audience members alike noticed all this peering and questioning, and they began to talk. Anna found it all rather grating. "You know, my dear," she told Dostoyevsky one evening on their way to a reading, "if you keep peering at me and searching for me in the audience today, I give you my word that I'll simply get up from my seat and walk past the stage and out of the hall."

"And I'll jump off the stage and run after you to find out what happened to you and where you went," he responded in complete seriousness. Realizing that his warning was sincere, Anna bit back her anger and kept silent. She had long since resolved to do what was necessary to be by his side, especially during this final summit of his career—and, truth be told, Anna, too, relished "those tumultuous ovations he was constantly being given by admiring Petersburg audiences."

And what a glorious summit it was turning out to be. *The Brothers Karamazov*, which came out in installments throughout 1879, was met with nearly universal acclaim, the first time a work by Dostoyevsky had enjoyed such an enthusiastic response since the appearance of *Crime and Punishment* thirteen years before. Only now that enthusiasm translated into commercial success, too, for *The Russian Messenger* was paying Dostoyevsky at nearly double his previous rate, and Anna was able to solicit opportunities to leverage her husband's escalating fame. This was all the more important, she knew, because Dostoyevsky's worsening emphysema was making it increasingly difficult for him to write, and his work was still their crucial source of income.

Soon she had found another. "After long reflection and questioning of experienced people," Anna recalled, "I decided to start a book service for out-of-towners, particularly since the several works I had already published had given me some familiarity with the book trade." Through her publishing business, Anna had learned that the bookselling business in rural Russia was extremely slow, and served by very few shops. And so, on January 1, 1880, she founded a new venture, to be called F. M. Dostoyevsky: Bookseller (to the Provinces Only).

One of the first successful businesses of its kind in Russia, the new company started off selling Dostoyevsky's work exclusively in the nation's outer reaches; later, she would expand its offerings to include "any books available for sale," regardless of author. In time, the business would also sell out-of-town customers subscriptions to newspapers and journals.

The arrangement had many advantages: the business could be conducted entirely from home, where Anna could look after her husband, the children, and the housekeeping. Since it was not a publishing venture but a distribution business, it also required very little overhead: she needed only to purchase a trade license and hire an errand boy, who bought books from local stores, printers, or secondhand booksellers, packed them, and took them to the post office. Because the quantity of each title Anna ordered was small, suppliers were unable to give her much of a discount; instead, she up-priced the books significantly for the long-distance market, resulting in "a very profitable enterprise." She also rented out a small flat near their apartment on Kuznechny Lane that served as a corner storefront for their book business.

There were other key business decisions to be made. They would have to advertise in newspapers—an expensive proposition, so Anna negotiated a deal to share ad costs with the publisher of another journal. As for her customer base, she was betting that the previous subscribers to *Diary of a Writer* for 1876 and 1877, "accustomed to its reliable editorial management, would also have confidence in a service operated by the same publisher." And she was right: former *Diary* subscribers made up a significant portion of her initial clientele. Anna minimized her financial risk by requiring customers to pay for their orders up front. "There were orders from educational institutions and *zemstvo** storehouses asking that books be sent to them on credit," she recalled. "But since we would need to lay out large sums of money to acquire these books, we had to decline such orders despite their potential profits."

In its first year, Anna's new business made a profit of around eight hundred rubles—not a huge windfall, but handsome enough to augment the family's income, which consisted mostly of the remainder of the payments for *The Brothers Karamazov*. Dostoyevsky made a total of about fourteen thousand rubles—nearly \$180,000 in today's money—on the novel, paid out between 1879 and 1880.

---

*A *zemstvo* was an elective district council in pre-revolutionary Russia.

Fifty years later, Anna's errand boy, a sixteen-year-old village peasant by the name of Pyotr Kuznetsov, wrote a colorful reminiscence of life in the Dostoyevsky home. After Fedya and Lyuba were put to bed at nine p.m., he recalled, the writer and his wife would set to work in the study, Dostoyevsky walking around and dictating the novel while Anna sat at the table writing furiously. The author enjoyed large, elaborate meals and had a particular fondness for expensive hen and other wild game, but "Anna Grigoryevna was very greedy, and from time to time her stinginess upset him." Dostoyevsky would buy himself expensive things, "and from this came an entire battle. F[yodor] M[ikhailovich] started screaming and stomping his feet that 'You think there's never enough, you're always imagining that you're a beggar.'" He "was not so tender with his wife and always firmly stood his ground," Kuznetsov wrote, while "Anna Grigoryevna would sometimes upset him with trifles, i.e., petty things, and he would go flying off the handle. . . . And she would always give in to him."

This, at any rate, is how Kuznetsov interpreted what his teenage eyes had seen fifty years before. Much, however, was hidden from his gaze. It is telling, for instance, that he called his memoir *At Work for Dostoyevsky*, when it was Anna who ran the business, advertised the position of errand boy, and hired him. Kuznetsov's perspective was no doubt shaped by the fact that Dostoyevsky was constantly sending the boy on minor errands unrelated to the publishing enterprise. He asked Kuznetsov to secretly mail a monthly gift of a hundred rubles to an old literary friend who'd come on hard times, for instance, commanding him not to tell Anna anything about it. Or the novelist would show up in the evening at Kuznetsov's city apartment unannounced, sit down at the kitchen table with the errand boy and his landlord, and press the landlord for details on the boy's living habits. Upon learning during one such visit that Kuznetsov gambled at cards, Dostoyevsky sternly chided the lad, "You're not to play cards any more. You will read books." Whereupon the writer started assigning Kuznetsov reading materials, including some of his own novels. This had the unintended consequence of lighting a literary fire inside the young man and inspiring him to one day start a successful Petersburg bookselling business of his own.

———

IT MAY HAVE FELT natural to Dostoyevsky to offer himself as a mentor to the young Kuznetsov, for he was now being asked to play the same role by countless Russians from every walk of life. Once the butt of literary jokes, the writer had become the toast of the town, receiving honorary invitations to literary evenings, balls, concerts, and social gatherings. During such visits, according to a family friend, he would often sit silently in a drawing room, his head bowed, lips twisted into a crooked half-smile, with Anna standing by to extract him from an unpleasant conversation with some literary enemy or the embrace of an overly enthusiastic acolyte. To spare him the burden of attending such events alone, Anna would often complain that she was bored at home. Dostoyevsky was overjoyed when she ordered an elegant black silk dress and two colored headdresses for their evenings out.

At the many benefits and other events he was invited to address, this "emaciated, unprepossessing, elderly man, with his piercing gaze fixed somewhere away on the distance and burning with mystic fire," hypnotized his audience with his spellbinding presentations. He was capable of transporting them to realms of consciousness through his spoken words no less rarefied than the ones he carried readers to in his novels.

In these years Dostoyevsky took on something of a prophetic stature in the popular imagination, with readers from across Russia sending him letters in search of spiritual advice. This new role was due to both the familiar story of his imprisonment and the ongoing publication of his masterwork, *The Brothers Karamazov*, in which he managed to distill a lifetime of ideas about man's tormented search for God, the irrationality of life, the tragedy of "accidental families," and the innate genius of the Russian people. His status as an oracle was such that audiences sometimes asked him to recite Pushkin's famous poem "The Prophet," swearing that Dostoyevsky himself must have composed those words.

As the story of *The Brothers Karamazov* progressed with each new serial installment, a sense of impending crime looms over Dmitry as his murderous rage toward his father becomes public knowledge. Determined to marry Grushenka, Dmitry becomes embroiled in a bitter struggle with his father for her heart—a struggle further complicated when Grushenka, "flying to her new life," goes off to meet "her former seducer," a Polish officer, upending the amorous designs of both Karamazovs, father and son. On the verge of suicide, Dmitry makes one final desperate dash after Grushenka and finds her in a shady tavern on the edge of town.

There, with Grushenka and other disreputable guests, he engages in an evening of ribaldry, drunkenness, and card-playing—"almost an orgy, a feast of feasts"—when suddenly Grushenka declares her love for Dmitry. "I'll be faithful, I'll be your slave," she swears to him. Intoxicated by her unexpected declaration (and the general debauchery), Dmitry's mind floods with sweet hopes for a new beginning. As he relaxes in Grushenka's arms, in the stink of the tavern, a small entourage barges into the tavern to interrupt his reverie. "Retired Lieutenant Karamazov, sir," says one of them, an attorney, "it is my duty to inform you that you are charged with the murder of your father, Fyodor Pavlovich Karamazov, which took place this night."

Aware of the mountain of potential evidence that might be used against him, Dmitry can already foresee his tragic fate. He is known to be a violent brawler constantly in need of money—the apparent motive for the crime—and his quarrels with his father, often including an express wish to see him dead, are a secret to no one. He rightly fears that the evidence would lead any jury to convict him of parricide. And yet he is not the one who committed the murder.

The story, the suspense, the profound moral conflict—readers couldn't put it down. And Dostoyevsky knew it. Buoyed by the public response, he kept writing at a feverish pitch, spinning his complex plot in ever new and unexpected directions, holding readers in his spell. Nor was it just the family drama–cum–murder mystery that so bewitched them. Readers sensed something else in the novel, too, an undercurrent that resonated deeply with the events of their times. The journeys of these characters— the tormented searchings of the Nihilist-atheist Ivan, the Christian piety of his younger brother, Alyosha, the murderous rage of Dmitry—were thinly veiled metaphors for the sociopolitical conflicts then raging throughout Russian society.

In particular, this story of parricide captivated a public that was gripped by shockingly regular reports about assassination attempts on their "Tsar-Father," whom many now considered no less corrupt than old Karamazov himself. One such attempt came on February 2, 1880, just before a diplomatic dinner to celebrate the twenty-fifth anniversary of the reign of Alexander II, when a bomb exploded in the Winter Palace just under the tsar's dining room. Ten soldiers were killed on guard duty and fifty-six others wounded. The assassination attempt was orchestrated by Narodnaya Volya, or the People's Will, an influential band of populist radicals who had orchestrated a number of similar assassination attempts in recent months—including some that succeeded in killing members of the extended royal family. Though he survived the February 2 attempt, the tsar immediately placed the country under martial law.

Given the cultural urgency of *The Brothers Karamazov*, all Dostoyevsky's hopes—literary and financial—were now pinned on the novel. Yet he worried that he might not be able to finish it. The previous summer, his doctor in Bad Ems had discovered that his worsening emphysema had caused his lung to become displaced, a shift that had also happened to his heart a few years earlier. "I can't not pay attention to the financial side of things," Dostoyevsky admitted in a letter to a friend. "After all, I'm a sick man, and I have a family. What will I leave them with? I could die any minute, and therefore, as long as I am alive, I must think about what fate will provide them with."

Anna was having similar thoughts. Reading his tortured letters from Bad Ems, full of complaints about his health and the obtuse Germans, she feared that her husband's riled nerves could fall to pieces at any moment. His loneliness was unbearable. "I keep thinking about my own death (I think about it seriously here), my darling, and about what I'll leave you and the children with. Everyone thinks that we have money, but we have nothing." He was worried not just about money but about his legacy: "I have *The Karamazovs* on my back now. I need to do a good job of finishing it, polish it like a jeweler, but this thing is a difficult and risky one; it will take a lot of energy. But it's also a fateful thing: it has to secure my name, otherwise there won't be any hope."

He dreamed of building a nest egg, buying an estate of his own. (Their vacation home in Staraya Russa was still owned by Anna's brother, Ivan, who had purchased it for the Dostoyevskys' use until they were able to afford it themselves.) "Would you believe I've gone nearly mad about that. I tremble for the children and their fate." Nor were these fears entirely unwarranted: although Anna's deft financial management had finally enabled him to pay off most of his long-standing debts, the family was far from affluent. What with constant business trips, invitations to literary evenings, and two growing children, they could not seem to amass any savings. Their only reserve was five thousand rubles still being held by *The Russian Messenger* for work Dostoyevsky had already completed on *The Brothers Karamazov*.

Dostoyevsky was little help in this regard, as a family friend wrote in her diary in October 1880. "Her husband is a curious fellow, judging from her words," this friend observed, relating a conversation she'd had with Anna:

> She does not sleep at night, thinking over ways to provide for the children, works like a convict, denies herself everything, never even taking a carriage to go anywhere. And he—to say nothing of the fact that he supports his brother and stepson [Pasha]—still concerns himself with the first person he meets, no matter what that person requests. . . . "That's how we live," [Anna] continued. "And if something happens, where do we turn? How will we live? We are poor! No pension will be coming our way."

The eminent Dostoyevsky scholar Joseph Frank, in the final installment of his seminal five-volume intellectual biography of Dostoyevsky, misquotes the first sentence ("She does not sleep at night"), replacing "She" with "He"—in Russian, as in English, there is only a one-letter difference between the two pronouns—suggesting that it was Dostoyevsky who couldn't sleep for worry over how to provide for the family. This honest mistake speaks volumes about the implicit bias readers and scholars alike have brought to their understanding of the Dostoyevskys' relationship. Indeed, Anna's presence can be felt everywhere in these final years of Dostoyevsky's life—in his writings, in his speeches, in the very fact of his physical survival—and yet, standing quietly in the shade of the giant, she is often erased from the historical record.

IN THE HIGHLY CHARGED ENVIRONMENT of the spring of 1880, after the attempt on the tsar's life, Dostoyevsky was invited to speak at the unveiling of a monument to Alexander Pushkin in Moscow. This was to be a major cultural event celebrating the great poet, often referred to as the father of modern Russian literature. Given the circumstances, this literary event—like many others in Russia—soon shaped up as an ideological battleground over the true significance of Pushkin's legacy in light of the current political moment. *Who are we? What is our destiny as a nation? How can Pushkin help us transcend our current morass?* These were the questions that dominated those days of terror, martial law, and spiritual disarray. And the audience at the Pushkin event would look to the two great literary lights of the time, Dostoyevsky and his longtime nemesis, Ivan Turgenev, for answers. (The third great voice of the age, of course, was Leo Tolstoy, but he declined the invitation, burdened by a spiritual crisis of his own, and in any event repelled by literary politics and public celebrations of all stripes.)

For Anna, attending these festivities with her husband would have been the proudest moment of her life—but she had to miss them. Though she tried to work out a scenario that would allow it, the cost of transporting their family of four from Staraya Russa to Moscow was just too high. She decided to stay behind with Fedya and Lyuba, sending her husband off to make the appearance on his own.

Her immense loss, however, is our gain, for during the trip Dostoyevsky wrote to her every day, sometimes twice a day. He recounted in detail the daily activities, festive dinners and toasts, the impromptu readings, the behind-the-scenes politics, the battles and backstabbing between the radicals and the conservatives. In particular, he kept a running narration of the mounting tensions between himself and his literary enemies, culminating in a great showdown between Turgenev and Dostoyevsky, with the two writers slated to take the stage to deliver their highly anticipated speeches on successive days.

Anna followed the unfolding drama with her heart in her throat, but her own letters in response, while full of genuine support, were also conspicuously restrained, shielding her husband once again from the burden of her emotional distress. But she missed him terribly—more so as the day of the unveiling kept getting postponed—and finally she opened up to him. "I dream about you in a very seductive way, and in the morning I think about how I wish you'd come soon," she admitted in one letter. "In general, my dear, I notice a certain coldness toward me in your letters," she wrote in another, echoing a common sentiment in Dostoyevsky's letters to her. "But enough about feelings, otherwise you'll get angry," she said. The frequent postponements upset her, but she urged him to stay, "otherwise it will be awkward if you're not present."

What Anna didn't share with her husband was that she was having nightmares about the dangers of all this nervous excitement to his health. In her mind, she concocted dreadful scenarios: That the stress could trigger a seizure, even a double seizure. That in his distress he would wander the hotel lobby looking for her, where he would surely be taken for a lunatic. That the spectacle would lead to mockery throughout Moscow. That no one there would come to his aid, which in turn would push him to undertake some desperate action. Grim detail upon detail piled up in Anna's imagination. At length she became so convinced by her own dark imaginings that she planned out an entire trip to Moscow, where she would watch over her husband from a distance, completely incognito. (She abandoned the plan only after realizing that the mere fact that she'd left the children behind might cause him to have a seizure.) For days this torment continued, only partially lifting after she finally arranged to have her friends in Moscow watch over her husband and telegraph her at once in the event of any distress.

As for Dostoyevsky, the Pushkin festivities were the crowning event of his career—of this he was certain—but he missed his family, and his money was running out, and he began to consider going home rather than waiting indefinitely for the unveiling and his speech. He pleaded with the event organizers that he needed to get back to work on his novel. Some of the organizers even proposed sending a mission to *The Russian Messenger* offices to demand that Mikhail Katkov revise his publication schedule to accommodate them. (These same supporters also considered wiring Anna to beg her further patience.) Dostoyevsky was all but ready to leave when he stopped himself: "I have fought for this my whole life, and I can't flee the field of battle now," he wrote Anna. As much as it pained them both, she exhorted him to stay.

The public showdown between Turgenev, an avowed Westernizer, and Dostoyevsky, the committed Slavophile, had been long in coming. Two years before, the writers had met backstage at an event where they'd been invited to present their radically different views of Russia. As far as we know, it was their first encounter in thirteen years, since their altercation in Baden-Baden, and according to one bystander Dostoyevsky refused to shake his rival's extended hand. A week later they met again, at another public event. As Turgenev was basking in an ovation, Dostoyevsky rushed onto the stage and shouted, "Tell me now, what is your ideal? Speak!" Dostoyevsky had never eased his animus toward the wealthier writer, who had spent the better part of two decades living abroad—further proof that he did not really love his homeland or even know her.

At last, the time arrived. The speech Dostoyevsky had prepared was a mesmerizing tribute to his literary forebear, hailing Pushkin as a "visionary" and a "prophet"—a fitting message from a writer whom many considered the new Prophet of the Russian people.

Turgenev had spoken the day before, but his much-awaited speech had been a failure, leaving the audience restless and dissatisfied. Turgenev, Dostoyevsky wrote to Anna immediately after the speech, "had denigrated Pushkin, denying him the title of national poet." His address, with its halting praise of Pushkin and Russian culture, felt tepid to an anxious crowd eager for affirmation. And that is precisely what Dostoyevsky was prepared to deliver.

Those present that day described the effect of Dostoyevsky's speech in terms that evoke a religious revival meeting. As one critic recalled: "When his turn came he as quietly as a mouse stepped up to the speaker's stand, and not five minutes had elapsed before everyone without exception present in the assemblage, all hearts, all thoughts, all souls, were in his power."

The message of Dostoyevsky's speech was one that everyone in his audience was hungry to hear: in Pushkin lay the solution not just to Russia's current problems, but to the world's. Pushkin's genius, he said, resided in his ability to "infuse himself fully within another nationality"—the model of that endlessly empathic Russian soul that will lead his country, and the world, away from the brink of disaster. It was Russia, Dostoyevsky insisted, that would "bring an ultimate reconciliation to Europe's contradictions, to indicate that the solution to Europe's anguish is to be found in the panhuman and all-unifying Russian soul, to enfold all our brethren within it with brotherly love, and at last, perhaps, to utter the ultimate word of great, general harmony, ultimate brotherly accord of all tribes through the law of Christ's Gospel!"

It was a message Russians needed now more than ever, he went on, as they had become as spiritually lost as Pushkin's wanderer, Aleko, from *The Gypsies*, or the superficial dandy Eugene Onegin. The truth every Russian sought was not "somewhere outside him, perhaps in some other land, in Europe, for instance, with her stable historical order and well-established social and civic life." If it was truth Russians were after, moreover, they would find it not in Pushkin's male characters but rather in his *women*—in characters like Tatyana Larina, the backwater country girl whose love Eugene Onegin cruelly rejects early in the novel. Only later, when he proposes to her after she has become the wife of an admired general, Tatyana flatly rejects him, saying: "But I'm now another's wife, / And I'll be faithful all my life." Pushkin's words expressed the ultimate power of the Russian woman, who chooses moral commitment over personal contentment.

Dostoyevsky's audience that day would have known that he was taking aim at Vissarion Belinsky's earlier, influential reading of Tatyana as weak-willed, because she allowed herself to be given in marriage by her mother rather than making her own free choice to marry for love. No enlightened woman, Belinsky maintained, would have accepted such a relationship. Dostoyevsky argued the exact opposite: perhaps, he said, "a southern woman or some Frenchwoman" (a possible allusion to Turgenev's longtime affair with Pauline García-Viardot) would have left her husband and gone with Eugene, but the *Russian* woman would always refuse to build her happiness on the unhappiness of others. A "pure Russian soul" like Tatyana would think, "Let no one, not even this old man, ever learn of my sacrifice and appreciate it; but I do not want to be happy after having destroyed another!" Tatyana therefore "is a positive, not a negative character. . . . She is the apotheosis of Russian womanhood."

As he was speaking, Dostoyevsky's listeners surely would have remembered his own Sonya in *Crime and Punishment*, who follows the repentant Raskolnikov to Siberian prison camp, or the real-life Decembrist wives the writer often praised for following their husbands to Siberia. In such acts of moral courage, Dostoyevsky argued, lay a deeper expression of love than anything Belinsky and his fellow Westernizers could ever have envisioned. This was a profoundly Russian sort of love, he said, the sort that Western-influenced Eugene Onegin was incapable of fathoming: Tatyana's "noble instinct alone tells her where and in what the truth is to be found, and this is expressed in the poem's ending," when she ultimately rejects Onegin. "Pushkin might have done better to name his poem after Tatyana rather than Onegin, for she is unquestionably the protagonist."

Another witness that day, the son of an assistant editor at *The Russian Messenger*, described the dramatic close of Dostoyevsky's address. As he recalled, the writer pronounced his final words

> in a sort of inspired whisper, lowered his head, and in a deathly silence, began rather hurriedly to leave the auditorium. The hall seemed to hold its breath, as if expecting something more. Suddenly from the back rows rang out a hysterical shriek, "You

have solved it!" [the secret of Pushkin, of Russia's national genius], which was taken up by several feminine voices in chorus. The entire auditorium began to stir.

The impact of the speech was overwhelming. When Dostoyevsky finished, he was answered by applause that lasted half an hour. Women fell before him and kissed his feet; some actually passed out in front of him. Enemies embraced and wept in one another's arms, telling Dostoyevsky, "It's you who reconciled us, you, our saint, our prophet!" One fellow novelist ran up to the podium and declared to the audience that what they had just witnessed was "not just a speech, but a historic event!" At one point during the speech even Turgenev was so moved that he blew Dostoyevsky a kiss from the audience.

After a chant of "Prophet! Prophet!" there was a "storm of applause, some sort of rumbling, stamping, feminine screeches. I do not think that the walls of the Hall of the Moscow Nobility either before or since had ever resounded with such a tempest of ecstasy."

Dostoyevsky's own response to what he had achieved was equally ecstatic. In the letter he wrote Anna a few hours later, we hear the voice of a gambler who hit the jackpot on his very last ruble: "No, Anya, no, you can never conceive of and imagine the effect that it produced! What are my Petersburg successes! Nothing, *zero*, compared to this!" He described how he "read loudly, with fire," and was "stopped by thunderous applause on absolutely every page, and sometimes even at every sentence." His remarks about Tatyana were "received with enthusiasm," he told his wife, but when he reached his climax, hailing "the *universal unity* of people, the hall was as though in hysteria." Dostoyevsky "rushed to the wings to escape, but everyone from the hall burst in there, and mainly women. They kissed my hands, tormented me. Students came running in. One of them, in tears, fell to the floor before me in hysteria and lost consciousness. A complete, absolutely complete victory!"

Anna read and reread the letter, beaming. Russia had finally discovered what she had known all along: this artist, who had once lifted her youthful heart to great spiritual heights, was now capable of doing the same for an entire nation. The wager for which she had sacrificed so much, over the past fourteen years, had paid off at last.

Anna would look back on her absence that day as "the greatest deprivation of my life." And yet she *had* been there with him on that podium. There can be little doubt that Dostoyevsky was thinking of his wife, if only subconsciously, when he offered his striking interpretation of Pushkin's most famous heroine. It was Anna who had followed him to hell and back, making countless excruciating career- and lifesaving decisions along the way. An integral part of his own creative trajectory and life journey, the idea of Anna flowed so deeply through Dostoyevsky's artistic blood by this point that he would have found it difficult to tell where she ended and he began. Not only had she made Dostoyevsky's creations possible; in a way, Anna *was* the ideal behind his creations. She was the living embodiment of the principles of Russian courage, moral integrity, and active love that had become central to his worldview, that he celebrated in his Pushkin speech—which would be remembered as one of the greatest in Russian literary history.

MEANWHILE, BACK AT HOME, Anna was laboring behind the scenes. Dostoyevsky's string of high-profile successes offered another opportunity to reach an even larger audience, and the couple decided to resume publication of *Diary of a Writer* after a two-and-a-half-year hiatus. They got to work preparing a single issue for the year, to feature his Pushkin speech in its entirety along with Dostoyevsky's reply to one of his fiercest critics. That issue came out in August, and to maximize sales Anna made a business trip to Petersburg, where in a matter of three days she succeeded in selling six thousand copies of the *Diary*—so many, in fact, that she had to print a second edition of the issue, and by autumn she'd managed to sell out that one, too.

Part four of *The Brothers Karamazov*—the final 320 pages—still had to be written to meet Anna's goal of publishing the novel as a stand-alone book by the end of the year. Dostoyevsky accomplished this tall order, and Anna brought out the novel in December in a print run of three thousand copies, half of which sold out within a matter of days.

With the lion's share of the novel so well received, Dostoyevsky might well have quit while he was ahead and brought his magisterial book to an early close. But the artist in him needed to keep testing the limits of his creative power, the gambler doubling down in the midst of a massive literary winning streak. He wrote on at full career, with a confidence in his artistic ability and control over his ever-deepening narrative that had often eluded him.

Dmitry Karamazov is found guilty and sentenced to twenty years of penal servitude, a bitter fate that he nonetheless embraces as a kind of atonement for a crime he never committed but knows he would and could have. This guilt-ridden realization marks the true beginning of his spiritual regeneration, as he internalizes one of the novel's deepest messages. As Father Zosima exhorts his followers:

> ... make yourself responsible for all the sins of men. For indeed it is so, my friend, and the moment you make yourself sincerely responsible for everything and everyone, you will see at once that it is really so, that it is you who are guilty on behalf of all and for all. Whereas by shifting your own laziness and powerlessness onto others, you will end by sharing in Satan's pride and murmuring against God.

Which is precisely the path taken by the actual murderer, who turns out to be the bastard son, Smerdyakov. Despite having killed the old man—whether out of deep-seated resentment or for the sheer evil thrill, Dostoyevsky never makes clear—Smerdyakov shifts the blame for Fyodor's death onto Ivan Karamazov. Smerdyakov tells Ivan that the latter's Nihilist doctrine that "everything is permitted" had inflamed his impressionable heart and inspired him to action. "The chief murderer is you alone, sir," he says to Ivan, "and I'm just not the real chief one, though I did kill him. It's you who are the most lawful murderer!" On the eve of Dmitry's trial, Smerdyakov hangs himself, while Ivan, excruciatingly aware

now of his own guilt in the murder of his father, succumbs to "brain fever." He remains in a state of crisis, unable to reconcile his former Nihilist
ideas and rebellion against God with this latest upheaval of his moral conscience.

Such, then, is the tragic fate of the Karamazov brothers—and, with it,
Dostoyevsky's harsh judgment on his "progressive" times, including the
recently imported European legal system that came to symbolize them.
Among other things, *The Brothers Karamazov* was the writer's bid to
demonstrate that this seemingly well-oiled legal machine was fundamentally problematic, ultimately incapable of pronouncing valid judgment on
matters of human guilt and innocence. The prosecution's rational arguments proving Dmitry's culpability may have won the day, but justice was
not served. As the novel shows, the drama behind the elder Karamazov's
tragic death stems from a web of conflicting human passions too complex
and subtle for any system of law to comprehend. Given this, Dostoyevsky
says more forcefully and clearly in this novel than in any other, Russians
must reclaim their own unique way of infusing life with meaning, of ef-
fecting true justice in a broken world.

In the novel's epilogue the writer returns to Alyosha Karamazov, now
outside the walls of the monastery, who is attempting to put Father Zosima's message of active love into practice in the world. Alyosha's final act is
to bring together a group of boys who once humiliated and abused the
poverty-stricken youngster Ilyusha Snegiryov, who is now dying. Through
the power of his love and concern, Alyosha successfully manages to reconcile the boys with Ilyusha, as the repentant adolescents comfort their
comrade on his deathbed. The novel's final scene takes place at Ilyusha's
grave, with the boys warmed by the glow of their newfound brotherhood.
They listen raptly as the youngest Karamazov brother exhorts them to
"never forget how good we once felt here, all together, united by such
good and kind feelings."

The Brothers Karamazov, like the Pushkin speech, was an absolute
triumph. The stand-alone edition of the novel was an immediate success,
and Dostoyevsky was deluged by event invitations throughout that fall
and winter. The venues he spoke at ranged from the Literary Fund at the

Nobility Assembly Hall, to the Society for Aid to Needy Students, to the Shelter of Saint Xenia at the home of Countess Mengden, where Princess Dagmar, the future wife of Tsar Alexander III, asked for a private meeting with her favorite writer.

Of all his audiences, though, Dostoyevsky most prized the young people. He viewed them as the future of the country—the Karamazovs of their generation, like the Alekos, Onegins, and Tatyanas before them—who were searching for an ideal to live by. It would be up to them to put into action the message of social reconciliation and active love he had been preaching in his art. Following Dostoyevsky in throngs after every speech, students asked him questions, listened closely to his long answers, and engaged him in heated debate about social issues.

These interactions with young people, Anna would recall, were among the happiest moments of these last months of her husband's life. Watching him enjoy his success, she escorted him home after each triumphant reading, events that left Dostoyevsky "physically exhausted but pleasantly aroused." Together they would sit until late into the night, the writer revisiting the details of that evening's heartening conversations with his young admirers, as if to make sure that Anna hadn't missed a single precious moment of his triumph. Which she certainly had not, she assured readers of her memoir, for "I was always present at these evenings, but used to stand aside, though never far away."

15.

Death of a Husband

On Sunday, January 25, 1881, Dostoyevsky's sister Vera came by for a visit under the pretext of wanting to spend some quality time with her brother and his family. Her real purpose in being there, however, was to persuade Dostoyevsky to renounce his portion of the inheritance from their aunt Kumanina, who had died ten years earlier. According to the terms of her will, Dostoyevsky was to inherit a portion of her Ryazan estate in 1881, but his sisters had spent the last decade urging their brother to cede his portion to them. Aware of how easily he could be manipulated, Anna had been trying for years to manage these negotiations behind her husband's back, even traveling to the estate in 1879 without his knowledge to look over the land and pick out the choicest piece for their family. On that Sunday afternoon, however, it was clear to Anna that the matter still had not been settled.

According to the memoirs of Dostoyevsky's daughter Lyubov', the conversation started off amicably enough. Dostoyevsky calmly explained that, while it was true he'd finally paid off most of his debts, he was still responsible for providing for three households—that of his ne'er-do-well stepson, Pasha; his alcoholic brother, Nikolai; and, of course, his own immediate family—and this had prevented him from realizing his longtime dream of purchasing land to leave to his wife and children after his death. The inheritance from his aunt would be his last opportunity to do so.

But Vera would have none of it. After reproaching her brother for his selfishness and cruelty to his sisters, she stormed out of the room sobbing, followed a few moments later by Dostoyevsky himself, who retreated alone to his study. Sinking into the chair at his writing desk, he held his flushed head in his shaking hands. He felt a strange moisture in his hands: they were covered with blood.

Anna sent at once for Dostoyevsky's regular doctor, but he was unavailable until later that evening. In the meantime, she told the children to distract their father by trying to make him laugh and playing games with him. Later Dostoyevsky suffered a second hemorrhage, his beard growing red with a thin stream of blood from his mouth. The doctor arrived soon thereafter, along with an eminent professor of medicine, who assured them that the hemorrhaging was slight and a "plug" (presumably a clot) might well form, sending the patient on the road to recovery. Over the next two days, the professor's prediction seemed to bear out: Dostoyevsky, noticeably more cheerful, chatted animatedly with his children and met with Anna and their typesetter, who had come by about the forthcoming issue of *Diary of a Writer*.

By this point, Anna was exhausted. She had spent the previous two nights sitting up in an armchair, and the better part of this day keeping watch over her husband, shielding him from the visitors who had begun showing up after hearing news of the novelist's illness. Of all those who came to their apartment, only Apollon Maikov, Dostoyevsky's oldest and closest friend, was able to offer Anna any comfort. Many others came armed with an agenda—including one minor scribe who'd built a career lampooning contemporary writers like Turgenev and Saltykov-Shchedrin, and had never before called on the Dostoyevskys. He came ostensibly to inquire about the health of the author, but his real mission became clear a few days later, when a tasteless article about the writer's final hours appeared in *The Moscow Gazette*.

That night Anna finally got some sleep on the mattress she'd laid on the floor next to Dostoyevsky's bed, although she awoke several times to see by the light of the night lamp that he was peacefully asleep. It seemed to her as if the plug was indeed forming. The next morning, Wednesday, January 28, when she awoke, her husband was looking straight into her eyes. He had been awake for hours, he told her, and had just now realized that he was going to die that day. "For God's sake, don't torture yourself with doubts," Anna insisted, "you're going to go on living, I tell you!"

"No. I know I have to die today. Light a candle, Anya, and give me the Gospel."

She did so at once. It was a copy that had been given to him by the widow of a former Decembrist when Dostoyevsky arrived in Tobolsk to begin his Siberian prison term in 1849. It was the only book he'd been allowed during those four years of hard labor, and it had never left his side since. Opening the book at random, Anna read from the book of Matthew, where Jesus says to John, "Do not hold me back, for thus it is fitting for us to fulfill a great truth."

"Do you hear? 'Do not hold me back.' That means I'm going to die," Dostoyevsky told Anna, who was trying to suppress her tears. He tried to comfort her, thanking her for the happy life she had given him, entrusting the children to her care, and telling her that he hoped she would love and protect them. "Remember this, Anya," he added, "I always loved you passionately and was never unfaithful to you even in my thoughts." Fearful that he was becoming too emotional, she begged him to rest.

By midday, letters and telegrams were pouring in, along with a new round of relatives, friends, and strangers. Among them was Pasha, Dostoyevsky's petty, self-centered stepson, whose character had not changed since Anna first met him in 1866. The ailing novelist, his longtime protector, kept spying him as he peeked through the crack of the door. "Anya, don't let him in here, he'll get me all upset!" Pasha's main objective that day, it seemed, was to inform every visitor that his "father" had no will and that a notary must be brought immediately so he might formally dispose of his possessions. Unbeknownst to Pasha, however, no notary was necessary, as Dostoyevsky had long since assigned Anna the rights to his work.

This was the last time Pasha would ever see his stepfather alive. One wonders whether he was capable of understanding the pain he was causing Dostoyevsky and his wife through his perversely selfish demands. It's impossible to know whether the stepfather and the prodigal son might ever have reconciled. Nor do we know much about what happened to Pasha after Dostoyevsky's death. He remained idle for the rest of his life, in every way except his diligent campaign to promote the fanciful notion that he was a Dostoyevsky by birth. He went so far as to name his own offspring after Dostoyevsky's children: Fyodor, Alexei, and Lyubov'. Pasha's claim to a place in literary history stems from his status as the unfortunate son of Dostoyevsky's first wife, upon whom the writer bestowed a great if often unwarranted pity—and from his insidious influence on the writer's relationship with his second wife, right to the end. Yet Anna came to love Pasha, the way a compassionate parent loves a wayward child. She took care never to disparage her stepson to others, and she continued supporting him, just as her husband had done, until Pasha's death in 1900, at the age of fifty-two.

Anna was well aware in these difficult hours that "aside from the five thousand rubles being held for him at *The Russian Messenger* Fyodor Mikhailovich had nothing at all, and that we were the heirs to this small sum, that is, the children and myself." This money—worth around sixty-three thousand dollars today—would be just enough for them to get by for two years. Beyond this five thousand rubles, the rights to Dostoyevsky's works were the family's only remaining assets, and that fact tortured the writer in the hours before his death. "My poor darling, my dearest . . . what am I leaving you with," he whispered to Anna, holding her hand as he lay limp on the bed. "My poor girl, how hard it will be for you to live!" Anna knew this, of course, but wasn't thinking about that; all her energy in those last hours was focused on easing her husband's suffering and praying for the strength to bear what was to come.

Throughout that Wednesday morning and afternoon, visitors assembled in the drawing room, with newcomers filing in every few minutes, but Anna stayed at her husband's side. At one point he asked her to call in the children, nine-year-old Fedya and twelve-year-old Lyuba. Dostoyevsky kissed and blessed them, told them in his feeble voice that he loved them dearly, and urged them always to remember that no matter how far they might go astray in life, they might always return to God, who would pardon and embrace them. The children crossed themselves fearfully; at one point Lyuba grabbed a stranger's hand and sobbed: "Pray, I beg you, pray for *papasha*, so that if he has any sins, God may forgive him!" The stranger, one of Dostoyevsky's writer colleagues, tried to comfort the little girl while quietly escorting her out of the room.

Dostoyevsky suffered another hemorrhage, then fell unconscious, a thin stream of blood once again darkening his face. As the bleeding grew more severe, Anna and the children knelt at the head of his bed and remained there, choking back their tears so as not to disturb him and prolong his agony. Holding her husband's hand in hers, Anna sensed his pulse growing steadily weaker, until, at last, at 8:38 p.m. on January 28, 1881, she felt it stop.

SHE WAS CERTAIN that she could not go on. Compounding her suffering, Anna was forced to endure this heartbreak "in the presence of a multitude, some of them deeply attached to him but others entirely indifferent both to him and to the inconsolable sorrow of our orphaned family." The arrival of Anna's brother, Ivan, later that evening was for her a veritable sign of God's grace. Having been away in Moscow on business, Ivan was unaware of the severity of Dostoyevsky's illness, and only upon arriving at the apartment did he learn that his brother-in-law had died. He immediately set to work helping with practical matters, sparing Anna the pain of having to handle it all herself.

Dostoyevsky's body remained on its raised catafalque, a stand with a lighted lamp and an icon near his head, for two and a half days. Anna recalled that time "as a kind of nightmare oppressing my soul," during which the steady stream of visitors caused the air in the study to grow so thick that the icon-lamp and the tapers surrounding the catafalque were extinguished. Anna was filled with bitter resentment at these crowds, who were robbing her of her very last opportunity to be alone with her husband, yet she had to hold back any show of feeling, lest some opportunistic reporter exploit her suffering for a sensationalist article. Her only refuge was the little room where her mother was staying, where from time to time she would hide behind a locked door and throw herself on the bed until someone knocked to tell her that a delegation had arrived.

The visitors who came to express their sympathy often prepared grandiose speeches about her husband's importance and "what Russia has lost in him." After a few days of such "condolences," Anna remembered:

> I finally became desperate and said to myself, "My God, how they torture me! What is it to me, 'what Russia has lost'? What do I care about Russia now? Can't you understand what *I've* lost? I've lost the best person in my life, my sun, my god! Take pity on me, take pity on me as a person, and don't tell me at this time about Russia's loss.'"
>
> When, out of the members of those many delegations, one person showed some pity for me as well as for "Russia," I was so touched that I seized this stranger's hand and kissed it.

Of course, Anna cared a great deal for Russia; she would consider it her obligation—indeed, her life's mission—to preserve her husband's art and ideas for the Russians of future generations. But in those precious days she needed to be nothing more than a mourning wife.

For days she stayed in that stifling apartment, refusing to eat anything but tea and rolls, while Ivan, Mama, and family friends took care of the children and prepared meals. After one of the requiem masses Anna felt a strange lump in her throat and asked a friend to bring her some valerian drops. "Get the valerian right away, where's the valerian?" people next to her began shouting. Suddenly, a strange thought came to Anna: Here she is, a widow in mourning, and for some reason everyone is calling for some unknown fellow named Valerian to come and comfort her! (Valerian was a common name in Russia; her husband's old friend Apollon Maikov had a brother by the name.) Delirious with grief as she was, the idea struck her as just absurd enough that she joined the wild chorus, shouting "Valerian, Valerian!" through sobs and laughter. When the maid returned from the apothecary, bringing both valerian drops and ammonia spirits in case Anna should faint, a crowd gathered as she poured drops of liquid into a wine-glass and forced them down Anna's throat. When Anna suddenly spit out the liquid, retching violently and screaming that her tongue was burning, they realized the maid had given her the ammonia spirits by accident. Luckily, she had spit out the spirits before swallowing; that night the skin peeled off her mouth and tongue, and if she had swallowed the ammonia, the same would have happened with her digestive tract.

On Friday, January 30, the evening before the start of the public funeral, Anna had one final opportunity to be with her husband. She was joined by her mother and Ivan, the two people who understood the depth of her love for Dostoyevsky. The three of them sat by the coffin in silence until four in the morning, when Ivan finally insisted that Anna go to bed to prepare for the trials to come.

At eleven a.m. on Saturday, January 31, Dostoyevsky's body was removed from their apartment at 5 Kuznechny Lane and carried to the Alexander Nevsky Monastery. Here Anna's parents had been married, and here, on the thirtieth of August, 1846, Anna herself had been born. And it was here, in the monastery's Tikhvin Cemetery, next to the gravesites of poets Vasily Zhukovsky and Nikolai Nekrasov, that Dostoyevsky had asked to be buried.

The funeral procession was a majestic affair, with a long file of wreaths borne aloft on tall poles, large choirs of young people singing funeral chants, and the elaborately decorated coffin raised high above the massive crowd at the end of the cortege. As news of the writer's death spread throughout the Russian capital, crowds of mourners spontaneously joined the silent procession; in a matter of a few hours the crowd grew to fifty thousand. According to contemporary newspaper reports, it was the largest public gathering of its kind in Russia in the nineteenth century.

Anna was aware of none of this. She would learn later, from stories she heard and read, of the full scale of the procession, but on that Saturday her eyes were focused on two things: the coffin in front of her and her young children, Fedya and Lyuba, by her side. "So heavy a responsibility to my husband's memory lay on me—would I be able to carry out my obligations with dignity?" she remembered wondering as she walked amid the sea of mourners. Just after two in the afternoon they arrived at the monastery, where the coffin was raised high in the center of the Church of the Holy Spirit. Anna was struck by the majestic beauty of the temple, by the many wreaths standing on tall poles along the walls, their inscriptions printed on ribbons in gold and silver.

The burial itself took place the following day. Ivan brought Fedya and Anna's mother to the monastery, while Anna and Lyuba were driven by a family acquaintance named Yulya Zasetskaya. As they were nearing the monastery, Madame Zasetskaya's carriage drew up next to a cab in which a colonel was sitting. He bowed, and Zasetskaya waved to him. An enormous crowd of several thousand was standing in the square, and it was impossible to drive up to the gates. They were forced to stop in the middle of the square. Anna and Lyuba got out and started walking toward the cathedral gates, while Zasetskaya stayed in the carriage to wait for the colonel to accompany her into the cathedral. Holding Lyuba's hand, Anna pushed her way with difficulty through the crowd before being stopped at the entrance and asked for her tickets. It had never occurred to her to bring them.

"I am the widow of the deceased and this is his daughter," she told the guard.

"There are plenty of Dostoyevsky's widows here who have gone inside already, and some of them are with children, too," was his reply.

"But you can see that I am in deep mourning."

"Oh, they were wearing veils, too." He asked to see her visiting card, but she had none with her. She begged them to call one of the funeral officials, citing the many prominent people who would vouch for her, but the guard rebuffed her: "How are we supposed to find them—do you think we can find them so fast in a crowd of thousands of people?"

In that moment Anna "felt desperate. Aside from the opinion [strangers] might form if they didn't see me at my husband's funeral rites, I myself had an agonizing need to say good-bye to him for the last time, to pray and cry a while at his coffin. I did not know what to do." At last a friend of Madame Zasetskaya's noticed her and came to vouch for her, and she was allowed inside.

After the service, a small group of Dostoyevsky's closest admirers carried the coffin to the Tikhvin Cemetery, which was filled with people—some standing near the gravesite, others clambering onto nearby monuments or fences or climbing trees, to watch the processional. Anna watched as the coffin was lowered into the ground, disappearing from view as attendees tossed in enough wreaths to cover the open grave almost to the very top of the crypt. The remaining wreaths were ripped to shreds by mourners who plucked leaves and flowers from them as keepsakes.

Some twenty-five years earlier, in the summer of 1856, ten-year-old Anna Snitkina had gazed from a private monastery apartment near Moscow's Kremlin at the majestic procession celebrating the coronation of Tsar Alexander II. Later that day, she had watched in confusion as polite ladies and gentlemen tore floral decorations from one another's hands, scrambling to secure their own piece of Russian imperial history. Now, on this cold January day a quarter century later, the thirty-four-year-old widow and mother of two watched as another massive crowd tore up wreaths in the Tikhvin Cemetery, vying for another piece of Russian history: a souvenir of the great Russian writer once imprisoned by Tsar Nicholas I and later liberated by his son, Alexander II.

On March 13, 1881, just over a month after Dostoyevsky's funeral, the same tsar who freed Dostoyevsky was killed by an exploding bomb tossed in front of his royal carriage by Narodnaya Volya, the revolutionary terrorist group. Two of the people who orchestrated the assassination were prominent radical feminists: Vera Figner and Sofya Perovskaya, six and seven years younger than Anna, respectively, all of them products of the women's emancipation movement of the 1860s. For their involvement in the assassination Perovskaya was executed by hanging and Figner was imprisoned for twenty years before being sent into exile. Later, the Soviet Union would embrace both women as revolutionary heroes.

In that moment of unrest after the assassination, it became clear to most Russians that the era of potential reconciliation between the state and the people had ended and another, far bloodier one had begun. And no one felt this more acutely than Anna, for whom the implacable march of history compounded her sense of personal loss. "I was clearly aware of one thing only," she later recalled:

that from that moment on, my personal life filled with immeasurable happiness was finished, and that I was orphaned in my heart forever. For me, who loved my husband so passionately, so utterly, who reveled in the love, friendship and respect of this man of such rare noble spirit, the loss was irretrievable. In those dreadful moments of parting I thought I could not survive my husband's passing, that my heart would burst any minute.

And yet, as the matriarch of their family, the head of its publishing business, and the keeper of her husband's memory, Anna knew she had no choice. Her children needed her, Russia needed her, and the legacy of her husband was at stake. She would have to find a way.

The widow, late in life, amid the trappings of her husband's legacy.

IV

THE LONG TWILIGHT

16.

High Priestess of Dostoyevsky

From the feminist movement that had once attracted her, Anna had internalized the values of independent-mindedness, hard work, and sacrifice for a cause greater than herself. From her traditional upbringing, she had inherited a love of family and country. And from her struggles—with an addict husband, with their yearslong exile, with crushing poverty, with the loss of two children and finally a husband, all by the age of thirty-four—she had learned to view compassion as the highest human value. "There's nothing in life more valuable than love," Anna told an acquaintance who cared for her in the weeks before her death in 1918. "One should forgive more often—assume guilt in oneself and soften the edges in others. Choose your god once and for all and without looking back serve him over the course of your entire life." She told this same acquaintance, "I gave myself to Fyodor Mikhailovich when I was twenty years old. Now I'm over seventy, and still I belong to him in my every thought, my every action. In my memory I belong to him, to his work, his children, his grandchildren."

Anna was exaggerating, of course. She had always had a strong, complex, and intense personality independent of her husband, and for many years after his death she led a rich and active life, continuing the publishing venture she had started with him, deriving as much personal satisfaction from her entrepreneurship and charitable activities as from her family. She adored the time she spent with her grandchildren. And she persisted with her stamp collection, the hobby she had started all the way back in 1867, in defiance of her husband's chauvinist remark that women lack character and perseverance.

Still, Anna dedicated most of her energy in her later years to shaping Dostoyevsky's legacy and presenting it to the world. Just as she had considered it her duty to shepherd her husband's art into the world, in the last thirty-eight years of her life she would serve as torchbearer of his memory for the benefit of future generations. This generosity had been a pattern since the very beginning of their relationship: Anna's first major gift was her dowry, pawned all those years before to save the couple's teetering young marriage. Her second was her steadfast support of her husband during their hard years of European exile, followed by ten years of ceaseless labor as Dostoyevsky's publisher and business manager. And now, in the years after his death, her determination to become the gatekeeper and high priestess of his memory would be perhaps her greatest contribution of all, to both her husband and the world at large.

At first, in the weeks and months following Dostoyevsky's death, she feared she wouldn't make it. Her nerves in a constant state of agitation, she was unable to sleep at night, and when she did she was racked by nightmares. "I cannot come to terms with the thought that I will never see him again, never hear him again," Anna wrote a friend, a few months after the writer's death. "I don't know what to do."

But she knew what she had to do. First, she needed to reimburse the subscribers of *Diary of a Writer* for the future issues they would not be receiving. Next, she had to decide what to do about her publishing venture and the book distribution business she had started the year before. As much as she wanted a break from these endeavors, she knew that she did not "have the moral right to delay the sale" of Dostoyevsky's books, since the grieving public "was feeling the need to enjoy the works of the late writer." In particularly high demand were *The Brothers Karamazov*, which Anna had brought out the previous year in a separate book edition, as well as *Notes from the House of the Dead* and the *Diary*. Within just a few days Anna sold out her entire surplus inventory of Dostoyevsky's works, netting around four thousand rubles.

"The strong demand for the works of Dostoyevsky did not go unnoticed by our booksellers and publishers," she recalled. In the aftermath of her husband's death, she was approached by several companies offering to buy out the rights to Dostoyevsky's work. One was a Polish bookseller who traveled from Warsaw to offer her twelve thousand rubles, an offer Anna's friends and family strongly encouraged her to accept. She could transfer that payment into interest-bearing government securities, they told her, adding five hundred rubles to her annual government-issued pension, yielding her a steady income of twenty-five hundred rubles a year. This was what most Russian attorneys made at the turn of the century, the high end of a physician's income, and more than nearly half of Russia's government officials. Given Anna's minimal living expenses— her modest apartment in Petersburg cost around five hundred rubles a year—she would have been able to live on this money, she calculated, "without difficulty." When added to the four thousand she'd just received from the sale of her extant Dostoyevsky inventory, as well as another five thousand from *The Russian Messenger* for the unpaid balance on *The Brothers Karamazov*, twelve thousand rubles for Dostoyevsky's copyrights was an attractive offer. It would also make her life so much easier to hand off the work and responsibility of running a publishing enterprise to somebody else.

Still, Anna went against the counsel of others and refused the bookseller's offer. She considered the dissemination of Dostoyevsky's works to be her duty, her responsibility to her husband, his audience, and his legacy. By publishing them herself, she reasoned, "I would be realizing a longtime dream of my unforgettable husband's to bring out his complete collected works."

To give herself time to focus on this project, she decided to close the book distribution side business she had started the previous year. When she announced this decision, businesspeople who recognized the value of the operation—and were interested in acquiring both the Dostoyevsky name and the relationships Anna had built—approached her with buyout offers. Once again, Anna refused. "To carry on an enterprise bearing the name of F. M. Dostoyevsky was something only I myself could do," she wrote, "since I held myself responsible for the firm's integrity." She would not risk subjecting "Fyodor Mikhailovich's name, so precious to me, to censure or mockery in the event the firm's management proved incompetent or dishonest." She recognized the value of what her distribution venture had accomplished in a short period: "I firmly believe," she wrote three decades later, "that if I had gone on with my own activity I would have a shop on a par with the *New Times* bookstore, one of the country's large booksellers." She took special pride in her loyal customer base, and in the high ethical standards she had maintained throughout the company's brief life span. "I think back on my short-lived enterprise with a pleasant feeling," she wrote, "chiefly because of the good relationships established between the business and its clients."

Going forward, she would devote her attention full-time to preparing the first uniform edition of her husband's collected works, her largest single publication venture yet. Anna made the risky decision to invest the entirety of the nine thousand rubles she'd recently acquired into its first edition. It wasn't enough, she knew, to cover even the cost of paper (twenty thousand rubles), but thanks to her strong business relationships, she was able to secure six months' credit from her suppliers, a rare accommodation in the Russian publishing business. One paper supplier told Anna that his firm was willing to take such a risk because "we know that you, and not your husband, published the previous books. . . . You brought us money and were always thorough."

Before anything could be printed, however, there were editorial issues for Anna to address. First and foremost, she needed to select which of her husband's many works should be included. After soliciting and reviewing opinions—many of them conflicting—from a range of literary voices, including several of her husband's former colleagues, she opted to include not only most of his major novels but a significant portion of his letters, excerpts from his notes for *Diary of a Writer*, and a number of articles written for *Time* and *Epoch* in the early 1860s. She also hired prominent authors and scholars to write biographical articles about Dostoyevsky. When she learned that some of them would not be able to complete their articles until the following year, however, she had to find a way to address both their needs and the urgent demand for Dostoyevsky's fiction among the reading public. Anna recognized that a swift publication of his best-known work was essential. "In light of this," she "decided to publish the complete collection of works not in order of volumes, that is, not starting from the first, as it's always done, but with the release of the sixth and seventh volumes, containing his novels." Every few months, between 1881 and 1883, she planned to issue a new volume of the fourteen-volume collection, charging twenty-five rubles for the entire set. It was a smart business decision, and a model that future Russian publishers would emulate.

After posting advertisements in newspapers, Anna waited "in great trepidation" for the market's verdict. In a matter of weeks, the enterprise "exceeded all of my expectations," with six thousand copies of the collection selling out easily. Within a few months, Anna could afford to pay off all the expenses incurred by the first two volumes, and was able to prepare the subsequent volumes using cash earned from the initial sales rather than relying on credit.

After business expenses of around seventy-five thousand rubles, the first edition of Dostoyevsky's works yielded a profit of seventy-five thousand—close to a million dollars today, more income than Dostoyevsky's entire body of work had generated during his lifetime. "I was, of course, very gratified by the material success of the collection, thanks to which our family had gained a certain independence," Anna remembered— a modest assessment, given the magnitude of her accomplishment. She was gratified that she could finally pay off the last of Dostoyevsky's personal debts, but one thought continued to bother her: "Why did this substantial income appear only so late, after my dear husband had gone from the earth? How much happiness it would have given him to know that his children wouldn't go uneducated, and his family wouldn't fall into destitution after his death." To her, the unexpected windfall seemed like "an irony of fate, which had so often been cruel to my dear husband." Had she never appeared in Dostoyevsky's life, of course, his fate would likely have been crueler still.

———

EVEN AS ANNA WRAPPED her husband's memory around her broken heart, the old Russia they had both loved was being violently uprooted. Everything the writer had fought against—the violence, the godlessness, the madness of revolution—was unfolding just as he'd predicted. There were calls for mercy toward Alexander II's assassin and the other revolutionaries, but Anna's voice was not among them: "Execute them!" she reportedly shouted while entering the publishing office one day.

She paid close attention to every mention of Dostoyevsky in the newspapers and journals of the day, and in those early years so much nonsense was written that she increasingly felt compelled to set the record straight. To that end, she began collecting materials for a memoir of her life with Dostoyevsky, in which she would present the writer the way she wanted the world to know him: as a loving husband and father, a compassionate soul, and a genius. She would work on the project throughout her later years, even as her health failed; when it finally appeared, seven years after her death, it was recognized immediately as a major literary event.

Even before his death the Pushkin speech had elevated Dostoyevsky in the public consciousness as a conservative torchbearer, and now everyone wanted to turn him into either a mascot or a whipping boy to further their own ideological agenda. To Anna, all of this missed the point. In a letter to one scholar, she insisted that her husband was to literature what the physicist Röntgen, who discovered the X-ray, was to the human body—the inventor of a wholly new means of peering inside the human soul. "To judge Dostoyevsky on the basis of his political (and other) views would be the same as judging Röntgen on a similar basis." The novelist's real contribution, Anna argued, was that he depicted "abysses and depths" of the human soul "that remained hidden from even Shakespeare and Tolstoy." Whatever we make of such comparisons, Anna was inarguably ahead of her time in her approach to reading Dostoyevsky. Most literary critics of the time viewed art through the lens of contemporary political and social debates, and a good half century would pass before Russian literary critics joined Anna in recognizing her husband's work as great art that transcends politics to touch the most irreducible truths of human existence.

In the months after her husband's death, Anna worked with almost maniacal focus. Word got out not to bother her during business hours. Eventually the throngs stopped coming, and only her close friends and a handful of random supplicants came by. One evening a man in his seventies with a thick woolen overcoat and a briefcase visited Anna with an urgent proposition. Like her husband, he had spent time in a Siberian prison camp, he told her, and had written his own prison memoirs. "If you don't want my competition, then buy my manuscript," he demanded in a deep guttural voice, shoving his briefcase in her face. "You can publish it as the second part of *Notes from the House of the Dead.*" Unsure whether to laugh or cry, Anna told him plainly, "I don't publish others' works," and showed him the door. When he was gone she fastened the lock, resolving never again to receive unknown visitors in the evening.

Scholars sent her their books on Dostoyevsky for potential publication, but she declined all such requests. There was only so much time in a day, and "I am not morally obligated to publish every work that appears about my husband," she told a friend, "no matter how talented the work." Even as she limited her scope to her husband's own work, her publishing enterprise remained sufficiently impressive to attract others who sought her advice.

One of those individuals was the wife of Leo Tolstoy. Sofya Tolstaya had heard about Anna's success from friends and came to ask her advice on how to create a publishing operation for her husband similar to the one Anna had created for Dostoyevsky. Without a hint of competitiveness, Anna shared her secrets of the trade, and she was deeply gratified when her counsel helped Countess Tolstaya to found a highly profitable publishing imprint of her own. The countess would return to Anna often for advice; in one of several letters from Anna in the Tolstaya archives, from October 1, 1885, she offers detailed advice on producing and selling a *Complete Works*. (At Sofya's request, Anna also used her government connections to intervene on behalf of a Tolstoyan conscientious objector who was arrested for refusal to participate in military service, playing a major role in getting the man's sentence reduced.)

Despite such acts of generosity, Anna developed a reputation for being a hard-driving businesswoman—some considered her a stingy egoist in pursuit of personal gain—and she often felt the need to defend herself. For the people closest to her, however, such justifications were unnecessary. They understood her deep sadness in the wake of her husband's death, and the burden of the responsibility she carried. "I feel my strength leaving me every year, yet there is so much more work still to do," Anna lamented to Andrei Dostoyevsky, the author's younger brother, in January 1889, when she was still just forty-two. "Fyodor Mikhailovich's books sell out fast . . . and I have no moral right to stop the circulation of the works, nor, moreover, the ideas, of my late husband." Although the publishing business provided for the family, it now served a second purpose: "I feel it is no longer the same work, as I do not now have the same keen desire to help, to ease his workload. Now I only have a sense of debt to him."

That debt would take many different forms; it would also take a serious toll on Anna's health. Her hard work allowed her to afford a decent education for their children—something she knew her husband valued—and she was proud to say she'd turned down the state's offer to pay for their education. "My children," she wrote of her decision, "must be educated not at the expense of the State but by the labor of their father and later the labor of their mother." But she was mindful that others were less fortunate, and she donated thousands of free copies of Dostoyevsky's books to libraries across Russia, and lent her personal and financial assistance to help open any number of others. In 1883 she founded a parish school for peasant children in Staraya Russa in Dostoyevsky's name. As its trustee, Anna would contribute thirty-two hundred rubles of her own money, as well as provide textbooks and works by her husband to the school's library. In its first few years, the school struggled because of lack of funds and had to turn away students, including many female students, which especially pained Anna. To rectify this, she solicited the help of the Chief Procurator of the Holy Synod (the highest church office in Russia), to fund a female division of the school. By all accounts, her efforts proved successful: by the time of its closing thirty-four years later, in 1917, the school had graduated more than a thousand girls.

In 1889, Anna founded a memorial devoted to her husband's life and career, the first of its kind to appear in Russia. Known formally as the F. M. Dostoyevsky Memorial Museum, the memorial, housed in a room within the Moscow Historical Museum, was designed to display a vast corpus of materials that she had collected in connection with her husband: manuscripts, editions of his essays, portraits, busts, and memorabilia. For years before its opening, she implored family, friends, and colleagues to send her any written work they could find on her husband and his work, in Russia or abroad. By the time it was ready for the public, in 1891, the room was such an impressive tribute that Tsar Alexander III himself visited the museum with his two sons.

As part of her ongoing project, Anna regularly consulted with Russia's leading writers, artists, theater directors, and composers on their adaptations of Dostoyevsky's works. And she also undertook the task of creating a bibliography of materials related to Dostoyevsky's life and art, a resource that one scholar of her time called "a unique work in the history of the Russian literary biography." Another academic, a world history professor who received a copy of the *Bibliographical Index* from Anna in 1906, wrote to her: "This is not only a monument to the great man, but a symbol of the love with which he was always surrounded by you. Literature will be forever grateful to you." His prediction was correct: to this day the *Bibliographical Index* remains a bedrock of Dostoyevsky studies. Anna also painstakingly preserved every detail of the couple's apartment in Petersburg and their vacation house in Staraya Russa (which she finally purchased from her brother after Dostoyevsky's death), so that future visitors would know exactly how they looked and felt during her husband's life.

IN 1885 AND 1886, Anna launched the second edition of Dostoyevsky's *Complete Collected Works* in six volumes. All six thousand copies were snatched up quickly. For this edition she had decided to lower the price to fifteen rubles, a wise move that allowed her to expand her customer base and would serve as a precedent for future editions. Anna released a third edition of the collected works in 1888 and 1889, and a fourth between 1888 and 1892. For both editions she charged only ten rubles per copy but quickly sold twelve thousand copies of each, making up the difference in revenue; each edition netted a profit of seventy-five thousand rubles. To give herself more time to work on the bibliography, the museum, and other charitable activities, Anna accepted another seventy thousand rubles to license a fifth edition to publisher Adolf Marx, who published it in 1893 as a literary supplement to the popular family journal *Niva*.

In fewer than fifteen years, *The Complete Collected Works* had brought in 375,000 rubles, or around five million dollars in today's money. Of this Anna received only her dower of 125,000 rubles; the other two-thirds went to her two children, Lyubov' and Fyodor, although they played no part in the business. Anna's account in *Reminiscences* also suggests that profits were taken out of the company rather than reinvested in the business, as companies often do today—a corporate structure that in time would prove devastating to the business, starving it of much-needed cash during an economic downturn.

For the twenty-fifth anniversary of Dostoyevsky's death, Anna published a lavish sixth edition of his collected works, which appeared between 1904 and 1906. This edition, printed in special large type on vellum paper, featured glossy photographs from the Dostoyevskys' personal collection. It also marked the first publication of excerpts from Dostoyevsky's notebooks to *The Possessed*, as well as previously censored parts of the chapter "At Tikhon's," in which Stravrogin confesses to having raped a twelve-year-old girl. The appearance of these materials created a literary sensation in Russia. Never one for false modesty, Anna proudly recalled that edition years later: "I can say that not one Russian writer up to the present day (1917) had ever been presented to the Russian public in as magnificent a way as I had succeeded in publishing my husband's works." She immediately followed the sixth edition with an equally attractive seventh, which she sought to make available to as wide an audience as possible by charging only ten rubles for the complete set.

Unfortunately, however, these editions "not only did not bring in the usual profits (which I, by the way, did not count on) but forced me to sustain a significant financial setback." Between the Russo-Japanese War of 1904–05 and the revolutionary uprisings that dominated headlines in 1905, the public was distracted from literary matters. These sixth and seventh editions sold only six thousand copies combined, bringing in a total of just over a hundred thousand rubles. Anna does not give a specific sum, but the loss must have been enormous—perhaps in the high tens of thousands—given the cost of publishing such elegant editions. Typographic services and paper had doubled in cost amid the rampant inflation, and the fixed costs of operating the business had also increased by two thousand a month. And the political unrest had more immediate consequences, as Anna was forced to buy additional insurance and increase her storage costs to protect her books from the fires being set by violent protesters throughout Petersburg.

The ultimate blow, however, came when her typographer, who had fallen on hard times himself, was no longer able to extend credit to Anna's company, demanding promissory notes from Anna that she was expected to pay off monthly. Even under normal operating conditions, this would have posed a significant financial challenge to her business. But now, with printing costs mounting and no ability to purchase services or materials on credit, Anna was faced with a dire situation. "For the first time in my life," she recalled, "I fell into the clutches of promissory notes, and I spent two or three years in great anxiety." At first she "succeeded in making ends meet each month," but then it became simply too difficult to manage.

Even with such financial challenges, though, hadn't Anna saved enough capital to weather the storm? According to her memoirs, she had not. All together she had only thirty thousand rubles in savings to draw on:

> Maybe it will seem strange that, having received such large revenues from the publications, I had saved up a relatively modest sum. But of these revenues I had only a widow's share [a dower of 125,000 rubles] and almost everything that came to me as

my portion I spent on affairs connected with the memory of
my unforgettable husband: the school in Staraya Russa in his
name, the memorial museum, the publication of two museum
catalogues, my stepson's education, etc.

She made a similar point in a letter to a friend in 1907: "It makes me
laugh when people speak about my 'wealth.' I have no wealth at all—I
spend all the income on the Staraya Russa school, on the Museum, and on
the publishing business. As for myself, I live a modest life." The extent of
her charitable activities begins to explain why she had insufficient cash
on hand for the publishing business during its most challenging time.

Did Anna show insufficient foresight in not holding on to more cash
for precisely such a downturn? From a purely economic point of view,
perhaps. Had she managed her finances differently, reinvesting more
earned income in the business, she might well have been able to keep her
publishing enterprise afloat. But her publishing enterprise was never
purely a financial concern for her; like the museum, school, and bibliographical index, it was an expression of her responsibility to make Dostoyevsky's legacy available to as wide an audience as possible. If she'd kept
more cash in the publishing enterprise, she might have shortchanged her
other legacy-building activities, whose influence would long outlive her.

Anna's business decisions in the years after Dostoyevsky's death might
be considered risky, then, but not reckless. Her career as a publisher was
marked by the same risk tolerance that had driven many of her decisions
in the past: turning down the offer of twelve thousand rubles for Dostoyevsky's copyrights, for instance, because she felt it her duty to bring out
her husband's works herself; even starting the publishing company in the
first place, to free her husband from his dependence on exploitive publishers and create a model that they themselves controlled. Such choices
might have appeared irresponsible in the moment—as they often did
to the Dostoyevskys' family and friends—but Anna had her rationale
for making them, and even from a purely financial perspective, she often proved more farsighted than those who counseled her to follow a
safer path.

HER CHILDREN WERE GROWING OLDER. Fyodor got married and divorced, and then married again. The second marriage was an unhappy one, but it produced two sons, Fyodor and Andrei, whom Anna adored. Fyodor's wife, Ekaterina Petrovna, got along well with her mother-in-law and made a point of visiting Anna often with the grandchildren. Anna reveled in the success of Fyodor, who at one point owned a large and lucrative racing stable in Petersburg and became one of Russia's foremost horse-breeding specialists. She reminisced with pleasure that her son's passion for horses could be traced back to the day she'd bought the boy his first foal, while Dostoyevsky was off in Moscow for the Pushkin Celebration festivities.

Lyubov', her daughter, was a different story. From a young age she had suffered from a mysterious nervous ailment, which she blamed on her unfortunate family circumstances. Long after her father's death, she clung to a delusion that he'd been nailed into his coffin in a lethargic sleep and would one day awaken and return to his family. Lyubov' had an increasingly strained relationship with her mother as she grew up, and after a serious quarrel Lyubov' moved out of the household altogether. Between 1911 and 1913, when she was in her early forties, Lyubov' published two mediocre novels, *The Barrister* and *The Female Émigré*, and a collection of short stories, *Sick Girls*, which was suffused with themes of hereditary pathology and degeneracy, phenomena she believed had marred her own life.

History's march, meanwhile, continued apace. The violent revolution of 1905 offered a grim preview of things to come, while the ensuing economic turbulence delivered a serious enough blow to Anna's publishing business that she had to decide whether to continue it at all. "I can say that I spent four years (1904–1908) in such financial straits and under such mental stress that I wouldn't wish it on my worst enemy," she wrote. Now in her early sixties, she was suffering from heart disease, and in 1910 her doctors insisted she take time off away from the bustle of city life to convalesce in the Sestroretski sanitarium on the outskirts of Petersburg. "I had to choose: either I was going to die while at work on the forthcoming eighth edition of the *Complete Collected Works*, or I would have to quit my publishing work. . . . This decision required long and difficult reflection."

Another factor made this decision all the more complicated and urgent. In 1910 the government announced a new law stipulating that an artist's family would lose the copyrights on their forebear's work thirty years after his death, rather than the previous limit of fifty. Anna was deeply insulted that "people who had nothing to do with literature and who knew nothing of the torments and deprivations of those genuine sufferers [i.e., writers] . . . could, with such a light heart, take away from those poor souls the only property they could leave children and grandchildren." With the thirtieth anniversary of Dostoyevsky's death less than a year away, this development posed a grave threat. "The thought of having unpaid debts in my old age was for me terrible," Anna recalled. Despite warnings from her doctors, she sprang immediately into action, using her connections to lobby government officials to change the law.

Against all odds, her efforts proved successful: Russia's legislative assembly reconsidered the matter, making a number of changes to the law that would protect the families of Russian artists, including reverting to the original limit of fifty years. It was a victory, on behalf of intellectual property rights for artists' families everywhere, for which Anna has never received proper credit.

But history, Anna well knew, was a roulette wheel, where fortunes can rise and fall in an instant. She feared that some government official might decide to revisit the copyright matter and change the law yet again. It was not out of the question, especially given the intensely anti-capitalist winds blowing across Russia stirred up by the revolutionary fervor. The very thought of having to go through another period of financial uncertainty seemed to Anna "a nightmare" she had no wish to relive. She had no choice but to consider the heartbreaking possibility that she might need to sell Dostoyevsky's copyrights to a private individual.

She approached a number of publishers about a potential sale, initially without success. Some of them were put off by her publishing firm's recent losses. Others feared government interference. Still others figured that there must be a catch, unable to believe that the great writer's wife, who had spent nearly forty years building his name and career, would now want to give it all away.

Anna did not view it that way, though. To her, selling the copyrights now appeared to be her last shot at saving Dostoyevsky's legacy, not to mention the future of their grandchildren. Her plan was to use the money to support her work on her memoir and the second edition of the *Bibliographical Index*, and to further develop the Dostoyevsky Museum in Moscow, while putting her grandchildren through school. And so, in perhaps the greatest gamble in a lifetime of gambles, Anna decided to sell all of Dostoyevsky's copyrights, for around 150,000 rubles, to the publishing house Prosvieshchenie.

With that sale, she recalled, "ended my former way of life, to which I had grown accustomed and which was so dear to me, and at the end of 1911 I had to begin a new and what at the time appeared to me to be an utterly useless and empty life." It was an excruciating decision, but it also gave her family enough to live on while she carried on her work of promoting Dostoyevsky's legacy. She probably was painfully aware of the irony that she had come into Dostoyevsky's life to help in his desperate bid to *avoid* losing his copyrights to Stellovsky, and now she was selling them off. Yet Anna had every reason to take pride in her stewardship of her husband's career: from that first critical impasse, through the rest of his life as a writer and the afterlife of his work, she had cleared the path for her husband to become one of the most revered voices in Russian literature—while becoming herself the first solo female publisher in Russian history.

The 150,000 rubles, of which Anna received her dower of 50,000 (a little over $700,000 today), ran low sooner than expected, although Anna does not say exactly why. By all accounts her personal living expenditures remained modest, under 5,000 a year; it seems likely that she continued to spend substantial amounts of her own money on the Dostoyevsky Museum, the *Bibliographical Index*, the Staraya Russa school, and other charitable activities—financial choices she likely made intentionally, despite the risks they posed to her own livelihood.

By February 1913 things had become desperate enough that Anna was forced to resort to an outlandish idea: making a personal appeal to the tsar. That month, she composed a letter to Tsar Nicholas II himself, who'd taken the throne after his father Alexander III's death in 1894. The letter, discovered in 2016 among Anna's archives in Moscow and never before published in English, was delivered to the tsar by a high-level government contact of Anna's. In it, she would channel every ounce of the persuasive power, sweet-talking cajolery, and literary skill she had honed over decades as a publisher—along with a sincere passion for her homeland—and ask the ruler of Russia for, well, money. "Your Great Majesty!" she emphasized, "I am not requesting anything for myself personally, but I am requesting Your Imperial Highness to bestow great mercy upon my grandchildren, Fyodor and Andrei Dostoyevsky, by assigning to them a yearly stipend until the end of their education."

It was a bold request—the widow of nineteenth-century Russia's most famous political prisoner asking the tsar to support her grandchildren. But Anna recognized that she had one great source of leverage: the name of that very political prisoner, who in his lifetime had gone from wanting to overthrow the government to becoming its most visible and passionate defender. Astonishingly, the gambit paid off. Nicholas II agreed to provide Fyodor and Andrei a yearly stipend of three thousand rubles for the duration of their studies, a sum that Anna, in the postscript to her letter, said "would give me the possibility of existing peacefully in the twilight of my life."

BUT THAT PEACEFUL EXISTENCE would be interrupted less than a year later by the outbreak of world war in 1914, and even more significantly by an unexpected attack aimed directly at Dostoyevsky's legacy. Back in 1883, Nikolai Strakhov, an old friend and colleague of her husband's—a man Anna had commissioned to write his biography, published as the first volume of the *Complete Collected Works*—had written a private letter to Tolstoy in which he offered a scathingly critical portrait of Dostoyevsky. Now, many years after Strakhov's death in 1896, that letter somehow found its way into the October 1913 issue of *Contemporary*

World. A year later, it was republished in the book *Correspondence Between L. N. Tolstoy and N. N. Strakhov.*

"I cannot consider Dostoyevsky either a good or happy man," Strakhov wrote. "He was malicious, envious, dissolute; and he lived his whole life in a state of agitation which made him pitiful and would make him ridiculous if he had not also been so malicious and so intelligent." Strakhov painted Dostoyevsky as spiteful and mean-spirited, claiming that he derived pleasure from dominating defenseless creatures far weaker than himself, like a Swiss waiter he had once treated poorly when they were traveling together in Europe. "And worst of all was that fact that he wallowed in it, that he never completely repented of all his nasty actions. He was drawn to nasty acts and he bragged about them." Dostoyevsky was full of animal lust, Strakhov went on, yet "had no taste, no feeling for feminine beauty and charm. This is evident from his novels. . . . In essence, however, all his novels are *self-justification*; they argue that every variety of loathsomeness can live side by side with nobility in the same human being." Dostoyevsky "was a truly unhappy and wicked person who imagined himself happy and a hero, and tenderly loved himself alone."

On and on it went, this character assassination, from the perspective of a respected Russian philosopher and literary critic. It was written for one reader's consumption, but now it was being read by all of literary Russia—and the portrait it paints continues to stain Dostoyevsky's reputation to this day. One of its most unfortunate elements, as damning as it was unsubstantiated, was Strakhov's suggestion that the shocking scene in *The Possessed* that Katkov had refused to publish, in which Stravrogin rapes a child, was based on a real-life crime Dostoyevsky had himself committed.

Over the course of her publishing career, Anna had dealt with her fair share of unscrupulous businesspeople. After her husband's death, she had been forced to respond to a number of sensationalist articles hawking falsehoods about the novelist. But Strakhov's letter was of a different order of magnitude. Here was a colleague and confidant of her husband's, a family friend who had traveled with Dostoyevsky through Europe and visited their home in Petersburg, who had played with their children, threatening (if only from the grave) to destroy the reputation Anna had dedicated her life to celebrating. It was the cruelest betrayal imaginable. Anna "was wounded for myself, for my trustfulness, for the fact that both my husband and I had been so deceived by this unworthy individual."

To this day it remains a mystery how the letter got out. Its publication was likely the work of one of Dostoyevsky's literary enemies, of whom he had many, even long after his death. Strakhov, of course, was not directly responsible for publishing the letter. But he would surely have known that any correspondence with Tolstoy would be published at some point after Tolstoy's death. The impetus for the letter likely came as Strakhov was studying Dostoyevsky's archive, which Anna had made available to him as he prepared the biography she had commissioned. There, among the writer's notes, Strakhov may well have come across a highly derogatory commentary about *him*, a personal insult that would put his own reputation at risk should it ever come to light.

To be charitable, when he wrote that letter back in 1883—two years after Dostoyevsky's death—Strakhov may have been betting on the hope that the preternaturally robust Tolstoy would live to a ripe old age (which he did), and that the damning letter would likely remain secret until many decades after Dostoyevsky's death. But it is equally possible that this high-minded idealist, as Strakhov fashioned himself, was also entirely capable of being a vindictive and jealous man. All of which points, in turn, to one of those inexplicable contradictions of human nature with which Dostoyevsky's own novels abound.

Yet for Anna this was no novel, but an all-too-real horror story featuring her husband, his late rival Tolstoy, and the perfidious Nikolai Strakhov, whose intemperate words threatened to destroy her life's work, uprooting the public narrative about Dostoyevsky that she had been trying for decades to construct.

She weighed her options. Any response she made might be dismissed as the words of a wounded widow coming to her late husband's defense— if it wasn't drowned out altogether by the sea of news about the world war, then dominating everybody's attention. If she were to remain silent, on the other hand, that "might appear to be a confirmation of the slander,"

Anna wrote. This was a possibility she could not risk. After weeks of angst-filled strategizing with friends, she decided to fight back by doing what she knew best: shaping the narrative from behind the scenes.

Calling on her network of friendly writers and colleagues, Anna organized a massive public relations campaign on her husband's behalf. Over the next year and a half, they would fill literary journals with glowing descriptions of Dostoyevsky's character, including vehement rebuttals to Strakhov's letter. Anna even got a group of writers and intellectuals to sign and publish a joint letter of condemnation of Strakhov's scurrilous accusations. Aware that even these efforts would be insufficient to repair the damage already done, Anna also decided to devote several pages in her memoir to a point-by-point rebuttal of each of Strakhov's claims. These pages, surely not what Anna had originally envisioned for one of the last chapters in her otherwise beautiful account of her life with Dostoyevsky, make for painful reading.

17.

Death of a Wife

I n 1917 it finally came to pass, the revolution Dostoyevsky had warned of for decades. So, too, did the crisis in European culture, which had long been strikingly evident to Anna, and now took the form of world war. To Anna, this must have come as definitive proof that her husband had been right all along: The path to a higher, more just civilization could not come from Europe. Only Russia could lead mankind there—although not through bloody violence, as these new revolutionaries believed, but through love, as Dostoyevsky had preached. Now in her seventies, Anna confronted this period of unrest with profound sadness, and with her customary single-minded focus on disseminating her husband's work and ideas.

In those years leading up to the revolution, Russian female activists played, in the words of historian Barbara Evans Clements, "a more important part in changing their society than did contemporary women in any other country." The feminist activists of early twentieth-century Russia organized on behalf of women's rights. They led enormous marches on the streets of Petersburg, including one with thirty-five thousand participants demanding that women's rights be written into the new Soviet constitution. They served in the army, forming special combat units that called themselves "Shock Battalions" and "Death Battalions" to emphasize their fierce determination to die for their country—a precursor to the savage valor displayed by women on the battlefields of the great civil war to come. Wanting to do their part in building the hoped-for utopia, women studied to become doctors and engineers and builders. The most extreme and dedicated among them—inspired by the exploits of nineteenth-century female revolutionary terrorists such as Vera Zasulich, who shot and nearly killed the governor of Petersburg, or Sofya Perovskaya, who helped to assassinate Tsar Alexander II—worked behind the scenes to do what they could to wipe out the tsarist state.

It was a heady time for the feminist movement in Russia, a period of daring and, in many cases, genuinely noble sacrifice for the cause of revolution, which women saw as the path not just to utopia but to their own ultimate liberation. In this sense, it was the culmination of decades of effort, dating back to the 1860s, when Anna Snitkina, the self-proclaimed emancipated "girl of the sixties," was coming of age. Now, as the new generation was pursuing their dream of female liberation with a degree of ruthlessness she could never have imagined, Anna was working. Quietly, steadily, she pored over materials she wanted to include in her husband's archives. She corresponded with Dostoyevsky scholars. She was hunched over a notebook atop a tiny wooden writing table, pen in hand, working on the second edition of her bibliography and the scholarly index to the holdings of the Dostoyevsky Museum in Moscow.

While the new generation of revolutionary feminists was seeking to uproot the past and replace it, Anna was trying desperately to preserve it. "I live not in the twentieth century, I have remained in the seventies of the nineteenth," she told Leonid Grossman, a prominent Dostoyevsky scholar and biographer, in the winter of 1916. "My people are the friends of Fyodor Mikhailovich, my society—the circle of those people who have passed who were close to Dostoyevsky. It is with them that I live."

He was her life's work. And this work was precisely what saved her own life, on February 28, 1917, some five days after the revolution had broken out and the Bolsheviks had taken power. On that morning, thanks to her worsening heart condition, seventy-year-old Anna was convalescing at the Sestroretski sanitarium. The sun had just come up, at five thirty a.m., when the chambermaid rushed in to announce that another workers' strike had broken out in the Russian capital. Anna, who had been coming to the facility for about seven years to recover, had a reputation for overexerting

herself and for disregarding cautionary advice. But today, in those dangerous early days of revolution, she heeded the chambermaid's warning. Removing the thick gray overcoat and large black fur hat she'd donned to run
some early-morning errands, Anna ambled over to her tiny writing table,
took up a pen with her arthritic fingers, and began to work. Then there was
another urgent knock at the door.

Anna opened it. The sanitarium librarian, pale and agitated, spoke in
a trembling voice:

"The factory workers are coming here. God save us!"

Anna hastened to the window and saw the wide alley stretching from
the train station to the sanitarium crammed with people carrying weap-
ons and red flags. These were the revolutionaries, who had overthrown
the tsarist regime, installed an emergency provisional government, and
were now in the process of destroying the Old Russia that Anna so loved.
Bolting the door, she found her money, tucked it all in a portmanteau,
and resolved to give them as much as they asked for. She stood behind the
door listening, her ailing heart "beating so loudly that it seemed it would
break any minute."

She went to get some water, in order to calm down. Walking past the
writing table, her eyes fell on the three folders with the papers and letters
from her husband's archives, which she'd been collecting and organizing
all that winter. "A terrible thought flashed through my mind: If they destroy, tear up or burn my papers I will be deprived of documents so interesting and important to literature. . . . I began stuffing the letters into
various boxes and sacks in order to save at least a portion of them."

A few minutes later she heard the shouts and whistles of the crowd,
now inside the building. Anna was hopeful that "they'd calm down, or,
God willing, Cossack [troops] would come to our aid. . . . But my hope
was in vain." From the first floor just below she heard loud knocking on
doors, and then a crash followed by the sound of breaking glass. After
that she could hear the group leaders yell, "Quiet! Begin with the first
number, in order!"

The cacophony of whooping and whistling and stomping feet echoed
through the stairwell and reached the second floor. Anna heard people

running up and down the corridor. Someone cried hysterically. Then silence. They must have gone into the sanitarium library, adjacent to her room, Number 10. Then she thought she overheard someone muttering the word "Dostoyevsky." She pressed her ear against the door. She heard it again. "Blood rushed to my head. 'What is this, a hallucination of my hearing, or what?'" she thought. But it was not.

When the dreaded knock came at last, Anna crossed herself, then opened the door. On the other side were thirty people or so, of all ages, some dressed in military apparel and others in shabby factory clothes, all staring at her.

"Dear friends, don't scare me, I'm an old woman!" she pleaded.

The Bolsheviks were not known for their mercy. From the very start of the revolution, they had rounded up and executed their political enemies without hesitation. That very summer, in the basement of an apartment building in Ekaterinburg, Tsar Nicholas II, who'd helped Anna's family just four years earlier, was savagely executed at gunpoint with his entire immediate family, their bodies later dumped into a giant hole in the earth and burned so that they could never be identified. The Bolsheviks had intended to disappear the royal family from history, as if in an illusionist's poof of smoke—as if the Russian people might suddenly forget their past, forget that they had been ruled over by a tsar for ten centuries. Anna of course would not have known about the assassinations, which were discovered only years later, but there was enough violence even in those early days for her to understand what was happening. As she stared at the men outside her door, she must have been thinking what they might do to her, the widow of nineteenth-century Russia's most passionate voice for conservatism, a man who had spent the last decade of his life warning Russians against these very revolutionaries.

Which is why, on that frigid February morning, she had every reason to believe that this was the end for her.

To Anna's shock, however, the group leader spoke in a calm, respectful voice. "We mean no harm," he said gently. "Don't be afraid. We're not here for you. We know who you are and won't do anything bad to you. We just need to have a look around your room."

After a few minutes, they were satisfied.

"So can I lock the door?" Anna asked.

"Lock it, lock it," the leader responded.

She later learned that the mob had been looking for a government official they believed was hiding in the building. Yet that didn't account for why she'd heard her husband's name spoken twice just before they knocked. Later, another sanitarium guest explained: when the men asked her who was living in Room 10, she told them it was the wife of Fyodor Dostoyevsky. On hearing this, the group leader softened, responding deferentially: "We won't bother her. We respect Dostoyevsky."

SAFE FOR THE MOMENT, Anna was nonetheless terrified for her country. Everything her husband had warned against, everything she had feared, was now a reality. This was a country she no longer recognized, an era she wished no part of.

She sought outlets for her troubled heart in her own family and in the soothing rhythms of life in Crimea, where before the war she had bought a small plot of land in the mountains with a three-story dacha with a charming apple orchard. In the summer of 1917, carrying Dostoyevsky's manuscripts with her, Anna traveled to this country home—Otrada, she named it, or "Happiness"—to spend a few months with her son and his family while working on the second edition of the *Bibliographical Index*. She spent much of her free time gardening, proud of the fact that she did the planting in the orchard with her own hands. One day she planned on bequeathing Otrada to her grandchildren, Anna's other great source of joy in those hard years. She visited them often, and they came to see her in the Crimea. Fyodor's wife, Ekaterina Petrovna, recalled one visit when she could hear Anna praying behind a closed door every evening,

> in the voice of passionate prayer, conviction, hope, at times with tears. That's the way a person prays in whom there has never arisen a shadow of doubt, who believes blindly, without reasoning. Anna Grigoryevna condemned and was indig-

nant toward mysticism or spiritual awakenings. She found that one can either believe as the Gospels command, or not believe at all.

Anna, it appears, was the last true believer in the Dostoyevsky family.

She had planned to spend a few more months at Otrada and then return to Petersburg, but in August a malaria epidemic broke out in the countryside around Otrada. Worse still, a local yardman who had just returned from a stint in the Red Army, probably taking the owner of the country home for a wealthy aristocrat, threatened to "liquidate" Anna—a favorite term of the Bolsheviks in those days—along with many other enemies of the new regime they planned to erase, one by one, from history. Anna knew she had to leave the area right away.

On August 22, 1917, she left for the train station with Ekaterina Petrovna and her grandchildren. They planned to travel together as far as Tuapse, where Ekaterina and the boys would head on to meet Fyodor, who was on business in Pyatigorsk, and Anna would return to Petersburg. But Anna fell ill and decided to remain in the Crimea, a place long familiar to her, moving on alone to Yalta, on the Black Sea. On the way she came down with full-blown malaria, and as soon as she arrived in Yalta she checked into a tiny room at the Hôtel de France. In that room, amid the soothing sounds of the Black Sea, she would rest until the disease had run its course.

Anna still had big plans. "I am seventy-two years old,* but I do not want to die yet," she told Leonid Grossman earlier that summer. "I have a feeling I will live as long as my mother did—making it into my late nineties! I have much work to do still." She dreamed of publishing a complete scholarly index to the materials contained in the Dostoyevsky Museum, opening another library in her husband's name, erecting a monument to him in Moscow. By now she had gathered more than two thousand new items for the second edition of the *Bibliographical Index*, and she

---

*Actually seventy-one; she would have turned seventy-two the following year, in August 1918.

continued to correspond with Dostoyevsky scholars and regularly sent new material to the Dostoyevsky Museum in Moscow. People who met her during this time were struck by Anna's determination, by the seemingly endless fount of energy that poured out of this gray-haired, emaciated woman, who refused to accept the limitations of age—or of the malaria she had never really conquered, and which now was slowly killing her.

She spent most of her final months lying in bed "in complete isolation," except for a few people who visited her daily, recalled an acquaintance who got to know Anna in this period. When she did emerge from her room, she would not allow others to speak of her illness and refused to take the medicine or follow the diet prescribed to her. Those around her believed that Anna's stubborn refusal to accept that she was seriously ill, and her obstinate commitment to her work, accelerated her illness. Neither warnings from her doctor nor entreaties from friendly hotel residents could persuade her to pace herself, to give herself time to get better.

On the morning of June 9, 1918, painful stomach paroxysms forced her back into her bed, where she lay for hours. There, in that tiny hotel room, with the sounds of gently lapping ocean waves outside her window, and amid vials of medicines and pens and voluminous bundles of well-organized papers, Anna slowly lost consciousness and never woke up.

The Afterlife of Anna Dostoyevskaya

Wartime complications prevented Anna from being buried next to her husband, despite a clear stipulation in her will and a wish she had repeated often to her family. Instead she was buried in a small local cemetery in the town of Yalta.

Throughout the 1920s, her grandson Andrei Fyodorovich Dostoyevsky and his mother, Ekaterina Petrovna, regularly visited Anna's grave. After Lyubov' died, childless, in 1926, they were all that remained of Dostoyevsky's family. (The writer's son, Fyodor, and *his* son, Fyodor, had both died of typhus in Moscow in 1921.) In 1932 the church in Yalta where Anna's remains were buried was destroyed, whereupon Andrei and Ekaterina Petrovna came to Yalta and hired workers to restore it. In July 1934, robbers dug up the grave.

During the Second World War, Andrei served as a frontline soldier and suffered serious wounds that made it difficult for him to travel to Yalta to check on his grandmother's gravesite. Word reached him that her grave had been "liquidated" during the war, but in 1959 the Yalta city government took the initiative to reinstate the grave and erect a marble headstone over it.

On June 9, 1968, the fiftieth anniversary of Anna's death, Andrei Fyodorovich, now well into his sixties and weak from illness, at last fulfilled his grandmother's most important wish. With the assistance of members of the Soviet Writers' Union, he arranged to have Anna's remains returned by train to Petersburg. After a three-day journey of more than a thousand miles, rolling past the snow-crested peaks of the Caucasus, the undulating landscape of Central Russia, and the great northern Russian steppe, her ashes were returned to the city she had always loved. They were brought to the Tikhvin Cemetery of the Alexander Nevsky Monastery, where she would be interred next to the man she loved.

Making your way today through the narrow, well-kept gravel pathways of the cemetery, canopied by great linden and oak trees, past the imposing tombs of poets Vasily Zhukovsky and Nikolai Nekrasov, you come to Dostoyevsky's impressive gravesite. Bordered by a low iron enclosure, his six-foot-high tombstone is surrounded by a modest, well-manicured garden. Beneath a stone cross is a sculpted bust of Dostoyevsky in his prime, wearing the neatly ironed frock coat in which he so often worked. Above that sculpture, boldly etched in the Old Church Slavonic script, is the writer's name, along with his favorite words from the Gospel of John, which serve as the epigraph to *The Brothers Karamazov*: "Verily, verily, I say unto you, Except a corn of wheat fall into the ground and die, it abideth alone: but if it die, it bringeth forth much fruit."

Adjacent to the tomb's base, about three feet above the ground, a second inscription is carved in script so small it can be read only when standing very close: "Anna Grigoryevna Dostoyevskaya. 1846–1918."

"I HAVE ALWAYS NEEDED AN IDEA IN LIFE," Anna told Leonid Grossman a few years before her death. "And I was always busy with some sort of activity, which consumed me entirely." Dostoyevsky became her idea, and the dissemination of his writings the activity that consumed her life. Yet, despite the crucial role she played in the novelist's life and career, Anna neither sought nor enjoyed the limelight. She had lived for her husband, she always insisted, "the joy and pride and happiness of my life, my sun, my god!"

To the many friends, publishers, and writers who knew her, Anna was the model of a valorous wife and mother. Leo Tolstoy, whose troubled relationship with his own wife was well-known at the time, told Anna during their one meeting after Dostoyevsky's death that "many Russian writers would feel better if they had wives like Dostoyevsky's." But there were others who considered Anna an enabler, a woman who failed to set boundaries for her husband and gave up her own identity in service of his needs. Some of Dostoyevsky's own relatives viewed her as an intruder who controlled her husband and stood between them and his pocketbook. In some quarters her toughness in business earned Anna the reputation of a "tight-fisted and shrewd businesswoman," one of the most insulting monikers you could receive in a Russian culture steeped in the Orthodox Christian value of self-abnegation and suspicion of moneymaking. The Soviet writer Lydia Chukovskaya went even further, calling Anna "frightening" and "terrible":

> I always hated wives of great people and thought: she is better than this. Even Sofya Andreyevna [Tolstaya] was better than the life she lived. Anna Grigoryevna is greedy and stingy. She forced [her husband], a poor sick person with asthma, with epilepsy, to work day and night, in order "to leave something for the children." What vulgarity! He writes her: "I ate lunch for a ruble." He earned tens of thousands and couldn't spend two rubles on lunch!

There is scant evidence to support these claims. If anything, Dostoyevsky was the one who'd felt the need to work like a dog and constantly suffered because of his inability to provide for the children, while Anna provided for them for many years after her husband's death. These skewed perspectives on Anna's character, which, like that of many spouses of great writers, have become the stuff of legend, say more about her critics than about Anna herself.

Whether idolized or demonized, Anna was not someone to be ignored. Her accomplishments had an undeniable significance to the course of Russian literary history, and her conduct as Dostoyevsky's partner would be the standard against which future generations of Russian writers' spouses measured themselves. Anna Dostoyevskaya would become for many the exemplar of how to be—and, for others, how *not* to be—in relationship with a creative genius.

Perhaps it is more useful to ask how Anna viewed her own life. Looking back on her years with Dostoyevsky and the decades following, she wrote in her memoir: "Despite all the material misfortunes and moral sufferings it has been my lot to bear I consider my life to have been one of exceptional happiness, and I would not wish to change anything in it." More than a century after Anna wrote these words, they still carry the moral force of the woman who came to embody one of nineteenth-century Russian literature's most prominent messages: life is what happens to us, but destiny is what we do with it. Navigating the competing ideologies of her time, working through one misfortune after another, Anna discovered in the end perhaps the most consequential freedom of all: the freedom to choose one's own individual response to one's life circumstances.

As a contrast, consider the life of Polina Suslova, a more typical feminist of her generation, who strove to achieve an ideal of independence so uncompromising that she was incapable of imagining other possible ways of being. "Better die of grief, but free, independent of things external, to one's convictions," Polina had resolved in her diary in 1865, during the period of her affair with Dostoyevsky, "and return one's soul to God as pure as it was, rather than to make concessions." She spent the rest of her life yoked to this extremist vision and went on to wreck the lives of multiple lovers and husbands before ruining her own. Polina died alone in Sevastopol, in the Crimea, at the age of seventy-nine, within just a few months and just a few miles of Anna. Both had known hardship and struggle, but these had taught Anna a different set of life lessons and led her to a different fate.

Deftly synthesizing the traditionalism of her parents' generation with the progressive ideas of her own, while never forgetting the lessons she had learned in those hard years of European exile, Anna Snitkina Dostoyevskaya found a purpose to guide her life: to honor her own experiences and potential while celebrating the work of the artist, the man, she loved. In so doing, she created a model of female agency that still has the power to inspire those of us—women and men alike—who seek meaning and fulfillment in our own troubled times.

ACKNOWLEDGMENTS

Writing and publishing a book can feel like a great gamble. I have been extremely fortunate to have had at my side over the past eight years of research and writing people without whom I never would have finished *The Gambler Wife*, or perhaps even dared to start it.

The day I met my agent, Rob McQuilkin, was one of my luckiest. With his signature combination of artistic and professional integrity, business savvy, and tenacity, as well as a gambler's instinct of his own, Rob has supported, inspired, and challenged me during the creation of this book and throughout my writing career. Rob remains my most cherished longtime guide through the vagaries of the publishing industry.

My editor, Calvert Morgan, believed in this book from the beginning, glimpsing many of its possibilities before I did. His sharp editorial eye, creative intelligence, and tough love allowed me to produce work far richer than it otherwise would have been. I also thank the team at Riverhead for transforming the finished manuscript into a work we can be proud of, and for their enthusiasm in bringing it to the world: Jynne Martin, Glory Plata, Catalina Trigo, Ashley Sutton, Brooke Halstead, and others. Many thanks, as well, to Lisa Pisani, my intrepid research assistant, whose knack for tracking down obscure sources anywhere in the world has benefited my work.

I am grateful to scholar Irina Andrianova, Russia's foremost researcher on Anna Dostoyevskaya, for introducing me to little-known or previously unseen documents from Anna's archives that have proven a boon to this book.

With love and appreciation I remember the late Sharon Leiter, a brilliant poet and scholar whose insights and editorial advice I will sorely miss.

I owe a debt of gratitude to the late Joseph Frank, the preeminent American scholar of Dostoyevsky, who was my mentor at Stanford graduate school and kindled my scholarly fascination with the writer. Frank's five-volume intellectual biography of Dostoyevsky, still the best such work, was always close at hand during the research and writing of this book.

I thank the European scholars who aided me on an extremely fruitful research trip I took to Germany and Switzerland in the summer of 2018. In Dresden, Olga and Gisbert Grossman escorted me to the key Dostoyevsky sites and shared their groundbreaking research on the Dostoyevskys' life in that town. In Baden-Baden, Renate Effern guided me on a tour of relevant sites and shared her original research on Dostoyevsky and Turgenev in Germany. Lutz Schenkel, director of the casino in Bad Homburg, gave me a private tour and helped me gain access to rare materials from the Bad Homburg city archives. And Thomas Schindler, director of Baden-Baden's casino, spent long hours in conversation with me and guided me through the gaming halls, including the very room where Dostoyevsky most often gambled.

I am grateful to writers and scholars Jay Parini and Briallen Hopper for reading early drafts of the manuscript, and to Carol Apollonio and Dana Gioia for their insights and advice, over the years. Many thanks, as well, to other colleagues whose support has aided the writing of *The Gambler Wife*: Wrenn Carlson, Pat Bristowe, Marva Barnett, Monica Patterson, Dorothe Bach, and Michael Palmer.

It is a well-known adage in Russian literary circles: One loves either Tolstoy or Dostoyevsky, but never both. As I look back on my journey with these two writers, now more than a quarter century long, I see that I was destined to be an exception to this rule. I attribute the shift in my scholarly focus from Tolstoy to Dostoyevsky to my decade-long experience of teaching Books Behind Bars: Life, Literature, and Leadership, a University of Virginia course where my undergraduate students meet with incarcerated youth to explore urgent life questions through conversations about classic works by Dostoyevsky and other Russian writers. This experience has given me a deeper appreciation of the genius of Dostoyevsky, who explores the themes of crime, punishment, and redemption, and who spent four harrowing years in a Siberian prison camp. I am indebted to my Books Behind Bars students from Beaumont Juvenile Correctional Center, Bon Air Juvenile Correctional Center, Virginia Department of Juvenile Justice Community Placement Program, and the University of Virginia. Their courage and insights have inspired me as a teacher and scholar, and led to the writing of this book.

I am grateful to my friend and fellow author Marietta McCarty, whose wisdom, intelligence, and warmth have been my steadfast companions on the writing journey. Marietta has helped pave the way for some of my most important creative breakthroughs, made during our regular fireside chats, replete with fine cheese, conversation, and friendship.

I would like to thank three close friends who whose moral and intellectual support aided me in the writing of *The Gambler Wife*: Mike Signer brought fierce intelligence and wisdom to our many clarifying conversations. James Yates deepened my thinking about the psychological and philosophical dimensions of the story. And John Gray helped me uncover important human truths that often eluded me. I also thank friends Jane Barnes, Jonathan Coleman, Pat Bristowe, Carolyn McGrath, Dorothy Kolomeisky, and Dawn Hunt.

I owe a debt of gratitude to my parents, my staunchest longtime supporters, who launched me on my path by suggesting, while I was still in high school, that I start studying Russian at a local college. My father, who passed away in 2018, was a businessman who instilled in me the values of risk-taking, self-discipline, and personal integrity. He was excited about *The Gambler Wife* and encouraged me to keep the faith when things became challenging. Were he still alive, he would be one of the book's most sympathetic readers.

I thank my three older brothers, Greg, Bob, and Mike, who have cheered me on in all my endeavors. Mike, a fellow author and academic, has aided me at key moments in my career and encouraged me to remain true to my intellectual and creative instincts.

My deepest appreciation goes to my immediate family. My wife, Corinne, a passionate and accomplished woman who finds creative solutions to the greatest challenges, is someone Anna Dostoyevskaya would have admired. Corinne has taken many risks in her life—not least her decision to marry me—and the payoff has been mine. Of our many gambles together, the most gratifying has been raising two boys, Evan and Ian. (At eight years old, Ian already insists that "writing is in my blood.") Corinne has stood by my side, sacrificed much, and loved me through every failure and triumph on my journey as a writer.

A NOTE ON SOURCES

The story told in *The Gambler Wife* is reconstructed from a wide range of sources, including archival materials previously unseen in English and other untapped Russian-language documents. Be it the color and material of the dress Anna wore on Dostoyevsky's birthday, or the weather on the day after the couple arrived in Baden-Baden, I have taken pains to ensure that every detail in this book is a documented fact. When a character says or thinks something, the fact is drawn directly from a diary, letter, or memoir, sources that until now have been mined largely by Slavic specialists contributing to scholarly publications.

One of those books, *Three Loves of Dostoyevsky*, by Soviet scholar Marc Slonim, was published first in Russian by the Chekhov Publishing House in New York and then in an English translation in 1955. Slonim argued that Dostoyevsky's marriage to Anna ended the cycle of sexual compulsion and self-destructive mania that had defined the writer's life to that point, giving Dostoyevsky "something constant . . . he could rely on when he was torn by the contradictions of his impulses and theories." Despite the crucial role that gambling played in Dostoyevsky's apprehension of the world and in his relationship with Anna, however, the subject received scant treatment in Slonim's account. Similarly, Slonim had little to say about Anna's place within the Russian feminist movement, her evolution into a successful businesswoman, or her important contributions to Russian culture as a publisher, bibliographer, and memoirist.

Soviet scholar Sergei Belov added to the portrait of Anna in *A Writer's Wife: Dostoyevsky's Last Love*, published in Russian in 1986. This biographical account included discussion of her important professional and personal role in Dostoyevsky's life and career, offering a fuller portrait of Anna's upbringing and social context, her role in keeping Dostoyevsky afloat, and her efforts to ensure his legacy.

And yet the books by Slonim and Belov, like other previous biographical accounts, present Anna in terms of what she meant to Dostoyevsky and his career, minimizing her own agency and accomplishments as a bold feminist and pioneering businesswoman. This is the case with the recent book *Dostoevsky in Love: An Intimate Life* by Alex Christofi, who describes Dostoyevsky's romantic relationships from the writer's perspective alone, and with significant omissions that reflect a lack of access to important Russian-language sources. This tendency to tell the story from Dostoyevsky's perspective is common to the major biographies of the writer. The best of these is the seminal five-volume series by Joseph Frank, recently condensed into a single 984-page volume, *Dostoevsky: A Writer in His Time*. Frank's work, like other estimable biographies, such as Avrahm Yarmolinsky's *Dostoevsky: A Life* (1934), Konstantin Mochulsky's *Dostoevsky: His Life and Work* (1967), Leonid Grossman's *Dostoevsky: A Biography* (1975), Richard Freeborn's *Dostoevsky (Life and Times)* (2005), and Anthony Briggs's *Brief Lives: Fyodor Dostoyevsky* (2011), devotes a very small part of the overall narrative to Anna, and is focused primarily on Anna's significance to Dostoyevsky as a writer, rather than what their relationship might have meant to her. American scholar Alexandra Popoff began to redress that balance in her 2012 book *The Wives: The Women Behind Russia's Literary Giants*, although Anna received but a brief chapter in that book.

What of Anna Dostoyevskaya's own memoir, *Reminiscences*? Does her story, told in her own voice, give us the richly textured account we might hope for? Yes and no. Immediately recognized as an important literary event upon its Russian publication seven years after her death, in 1925, Anna's portrait of her life with Dostoyevsky remains an invaluable source of information about many aspects of both her life and her husband's, as well as the milieu in which they lived. Yet her manuscript was not published in its entirety; the original edition omitted crucial sections related to Anna's publishing enterprise after her husband's death, as well as other important episodes in her life that I recount in this book—including her attendance at the coronation of Tsar Alexander II in 1856, her parents' matchmaking efforts on her behalf when she was still a teenager, and her terrifying confrontation with revolutionaries at a Petersburg sanitarium in 1917. Thanks to the first complete edition of *Reminiscences*, finally published in Russia in 2015 as *Reminiscences 1846–1917: Sun of My Life—Fyodor Dostoyevsky*, I have been able to fill in significant gaps in our understanding of the details of Anna's life.

Yet even this complete edition of Anna's memoir lacks the sort of historical perspective that can only be gained with the passage of time. Anna's primary aim in writing *Reminiscences* was to present an idealized portrait of her husband, not to offer an unvarnished portrait of their marriage. The couple's four tumultuous years in Europe, for instance, constitute but a brief section of *Reminiscences*, and even then she omits some telling details—making no mention of her husband's mistress Polina Suslova, for example, or of the distress Anna experienced after discovering their correspondence.

Moreover, in the memoir Anna takes pains to cast herself in a supporting role to Dostoyevsky, telling readers in the opening paragraph of her preface that "I am utterly lacking in literary talent." As scholars have noted, the memoir itself belies her assessment, while her well-documented achievements as an editor, publisher, and bibliographer offer ample proof of her independent professional accomplishment. Anna minimized her significance out of genuine humility, to be sure, but also to avoid violating Russian expectations about how a writer's widow should present herself—as little more than an ambassador. In her effort to downplay her significance, Anna made herself appear more traditional, more passive, and less complex than she was. *The Gambler Wife* is an attempt to offer a fuller portrait that draws on Anna's letters, personal diaries, and the recollections of others to capture her intelligence, complexity, and agency.

Some of these sources have never been seen before in English. The memoir of Marya Nikolayevna Stoyunina, Anna's gymnasium classmate and lifelong friend, offers a brief but colorful portrait of Anna as an intelligent, bold, and mischievous gymnasium student. The compact, valuable memoir by Z. S. Kovrigina, Anna's acquaintance from her last months, provides us with the most intimate picture we have of Anna in her final days as she lay slowly dying of malaria. Both of these memoirs were published in the two-volume scholarly Russian work *F. M. Dostoyevsky: Articles and Materials*.

Another useful Russian source, *F. M. Dostoyevsky in Forgotten and Unknown Reminiscences of Contemporaries*, includes Marya Stoyunina's account of the later years of the Dostoyevskys' marriage, as well as critic and poet Alexander Alekseyevich Izmailov's account of his conversations with Anna in the last years of her life. Other valuable Russian sources that present Anna's intimate, previously unpublished letters to extended family and friends are *Dostoyevsky in Unpublished Correspondence with Contemporaries* and "Correspondence of Anna Dostoyevskaya with Contemporaries," a 1976 article in the Soviet journal *Baikal*.

My research also uncovered little-known materials from Anna's archives that have never before been seen in English. In the past decade, a researcher named Irina Andrianova of Petrozavodsk State University has begun to mine these materials, and she generously shared with me her research. Andrianova's scholarly works—in particular her 2013 Russian-language book *Anna Dostoyevskaya: Calling and Confession*—contain selections that have enriched the portrait of Anna in *The Gambler Wife*: unpublished drafts of Anna's *Reminiscences*, her private notebooks and notes on her husband's literary work, her personal correspondence with Dostoyevsky and others, as well as business and housekeeping documents.

One fascinating archival document Professor Andrianova discovered is Anna's 1913 letter to Tsar Nicholas II, in which she solicits his financial assistance. This remarkable letter, which proved pivotal to Anna's final years after the tsar agreed to pay for her grandchildren's education, reveals Anna's entrée into the highest political circles—ironic, given Dostoyevsky's revolutionary past—while reflecting how fully the writer had come to accept the realities of the Russian political system in his later years.

The Gambler Wife also draws on materials that neither Anna nor her husband ever intended to be made public. "Anya, give me your word that you'll never show anyone these letters," Dostoyevsky wrote to her from Bad Homburg in 1867. "I don't want tongues to wag about this abominable situation of mine." Anna was no less determined to preserve the secrecy of her own correspondence. "In the event that my letters to my husband should be found," she wrote in her will, "I request that my heirs destroy them, since it would be extremely difficult for me if they should ever appear in print." Not only were these letters never destroyed, but many of them were published in the thirty-volume Russian edition of the *Complete Collected Works of F. M. Dostoyevsky,* published between 1972 and 1990. American scholars David Lowe and Ronald Meyer subsequently translated the letters and compiled them in a five-volume English-language edition, still the best resource in English on Dostoyevsky's correspondence.

Unfortunately, Anna's side of the epistolary conversation is missing from Lowe and Meyer's compilation, a lacuna that has yet to be filled by any English-language source. In 1976 the material became available in Russian when the Leningrad-based publisher Nauka issued an annotated scholarly volume of the complete correspondence between Anna and her husband. A crucial source for my book, this Russian volume contains many letters from Anna that have never been translated into English. It also allowed me to reconstruct key moments from the couple's later years together—not least the writer's 1880 appearance and address at the famous Pushkin Celebration.

Finally, I draw extensively on the personal diary Anna kept during the year of 1867, which chronicles in painstaking detail every moment of debasement and ecstasy she experienced as a newlywed. "I'd give a lot, Anyechka, to find out what it is you're writing in those little squiggles of yours," Dostoyevsky said one evening early in their honeymoon. "You're saying bad things about me, no doubt?" Indeed she was, along with other, more touching and poignant things—almost all of it in shorthand, to ensure that her personal diary would remain hers alone. Later in life, as she realized that her diary could not be kept confidential indefinitely, she doctored it to whitewash its portrayal of her husband. But she only partially succeeded in this effort, and thanks to the work of Soviet-era Dostoyevsky scholars we now have access to much of the original diary. Critical chunks of this document are still available only in Russian, under the title *The Diary of 1867*—including Anna's account of their stay in Geneva in 1867, a critical moment in the writer's career and a turning point in the Dostoyevskys' marriage. These pages allow us to witness Anna's reactions to the historic Peace Congress of 1867, as well as the last known episode in her protracted clandestine battle with Polina Suslova.

Another important goal of *The Gambler Wife* is to situate Anna's story within its proper social and cultural context, an effort enabled by a number of excellent works of historical scholarship. For an understanding of the Russian feminist movement of the nineteenth and early twentieth centuries, I have relied on Richard Stites's *The Women's Liberation Movement in Russia: Feminism, Nihilism, and Bolshevism, 1860–1930* and Barbara Alpern Engel's *Mothers and Daughters: Women of the Intelligentsia in Nineteenth-Century Russia.* My portrayal of the Russian feminist movement was enriched by the private diary of Polina Suslova, as well as

the memoir of Sofya Kovalevskaya, a pioneering mathematician who also happened to be the sister of the writer's love interest Anna Korvin-Krukovskaya. For
an understanding of the literary and intellectual milieu in which Dostoyevsky
worked, I have drawn in part on Joseph Frank's magisterial five-volume intellectual biography of Dostoyevsky, still the best on the writer in any language.

One of the joys of writing this book was an extremely fruitful research trip to
Europe I took in the summer of 2018. During this trip I retraced the Dostoyevskys'
footsteps through Germany and Switzerland, visiting not only Dresden, where
they spent nearly a year and a half, and Geneva, the setting for "Life and Fate,"
chapter 9 in part two of *The Gambler Wife*, but also the casinos in Wiesbaden, Bad
Homburg, and Baden-Baden, where the book's major gambling scenes take place.
In Baden-Baden, I visited the very gaming hall where Dostoyevsky most often
gambled; it is still in use today and has been preserved to look almost identical to
the way it did in the 1860s. In Bad Homburg, I was given access to rare archival
documents that provided me with historical detail about the culture of gambling
in that town—down to the nationalities and even names of other guests at Dostoyevsky's hotel. In Wiesbaden, I visited the famed casino where Dostoyevsky played
roulette, and the former site of the synagogue that figured in his final gambling
spree and cessation of his addiction. And in Geneva I spent an afternoon at the
gravesite of the Dostoyevskys' first child, Sonya, who was born in February 1868 and
died three months later. As I breathed the fresh air of Lake Geneva, I understood—
more powerfully than any document could have conveyed—why this town seemed
to offer the couple a respite from their persistent troubles.

A WORD ON TRANSLATION AND DATES

My translation of passages from Anna Dostoyevskaya's memoir, *Reminiscences*, is
based on that of Beatrice Stillman, published in the United States by Liveright in
1975. I have cross-checked her work against the Russian original, silently correct-
ing errors when necessary and making every effort to reflect the locution and ca-
dence of Anna's original while making it sound as natural to contemporary
American ears as it would have to a Russian reader of her time. My translation of
Anna's private diary of 1867 is based on that of René Fülöp-Miller and Dr. Eckstein, published by Macmillan in 1928 under the title *The Diary of Dostoyevsky's
Wife*. However, this translation contains omissions, errors, and certain stylistic
infelicities, which I have silently emended as necessary. In instances where I cite
third-party quotations of Dostoyevsky or others, I have cross-checked against Russian originals whenever possible. Unless otherwise specified, all other translations
from Russian-language sources as well as German-language sources are my own.

A number of works by Dostoyevsky mentioned in this book have been published under varying titles. *The Insulted and Injured* is sometimes translated as *The
Insulted and Humiliated* or *The Humiliated and Wronged*; *Notes from the House of
the Dead* as *Notes from the Dead House* or simply *The Dead House*; *Notes from*

Underground as *Notes from the Underground*; *The Possessed* as *The Devils* or *Demons*; and *The Adolescent* as *A Raw Youth* or *An Accidental Family*.

Dates in this book are given according to the old-style Julian calendar, in effect in Russia until 1918. The Julian calendar was twelve days behind the Western (Gregorian) calendar in the nineteenth century, and thirteen days behind it in the twentieth.

NOTES

INTRODUCTION

x **"It was dim and hushed"**: Anna Dostoevsky, *Dostoevsky: Reminiscences*, trans. and ed. Beatrice Stillman (New York: Liveright, 1975), 17. I have taken my translations from this edition, cross-checking with the Russian original in A. G. Dostoevskaia, *Vospominanii 1846–1917: Solntse moei zhizni—Fedor Dostoevskii*, ed. Irina S. Andrianova and Boris N. Tikhomirov (Moscow: Boslen, 2015). When necessary, I silently make corrections to the Stillman translation.

x **"Well now, what kind of writers"**: Ibid., 58.

xi **"I really puffed him up"**: Quoted in Joseph Frank, *Dostoevsky: A Writer in His Time* (Princeton, NJ: Princeton University Press, 2010), 113.

xii **"can have a place"**: Quoted ibid., 97.

xii **"a realist in the higher sense"**: "They call me a psychologist," Dostoyevsky wrote in a notebook of 1880–81. "Untrue: I am simply a realist in the higher sense—that is, I depict all the depth of the human soul." Cited from F. M. Dostoevskii, *Polnoe sobranie sochinenii v tridtsati tomakh* (Leningrad: Nauka, 1986), vol. 27, 65.

xiii **"I was quite a daydreamer"**: Anna Dostoevsky, *Dostoevsky: Reminiscences*, 59.

xiii **"How long have you"**: Ibid., 19.

xiv **"I felt I was setting out"**: Ibid., 15.

xv **"Educated women need"**: Quoted in Richard Stites, *The Women's Liberation Movement in Russia: Feminism, Nihilism, and Bolshevism, 1860–1930* (Princeton, NJ: Princeton University Press, 1978), 79.

xv **"Christian love"**: Frank, *Dostoevsky: The Stir of Liberation, 1860–1865* (Princeton, NJ: Princeton University Press, 1986), 97.

xv **"debauch of acquisition"**: This phrase is quoted in Stites, *The Women's Liberation Movement in Russia*, 79.

xv **"serious, almost stern"**: Anna Dostoevsky, *Dostoevsky: Reminiscences*, 60.

xvi **"I was glad"**: Quoted ibid., 19.

xvii **"I left Dostoyevsky's apartment"**: A. G. Dostoevskaia, *Vospominanii 1846–1917: Solntse moei zhizni—Fedor Dostoevskii*, 18.

xvii **"Earning one's own way"**: Entry of October 6, 1866, quoted in A. G. Dostoevskaia, *Dnevnik 1867 goda* (Moscow: Nauka, 1993), 316.

xvii **"simply, seriously, almost sternly"**: Anna Dostoevsky, *Dostoevsky: Reminiscences*, 21.

xviii **"As I watched"**: Ibid., 21–22.

xviii **"It would seem"**: Entry of October 4, 1866, quoted in A. G. Dostoevskaia, *Dnevnik 1867 goda*, 307.

xix **thirty thousand dollars in today's money**: Historical conversion rates remain a subject of scholarly controversy. For conversations from historical rubles into historical dollars until the year 1880, I use as benchmark the well-known 1867 purchase of Alaska by the United States from Russia. The exchange rate of the transaction was 1.6 rubles for one dollar, meaning that one ruble was valued at $0.625. (I am grateful to Larissa Kochetkova, senior vice president of PNC Investments in Virginia, for providing me with this figure.) For conversions from historical rubles currencies into historical dollars beginning in the year 1880, I rely on the historical currency converter published by Professor Rodney Edvinsson at http://www.historicalstatistics.org/currencyconverter.html. To calculate the present-day value of historical dollars, I use the inflation calculator based on official records published by the U.S. Department of Labor: https://www.officialdata.org/.

xix **for *Fathers and Sons* alone**: On Turgenev's honorarium, see Anastasia Tuliakova, "Skol'ko zarabatyvali russkie pisateli?," *Arzamas*, July 8, 2016, https://arzamas.academy/mag/315-money.

xix **the equivalent of a year and a half's living wage**: Cited from William Mills Todd III, "'To Be Continued': Dostoevsky's Evolving Poetics of Serialized Publication," *Dostoevsky Studies* 18 (2014): 27. To put Dostoyevsky's gamble into context: At the time you could buy a four-person horse-drawn carriage for two thousand rubles, or a three-story home in the country for six thousand. A Russian lawyer could earn as much as three thousand to five thousand rubles a year, while a writer like Dostoyevsky, without independent means, would have been able to just get by on two thousand a year, or about twenty thousand dollars today.

xx **"My cherished dream"**: Anna Dostoevsky, *Dostoevsky: Reminiscences*, 15.

xxi **"The storm is approaching"**: Alexander Herzen, "The Russian People and Socialism. A Letter to Michelet" (1851), in *My Past and Thoughts: The Memoirs of Alexander Herzen*, trans. Constance Garnett (New York: Alfred A. Knopf, 1928), vol. 4, 1649.

xxiv **"You are the rarest"**: Letter to Anna Dostoyevskaya, July 24, 1876, in F. M. Dostoevskii, *Polnoe sobranie sochinenii v tridtsati tomakh*, vol. 29, book 2, 112.

xxiv **"You are the only woman"**: Quoted in S. V. Belov, *Zhena pisatelia: Posledniaia liubov' F. M. Dostoevskogo* (Moscow: Sovetskaia Rossiia, 1986), 204. Also in Anna Dostoevsky, *Dostoevsky: Reminiscences*, 384.

I. THE DECENT THING TO DO

4 **"quiet, measured, and serene"**: Anna Dostoevsky, *Dostoevsky: Reminiscences*, trans. and ed. Beatrice Stillman (New York: Liveright, 1975), 10.

4 **"No one tried"**: Ibid., 11.

5 **"as luck would have it"**: Ibid., 10.

5 **"a man of very exuberant"**: Ibid., 5.

6 **"I would have felt"**: Ibid., 9.

6 **"real head of the house"**: Ibid.

7 **a passionate devotee**: These facts taken from Aimée Dostoyevsky, *Fyodor Dostoyevsky: A Study* (London: William Heinemann, 1921), 126–27.

7 **she was pained to read**: "My heart," she would write, "was full of sympathy and pity for Dostoevsky, who had to endure a horrible life in prison at hard labor." Anna Dostoevsky, *Dostoevsky: Reminiscences*, 59.

8 **"It seemed to me"**: Ibid.

8 **"depict a talented"**: Scholar Joseph Frank writes that "Dostoevsky's aim, unprecedented in the Russian novel of his time, was to depict a talented and strong-willed woman who refuses to allow herself to be crushed—who becomes the main *positive* heroine of a major novel." See Joseph Frank, *Dostoevsky: A Writer in His Time* (Princeton, NJ: Princeton University Press, 2010), 115.

9 **"Ladies. Stop being children"**: Quoted in Barbara Alpern Engel, *Mothers and Daughters: Women of the Intelligentsia in Nineteenth-Century Russia* (Cambridge: Cambridge University Press, 1983), 53–55.

10 **"I will never fall"**: N. D. Khvoshchinskaia, *Povesti i rasskazy* (Moscow: Khudozhestvennaia Literatura, 1963), 18–56.

10 **"Value us as your comrades"**: Quoted in Engel, *Mothers and Daughters*, 80.

11 **"there is no destiny"**: Quoted ibid., 58.

12 **"the military and court personnel"**: Quoted in A. G. Dostoevskaia, *Vospominaniia 1846–1917: Solntse moei zhizni—Fedor Dostoevskii*, ed. Irina S. Andrianova and Boris N. Tikhomirov (Moscow: Boslen, 2015), 75–76. Translation mine.

13 **of a "patriarchal" time**: Ibid., 76.

13 **"It was easier"**: Quotation and previous details, ibid., 78.

13 **"People were not ashamed"**: A. G. Dostoevskaia, *Vospominaniia 1846–1917: Solntse moei zhizni—Fedor Dostoevskii*, 85.

14 **"The young man's deception"**: Ibid., 92.

14 **"lively, firm, ardent"**: "Iz Vospominanii M. N. Stoiunina ob A. G. Dostoevskoi," in A. S. Dolinin, ed., *F. M. Dostoevskii: Stat'i i materialy* (Moscow and Leningrad: Mysl', 1924), vol. 2, 578.

15 **"her father and mother"**: Ibid.

15 **"an oval face"**: Ibid., 579.

15 **"All she'd have to do"**: Ibid.

15 **"the singularity of her spiritual qualities"**: "Poslednie mesiatsy zhizni A. G. Dostoevskoi," in Dolinin, *F. M. Dostoevskii: Stat'i i materialy*, vol. 2, 587. Translation mine.

16 **"physics, chemistry and zoology"**: Anna Dostoevsky, *Dostoevsky: Reminiscences*, 11.

16 **The opportunity presented itself**: Details taken from the introductory essay by I. S. Andrianova and B. N. Tikhomirov, "Liubit' Dostoevskogo: Anna Grigorievna Dostoevskaia i ee vospominaniia," in A. G. Dostoevskaia, *Vospominaniia 1846–1917: Solntse moei zhizni—Fedor Dostoevskii*, 16.

16 **"My whole life"**: Entry of October 3, 1867, in A. G. Dostoevskaia, *Dnevnik 1867 goda*, 301.

17 **"It was the first"**: Anna Dostoevsky, *Dostoevsky: Reminiscences*, 12–13.

17 **"Who is offering"**: Ibid., 15.

2. THE GAMBLER

18 **"What's that, 'She returned'"**: Anna Dostoevsky, *Dostoevsky: Reminiscences*, trans. and ed. Beatrice Stillman (New York: Liveright, 1975), 23.

18 **this portmanteau word**: This was not the first time the name "Roulettenberg" had been used for a gambling town in Russia. The Russian translator of William Thackeray's sketch *The Kickleburys on the Rhine*, which appeared in 1851 in *Fatherland Notes* in the same number (6) as a comedy by Dostoyevsky's brother, had rendered "Rougetnoirbourg" as "Rouletteburg." Dostoyevsky in all likelihood remembered this when he sat down to write *The Gambler*.

19 **"With what triumph"**: Anna Dostoevsky, *Dostoevsky: Reminiscences*, 31–32.

19 **"Chatting with me"**: Ibid., 27.

20 **"it seemed strange"**: Ibid., 56.

20 **a passing liaison:** Dostoyevsky had remarked to Mikhail on the difficulty he had when their youngest brother, Andrei, came to visit Dostoyevsky in Petersburg. "Impossible to work or to amuse oneself—you understand." Cited from Joseph Frank, *Dostoevsky: A Writer in His Time* (Princeton, NJ: Princeton University Press, 2010), 62. The amusement Dostoyevsky was likely referring to was the sort that would have been made especially inconvenient by the overnight stay of a prudish younger brother.

21 **"I can't help feeling"**: Letter to Mikhail Dostoyevsky, December 17, 1846, in F. M. Dostoevskii, *Polnoe sobranie sochinenii v tridtsati tomakh* (Leningrad: Nauka, 1985), vol. 28, 135.

21 **"Dostoyevsky never was"**: Quoted in Kenneth Lantz, *The Dostoevsky Encyclopedia* (Westport, CT: Greenwood Press, 2004), 302.

21 **"criminal intentions of overthrowing"**: Ibid., 310.

22 **"Life is everywhere"**: Quoted in Joseph Frank, *Dostoevsky: The Stir of Liberation, 1860–1865* (Princeton, NJ: Princeton University Press, 1986), 5.

22 **"pity for an unfortunate man"**: Cited from Lantz, *The Dostoevsky Encyclopedia*, 104.

23 **"In fact, the more unhappy"**: Quoted ibid., 105.

23 **"At one time"**: Leonid Grossman, *Dostoevsky: A Biography*, trans. Mary Mackler (Indianapolis and New York: Bobbs-Merrill, 1975), 295.

24 **"My nerves are shot"**: Quoted in Frank, *Dostoevsky: The Stir of Liberation*, 294.

24 **"Anna, I'm standing"**: Anna Dostoevsky, *Dostoevsky: Reminiscences*, 30.

25 **"apparently abandoned by everyone"**: Ibid., 24.

25 **"utterly fascinating conversations"**: Ibid., 32.

25 **"I think around four hundred"**: Fyodor Dostoevsky, *The Double* and *The Gambler*, trans. Richard Pevear and Larissa Volokhonsky (New York: Vintage Books, 2007), 195.

25 **"It came to one thousand"**: Ibid., 322.

27 **"naïve, poetic letter"**: "Her letter," Aimée (Lyubov') Dostoyevsky writes, "was reserved among my father's papers; it is simple, naïve, and poetic. She might have been some timid young girl, dazzled by the genius of the great writer." Aimée Dostoyevsky, *Fyodor Dostoyevsky: A Study* (London: William Heinemann, 1921), 105. Subsequent scholarship, however, has raised serious questions about the existence of this letter.

27 **"All my friends"**: Fyodor Dostoevsky, *The Gambler with Polina Suslova's Diary*, trans. Victor Terras, ed. Edward Wasiolek (Chicago: University of Chicago Press, 1972), 208.

27 **"during my first youth"**: Grossman, *Dostoevsky: A Biography*, 277.

28 **worried about his failing wife:** Letter to Varvara Konstant, August 20, 1863: "I'm terribly and sincerely worried about [Marya Dmitriyevna's] health," in Fyodor Dostoevsky, *Complete Letters*, vol. 2 (1860–1867), ed. and trans. David A. Lowe (Ann Arbor, MI: Ardis, 1989), 59.

28 **"for the treatment of my health"**: Letter to Yegor Kovalevsky, Chairman of the Society, July 23, 1863, ibid., 53.

28 **"To seek happiness"**: Letter to Mikhail Dostoyevsky, September 8, 1863, ibid., 62.

29 **sixty-two thousand dollars in today's money:** For conversion from historical francs to historical dollars I rely on the historical currency converter published by Professor Rodney Edvinsson at http://www.historicalstatistics.org/currencyconverter.html. Unless otherwise stated, all other conversions from historical currencies into historical dollars are calculated using the historical currency converter. The only exceptions are conversions from rubles to dollars before the year 1880; the currency converter has no data on ruble exchange rates before 1880. To calculate the present-day value of historical dollars, I use the inflation calculator based on official records published by the U.S. Department of Labor: https://www.officialdata.org/.

29 **"The point here"**: Fyodor Dostoevsky, *The Double and The Gambler*, 320.

29 **As soon as he arrived:** These details taken from Karla Hielscher, *Dostojewski in Deutschland* (Frankfurt am Main: Insel Verlag, 1999), 28.

30 **"How could I fail":** Letter to Mikhail Dostoyevsky, September 8, 1863, in Fyodor Dostoevsky, *Complete Letters*, vol. 2 (1860–1867), 63.

30 **Gambling addiction researchers:** Researcher Sanju George writes: "Another classic cognitive characteristic of people with gambling addiction is 'magical' thinking, that is, they hold irrational beliefs in particular outcomes—it can be a very strong hunch or a belief that following certain rituals will guarantee success. Quoted in George Sanju, "From the Gambler Within: Dostoyevsky's *The Gambler*," *Advances in Psychiatric Treatment* 18, no. 3 (2012): 228.

30 **an irrational, compulsive belief:** Alexei in *The Gambler* engages in a similar sort of thinking: "I drew one conclusion that seems to be correct: in the sequence of accidental chances, there is indeed, if not a system, at any rate the semblance of some order—which, of course, is very strange." Fyodor Dostoevsky, *The Double and The Gambler*, 194. Fifteen years later, in *The Adolescent*, Dostoyevsky would once again give voice to this belief through his hero: "To this day I firmly believe that in gambling complete calm and self-control, which enable one to preserve subtle thinking and careful calculation, will always overcome the crudeness of blind chance." Cited from Fyodor Dostoevsky, *The Adolescent*, trans. Andrew R. MacAndrew (New York and London: W. W. Norton, 1971), 281.

30 **The next day:** These details taken from letter to Varvara Konstant, August 20, 1863, in Fyodor Dostoevsky, *Complete Letters*, vol. 2 (1860–1867), 58.

31 **"It simply consists":** Letter to Varvara Konstant, August 20, 1863, ibid., 57–58.

31 **"A true gentleman":** Fyodor Dostoevsky, *The Double and The Gambler*, 186.

31 **"plebeian, mercenary":** Ibid.

31 **"higher, better society":** Robert Erhard, *Aus der Chronik der Kaiserallee: Geschichte und Geschichten vom Promenade-, Konversations- und Kurhaus* (Baden-Baden, Germany: Kurhaus, 2005), part 2, https://kurhaus-Baden-Baden.de/en/at-the-kurhaus.

32 **"Here in this den":** F. Dershau, "Iz zapisok igroka," *Russkoe slovo* 4 (1859): 57.

32 **"This sad event":** Ibid.

33 **"In all, all that portends":** S. V. Belov, *Zhena pisatelia: Posledniaia liubov' F. M. Dostoevskogo* (Moscow: Sovetskaia Rossiia, 1986), 91–92.

33 **After his stint in Wiesbaden:** According to Frank, *Dostoevsky: A Writer in His Time*, 390.

33 **"I thought you weren't":** This scene with Polina is drawn from Fyodor Dostoevsky, *The Gambler with Polina Suslova's Diary*, 205–7.

34 **"I did not say anything":** Diary entry of September 6, 1863, ibid., 214–15.

35 **"It's absolutely essential":** Letter to Mikhail Dostoyevsky, March 20, 1864, in Fyodor Dostoevsky, *Complete Letters*, vol. 2 (1860–1867), 95.

35 **"the only person I have left":** Letter to Alexander Vrangel, March 31, 1865, ibid., 152.

36 **"His family was left":** Ibid., 153.

36 **"The public," he said, "did not":** Ibid., 154.

36 **"I would gladly":** Ibid., 155.

37 **"I'm alone":** Ibid.

37 **"did so hate women writers":** Sonya Kovalevsky, *Her Recollections of Childhood*, trans. Isabel F. Hapgood (New York: Century, 1895), 109.

37 **"youthful directness, sincerity":** Ibid., 107.

38 **"Anything may be expected":** Ibid., 116.

38 **"Remember, Liza":** Ibid., 121.

38 **"the height of success":** Ibid., 123.

38 **"stately, airy, and colorless":** Ibid., 130.

39 **"But were the Gospels":** Ibid., 134.

39 **"You are an empty-headed":** Ibid., 136.

39 **dismissed the young people:** Ibid.

40 **"eternal mate":** Dostoyevsky would use this phrase in a letter he sent to Polina on April 23, 1867. In Fyodor Dostoevsky, *Complete Letters*, vol. 2 (1860–1867), 229.

40 **"Apollinaria is a sick egoist":** Letter to Nadezhda Suslova, April 19, 1865, ibid., 157.

41 **more than a thousand dollars today:** According to the Deutsche Bundesbank website, "The Coinage Act of 9 July 1873 set the exchange rate of the Prussian thaler against the Mark at 1 thaler = 3 Mark"; see "Purchasing Power Comparisons of Historical Monetary Amounts" at https://www.bundesbank.de/en/statistics/economic-activity-and-prices/producer-and-consumer-prices/purchasing-power-comparisons-of-historical-monetary-amounts-795290. In 1873, one Mark was worth about $0.27. This means that one thaler was worth around $0.81.

41 **"my situation has worsened":** Letter to Polina Suslova, August 10, 1865, in Fyodor Dostoevsky, *Complete Letters*, vol. 2 (1860–1867), 167.

41 **"abominable to the point":** Letter to Polina Suslova, August 12, 1865, ibid., 168–69.

42 **"Save me and deliver me":** Letter to Alexander Vrangel, August 24, 1865, ibid., 171–72.

42 **"after yielding to certain strange":** Letter to Mikhail Katkov, September 10–15, 1865, ibid., 174.

42 **"some painful and cowardly":** Fyodor Dostoevsky, *Crime and Punishment*, trans. Richard Pevear and Larissa Volokhonsky (New York: Vintage Books, 1992), 3.

43 **"I have to put myself":** Letter to Ivan Yanyshev, November 22, 1865, in Fyodor Dostoevsky, *Complete Letters*, vol. 2 (1860–1867), 181.

43 **"Today F[yodor] M[ikhailovich] was here":** Entry of November 2, 1865, cited from Fyodor Dostoevsky, *The Gambler with Polina Suslova's Diary*, 301.

44 **"You and brother Andrei":** Letter to Domnika Dostoyevskaya, February 13, 1866, in Fyodor Dostoevsky, *Complete Letters*, vol. 2 (1860–1867), 187.

44 **"I'm working like a convict":** Letter to Alexander Vrangel, February 18, 1866, ibid., 189–90.

44 **"Petrified by the years":** These details taken from Joseph Frank, *Dostoevsky: The Miraculous Years, 1865–1871* (Princeton, NJ: Princeton University Press, 1995), 47.

44 **"With God's help":** Letter to Alexander Vrangel, February 18, 1866, in Fyodor Dostoevsky, *Complete Letters*, vol. 2 (1860–1867), 189–91.

44 **"At the present moment":** Letter to Alexander Vrangel, May 9, 1866, ibid., 197.

45 **"psychological account of a crime":** Letter to Mikhail Katkov, September 10–15, 1865, ibid., 174.

45 **"straight out":** Letter to Anna Korvin-Krukovskaya, June 17, 1866, ibid., 200.

46 **"I want to do":** Ibid.

46 **"worries me to the point":** Letter to Alexander Milyukov, June 10, 1866, ibid., 208.

46 **"amazed by my own boldness":** Anna Dostoevsky, *Dostoevsky: Reminiscences*, 32.

46 **"whose irresoluteness I could":** Ibid.

47 **more than a little distasteful:** "Both of us became involved with the lives of the characters of the new novel," Anna wrote, "and I began to have my favorites and my antagonists, just as he did. I was sympathetic to the grandmother who gambled away her fortune, and to Mr. Astley; but my contempt was aroused by Polina and by the hero himself, whose irresoluteness I could not forgive. Whereas Dostoevsky was wholly on the gambler's side, and told me that he had experienced many of his hero's emotions and feelings himself. He maintained that it is possible to possess a strong character, to prove that fact by your own life, and nonetheless lack the strength to conquer in yourself the passion for roulette." Ibid.

In a letter to critic and philosopher Nikolai Strakhov, Dostoyevsky described his hero as "a gambler, and not merely an ordinary gambler, just as Pushkin's Covetous Knight is not an ordinary miser. . . . He is a *poet in his own way*, but the fact is that he himself is ashamed of the poetic element in him, because deep down he feels it is despicable, although the need to take risks ennobles him in his own eyes." Quoted in Frank, *Dostoevsky: The Miraculous Years*, 170–71 (emphasis mine).

47 **"Leaving his house"**: Anna Dostoevsky, *Dostoevsky: Reminiscences*, 32.

47 **"the genuine warmth"**: Ibid., 60–61.

3 · A NOVEL PROPOSAL

48 **"*The Gambler* was finished"**: Anna Dostoevsky, *Dostoevsky: Reminiscences*, trans. and ed. Beatrice Stillman (New York: Liveright, 1975), 33.

49 **"was very pleased to hear"**: Ibid., 34.

49 **"When can I"**: Ibid., 35.

50 **"the merry rush"**: Ibid., 36.

51 **"I'll do it gladly"**: Ibid., 38.

51 **"all for nothing"**: Ibid., 39.

51 **"Was I really"**: Ibid.

52 **"immerse myself in some other"**: Ibid.

52 **"heartfelt, interesting talks"**: Ibid., 40.

52 **"Do you know"**: Ibid.

52 **"But how cold"**: Ibid., 41.

52 **"Please don't trouble"**: Ibid.

53 **"all those Hintzes"**: Fyodor Dostoevsky, *The Double* and *The Gambler*, trans. Richard Pevear and Larissa Volokhonsky (New York: Vintage Books, 2007), 321.

53 **"You've turned to wood"**: Ibid., 324.

53 **"I've driven it all"**: Ibid.

54 **"There's what your last gulden"**: Ibid., 329.

55 **"So you're here"**: Anna's visit to Dostoyevsky and the details of his imaginary novel are drawn from Anna Dostoevsky, *Dostoevsky: Reminiscences*, 43–44.

56 **"But, Fyodor Mikhailovich"**: These are Dostoyevsky's exact words as Anna recounted them in *Reminiscences*. Ibid., 45.

57 **"But why would that be impossible?"**: Dostoyevsky's exact words, quoted ibid., 46.

58 **"How can I make"**: Ibid.

58 **"Anna Grigoryevna"**: This final piece of dialogue is reconstructed; ibid., 46–47.

58 **was concerned**: Anna wrote of her mother's reaction: "As a person with experience of the world, she could not help foreseeing that such a marriage had much torment and grief in store for me, as much because of my future husband's terrible disease as from lack of financial means." Ibid., 48.

58 **He visited the Snitkins**: Ibid., 53.

59 **"I ran away"**: Ibid., 54.

59 **"What has become"**: Ibid., 55.

59 **Anna was eager**: "I want to know everything there is to know about you," she told Dostoyevsky, "to see your past clearly, to know you through and through." Ibid., 56.

59 **"strange, mistrustful, and sickly-fanciful"**: See ibid., 394, note 29.

59 **Of Polina Suslova**: Curiously, in her nearly four-hundred-page memoir, Anna never once mentions Polina, despite the significant and troubling role the woman would play in the early years of her relationship with Dostoyevsky. Perhaps this was, as some scholars have surmised, because she worked so hard to cast her relationship with Dostoyevsky in the most idyllic terms possible,

so as not to besmirch his reputation in the eyes of posterity. A. S. Dolinin, for example, has written that in *Reminiscences*, Anna attempted to "create out of the history of her life with Dostoyevsky a kind of idyl in the spirit of English family novels." (Quoted in Irina Sviatoslavovna Andrianova, *Anna Dostoevskaia: Prizvanie i priznaniia* [Petrozavodsk: PetrGU, 2013], 72.) Or perhaps, too, it was because she herself wished to forget about that most trying episode in her marriage, in order not to soil his memory for herself.

60 **"diametrically opposed"**: Anna Dostoevsky, *Dostoevsky: Reminiscences*, 56–57.

60 **"nervous and exacting"**: Sonya Kovalevsky, *Her Recollections of Childhood*, trans. Isabel F. Hapgood (New York: Century, 1895), 148–49. Everything we know about Dostoyevsky's courtship of Anna Korvin-Krukovskaya comes from the memoirs of Anna's sister, Sofya Kovalevsky (née Sofya Vasilievna Korvin-Krukovskaya), who would go on to an illustrious career as both a distinguished mathematician and the first woman ever appointed to a full professorship at a European university.

61 **"frivolous novels"**: Anna Dostoevsky, *Dostoevsky: Reminiscences*, 68.

61 **"shield me"**: Ibid., 67.

61 **"Then why do *you* read"**: Ibid.

61 **"God entrusted you to me"**: Letter to Anna Dostoyevskaya, May 5, 1867, in Fyodor Dostoevsky, *Complete Letters*, vol. 2 (1860–1867), ed. and trans. David A. Lowe (Ann Arbor, MI: Ardis, 1989), 230.

62 **"to know everything"**: Anna Dostoevsky, *Dostoevsky: Reminiscences*, 67.

62 **Why hadn't he just proposed**: Ibid., 63.

62 **"So it follows"**: Ibid.

63 **"no one, no one"**: Fyodor Dostoevsky, *Crime and Punishment*, trans. Richard Pevear and Larissa Volokhonsky (New York: Vintage Books, 1992), 412.

64 **"might make the subject"**: Ibid., 551.

65 **"The moment Fyodor Mikhailovich"**: Ibid., 69.

65 **Anna broke into sobs**: Ibid., 65.

65 **that of a "madwoman"**: Ibid.

65 **"for the scene"**: Ibid., 66.

66 **"This was the only"**: Ibid.

4. WHAT IS TO BE DONE?

68 **"Everything is based on money"**: Nikolai Chernyshevsky, *What Is to Be Done?*, trans. Michael R. Katz (Ithaca and London: Cornell University Press, 1989), 144.

68 **"almost like worshippers"**: Richard Stites, *The Women's Liberation Movement in Russia: Feminism, Nihilism, and Bolshevism, 1860–1930* (Princeton, NJ: Princeton University Press, 1978), 98.

68 **"Who has not read"**: Rufus W. Mathewson, *The Positive Hero in Russian Literature*, 2nd ed. (Stanford, CA: Stanford University Press, 1975), 81. Also quoted in introduction to Chernyshevsky, *What Is to Be Done?*, 32.

69 **"that supplies energy"**: Cited from introduction to Chernyshevsky, *What Is to Be Done?*, 32.

69 **every schoolgirl in the mid-1860s**: Stites, *The Women's Liberation Movement in Russia*, 97.

69 **"symbolized the women's movement"**: Quoted ibid., 98–99.

69 **"girls, bred in the most aristocratic families"**: Ibid., 105.

69 **up to twenty-five rubles for a copy**: Ibid., 98.

70 **"my dreams of independence"**: Anna Dostoevsky, *Dostoevsky: Reminiscences*, trans. and ed. Beatrice Stillman (New York: Liveright, 1975), 20.

70 **"An obedient daughter"**: Aimée Dostoyevsky, *Fyodor Dostoyevsky: A Study* (London: William Heinemann, 1921), 135–36.

71 **"No one ever held"**: Quoted in Barbara Alpern Engel, *Mothers and Daughters: Women of the Intelligentsia in Nineteenth-Century Russia* (Cambridge: Cambridge University Press, 1983), 94.

71 **"punished us cruelly"**: Quoted ibid., 128.

71 **so feared her husband**: Ibid., 128–29.

72 **"did not attempt"**: Ibid., 48.

72 **a fully empowered woman**: Intriguingly, in 1848, the same year Dostoyevsky was working on *Netochka Nezvanova*, novelist Karolina Pavlova published *A Double Life*, the coming-of-age story of a sensitive teenage girl, Cecily, who marries a man she doesn't love in order to gain acceptance from her high-society world. Only in her poetic dream life is she able to express her mute suffering, her recognition that to remain spiritually and emotionally unfulfilled is the fate of a woman in her time. Cecily could hardly be considered any kind of protofeminist figure, whereas Netochka Nezvanova could. More surprising still is that Netochka was created by a man, who, by composing the novel in the form of a first-person confession, gives Netochka full authority to narrate the story in her own voice.

73 **"I watched, I noticed"**: Fyodor Dostoyevsky, *Netochka Nezvanova*, trans. Jane Kentish (London: Penguin Books, 1985), 122–23.

73 **"long and hopeless suffering"**: Ibid., 145.

73 **"I was shocked and frightened"**: Ibid., 144.

74 **"a revelation, the unlocking"**: Ibid., 139.

74 *The Story of a Woman*: The Petrashevskyite Ipolit Debu recalls how at their Friday gatherings Dostoyevsky recounted his "Story of a Woman" "in far more detail than appeared in the printed version." Cited from N. F. Budanova and G. M. Fridlender, eds., *Letopis' zhizni i tvorchestva F. M. Dostoevskogo, 1821–1881, 3* vols. (Saint Petersburg: Gumanitarnoe Agentstvo Akademicheskii Projekt, 1993), vol. 1, 146.

74 **his first big novel**: Letter to Mikhail Dostoyevsky, October 7, 1846, in F. M. Dostoevskii, *Polnoe sobranie sochinenii v tridtsati tomakh*, 30 vols. (Leningrad: Nauka, 1985), vol. 28, book 1, 128. In this letter Dostoyevsky informs his brother that he was hard at work on the novel and obligated to provide the manuscript for the first part to Kraevsky, the editor of *Fatherland Notes*. By the end of the year he told Mikhail that he was certain this novel would arouse the same level of excitement as his debut epistolary novel, *Poor Folk*, had at the beginning of the year.

75 **complex inner life**: As scholar Joseph Frank astutely observes, this novel offers an early glimpse into what would prove one of Dostoyevsky's most important contributions to Russian literature: "Even though social position and relations of the characters serve to frame and motivate the action, Dostoyevsky's focus is no longer on external social conditions and their reflection in the consciousness and in behavior.... Rather, it is on the personal qualities that the characters display in the battle against the instinctive tendency of the injured ego to hit back for what social-psychic traumas it has been forced to endure. The world of *Netochka Nezvanova* is thus no longer exclusively social-psychological but already has become the moral-psychological universe of his later fiction." Joseph Frank, *Dostoevsky: A Writer in His Time* (Princeton, NJ: Princeton University Press, 2010), 117.

75 **"I had only one pleasure"**: Fyodor Dostoyevsky, *Netochka Nezvanova*, 48.

75 **"How should I"**: Ibid., 144.

75 **"I was destined"**: Ibid., 130.

76 **"compassionate *motherly* feeling"**: Ibid., 32.

76 **"half-crazy man"**: Ibid., 48.

76 **"quite a daydreamer"**: A. G. Dostoevskaia, *Vospominanii 1846–1917: Solntse moei zhizni— Fedor Dostoevskii*, ed. Irina S. Andrianova and Boris N. Tikhomirov (Moscow: Boslen, 2015), 148.

76 **"Those were my feelings"**: Ibid., 59.

77 **"You know, it was fate"**: Ibid., 60.

5. CROSSING THE THRESHOLD

78 **"Freedom, a new life"**: Fyodor Dostoevsky, *The House of the Dead*, trans. David McDuff (London: Penguin Books, 1985), 357.

78 **"future everything"**: Quoted in S. V. Belov, *Zhena pisatelia: Posledniaia liubov' F. M. Dostoevskogo* (Moscow: Sovetskaia Rossiia, 1986), 78.

78 **"For half the wedding ceremony"**: Anna Dostoevsky, *Dostoevsky: Reminiscences*, trans. and ed. Beatrice Stillman (New York: Liveright, 1975), 76.

79 **"What a dreadful night"**: Ibid., 80.

79 **"To be conscious"**: A. A. Izmailov, "U A. G. Dostoevskoi (k 35-letiiu so dnia konchiny F. M. Dostoevskogo)," in *F. M. Dostoevskii v zabytykh i neizvestnykh vospominaniiakh sovremennikov*, ed. S. V. Belov (Saint Petersburg: Andreev i Synov'ia, 1993), 194.

80 **"patriarchal and hospitable family"**: Anna Dostoevsky, *Dostoevsky: Reminiscences*, 82.

81 **"My primordial enemy"**: Quoted in footnote 4 to letter from E. F. Dostoevskaia to A. P. Ivanov, August–September 1865, in *Dostoevskii v neizdannoi perepiske s sovremennikami*, http://dostoevskiy-lit.ru/dostoevskiy/pisma-dostoevskomu/neizdannaya-perepiska/neizdannaya-perepiska-4.htm.

81 **"Well, papa, such things"**: Anna Dostoevsky, *Dostoevsky: Reminiscences*, 89.

82 **"Anyechka," he would say**: Ibid., 88.

82 **"outraged" by her husband's failure**: Ibid., 90–91.

83 **"But let's not forget"**: Ibid., 89.

83 **"Pasha was already"**: Ibid.

83 **"I loved Fyodor"**: Ibid., 90.

84 **"colossal mistake"**: Ibid., 92.

85 **"How about it"**: Ibid., 94.

86 **"they saw a young woman"**: Ibid., 97.

86 **Her brother, Ivan**: Ibid., 101–2.

86 **"salvation lies not"**: V. G. Belinsky, "Letter to N. V. Gogol," July 3, 1847, transcribed from V. G. Belinsky, *Selected Philosophical Works* (Moscow: Foreign Languages Publishing House, 1948), at Marxists Internet Archive, https://www.marxists.org/subject/art/lit_crit/works/belinsky/gogol.htm.

87 **"A commune"**: Cited from Nicholas V. Riazanovsky, *Nicholas I and Official Nationality in Russia, 1825–1855* (Berkeley: University of California Press, 1969), 96.

87 **privileged reason and argument**: These dichotomies adapted from Andrew Baruch Wachtel and Ilya Vinitsky, *Russian Literature* (Cambridge, UK, and Malden, MA: Polity Press, 2009), 94–96.

87 **"We have at last"**: Kenneth Lantz, *The Dostoevsky Encyclopedia* (Westport, CT: Greenwood Press, 2004), 400.

88 **"more solid and moral foundations"**: Cited from Joseph Frank, *Dostoevsky: The Years of Ordeal, 1850–1859* (Princeton, NJ: Princeton University Press, 1983), 229.

88 **"The ancient truth"**: Cited from Joseph Frank, *Dostoevsky: The Mantle of the Prophet, 1871–1881* (Princeton, NJ: Princeton University Press, 2002), 481.

91 **"Anna Grigoryevna"**: This scene and dialogue are reconstructed from Anna Dostoevsky, *Dostoevsky: Reminiscences*, 107.

92 **"Fate is against us"**: Ibid., 108–9.

93 **"If we were to save"**: Ibid., 109.

93 **"the good habits"**: Ibid., 110.

93 **"feared my mother's displeasure"**: Ibid., 109–10.

93 **"What else is to be done"**: Ibid., 111.

94 **"Are you still dreaming"**: Ibid.

94 **"How happy I am"**: Ibid., 112.

94 **"begging him to let me"**: Ibid.

94 **"burst into such violent sobbing"**: Ibid.

96 **"Permit me, *papa*"**: Ibid., 113.

97 **"measure swords and see"**: Ibid.

6. A NEW BEGINNING

102 **"There was nobody"**: Anna Dostoevsky, *Dostoevsky: Reminiscences*, trans. and ed. Beatrice Stillman (New York: Liveright, 1975), 118.

102 **"We are supremely happy"**: A. G. Dostoyevskaya, *The Diary of Dostoyevsky's Wife*, ed. René Fülöp-Miller and Dr. Eckstein, trans. Madge Pemberton (New York: Macmillan, 1928), 59.

102 **on the Brülsche Terrasse:** The Brülsche Terrasse has been preserved to appear today much as it would have in 1867.

102 **Anna would never forget:** In 2018, as part of a research trip for this book, I visited each of these places. For my description of their appearance in the Dostoyevskys' time, I have drawn from Anna's secret diary as well as the unpublished article, Ol'ga Grossman and Gizbert Grossman, "Progulki po staromu Drezdenu s chetoi Dostoevskikh," 4.

102 **"land of holy wonders"**: Fyodor Dostoevsky, *Winter Notes on Summer Impressions*, trans. David A. Patterson (Evanston, IL: Northwestern University Press, 1997), 2; see also the footnote on p. 75.

103 **"How they struggle"**: Ibid., 35.

103 **"The question occurred to me"**: Letter to Apollon Maikov, August 16, 1867, quoted in Fyodor Dostoevsky, *Complete Letters*, vol. 2 (1860–1867), ed. and trans. David A. Lowe (Ann Arbor, MI: Ardis, 1989), 253.

103 **"scrape away"**: Cited from Joseph Frank, *Dostoevsky: The Miraculous Years, 1865–1871* (Princeton, NJ: Princeton University Press, 1995), 250.

104 **"Oh, these Germans"**: A. G. Dostoyevskaya, *The Diary of Dostoyevsky's Wife*, 297.

104 **"Germans really are"**: Ibid., 46.

104 **"when you go inside"**: Ibid., 37.

105 **"I think there must"**: Ibid., 95.

105 **"Never has any picture"**: Ibid., 36.

106 **"He called me"**: Ibid., 38.

106 **"When I think of him"**: Entry of May 1, 1867, in A. G. Dostoyevskaya, *The Diary of Dostoyevsky's Wife*, 64.

106 **Some recent scholars:** Addiction researchers Lorne Tepperman, Patrizia Albanese, Sasha Stark, and Nadine Zahlan write: "By giving Dostoevsky the semblance of support for his gambling, Anna enabled it and, in this way, perpetuated it. So, Anna's cooperation kept Dostoevsky's affection but it did not improve their financial situation." Lorne Tepperman, Patrizia Albanese, Sasha Stark, and Nadine Zahlan, *The Dostoevsky Effect: Problem Gambling and the Origins of Addiction* (Don Mills, ON: Oxford University Press, 2013), 58.

108 **scolding her gently:** Entry of May 4, 1867, in A. G. Dostoyevskaya, *The Diary of Dostoyevsky's Wife*, 73.

108 **"It's not good"**: Entry of April 27, 1867, ibid., 50.

108 **"It was a very stupid"**: Entry of May 4, 1867, ibid., 74.

108 **scholars have since confirmed**: See note 35 in A. G. Dostoevskaia, *Dnevnik 1867 goda* (Moscow: Nauka, 1993), 426.

109 **"calls me Brylkina"**: Entry of May 4, 1867, in A. G. Dostoyevskaya, *The Diary of Dostoyevsky's Wife*, 74.

109 **"the rebellious girl"**: The word in Russian is *bryklivyi*, which is colloquial for "inclined to kick" or "inclined to rebel."

109 **actually *was* named Brylkina**: See note 35 in A. G. Dostoevskaia, *Dnevnik 1867 goda*, 426.

109 **perhaps even a few years**: Their last known meeting happened on November 2, 1865, according to the biographical timeline in Liudmila Saraksina, *Voszliubliennaia Dostoevskogo: Apollinariia Suslova: Biografiia v dokumentakh, pis'makh, materialakh* (Moscow: Soglasie, 1994), 453. However, Marc Slonim, in *Three Loves of Dostoevsky*, 177, suggests, without evidence, that Dostoevsky last saw Polina in the spring of 1866, just before she went to her brother's place in the country.

109 **"My stenographer, Anna"**: Letter to Polina Suslova, April 23, 1867, in Fyodor Dostoevsky, *Complete Letters*, vol. 2 (1860–1867), 227–28.

110 **"weak-willed, muddled"**: Letter to Anna Dostoyevskaya, May 5, 1867, ibid., 230.

111 **The roulette wheel**: This fact we know from Polina's own diary, where she recorded how, a few days after their separation, Dostoevsky begged her to send him money in Bad Homburg: "Yesterday I received a letter from F[yodor] M[ikhailovich]. He had lost all his money gambling and asked me to send him some money." Entry of October 27, 1863, quoted in Fyodor Dostoevsky, *The Gambler with Polina Suslova's Diary*, trans. Victor Terras, ed. Edward Wasiolek (Chicago: University of Chicago Press, 1972), 223.

111 **By the time he arrived in Bad Homburg**: Details taken from letter to Anna Dostoyevskaya, May 17, 1867, in Fyodor Dostoevsky, *Complete Letters*, vol. 2 (1860–1867), 230–31.

111 **traveling dignitaries and statesmen**: The guests that day included a Parisian consul named Lammére, who had come with his family; the well-known British Major Tevor; and a dashing fifty-year-old American statesman with wavy hair, who'd recently become governor of Pennsylvania. Details taken from Johannes Latsch, "'Schlimmer als Sibierien': Dostojewskij am Schicksalsrad—Der 'Spieler'-Dichter 1867 in Homburg," in *Aus dem Stadtarchiv: Vorträge zur Bad Homburger Geschichte* (Bad Homburg, Germany: Gotisches Haus, 2009), 68. Names of hotel guests were meticulously tracked and published in a daily log. (Ibid., 88, note 5.)

111 **By the time of Dostoyevsky's first trip**: I am grateful to Mr. Lutz Schenkel, managing director of the François-Blanc-Spielbank GmbH, as the casino is now called, for these and other details about the history of the Kurhaus and Bad Homburg. Mr. Schenkel also gave me a copy of the definitive book about the casino's history and founder, François Blanc, from which I gleaned many other fascinating details: Egon Caesar Conte Corti, *Der Zauberer von Homburg und Monte Carlo: 1841–1872* (Frankfurt: Societäts-Verlag, 2008; dual publication with Eva Schweiblmeir, *Die Rückkehr des Glücks 1872–2008*).

112 **Inside, visitors breezed**: Details taken from Latsch, "Schlimmer als Sibierien," 69.

112 **"crowding, closeness, pushing"**: Letter to Anna Dostoyevskaya, May 8, 1867, in Fyodor Dostoevsky, *Complete Letters*, vol. 2 (1860–1867), 234.

112 **"About your travels, about your impressions"**: Quoted in Karla Hielscher, *Dostojewski in Deutschland* (Frankfurt am Main: Insel Verlag, 1999), 27.

112 **"the place here is charming"**: Letter to Anna Dostoyevskaya, May 19, 1867, in Fyodor Dostoevsky, *Complete Letters*, vol. 2 (1860–1867), 233.

113 **"already in my hands"**: Letter to Anna Dostoyevskaya, May 5, 1867, quoted ibid., 231–32.

113 **"If one is prudent"**: Letter to Anna Dostoyevskaya, May 6, 1867, ibid., 232.

113 **"rational design"**: The underground man addresses the reader: "You believe in the Crystal Palace, forever indestructible, that is to say, in one at which *you won't be able to stick out your tongue* even in stealth or thumb one's nose even in your pocket. Well, perhaps I am afraid of this palace just because it is made of crystal and is forever indestructible, and just because *I won't be able to poke my tongue out at it* even by stealth." Fyodor Dostoevsky, *Notes from Underground*, trans. David Magarshack, in *Great Short Works of Fyodor Dostoevsky* (New York: Perennial Classics, 2004), 292 (emphasis mine).

114 **could not have seen himself as an addict**: In their illuminating book *The Dostoevsky Effect: Problem Gambling and the Origins of Addiction*, the authors, professional gambling researchers, point out that this sort of rational self-justification is typical of problem gamblers: "Many of the problem gamblers we have studied, including Dostoevsky, imagine their motive for gambling is mainly instrumental—to make money or even take risks—but in fact their motive is emotional or expressive—to experience the rush associated with taking the risk." See Tepperman, Albanese, Stark, and Zahlan, *The Dostoevsky Effect*, 101.

114 **"Without any exaggeration"**: Letter to Anna Dostoyevskaya, May 6, 1867, in Fyodor Dostoevsky, *Complete Letters*, vol. 2 (1860–1867), 232.

114 **"My longing to see"**: Letter to Anna Dostoyevskaya, May 10, 1867, ibid., 239.

114 **"this is even all"**: Letter to Anna Dostoyevskaya, May 9, 1867, ibid., 238.

115 **"About twenty times now"**: Letter to Anna Dostoyevskaya, May 10, 1867, ibid., 239.

115 **"The future is simply a riddle"**: Letter to Anna Dostoyevskaya, May 13, 1867, ibid., 244–45.

115 **"Try to understand"**: Ibid., 245.

115 **"It was as if I was risen"**: Letter to Anna Dostoyevskaya, May 9, 1867, ibid., 237.

116 **He reproached himself**: "My whole mistake was in parting from you and not taking you with me," he wrote in the letter to Anna Dostoyevskaya, May 10, 1867, ibid., 240.

116 **"Your judgment alone"**: Letter to Anna Dostoyevskaya, May 12, 1867, ibid., 243.

116 **"At least I know"**: Letter to Anna Dostoyevskaya, May 11, 1867, ibid., 241.

116 **"countless new thoughts"**: Entry of July 26, 1867, in A. G. Dostoyevskaya, *The Diary of Dostoyevsky's Wife*, 337.

116 **she was "overjoyed"**: Entry of May 6, 1867, ibid., 82.

117 **"If only Fedya would come back"**: Entry of May 7, 1867, in response to Dostoyevsky's letter to Anna Dostoyevskaya, May 6, ibid., 84.

117 **wrote letters home**: Entry of May 8, 1867, ibid., 90.

117 **"So gorgeous was it"**: Entry of May 9, 1867, ibid., 97.

118 **"If death were coming my way"**: Entry of May 9, 1867, ibid., 98.

118 **"a little bit different"**: Entry of May 15, 1867, ibid., 115.

118 **"precious piece of writing"**: Ibid., 115–16.

119 **"I am so afraid"**: "How often, I wonder, must I continue to keep my activities secret, and even to tell falsehoods, in order not to anger him and get him over-excited!" she wrote. "I hate it, but what else can I do? I am so afraid of this temper of his resulting in a fit." Entry of June 21, 1867, ibid., 205.

119 **"There is only one thing"**: Entry of August 9, 1867, ibid., 391.

119 **"looked on me as a rock"**: Anna Dostoevsky, *Dostoevsky: Reminiscences*, 384.

120 **"better not dare interfere"**: Entry of June 14, 1867, in A. G. Dostoevskaia, *Dnevnik 1867 goda*, 101–2.

120 **"I don't like to hear"**: Anna Dostoevsky, *Dostoevsky: Reminiscences*, 122–23.

120 **"we could be the happiest"**: Entry of June 8, 1867, in A. G. Dostoyevskaya, *The Diary of Dostoyevsky's Wife*, 171.

120 **"Even if I don't"**: Ibid.

121 **"Money means nothing"**: Ibid., 171–72.

121 **"I'm going to write":** Ibid.

121 **"How often, I wonder":** Entry of June 21, 1867, ibid., 205.

122 **"positively eats out of my hand!":** Entry of June 13, 1867, ibid., 156.

122 **"as if I were at home":** Anna Dostoevsky, *Dostoevsky: Reminiscences*, 124.

122 **To Anna the evening was a "triumph":** Ibid., 125.

122 **"a Russian lady":** Details, ibid., and from 391, note 9.

123 **"recruited into the ranks":** Ibid., 125.

123 **"to be more careful":** Ibid.

123 **"I simply cannot bear":** Entry of June 9, 1867, in A. G. Dostoyevskaya, *The Diary of Dosto-yevsky's Wife*, 163.

124 **"never to cry":** Entry of April 29, 1867, ibid., 58.

124 **"to appear in good spirits":** Entry of July 7, 1867, ibid., 269.

124 **"making money by roulette":** Entry of May 7, 1867, ibid., 84.

124 **"would get this miserable idea":** Entry of May 11, 1867, ibid., 103.

124 **allowed herself to get excited:** Entry of May 8, 1867, ibid., 84.

124 **"my suffering is greater":** Entry of May 7, 1867, ibid.

124 **such an "interesting and enigmatic" man:** Anna Dostoevsky, *Dostoevsky: Reminiscences*, 121.

124 **"thanked God that Olkhin had chosen me":** Ibid., 59.

124 **"Destiny has in store":** Entry of May 9, 1867, in A. G. Dostoyevskaya, *The Diary of Dostoyevsky's Wife*, 98.

125 **"a whole new world":** Entry of April 23, 1867, ibid., 45.

125 **"My spirits were":** Entry of June 14, 1867, ibid., 185.

126 **"He spoke so persuasively":** Anna Dostoevsky, *Dostoevsky: Reminiscences*, 127.

126 **"Good-bye now":** Entry of June 21, 1867, in A. G. Dostoyevskaya, *The Diary of Dostoyevsky's Wife*, 206.

7. THE "GAMBLER WIFE"

127 **"indisputably the most glamorous":** The description of Baden-Baden is drawn from the entry of June 21, 1867, in A. G. Dostoyevskaya, *The Diary of Dostoyevsky's Wife*, ed. René Fülöp-Miller and Dr. Eckstein, trans. Madge Pemberton (New York: Macmillan, 1928), 217–18. The quotation from *Reichard's* guide is from Karla Hielscher, *Dostojewski in Deutschland* (Frankfurt am Main: Insel Verlag, 1999), 99.

128 **a little over two hundred dollars:** There were 3.237 ducats per thaler, according to a post on "How to Sort Gold Ducats in the Thaler World?" Numista, https://en.numista.com/forum /topic53429.html.

128 **such "legal norms":** Cited from Ian M. Helfant, "His to Stake, Hers to Lose: Women and the Male Gambling Culture of Nineteenth-Century Russia," *Russian Review* 62, no. 2 (2003): 231.

129 **"I got up":** Entry of June 24, 1867, in A. G. Dostoyevskaya, *The Diary of Dostoyevsky's Wife*, 221.

129 **"He's had a seizure":** Ibid.

129 **"He would spare me":** Ibid., 221–22.

130 **"What do you mean":** Entry of August 1, 1867, ibid., 356.

130 **"There is no doubt":** Entry of July 23, 1867, ibid., 325.

130 **"I am very concerned":** Entry of July 25, 1867, ibid., 337.

130 **"There they are":** Entry of July 1, 1867, ibid., 251.

131 **"bright and shining" casino:** Robert Erhard, *Aus der Chronik der Kaiserallee: Geschichte und Geschichten vom Promenade-, Konversations- und Kurhaus* (Baden-Baden, Germany: Kurhaus, 2005).

131 **"In the gaming rooms":** Ivan Turgenev, *Smoke*, trans. Michael Pursglove (Richmond, UK: Alma Classics, 2013), 3. I have emended Pursglove's translation slightly for clarity and readability.

131 **"The sight of a roulette wheel":** Ibid., 122.

132 **"could not help noticing":** Entry of July 7, 1867, in A. G. Dostoyevskaya, *The Diary of Dostoyevsky's Wife*, 225.

132 **One hot July afternoon:** Ibid., 254–55.

133 **"He looked dreadful":** Entry of August 1, 1867, ibid., 357.

133 **"lay on the sofa":** Entry of June 28, 1867, ibid., 233. The closest approximation to what Anna must be referring to is the Deutsches Kaiserreich gold coins, which were first circulated only in 1871. Still, this coin provides the best proxy we have for the "gold" coins Anna must have been referring to. The Deutsches Kaiserreich gold coin contained just under eight grams of gold, which in 1867 would have been valued at $7.30, the equivalent of $128.20 today. Information about the Deutsches Kaiserreich gold coin from "German Empire Gold Mark Coins," Coininvest, https://www.coininvest.com/en/gold-coins/deutsches-kaiserreich/.

134 **"It really did seem":** Entry of June 28, 1867, in A. G. Dostoyevskaya, *The Diary of Dostoevsky's Wife*, 235–36.

134 **"Oh God, how all this":** Entry of July 22, 1867, ibid., 319.

134 **not "a simple weakness":** Anna Dostoevsky, *Dostoevsky: Reminiscences*, trans. and ed. Beatrice Stillman (New York: Liveright, 1975), 131–32.

134 **hope that "my presence":** Ibid., 127.

134 **"My God, when shall we":** Entry of July 22, 1867, in A. G. Dostoyevskaya, *The Diary of Dostoyevsky's Wife*, 320.

135 **"I call that disgusting egotism!":** Entry of July 21, 1867, ibid., 313.

135 **"I can see that":** Entry of July 21, 1867, ibid., 313–14.

135 **"he ought to try":** Entry of July 21, 1867, ibid., 314.

136 **"our former difficult life":** Entry of July 31, 1867, ibid., 349.

136 **Anna wrote her mother:** Ibid., 349–50.

136 **"I simply hated":** Entry of July 9, 1867, ibid., 278.

137 **"accursed race of Baden-Baden":** Entry of August 4, 1867, ibid., 370.

137 **"I would dearly love":** Entry of July 18, 1867, in A. G. Dostoevskaia, *Dnevnik 1867 goda* (Moscow: Nauka, 1993), 169.

137 **"I don't care":** Entry of August 9, 1867, in A. G. Dostoyevskaya, *The Diary of Dostoyevsky's Wife*, 391.

137 **The "grizzling heat":** Entry of July 29, 1867, ibid., 343.

138 **the "pernicious place":** Entry of July 10, 1867, ibid., 281.

138 **It wasn't much:** Starting in 1837, 1.75 German guldens were the equivalent of 1 thaler, making 1 gulden worth .57 thalers. Cited from "Thaler: 19th-Century Germany," Wikipedia, https://en.wikipedia.org/wiki/Thaler#19th-century_Germany. See also the Historical Currency Converter, http://www.historicalstatistics.org/currencyconverter.html.

138 **"That was idiotic":** Entry of July 29, 1867, in A. G. Dostoyevskaya, *The Diary of Dostoyevsky's Wife*, 344.

138 **her mother's "damned furniture":** Entry of August 5, 1867, ibid., 371.

138 **"The whole time":** Entry of August 6, 1867, ibid., 379.

138 **his gambling "fever":** Entry of August 6, 1867, ibid., 375–76.

139 **"If he thinks"**: Entry of August 6, 1867, ibid., 379.

139 **sixteen hundred dollars**: Rodney Edvinsson. "Historical Statistics Currency Converter," January 10, 2016, https://www.historicalstatistics.org/Currencyconverter.html.

139 **"For the first time"**: Entry of August 8, 1867, in A. G. Dostoyevskaya, *The Diary of Dostoyevsky's Wife*, 383.

139 **"but could never carry out"**: Entry of August 7, 1867, ibid., 383.

139 **he "cannot bring himself"**: Entry of August 7, 1867, ibid., 382.

139 **"almost as if he were ashamed"**: Entry of August 5, 1867, ibid., 371–72.

140 **simple rough white straw**: Entry of April 19 or 20, 1867, ibid., 37.

140 **"my strength of mind"**: Entry of August 8, 1867, ibid., 383.

140 **"something seemed to tempt me"**: Entry of August 8, 1867, ibid.

141 **"I'd like Fedya"**: Entry of August 8, 1867, ibid., 383–84.

141 **"I could've easily crept"**: Entry of August 8, 1867, ibid., 384.

141 **"I've noticed things"**: Entry of August 8, 1867, ibid.

141 **she "felt horrible"**: Entry of August 8, 1867, ibid.

142 **"a demented couple"**: Entry of August 9, 1867, ibid., 389.

142 **she was his "gambler wife"**: Entry of August 8, 1867, ibid., 384. The phrase Dostoyevsky used was *igrok-zhena*, or literally: "gambler-wife." Madge Pemberton translates the phrase as "gambling fiend," which captures the spirit of Dostoyevsky's remark but not his exact words. I have opted for the more literal translation, which, in this case, seems to me to be more accurate.

142 **"undermined my will power"**: Entry of July 31, 1867, ibid., 352.

142 **"We are poor"**: Entry of August 6, 1867, ibid., 376.

143 **"All our energy"**: Entry of August 7, 1867, ibid., 382.

8. TURGENEV

144 **there was no way around it**: Entry of June 25, 1867, in A. G. Dostoyevskaya, *The Diary of Dostoyevsky's Wife*, ed. René Fülöp-Miller and Dr. Eckstein, trans. Madge Pemberton (New York: Macmillan, 1928), 223.

144 **"a pimple on the nose"**: Quoted in Joseph Frank, *Dostoevsky: The Miraculous Years, 1865–1871* (Princeton, NJ: Princeton University Press, 1995), 211.

145 **"exhibits *lack of faith*"**: Cited ibid.

145 **"He is an atheist"**: Letter to Apollon Maikov, August 16, 1867, in Fyodor Dostoevsky, *Complete Letters*, vol. 2 (1860–1867), ed. and trans. David A. Lowe (Ann Arbor, MI: Ardis, 1989), 257.

145 **"in the course of ten"**: Ivan Turgenev, *Smoke*, trans. Michael Pursglove (Richmond, UK: Alma Classics, 2013), 29.

146 **"exhibition of everything"**: Ibid., 90.

146 **"We have given"**: Cited from Andrzej Walick, *A History of Russian Thought from the Enlightenment to Marxism*, trans. Hilda Andrews-Rusiecka (Stanford, CA: Stanford University Press, 1979), 86.

146 **nicknamed him "the American"**: Victor Terras, ed., *Handbook of Russian Literature* (New Haven, CT: Yale University Press, 1985), 488.

146 **"frightened by a novel"**: Quoted in Frank, *Dostoevsky: The Miraculous Years, 1865–1871*, 214.

147 **"One can't listen"**: Letter to Apollon Maikov, August 16, 1867, in Fyodor Dostoevsky, *Complete Letters*, vol. 2 (1860–1867), 257–59.

147 **two-story house**: This detail taken from Walter G. Moss, *Russia in the Age of Alexander II, Tolstoy and Dostoevsky* (London: Anthem Press, 2002), 128.

147 **The meeting began:** Details of this encounter are drawn from A. G. Dostoyevskaya, *The Diary of Dostoyevsky's Wife*, 238; and Dostoyevsky's letter to Maikov, August 16, 1867, in Fyodor Dostoyevsky, *Complete Letters*, vol. 2 (1860–1867), 257–59.

148 **More than a decade:** Unsurprisingly, Turgenev's recollection of the meeting differed from Dostoyevsky's. This came to light many years later, when Turgenev learned from a literary friend, P. V. Annenkov, that the letter in which Dostoyevsky described to Maikov his meeting with Turgenev had been given "for posterity" to the editor of a journal called *Russian Archives* (*Russkii Arkhiv*) with the stipulation that its contents could not be published before 1890. Turgenev assumed that it was Dostoyevsky who'd sent this letter to the journal, but in fact he had nothing to do with it. Maikov had shown the letter to the nephew of the editor of *Russian Archives*, and that editor, without Dostoyevsky's permission, had transcribed the pages describing the famous encounter and sent them to his uncle. Upon learning that these contents were in the possession of *Russian Archives*, Turgenev sent a disclaimer to the editors, flatly denying the "shocking and absurd opinions about Russia" attributed to him, and insisting that he considered Dostoyevsky "a person who, as a consequence of morbid seizures and other causes, is not in full control of his own rational capacities; and this opinion of mine is shared by many others." Dostoyevsky's mental imbalance, Turgenev maintained, was evident during their visit, in which Dostoyevsky "relieved his heart by brutal abuse against the Germans, against me and my last book, and then departed; I hardly had the time or desire to contradict him; I repeat that I treated him as somebody who was ill. Probably his disordered imagination produced those arguments that he attributed to me, and on whose basis he composed against me his . . . message to posterity." Quoted in Frank, *Dostoevsky: The Miraculous Years*, 219–20.

149 **"all those Turgenevs":** Dostoyevsky's letter to Maikov, August 16, 1867, in Fyodor Dostoyevsky, *Complete Letters*, vol. 2 (1860–1867), 255.

149 **"convince themselves that":** Fyodor Dostoyevsky, *Winter Notes on Summer Impressions*, trans. David A. Patterson (Evanston, IL: Northwestern University Press, 1997), 35, 44.

150 **"What liberty?":** Ibid., 48.

150 **"the chief stumbling block":** Ibid., 48–49.

151 **"One does not find":** Ibid., 55.

151 **"Europe and its task":** Ibid., 46.

151 **"Our people are infinitely higher":** Letter to Apollon Maikov, December 31, 1867, in Fyodor Dostoevsky, *Complete Letters*, vol. 2 (1860–1867), 300.

152 **"My future seems":** Letter to Apollon Maikov, August 16, 1867, ibid., 259.

152 **"To go the way":** Ibid., 251.

152 **"I know this conversation":** Entry of July 10, 1867, in A. G. Dostoyevskaya, *The Diary of Dostoyevsky's Wife*, 239.

153 **as mere echoes:** In her essay that accompanies her 1993 compilation of Anna's personal diary of 1867, for instance, Russian scholar S. V. Zhitmirskaia writes that Anna's views about Europe are an "echo of the judgments of the writer," a shortsighted view held by other scholars, as well. Cited from A. G. Dostoevskaia, *Dnevnik 1867 goda* (Moscow: Nauka, 1993), 410.

153 **"as if condemned":** Entry of August 10, 1867, ibid., 396.

155 **"I was overjoyed":** Entry of August 11, 1867, ibid., 404.

9. LIFE AND FATE

157 **"when the child":** Entry of September 22, 1867, in A. G. Dostoevskaia, *Dnevnik 1867 goda* (Moscow: Nauka, 1993), 279.

157 **"Anya, we have grown":** Ibid.

158 **"a young, kind, and wonderful":** Citations taken from letter to Apollon Maikov, August 16, 1867, in Fyodor Dostoevsky, *Complete Letters*, vol. 2 (1860–1867), ed. and trans. David A. Lowe (Ann Arbor, MI: Ardis, 1989), 252–59.

158 **Dostoyevsky did confess:** Letter to Apollon Maikov, August 16, 1867, ibid., 252.

158 **"It was his mind":** Entry of June 8, 1867, in A. G. Dostoevskaya, *The Diary of Dostoyevsky's Wife*, ed. René Fülöp-Miller and Dr. Eckstein, trans. Madge Pemberton (New York: Macmillan, 1928), 171–72.

159 **"On the final day":** Entry of August 26, 1867, in A. G. Dostoevskaia, *Dnevnik 1867 goda*, 241.

159 **"They began with the fact":** Letter to Sofya Ivanova, September 29, 1867, quoted in Fyodor Dostoevsky, *Complete Letters*, vol. 2 (1860–1867), 276.

160 **"Down with papacy!":** Entry of August 30, 1867, in A. G. Dostoevskaia, *Dnevnik 1867 goda*, 249.

160 **"What's this stupid congress for?":** Ibid.

160 **Many of the attendees agreed with her:** A. P. Campanella, "Garibaldi and the First Peace Congress in Geneva in 1867," *International Review of Social History* 5, no. 3 (1960): 456–86, https://www.cambridge.org/core/services/aop-cambridge-core/content/view/S0020859000001693.

161 **"I'm a terribly rotten person!":** Entry of August 30, 1867, in A. G. Dostoevskaia, *Dnevnik 1867 goda*, 249.

161 **"After all, he'd betrayed":** Entry of August 30, 1867, ibid., 250.

161 **"I bit my hands":** Entry of August 30, 1867, ibid., 250–51.

162 **"was a lot more fighting":** Entry of August 30, 1867, ibid., 251.

162 **"I would've given her":** Entry of August 31, 1867, ibid., 252.

163 **"To hell with her":** Entry of October 17, 1867, ibid., 336.

163 **the last we hear:** As for Polina, little is known about her after that point. She went on to marry Vasily Rozanov, a prominent philosopher and Dostoyevsky scholar whose book *The Legend of the Grand Inquisitor* still stands as a monument of Dostoyevsky studies. Polina was an experienced thirty-seven-year-old coquette when she first met Rozanov, a naive if brilliant seventeen-year-old student—a pairing that eerily echoed and reversed the roles once played by the seventeen-year-old Polina and forty-year-old Dostoyevsky when they first became lovers. Adding to this odd Dostoyevskian subtext of their union was the fact that Rozanov apparently once waxed lyrical about how he, a passionate Dostoyevsky scholar, was granted the rarest of opportunities: to get close to his object of study by sleeping with the very woman who once copulated with Dostoyevsky himself. After six years of marriage, Polina ran away from Rozanov with a Jewish bookseller.

163 **"She and Dostoyevsky":** Marc Slonim, *Three Loves of Dostoevsky* (New York: Rinehart, 1955), 177.

164 **"I absolutely cannot":** Letter to Apollon Maikov, August 16, 1867, in Fyodor Dostoevsky, *Complete Letters*, vol. 2 (1860–1867), 261.

164 **"This has to be":** Letter to Apollon Maikov, October 9, 1867, ibid., 278.

165 **"I don't think":** Letter to Apollon Maikov, December 31, 1867, ibid., 297.

165 **"My God, how I hope":** Entry of October 3, 1867, quoted in A. G. Dostoevskaia, *Dnevnik 1867 goda*, 298.

166 **"He definitely has":** Entry of September 6, 1867, ibid., 257.

166 **"To distract him":** Anna Dostoevsky, *Dostoevsky: Reminiscences*, trans. and ed. Beatrice Stillman (New York: Liveright, 1975), 137.

166 **"Oh, darling":** Letter to Anna Dostoyevskaya, November 5, 1867, in Fyodor Dostoevsky, *Complete Letters*, vol. 2 (1860–1867), 290.

166 **"Anya, darling, my dear":** Letter to Anna Dostoyevskaya, November 6, 1867, quoted ibid., 291.

167 **"I didn't especially grieve":** Entry of November 8, 1867, in A. G. Dostoevskaia, *Dnevnik 1867 goda*, 379.

167 **"My friend, don't be sad"**: Letter to Anna Dostoyevskaya, November 6, 1867, in Fyodor Dostoevsky, *Complete Letters*, vol. 2 (1860–1867), 291.

168 **"Anna Grigoryevna has been waiting"**: Letter to Apollon Maikov, February 18, 1868, in Fyodor Dostoevsky, *Complete Letters*, vol. 3 (1868–1871), 25.

169 **"I'm so sorry"**: Anna Dostoevsky, *Dostoevsky: Reminiscences*, 140–41.

169 **"my only guardian"**: Ibid., 141.

170 ***"Oh, ces russes"***: Ibid., 142.

170 **"His face showed"**: Ibid., 142.

171 **"Anya, look"**: Ibid., 143.

171 **her husband's tenderness**: Ibid., 146.

171 **"Well, what can I say"**: Letter to Anna Dostoyevskaya, March 23, 1868, in Fyodor Dostoevsky, *Complete Letters*, vol. 3 (1868–1871), 60.

171 **"if this vile"**: Letter to Anna Dostoyevskaya, March 23, 1868, ibid., 63.

172 **He would write Katkov**: Letter to Anna Dostoyevskaya, March 23, 1868, ibid., 66.

173 **"but the coldness and heartlessness"**: Anna Dostoevsky, *Dostoevsky: Reminiscences*, 148.

173 **"For the first time"**: Ibid.

173 **"There are moments"**: Letter to Apollon Maikov, June 22, 1868, in Fyodor Dostoevsky, *Complete Letters*, vol. 3 (1868–1871), 81–82.

174 **"In all the fourteen years"**: Anna Dostoevsky, *Dostoevsky: Reminiscences*, 149.

174 **"How happy we were"**: Letter to N. M. Dostoyevsky, September 1868, in F. M. Dostoevskii,"Dostoevskii v neizdannoi perepiske sovremennikov (1837–1881)," ed. L. P. Lanskii, *Literaturnoe nasledstvo* 86 (1973), 412, http://dostoevsky-lit.ru/dostoevskiy/pisma-dostoevsko mu/neizdannaya-perepiska/neizdannaya-perepiska-5.htm.

174 **"I cannot live"**: Entry of September 22, 1867, in A. G. Dostoevskaia, *Dnevnik 1867 goda*, 279.

IO. THE POSSESSED

175 **"How unpleasant and disgusting"**: Letter to Sofya Ivanova, July 23, 1868, in Fyodor Dostoevsky, *Complete Letters*, vol. 3 (1868–1871), ed. and trans. David A. Lowe (Ann Arbor, MI: Ardis, 1990), 86.

175 **"At every moment"**: Quoted in Joseph Frank, *Dostoevsky: The Miraculous Years, 1865–1871* (Princeton, NJ: Princeton University Press, 1995), 287.

175 **"Everything, my entire fate"**: Letter to Apollon Maikov, February 18, 1868, in Fyodor Dostoevsky, *Complete Letters*, vol. 3 (1868–1871), 30.

176 **"Anna Grigoryevna is patient"**: Letter to Apollon Maikov, October 26, 1868, ibid., 104.

176 **"My only reader"**: Letter to Apollon Maikov, December 31, 1867, in Fyodor Dostoyevsky, *Complete Letters*, vol. 2 (1860–1867), 298.

177 **"bitterly convinced that"**: Letter to Apollon Maikov, October 26, 1868, in Fyodor Dostoyevsky, *Complete Letters*, vol. 3 (1868–1871), 103.

177 **"the chief criticism"**: Quoted in Frank, *Dostoevsky: The Miraculous Years*, 308.

178 **his angelic "Prince Christ"**: Myshkin, then, is the perfect illustration of philosopher Reinhold Niebuhr's sobering observation, in *The Nature and Destiny of Man*, that "it is impossible to symbolize the divine goodness in history in any other way than by complete powerlessness."

178 **"the highest degree"**: Fyodor Dostoevsky, *The Idiot*, trans. Richard Pevear and Larissa Volokhonsky (New York: Vintage, 2003), 226.

178 **once again so financially desperate**: Letter to Sofya Ivanova, March 8, 1869, in Fyodor Dostoevsky, *Complete Letters*, vol. 3 (1868–1871), 142.

179 **"It's not for me"**: Letter to Apollon Maikov, December 11, 1868, ibid., 114–15.

179 **Together they composed limericks:** Anna Dostoevsky, *Dostoevsky: Reminiscences*, trans. and ed. Beatrice Stillman (New York: Liveright, 1975), 154.

180 **"For two years we've been living in poverty"**: The original text of this poem appeared in a 1993 Russian edition of Anna's diaries:

> Два года мы бедно живём
>
> Одна чиста у нас лишь совесть.
>
> И от Каткова денег ждём
>
> За неудавшуюся повесть.
>
> Есть ли у тебя, брат, совесть?
>
> Ты в "Зарю" затеял повесть,
>
> Ты с Каткова деньги взял,
>
> Сочиненье обещал.
>
> Ты последний капитал
>
> На рулетке просвистал,
>
> И дошло, что ни алтына
>
> Не имеешь ты, дубина!

Quoted in diary entry of June 12, 1868, in Anna Dostoevskaia, *Dnevnik 1867 goda* (Moscow: Nauka, 1993), 388.

180 **would go by "Lyuba"**: The baby's name, Lyubov', or "love" in Russian, would belie the great pain this beloved child would cause her mother later in life. In adulthood Lyubov' abandoned Russia for good, not only proudly declaring herself an Englishwoman but committing herself to spreading the outlandish idea that her father, the revered Russian patriot, in fact had little Russian blood in him at all. Scholars unanimously agree that there are no grounds for this argument, which Lyubov' pushes in a popular biography she wrote of her father published in 1921. Tellingly, she calls herself not Lyubov' but Aimée Dostoyevsky, Aimée meaning "loved" in French. See Aimée Dostoyevsky, *Fyodor Dostoyevsky: A Study* (London: William Heinemann, 1921).

180 **"Oh, why are you not married"**: Letter to Nikolai Strakhov, February 26, 1870, in Fyodor Dostoevsky, *Complete Letters*, vol. 3 (1868–1871), 240.

181 **"I'll lose touch"**: Letter to Apollon Maikov, March 25, 1870, ibid., 245.

181 **social and political crisis:** Anna Dostoevsky, *Dostoevsky: Reminiscences*, 158.

182 **"Strike me dead"**: Quoted in Fyodor Dostoevsky, *The Possessed*, trans. Constance Garnett (New York: Barnes and Noble Classics, 2005), 2.

182 **healing powers of the Russian spirit:** "The essence of religious feeling," says Myshkin, "does not come under any sort of reasoning or atheism, and has nothing to do with any crimes or misdemeanors. . . . But the chief thing is that you will notice it more clearly and quickly in the Russian heart than anywhere else." Frank, *Dostoevsky: The Miraculous Years*, 328.

183 **The professors and artists:** On December 30, 1870, he wrote to Maikov of a "hoary and influential scholar" in a reading room who shouted: "'Paris muss bombardiert sein!' [Paris must be bombarded.] There are the results of their learning. If not of their learning, then of their stupidity. They may be scholars, but they're horribly stupid!" In Fyodor Dostoevsky, *Complete Letters*, vol. 3 (1868–1871), 297.

184 **"And note, dear friend"**: Letter to Apollon Maikov, October 9, 1870, ibid., 280.

184 **"Nikolai Stavrogin is a gloomy"**: Quoted in Leonid Grossman, *Dostoevsky: A Biography*, trans. Mary Mackler (Indianapolis and New York: Bobbs-Merrill, 1975), 474.

185 **"Shatov spoke"**: Fyodor Dostoevsky, *The Possessed*, 592–93.

185 **the four "people":** Anna Dostoevsky, *Dostoevsky: Reminiscences*, 162.

186 **praying "to God":** Ibid., 161–62.

186 **"Living abroad seemed":** Ibid., 162.

187 **Dostoyevsky, meanwhile, was going:** All of these details Dostoyevsky relays in a letter to his niece, Sofya Ivanova, written on January 6, 1871:

"Anna Grigoryevna has even fallen ill from missing Russia, and that torments me. She is sad and pining away. True, she is very exhausted physically from nursing the baby a whole year. Since then her health has been severely shaken, and add to that her homesickness. The doctors said that she has symptoms of severe exhaustion of the blood, and specifically from nursing. The last week she's even been very bad. She's been walking little, mostly sitting or lying down. I'm terribly afraid. You can imagine my situation. But meanwhile she doesn't want to be treated; she says that the doctors don't understand anything. They prescribed iron for her; she refuses to take it. I am utterly at a loss and am losing my mind. This situation in general has been continuing a long time. You can imagine after that whether I've been able to work successfully.

"I, however, am at least working and busy with that, although I don't like my work and it constitutes torment for me. But Anna just pines. As usual, she's been helping me rewrite until recently; but there's no way her inner longing, her homesickness can be chased away."

Quoted in Fyodor Dostoevsky, *Complete Letters*, vol. 3 (1868–1871), 300–301.

187 **"If only you knew":** Letter to Apollon Maikov, December 30, 1870, ibid., 296.

II. THE FINAL SPIN

188 **a recent advertisement:** Letter to Apollon Maikov, December 15, 1870, in Fyodor Dostoevsky, *Complete Letters*, vol. 3 (1868–1871), ed. and trans. David A. Lowe (Ann Arbor, MI: Ardis, 1990), 291.

189 **"At first," Anna recalled:** Anna Dostoevsky, *Dostoevsky: Reminiscences*, trans. and ed. Beatrice Stillman (New York: Liveright, 1975), 163.

190 **"Why, all of Stellovsky":** Letter to Apollon Maikov, April 1, 1871, in Fyodor Dostoevsky, *Complete Letters*, vol. 3 (1868–1871), 336.

190 **"the way the Tolstoys":** Letter to Nikolai Strakhov, December 2, 1870, ibid., 286.

190 **"I have tackled":** Letter to Apollon Maikov, February 12, 1870, ibid., 235.

191 **"I'm afraid":** Letter to Apollon Maikov, March 2, 1871, ibid., 324.

191 **"In order to soothe":** Anna Dostoevsky, *Dostoevsky: Reminiscences*, 165.

191 **"He'd won a few times":** Ibid.

192 **Dostoevsky suggested:** These details are taken from Dostoyevsky's letter sent to Anna on April 16, 1871. Quoted in Fyodor Dostoevsky, *Complete Letters*, vol. 3 (1868–1871), 339.

193 **Thursday, April 15:** The details of Dostoyevsky's final gambling spree are described in a letter he sent to Anna from Wiesbaden on April 16, the day after he arrived. See letter to Anna Dostoyevskaya, April 16, 1871, ibid., 339–43.

193 **"vile and cruel letter":** Ibid., 339–40.

193 **"I swear to you":** Letter to Anna Dostoevsky, April 16, 1871, ibid., 340.

194 **thirty-five times his bet:** For a description of the roulette rules at this time in Europe, see Ian Helfant, *The High Stakes of Identity: Gambling in the Life and Literature of Nineteenth-Century Russia* (Evanston, IL: Northwestern University Press, 2002), 122–23.

194 **"I'm not a scoundrel":** Letter to Anna Dostoyevskaya, April 16, 1871, in Fyodor Dostoevsky, *Complete Letters*, vol. 3 (1868–1871), 340.

194 **"Anya, please, for the sake":** Letter to Anna Dostoyevskaya, April 16, 1871, ibid., 339.

195 **"My priceless one":** Ibid.

195 **deadening Western values:** In an eerie twist of fate, the synagogue resembling a church onto which Dostoyevsky projected his pro-Russian, anti-Semitic fantasies, and which played a role in the cessation of his gambling addiction, would be bombed in World War II. Later, a memorial would be erected in its place to the Jews of Wiesbaden killed during the Holocaust. As both a Jew and an admirer of Dostoyevsky, I found myself overcome by conflicting emotions when I stood at the sight of this memorial, studying the many hundreds of names of the deceased etched into the marble wall. To this day, I find it difficult to reconcile my appreciation of the profound spiritual beauty of so much of Dostoyevsky's fiction with his hateful, anti-Semitic rhetoric, which, as history has tragically shown, did for a time prevail in twentieth-century Europe.

195 **"I *won't go see*":** Letter to Anna Dostoyevskaya, September 16, 1871, in Fyodor Dostoevsky, *Complete Letters*, vol. 3 (1868–1871), 342.

195 **"a knife couldn't":** Entry of Friday, September 22, 1867, in A. G. Dostoevskaia, *Dnevnik 1867 goda* (Moscow: Nauka, 1993), 279.

196 **"I know that you'll die":** Letter to Anna Dostoyevskaya, April 16, 1871, in Fyodor Dostoevsky, *Complete Letters*, vol. 3 (1868–1871), 341.

196 **"Anya, believe that":** Letter to Anna Dostoyevskaya, April 16, 1871, ibid., 343.

196 **"His fantasy of winning":** Anna Dostoevsky, *Dostoevsky: Reminiscences*, 166.

196 **psychological and biological factors:** See chapter 4, "Explanations of Dostoevsky's Gambling," in Lorne Tepperman, Patrizia Albanese, Sasha Stark, and Nadine Zahlan, *The Dostoevsky Effect: Problem Gambling and the Origins of Addiction* (Don Mills, ON: Oxford University Press, 2013), 80–109.

197 **"the semiotic system":** In W. J. Leatherbarrow, ed., *Dostoevsky's The Devils: A Critical Companion* (Evanston, IL: Northwestern University Press, 1999), 30.

197 **"You alone are my savior":** Letter to Anna Dostoyevskaya, April 16, 1871, in Fyodor Dostoevsky, *Complete Letters*, vol. 3 (1868–1871), 339–40.

198 **"I have in store":** Letter to Anna Dostoyevskaya, April 17, 1871, ibid., 344.

198 **"I realize how":** Letter to Anna Dostoyevskaya, April 17, 1871, cited from F. M. Dostoevskii, *Polnoe sobranie sochinenii v tridtsati tomakh* (Leningrad: Nauka, 1972–1990), vol. 29, book 1, 202.

199 **to assure Anna:** Letter to Anna Dostoyevskaya, April 19, 1871, in Fyodor Dostoevsky, *Complete Letters*, vol. 3 (1868–1871), 347.

199 **"if you're completely":** Letter to Anna Dostoyevskaya, April 19, 1871, ibid., 347–48.

200 **"I felt so badly":** Anna Dostoevsky, *Dostoevsky: Reminiscences*, 166–67.

201 **"Mama, give me":** Ibid., 167.

201 **"Our consciousness of the fact":** Ibid., 169.

12. THE PUBLISHER

205 **"I had developed":** Anna Dostoevsky, *Dostoevsky: Reminiscences*, trans. and ed. Beatrice Stillman (New York: Liveright, 1975), 170.

205 **"more like an adoration":** Ibid., 90.

206 **"Let everybody see":** Ibid., 179.

206 **"Well, how's *papa*":** Ibid., 187.

206 **"I have turned":** Ibid., 175.

207 **seeking outside work:** That Anna worked fourteen hours a day was reported by Z. S. Kovrigina, an acquaintance who knew Anna in her final months, between the end of 1917 and early 1918. Anna told Kovrigina many stories about her life like this one. See Z. S. Kovrigina, "Poslednie mesiatsy zhizni A. G. Dostoevskoi," in A. S. Dolinin, ed., *F. M. Dostoevskii: Stat'i i materialy* (Moscow and Leningrad: Mysl', 1924), vol. 2, 581.

207 **"Troubles don't come singly":** Quoted in Anna Dostoevsky, *Dostoevsky: Reminiscences*, 203.

207 **"a cruel talent":** The article was published in 1883, two years after Dostoyevsky's death. See N. K. Mikhailovsky, "Dostoevskii—zhestokii talant," in *F. M. Dostoevskii v russkoi kritike: Shornik stat'ei*, ed. A. A. Belkin (Moscow: Khudozhestvennaia Literatura, 1956), 306–84.

208 **"So ended my effort":** Anna Dostoevsky, *Dostoevsky: Reminiscences*, 210.

209 **"In those days":** Ibid., 215.

209 **only one translation and publication company:** See Irina Sviatoslavovna Andrianova, "Aspiration for Independence: Anna Dostoevskaia's Publishing Commerce," *Canadian-American Slavic Studies* 50 (2016): 301. See also Richard Stites, *The Women's Liberation Movement in Russia: Feminism, Nihilism, and Bolshevism, 1860–1930* (Princeton, NJ: Princeton University Press, 1978), 69.

210 **Anna went about researching:** Anna Dostoevsky, *Dostoevsky: Reminiscences*, 214.

211 **She ordered paper:** According to scholar David Lowe, "The Dostoevskys had gotten paper from the Varguinins on credit for their own editions of *The Idiot*, *The Possessed*, and *Notes from the House of the Dead*." Fyodor Dostoevsky, *Complete Letters*, vol. 4 (1872–1877), ed. and trans. David A. Lowe (Ann Arbor, MI: Ardis, 1991), 185, footnote 2.

211 **"Why so little?":** Anna Dostoevsky, *Dostoevsky: Reminiscences*, 216–17.

211 **an elegantly dressed salesman:** Ibid., 217.

212 **"Well, Anyechka":** Ibid., 218.

213 **"Our publishing business":** Ibid., 219.

213 **"I felt a rare sense":** Ibid., 218.

213 **"I came for the demons":** Ibid., 220.

214 **control over the copyrights:** In *Reminiscences*, Anna writes, "Fyodor Mikhailovich had assigned the literary rights to his works to me back in 1873." Anna Dostoevsky, *Dostoevsky: Reminiscences*, 347.

214 **a solid passport:** See footnote 12 to Dostoyevsky's letter to Anna Dostoyevskaya, July 5, 1873, in Fyodor Dostoevsky, *Complete Letters*, vol. 4 (1872–1877), 77.

214 **Several years later:** Ibid., 240.

214 **"such understanding, such feeling":** Irina Sviatoslavovna Andrianova, *Anna Dostoevskaia: Prizvanie i priznaniia* (Petrozavodsk: PetrGU, 2013), 48.

214 **try her hand at fiction:** Details about Anna's fiction cited from Irina Sviatoslavovna Andrianova, "'Neprochitannoe' literaturnoe nasledie zheny F. M. Dostoevskogo (s prilozheniem tekstov ee neopublikovannykh proizvedenii)," *Neizvestnyi Dostoevskii*, no. 4 (2018): 228–34; entire article, 224–60, https://cyberleninka.ru/article/n/neprochitannoe-literaturnoe-nasledie-zheny -f-m-dostoevskogo-s-prilozheniem-tekstov-ee-neopublikovannyh-proizvedeniy/viewer.

215 **"I admire your letters":** Letter to Anna Dostoyevskaya, June 16, 1874, quoted in Fyodor Dostoevsky, *Complete Letters*, vol. 4 (1872–1877), 142.

215 **Sometimes he would steal:** I. S. Iarsheva, "Pomoshchnitsa i soavtor Dostoevskogo," *Znanie. Ponimanie. Umenie* 2 (2011): 142–43.

217 **sell every copy:** Anna Dostoevsky, *Dostoevsky: Reminiscences*, 244.

218 **an unscrupulous businessman:** Entry of October 4, 1867, in A. G. Dostoevskaia, *Dnevnik 1867 goda* (Moscow: Nauka, 1993), 308.

219 **"I cannot give you":** The account of Nekrasov's visit is drawn from Anna Dostoevsky, *Dostoevsky: Reminiscences*, 228–30.

220 **"I beg you not":** Letter to Dostoyevsky, June 22, 1874, in F. M. Dostoevskii and A. G. Dostoevskaia, *Perepiska*, ed. S. V. Belov and V. A. Tunimanov (Leningrad: Nauka, 1976), 110–11.

221 **"the storm which cleared":** The phrase belongs to scholar Jacques Catteau, who links it to a passage from *The Gambler*. Cited from Jacques Catteau, *Dostoyevsky and the Process of Literary Creation*, trans. Audrey Littlewood (Cambridge: Cambridge University Press, 1989), 145.

221 **"I kiss all of you"**: Fyodor Dostoevsky, *Complete Letters*, vol. 4 (1872–1877), 145.

221 **"My dear, dear"**: Letter to Anna Dostoyevskaya, June 22, 1874, in F. M. Dostoevskii and A. G. Dostoevskaia, *Perepiska*, 111.

222 **"Even if we have to ask"**: Letter to Anna Dostoyevskaya, December 20, 1874, in Fyodor Dostoevsky, *Complete Letters*, vol. 4 (1872–1877), 189.

222 **"The whole idea"**: Kenneth Lantz, *The Dostoevsky Encyclopedia* (Westport, CT: Greenwood Press, 2004), 345.

222 *Disorder* **as a title:** In his notes to the novel he wrote: "Title of the novel: *Disorder.*" Ibid.

223 **"ever-modest living quarters"**: Anna Dostoevsky, *Dostoevsky: Reminiscences*, 235.

223 **"a diary in the literal sense"**: Cited from F. M. Dostoevskii, *Polnoe sobranie sochinenii v tridtsati tomakh* (Leningrad: Nauka, 1972–1990), vol. 22, 265.

224 **"most beautiful memories"**: Anna Dostoevsky, *Dostoevsky: Reminiscences*, 238.

224 **"having great success"**: Ibid., 238, 244.

224 **"I have a premonition"**: Letter to Anna Dostoyevskaya, December 19, 1874. Quoted in Fyodor Dostoevsky, *Complete Letters*, vol. 4 (1872–1877), 187.

224 **Anna persuaded the bookseller:** Ibid., 187, footnote 3.

225 **"My dear, here's when"**: Letter to Dostoyevsky, June 24, 1875, in F. M. Dostoevskii and A. G. Dostoevskaia, *Perepiska*, 205.

225 **chemises from the best shop:** Anna Dostoevsky, *Dostoevsky: Reminiscences*, 270.

226 **"I'm nothing but"**: Fyodor Dostoevsky, *The Adolescent*, trans. Andrew McAndrew (New York and London: W. W. Norton, 1971), 265.

227 **seems to be transmuting:** With *The Adolescent*, Dostoyevsky was also attempting to write a novel that would compete with the latest work of his great literary rival, Leo Tolstoy. *Anna Karenina*, just then being serialized in *The Russian Messenger*, was fast becoming regarded as the defining encyclopedia of Russian life in the 1870s. Determined to carve out a niche of his own, Dostoyevsky strove to redefine Russian reality for his readers, showing them that the truth about who they had become was not to be found in the "gentry-landowner" literature produced by insulated aristocrats like Tolstoy but in the frenzied portraits of social fragmentation and "accidental families" found only in *The Adolescent*. "It really is all gentry-landowner literature," Dostoyevsky remarked of Tolstoy's novels, by which he meant the sort of literature created by privileged aristocrats ensconced in their private kingdoms, envisioning an idyllic, orderly Russia that no longer existed." Quoted in Joseph Frank, *Dostoevsky: The Miraculous Years, 1865–1871* (Princeton, NJ: Princeton University Press, 1995), 434.

227 **"this chaos"**: Quoted in Leonid Grossman, *Dostoevsky: A Biography*, trans. Mary Mackler (Indianapolis and New York: Bobbs-Merrill, 1975), 507. Most critics today agree *The Adolescent* is the weakest of Dostoyevsky's major post-Siberian novels.

228 **"Guard, open up"**: Anna Dostoevsky, *Dostoevsky: Reminiscences*, 257–58. This episode and the quotations are from Anna Dostoevsky, *Dostoevsky: Reminiscences*, 257–59.

229 **"simple and angelic"**: In a letter written to Anna from Bad Ems in 1874, for instance, he implored her to stop frightening him with "prophecies of your iron character, Anechka. That's the only bad thing in you. Your natural character is simple and angelic—that's what." But was it really? Letter to Anna Dostoyevskaya, July 6, 1874, quoted in Fyodor Dostoevsky, *Complete Letters*, vol. 4 (1872–1877), 151.

13. A TEST

230 **"The editorial work"**: K. M. Nakoriakova, *Ocherki po istorii redaktirovaniia v Rossii 16–19 vekov: Opty i problemy* (Moscow: VK, 2004), quoted in Irina Sviatoslavovna Andrianova,

"Aspiration for Independence: Anna Dostoevskaia's Publishing Commerce," *Canadian-American Slavic Studies* 50 (2016): 305.

231 **"unquestionably anti-Semitic"**: Cited from Frank's foreword to David I. Goldstein, *Dostoyevsky and the Jews* (Austin and London: University of Texas Press, 1981), xiii–xiv.

231 **"morally reprehensible"**: Gary Saul Morson, "Dostoevsky's Anti-Semitism and the Critics: A Review Article," *Slavic and East European Journal* 27, no. 3 (1983): 310.

232 **"Anna Grigoryevna helps me"**: Letter to Andrei Dostoyevsky, March 1876, quoted in Fyodor Dostoevsky, *Complete Letters*, vol. 4 (1872–1877), ed. and trans. David A. Lowe (Ann Arbor, MI: Ardis, 1991), 274.

232 **"to God, well-developed, directed, preserved"**: Letter to Anna Dostoyevskaya, May 5, 1867, in Fyodor Dostoevsky, *Complete Letters*, vol. 2 (1860–1867), 230.

233 **"My Darling Anya"**: Letter to Anna Dostoyevskaya, July 13, 1876, in Fyodor Dostoevsky, *Complete Letters*, vol. 4 (1872–1877), 300.

233 **"I'm so in love"**: Letter to Anna Dostoyevskaya, July 15, 1876, ibid., 301–3.

233 **"My angel"**: Ibid., 301.

234 **"But, not remaining satisfied"**: Letter to Andrei Dostoyevsky, March 11, 1876, in F. M. Dostoevskii, "Dostoevskii v neizdannoi perepiske sovremennikov (1837–1881)," ed. L. P. Lanskii, *Literaturnoe nasledstvo* 86 (1973), 447, http://dostoevskiy-lit.ru/dostoevskiy/pisma-dostoevsko mu/neizdannaya-perepiska/neizdannaya-perepiska-7.htm.

234 **"this most placid"**: Anna Dostoevsky, *Dostoevsky: Reminiscences*, trans. and ed. Beatrice Stillman (New York: Liveright, 1975), 261.

235 **"And if perchance"**: Ibid.

235 **"Why are you so gloomy, Fedya?"**: This exchange, ibid., 263–64.

236 **"I myself was infinitely happy"**: Ibid., 264.

237 **"have a good laugh"**: Ibid., 261.

237 **"Whether it is good"**: Fyodor Dostoevsky, *Great Short Works of Fyodor Dostoevsky* (New York: Perennial Classics, 2004), 291.

238 **"My dear: Whom"**: Letter to Dostoyevsky, July 9, 1876, in F. M. Dostoevskii and A. G. Dostoevskaia, *Perepiska*, ed. S. V. Belov and V. A. Tunimanov (Leningrad: Nauka, 1976), 219.

238 **"I'm afraid, really afraid"**: Letter to Anna Dostoyevskaya, July 15, 1876, in Fyodor Dostoevsky, *Complete Letters*, vol. 4 (1872–1877), 303–4.

238 **"To be enslaved"**: Fyodor Dostoevsky, *The Double* and *The Gambler*, trans. Richard Pevear and Larissa Volokhonsky (New York: Vintage Books, 2007), 203, 205.

238 **her former fiancé**: Letter to Dostoyevsky, July 13, 1876, in F. M. Dostoevskii and A. G. Dostoevskaia, *Perepiska*, 222.

239 **"I kiss you"**: Letter to Anna Dostoyevskaya, July 18, 1876, in Fyodor Dostoevsky, *Complete Letters*, vol. 4 (1872–1877), 309.

239 **"The fact that you're jealous"**: Letter to Dostoyevsky, July 19, 1876, in F. M. Dostoevskii and A. G. Dostoevskaia, *Perepiska*, 232.

239 **seven thousand subscribers:** The figure of seven thousand cited from the "Chronology" in Kenneth Lantz, *The Dostoevsky Encyclopedia* (Westport, CT: Greenwood Press, 2004), xxxi.

239 **living expenses of around 3,500 rubles:** This estimate is based on Anna's recollection that a few years earlier, in 1874, their expenses were at least three thousand a year. A baby boy, Alexei, was born in 1875, adding one more mouth to feed.

239 **five hundred rubles:** Anastasia Tuliakova, "Skol'ko zarabatyvali russkie pisateli?" *Arzamas*, July 8, 2016, https://arzamas.academy/mag/315-money.

239 **"the burdens of"**: Anna Dostoevsky, *Dostoevsky: Reminiscences*, 282.

240 **"You yourself don't"**: Letter to Anna Dostoyevskaya, July 24, 1876, in F. M. Dostoevskii, *Polnoe sobranie sochinenii v tridtsati tomakh* (Leningrad: Nauka, 1986), vol. 29, book 2, 112.

240 **"Memento—for the rest"**: Anna Dostoevsky, *Dostoevsky: Reminiscences*, 285.

241 **"When I die"**: Ibid., 287–88.

241 **That story would**: Details about Alyosha's death, ibid., 291–92.

242 **Darkness fell upon the household**: Details about the days just after Alyosha's death are taken from Joseph Frank, *Dostoevsky: The Mantle of the Prophet, 1871–1881* (Princeton, NJ: Princeton University Press, 2010), 383.

242 **After a short service**: These details are taken from the memoir of Dostoyevsky's daughter Lyubov' Dostoyevskaya, in Aimée Dostoyevsky, *Fyodor Dostoyevsky: A Study* (London: William Heinemann, 1921), 180.

243 **"This summer is"**: Letter to Nikolai Dostoyevsky, July 17, 1878, in F. M. Dostoevskii, "Dostoevskii v neizdannoi perepiske sovremennikov (1837–1881)," 464.

243 **"'And I will remember'"**: Fyodor Dostoevsky, *The Brothers Karamazov*, trans. Richard Pevear and Larissa Volokhonsky (New York: Farrar, Straus and Giroux, 1990), 50.

244 **"I so lost my bearing"**: Anna Dostoevsky, *Dostoevsky: Reminiscences*, 293.

245 **"deeply tragic story"**: Quoted in Leonid Grossman, *Dostoevsky: A Biography*, trans. Mary Mackler (Indianapolis and New York: Bobbs-Merrill), 570.

247 **a "strange man"**: Fyodor Dostoevsky, *The Brothers Karamazov*, 3.

248 **"These are authentic Russians"**: Anna Dostoevsky, *Dostoevsky: Reminiscences*, 296.

14. AT THE PROPHET'S SIDE

249 **"faithful armor-bearer"**: Anna Dostoevsky, *Dostoevsky: Reminiscences*, trans. and ed. Beatrice Stillman (New York: Liveright, 1975), 311.

249 **"Go to him!"**: Ibid., 312–13.

250 **"You know, my dear"**: Ibid., 311.

251 **"After long reflection"**: Ibid., 319.

251 **the new company**: This is according to a well-known secondhand Petersburg bookseller, Fyodor Grigoryevich Shilov, who knew Anna well. Shilov recalled: "In 1880 in *Russian Bibliography* an announcement appeared that F.M. Dostoyevsky: Bookseller is sending any books available for sale to institutions as well as private individuals, and orders will be fulfilled promptly and accurately." Cited from F. G. Shilov, *Zapiski starogo knizhnika* (Moscow: Kniga, 1990; dual publication with P. N. Martynov, *Polveka v mire knig*), 156.

252 **"a very profitable enterprise"**: Anna Dostoevsky, *Dostoevsky: Reminiscences*, 319.

252 **a small flat**: "Nearby their flat on Kuznechny Lane (now renamed Dostoyevsky Street)," recalled Shilov, "the Dostoyevskys had a corner storefront for their book business." Cited from Shilov, *Zapiski starogo knizhnika*, 156.

252 **"accustomed to its reliable"**: Anna Dostoevsky, *Dostoevsky: Reminiscences*, 318.

252 **"There were orders"**: Ibid., 319.

252 **fourteen thousand rubles**: This figure was calculated based on Anna's statement in her memoir that he was now earning three hundred rubles per signature of sixteen pages.

253 **"Anna Grigoryevna was very greedy"**: P. G. Kuznetsov, "Na Sluzhbe u Dostoevskogo v 1879–1881," *Literaturnoe nasledstvo* 86 (1973), 335, http://www.litnasledstvo.ru/site/download_arti cle/id/1690.

253 **"You're not to play"**: Ibid., 335.

254 **During such visits:** E. A. Shtakenshneider, diary entry of October 15, 1880. In *F. M. Dostoevskii v vospominaniiakh sovremennikov*, ed. K. I. Tiun'kin and M. Tiun'kina (Moscow: Khudozhestvennaia Literatura, 1990), vol. 2, 360.

254 **"emaciated, unprepossessing, elderly man":** Quoted in Anna Dostoevsky, *Dostoevsky: Reminiscences*, 324.

255 **"flying to her new life":** Fyodor Dostoevsky, *The Brothers Karamazov*, trans. Richard Pevear and Larissa Volokhonsky (New York: Farrar, Straus and Giroux, 1990), 364, 365.

255 **"almost an orgy":** Ibid., 432.

255 **"I'll be faithful":** Ibid., 442–44.

256 **"I can't not pay":** Memoir of M. A. Polivanova, "Zapis' o poseshchenii Dostoevskogo 9 Iiulia 1880 goda," in *F. M. Dostoevskii v vospominaniiakh sovremennikov*, vol. 2, 435.

256 **"I keep thinking about":** Letter to Anna Dostoyevskaya, August 13, 1879, quoted in Fyodor Dostoevsky, *Complete Letters*, vol. 5 (1878–1881), ed. and trans. David A. Lowe (Ann Arbor, MI: Ardis, 1991), 139.

257 **"Would you believe":** Letter to Anna Dostoyevskaya, August 16, 1879, ibid., 145.

257 **"Her husband is":** E. A. Shtakenshneider, diary entry of October 19, 1880, in *F. M. Dostoevskii v vospominaniiakh sovremennikov*, vol. 2, 363.

257 **misquotes the first sentence:** Joseph Frank, *Dostoevsky: The Mantle of the Prophet, 1871–1881* (Princeton, NJ: Princeton University Press, 2002), 561.

259 **"I dream about you":** Letter to Dostoyevsky, June 1, 1880, in F. M. Dostoevskii and A. G. Dostoevskaia, *Perepiska*, ed. S. V. Belov and V. A. Tunimanov (Leningrad: Nauka, 1976), 336.

259 **"In general, my dear":** Letter to Dostoyevsky, May 31, 1880, ibid., 334.

260 **"I have fought":** Letter to Anna Dostoyevskaya, May 28/29, 1880, in Fyodor Dostoevsky, *Complete Letters*, vol. 5 (1878–1881), 216.

260 **Two years before:** Frank, *Dostoevsky: The Mantle of the Prophet*, 415–16.

260 **A week later:** Ibid., 418.

260 **a mesmerizing tribute:** Cited from Katherine Bowers, Connor Doak, and Kate Holland, eds., *A Dostoevskii Companion: Texts and Contexts* (Boston: Academic Studies Press, 2018), 478.

260 **"had denigrated Pushkin":** Letter to Anna Dostoyevskaya, June 7, 1880, in Fyodor Dostoevsky, *Complete Letters*, vol. 5 (1878–1881), 233.

261 **a religious revival meeting:** I am grateful to scholar Joseph Frank for suggesting this apt comparison. See Frank, *Dostoevsky: The Mantle of the Prophet*, 527.

261 **"When his turn came":** Quoted ibid., 519.

261 **Pushkin's genius:** Bowers, Doak, and Holland, *A Dostoevskii Companion*, 476.

261 **It was Russia:** Ibid., 479.

261 **"somewhere outside him":** Ibid., 467.

261 **"But I'm now":** Alexander Pushkin, *Eugene Onegin*, trans. James E. Falen (Oxford: Oxford University Press, 1995), 210.

262 **"a southern woman":** Bowers, Doak, and Holland, *A Dostoevskii Companion*, 469–72.

262 **Tatyana's "noble instinct":** Ibid., 469.

262 **"in a sort of inspired whisper":** Quoted ibid., 527.

263 **"It's you who reconciled us":** Quoted ibid.

263 **"No, Anya, no":** The quotations are cited from Dostoyevsky's letter to Anna Dostoyevskaya, June 8, 1880. In Fyodor Dostoevsky, *Complete Letters*, vol. 5 (1878–1881), 236–37.

264 **"the greatest deprivation":** Anna Dostoevsky, *Dostoevsky: Reminiscences*, 329.

265 **"make yourself responsible":** Fyodor Dostoevsky, *The Brothers Karamazov*, 320.

265 **"everything is permitted"**: Ibid., 627.

266 **"never forget how good"**: Ibid., 774.

267 **"physically exhausted"**: Anna Dostoevsky, *Dostoevsky: Reminiscences*, 338.

267 **"I was always present"**: Ibid.

15. DEATH OF A HUSBAND

268 **the conversation started:** These details are taken from the memoirs of the Dostoyevskys' daughter Lyubov'. See Aimée Dostoyevsky, *Fyodor Dostoyevsky: A Study* (London: William Heinemann, 1921), 272.

269 **tasteless article:** "I did not recognize even myself in the words attributed to me," Anna later wrote of the piece, "so little did they correspond either to my character or to my frame of mind in those agonizing moments." See Anna Dostoevsky, *Dostoevsky: Reminiscences*, trans. and ed. Beatrice Stillman (New York: Liveright, 1975), 349–50.

270 **"For God's sake"**: Ibid., 345.

270 **"Remember this, Anya"**: Ibid., 347.

270 **"Anya, don't let him"**: Ibid.

271 **his own offspring:** Pasha's own children, according to Lyubov' Dostoyevskaya's memoirs, were raised well by their mother and became productive members of society. See Aimée Dostoyevsky, *Fyodor Dostoyevsky: A Study*, 196.

271 **She took care:** By contrast, in the years following Dostoyevsky's death Russian intellectuals refused to help Pasha and his family on the grounds that he had poisoned Dostoyevsky's life. "I think myself that they would have shown their admiration for my father better by a little kindness to this family, which was dear to him," Lyubov' Dostoyevskaya would later reflect. Which is exactly the approach Anna would take toward this man who'd caused her and her husband so much pain over the years. See Aimée Dostoyevsky, *Fyodor Dostoyevsky: A Study*, 198.

271 **"aside from the five thousand"**: Anna Dostoevsky, *Dostoevsky: Reminiscences*, 347–48.

271 **"My poor darling"**: Ibid., 348.

272 **"Pray, I beg you"**: Quoted in S. V. Belov, *Zhena pisatelia: Posledniaia liubov' F. M. Dostoevskogo* (Moscow: Sovetskaia Rossiia, 1986), 155.

272 **"in the presence"**: Anna Dostoevsky, *Dostoevsky: Reminiscences*, 349.

272 **"a kind of nightmare"**: Ibid., 351.

273 **"I finally became desperate"**: Ibid., 356.

273 **Anna felt a strange lump:** Ibid., 357.

274 **"So heavy a responsibility"**: Ibid., 359.

275 **"I am the widow"**: Ibid., 360.

275 **Anna "felt desperate"**: Ibid., 360–61.

276 **"I was clearly aware"**: Ibid., 349.

16. HIGH PRIESTESS OF DOSTOYEVSKY

281 **"There's nothing in life"**: S. V. Belov, *Zhena pisatelia: Posledniaia liubov' F. M. Dostoevskogo* (Moscow: Sovetskaia Rossiia, 1986), 174–75.

282 **"I cannot come to terms"**: Letter to Sofia Viktorovna Averkieva, July 22, 1881, in A. G. Dostoevskaia, "Perepiska A. G. Dostoevskoi s sovremennikami," *Baikal: Literaturno-khudozhestvennyi i obshchestvenno-politicheskii zhurnal*, no. 5 (1947), 138.

282 **what she had to do:** A. G. Dostoevskaia, *Vospominaniia, 1846–1917: Solntse moei zhizni—Fedor Dostoevskii*, ed. Irina S. Andrianova and Boris N. Tikhomirov (Moscow: Boslen, 2015), 480.

283 **"The strong demand":** Ibid., 481.

283 **what most Russian attorneys made:** I was unable to find data for the middle of the nineteenth century, and instead use as a proxy data from the turn of the century. If anything, salaries would have been lower in 1866, making Anna's gamble all the greater. According to historian Christine Ruane, in 1905, "90 percent of 12,473 lawyers earned over 2,000 rubles a year and over a third of these earned over 5,000 rubles. The earnings of government bureaucrats were equally high. Of the 91,204 salaried government officials employed in 1905, 46 percent earned more than 2,000 rubles per year. Among physicians, annual incomes ranged from somewhat under 500 to 3,000 rubles." Cited from Christian Ruane, *Gender, Class, and the Professionalization of Russian City Teachers, 1860–1904* (Pittsburgh: University of Pittsburgh Press, 1994), 59; and Peter H. Lindert and Steven Nafziger, "Russian Inequality on the Eve of Revolution," *Journal of Economic History* 74, no. 3 (September 2014): 767–98.

283 **minimal living expenses:** The cost of a single room in Petersburg at the turn of the century ranged between three hundred and five hundred rubles a year. See Christopher Williams, *Health & Welfare in St. Petersburg, 1900–1941: Protecting the Collective* (London and New York: Routledge, 2018), 19.

283 **"without difficulty":** A. G. Dostoevskaia, *Vospominaniia, 1846–1917: Solntse moei zhizni— Fedor Dostoevskii*, 481.

283 **"I would be realizing":** Ibid.

283 **"To carry on":** Anna Dostoevsky, *Dostoevsky: Reminiscences*, trans. and ed. Beatrice Stillman (New York: Liveright, 1975), 320.

284 **"I firmly believe":** Ibid.

284 **One paper supplier:** A. G. Dostoevskaia, *Vospominaniia, 1846–1917: Solntse moei zhizni— Fedor Dostoevskii*, 482.

285 **"In light of this":** Ibid., 485. The phrase "Complete Collected Works" was something of a publishing convention in Russia, but this was not a truly complete set. The much later *Polnoe sobranie sochinenii v tridtsati tomakh* (Complete Collected Works in Thirty Volumes), brought out by the Leningrad-based Nauka, came much closer to including everything Dostoevsky ever wrote, but that collection took nearly twenty years to publish: from 1972 to 1990.

285 **"in great trepidation":** A. G. Dostoevskaia, *Vospominaniia, 1846–1917: Solntse moei zhizni— Fedor Dostoevskii*, 486.

285 **"I was, of course":** Ibid.

285 **"Why did this substantial income":** Ibid., 487–88.

286 **"Execute them!":** Quoted in Irina Sviatoslavovna Andrianova, "'Velikii Gosudar'! Ia nichego ne proshchu dlia sebia lichno . . . ': Vdova Dostoevskogo i imperatorskii dom," *Vestnik slavianskikh kultur* 42 (2016): 55.

286 **"To judge Dostoyevsky":** Quoted in Belov, *Zhena pisatelia*, 123–24.

287 **"If you don't want":** Quoted in A. G. Dostoevskaia, *Vospominaniia, 1846–1917: Solntse moei zhizni—Fedor Dostoevskii*, 590.

287 **"I am not morally obligated":** Letter to V. V. Rozanov, October 28, 1897, in A. G. Dostoevskaia, "Perepiska A. G. Dostoevskoi s sovremennikami," *Baikal: Literaturno-khudozhestvennyi i obshchestvenno-politicheskii zhurnal*, no. 5 (1947), 142.

287 **Anna shared her secrets:** Anna Dostoevsky, *Dostoevsky: Reminiscences*, 363.

287 **several letters from Anna:** Cited from Irina Sviatoslavovna Andrianova, "Aspiration for Independence: Anna Dostoevskaia's Publishing Commerce," *Canadian-American Slavic Studies* 50 (2016): 308.

287 **Anna also used her government connections:** Sergei Belov discusses this and Anna's other accomplishments after Dostoyevsky's death in Belov, *Zhena pisatelia*, 175–77.

288 **"I feel my strength"**: Quoted in Andrianova, "Aspiration for Independence," 306.

288 **"I feel it is no longer"**: Ibid.

288 **"My children"**: Anna Dostoevsky, *Dostoevsky: Reminiscences*, 352. Although scholar Joseph Frank points out that Anna similarly claimed to have turned down the government's offer to pay for the funeral, there is no record of this in the official report. See Joseph Frank, *Dostoevsky: The Mantle of the Prophet, 1871–1881* (Princeton, NJ: Princeton University Press, 2002), 748.

288 **she founded a parish school**: Details cited from Belov, *Zhena pisatelia*, 172.

288 **she solicited the help**: Sections of the letter are quoted ibid., 172.

289 **"a unique work"**: Cited from the introductory essay by L. P. Grossman, "A. G. Dostoevskaia i ee 'Vospominanii,'" in A. G. Dostoevskaia, *Vospominaniia A. G. Dostoevskoi*, ed. Leonid P. Grossman (Moscow: Gosudarstvennoe Izdatel'stvo, 1925), 12.

289 **"This is not only a monument"**: Cited from Irina Sviatoslavovna Andrianova, "Dostoyevsky's First Bibliographer," *Slavic and East European Information Resources* 17, no. 1–2 (2016): 4–15, DOI: 10.1080/15228886.2016.1129684.

290 **a profit of seventy-five thousand**: This assumes Anna was telling the truth during her negotiations with the publisher Adolf Marx, to whom she was considering selling the rights to the fifth edition of Dostoyevsky's collected works. Always a tough, shrewd negotiator, Anna was also known for her high standards of honesty and ethical behavior. Her conversation with Marx can be found in A. G. Dostoevskaia, *Vospominaniia 1846–1917: Solntse moei zhizni—Fedor Dostoevskii*, 542.

290 **Anna received only her dower**: I am grateful to Russian scholar Irina Andrianova for this clarification in an email to me.

290 **previously censored parts**: Andrianova, "Aspiration for Independence," 307. But the full material was only published in 1922, as part of a brilliant wave of Dostoyevsky scholarship; see Anna Dostoevsky, *Dostoevsky: Reminiscences*, 412, note 10.

290 **"I can say"**: A. G. Dostoevskaia, *Vospominaniia 1846–1917: Solntse moei zhizni—Fedor Dostoevskii*, 575.

290 **"not only did not bring"**: Ibid.

291 **"For the first time"**: Ibid., 576–77.

291 **"Maybe it will seem"**: Ibid., 577.

292 **"It makes me laugh"**: Letter to Vasilii Vasilievich Rozanov, October 27, 1907, quoted in A. G. Dostoevskaia, "Perepiska A. G. Dostoevskoi s sovremennikami," *Baikal: Literaturno-khudozhestvennyi i obshchestvenno-politicheskii zhurnal*, no. 5 (1947), 141–42.

293 **a mysterious nervous ailment**: Taken from Anna Dostoevsky, *Dostoevsky: Reminiscences*, 420.

293 **her own life**: Fed up with Russia, in 1913, at the age of forty-four, Lyubov' permanently emigrated to Germany, whereupon, rejecting her Russian past, she proudly declared herself a European. From Germany she sent her mother long, weepy letters about how unfairly life was treating her, and then begging Anna for money, without a hint of acknowledgment that her aged mother may herself have been short on funds and struggling. In 1921, three years after Anna's death, Lyubov' published her titillating biography of Dostoyevsky, in which she argued, contrary to all available evidence, that her father was, in fact, mostly of Lithuanian stock and had little Russian blood. Given all this, it is hardly any wonder that Anna often mentioned to family and friends that Lyubov', whose name means "love" in Russian, and on whom they had pinned such high hopes, broke her mother's heart over and over again.

293 **"I can say that"**: A. G. Dostoevskaia, *Vospominaniia 1846–1917: Solntse moei zhizni—Fedor Dostoevskii*, 578.

293 **"I had to choose"**: Ibid.

294 **"people who had nothing"**: Ibid., 582.

294 **"The thought of having"**: Ibid., 579–80.

294 **seemed to Anna "a nightmare"**: Ibid., 584.

295 **"ended my former way"**: Ibid., 587.

296 **"Your Great Majesty!"**: Quoted in Irina Sviatoslavovna Andrianova, "'Velikii Gosudar'! Ia nichego ne proshchu dlia sebia lichno . . .': Vdova Dostoevskogo i imperatorskii dom." *Vestnik slavianskikh kultur* 42 (2016), 64.

296 **"would give me the possibility"**: Ibid.

297 **"I cannot consider Dostoyevsky"**: Quoted in Anna Dostoevsky, *Dostoevsky: Reminiscences*, 372–73.

298 **Anna "was wounded"**: Ibid., 375.

298 **a highly derogatory commentary:** Dostoyevsky had written that Strakhov "has no civic feeling or sense of duty, no outrage at any kind of filth, despite his strictly moral appearance. He is secretly lustful and, for any kind of coarse, nasty trick, is ready to sell everyone and everything, and his civic duty, which he doesn't feel, and his work, about which he is indifferent, and the ideal, of which he has none." Cited in notes to letter from A. N. Peshkova-Toliverova to A. G. Dostoevskaia, October 27, 1915, in A. G. Dostoevskaia, "Perepiska A. G. Dostoevskoi s sovremennikami," 143.

298 **"might appear to be"**: Anna Dostoevsky, *Dostoevsky: Reminiscences*, 380.

17. DEATH OF A WIFE

300 **"a more important part"**: Barbara Evans Clements, *A History of Women in Russia: From Earliest Times to the Present (Bloomington: Indiana University Press, 2012)*, 209.

300 **The feminist activists:** For more on the evolution of the Russian feminist movement during this time, see chapter 9, "Women Against Women," in Richard Stites, *The Women's Liberation Movement in Russia: Feminism, Nihilism, and Bolshevism, 1860–1930* (Princeton, NJ: Princeton University Press, 1978), 278–313.

301 **"I live not"**: Quoted in introductory article by L. P. Grossman, "A. G. Dostoevskaia i ee 'Vospominanii,'" in A. G. Dostoevskaia, *Vospominaniia A. G. Dostoevskoi*, ed. Leonid P. Grossman (Moscow: Gosudarstvennoe Izdatel'stvo, 1925), 14.

302 **"The factory workers"**: A. G. Dostoevskaia, *Vospominanii 1846–1917: Solntse moei zhizni— Fedor Dostoevskii*, ed. Irina S. Andrianova and Boris N. Tikhomirov (Moscow: Boslen, 2015), 639.

302 **"A terrible thought"**: Ibid.

302 **"they'd calm down"**: Ibid., 640.

302 **"Quiet! Begin"**: Ibid.

303 **muttering the word "Dostoyevsky"**: Ibid.

303 **"Dear friends"**: Ibid.

303 **"We mean no harm"**: Details taken from A. G. Dostoevskaia, *Vospominanii 1846–1917: Solntse moei zhizni—Fedor Dostoevskii*, 640; and A. G. Dostoevskaia, *Vospominaniia A. G. Dostoevskoi*, 16.

304 **"We won't bother her"**: A. G. Dostoevskaia, *Vospominanii 1846–1917: Solntse moei zhizni— Fedor Dostoevskii*, 641.

304 **"in the voice of passionate prayer"**: S. V. Belov, *Zhena pisatelia: Posledniaia liubov' F. M. Dostoevskogo* (Moscow: Sovetskaia Rossiia, 1986), 199.

305 **She had planned**: Ibid., 200.

305 **"I am seventy-two"**: A. G. Dostoevskaia, *Vospominaniia A. G. Dostoevskoi*, 14.

306 **"in complete isolation"**: Z. S. Kovrigina, "Poslednie mesiatsy zhizni A. G. Dostoevskoi," in A. S. Dolinin, *F. M. Dostoevskii: Stat'i i materialy* (Moscow and Leningrad: Mysl', 1924), vol. 2, 589.

EPILOGUE: THE AFTERLIFE OF ANNA DOSTOYEVSKAYA

308 **"I have always needed"**: A. G. Dostoevskaia, *Vospominanii A. G. Dostoevskoi*, ed. Leonid P. Grossman (Moscow: Gosudarstvennoe Izdatel'stvo, 1925), 14–15.

308 **"the joy and pride"**: Ibid., 356.

309 **"many Russian writers"**: Z. S. Kovrigina, "*Poslednie mesiatsy zhizni* A. G. Dostoevskoi," in A. S. Dolinin, *F. M. Dostoevskii: Stat'i i materialy* (Moscow and Leningrad: Mysl', 1924), vol. 2, 587.

309 **"tight-fisted and shrewd"**: Quoted in A. G. Dostoevskaia, *Vospominanii A. G. Dostoevskoi*, 13.

309 **"I always hated wives"**: Quoted in Irina Sviatoslavovna Andrianova, *Anna Dostoevskaia: Prizvanie i priznaniia* (Petrozavodsk: PetrGU, 2013), 28.

309 **inability to provide:** "We have to stash away, Anya," Dostoyevsky wrote to his wife in a letter in July 1879, "we have to leave the children something; this thought torments me." Quoted ibid., 29.

310 **the standard against:** It is no coincidence that in *The Wives: The Women Behind Russia's Literary Giants*, a very good overview of the subject of Russian writers' wives, Alexandra Popoff begins her discussion with the example of Anna Dostoyevskaya. See chapter 1, "Anna Dostoevsky: Cherishing a Memory," in Alexandra Popoff, *The Wives: The Women Behind Russia's Literary Giants* (New York: Pegasus Books, 2012), 1–60.

310 **how *not* to be:** American scholar Alexandra Popoff is clearly put off by what she views as Anna's unquestioning submission to societal expectations of how a Russian writer's wife and widow was to behave. By contrast, Popoff argues, Leo Tolstoy's wife, Sofya, was far more determined "to speak her mind and become Lev Tolstoy's critic." See Alexandra Popoff, "Sophia Tolstaia's and Anna Dostoevskaia's Autobiographical Writing," *Aspasia: The International Yearbook of Central, Eastern, and Southeastern European Women's and Gender History* 7, no. 1 (2013): 19–41.

310 **"Despite all the material":** Anna Dostoevsky, *Dostoevsky: Reminiscences*, trans. and ed. Beatrice Stillman (New York: Liveright, 1975), 5–6.

310 **"Better die of grief"**: Entry of September 17, 1865, quoted in Fyodor Dostoevsky, *The Gambler with Polina Suslova's Diary*, trans. Victor Terras, ed. Edward Wasiolek (Chicago: University of Chicago Press, 1972), 301.

BIBLIOGRAPHY

PRIMARY SOURCES

Anna Dostoyevskaya

Dostoevskaia, A. G. *Dnevnik A. G. Dostoevskoi, 1867 g.* Moscow: Novaia Moskva, 1923.

Dostoevskaia, A. G. *Dnevnik 1867 goda.* Moscow: Nauka, 1993.

Dostoevskaia, A. G. "Perepiska A. G. Dostoevskoi s sovremennikami." *Baikal: Literaturno-khudozhestvennyi i obshchestvenno-politicheskii zhurnal*, no. 5 (1947): 137–45.

Dostoevskaia, A. G. "Rasshifrovannyi dnevnik A. G. Dostoevskoi." *Literaturnoe nasledstvo* 86 (1973): 155–290. http://www.litnasledstvo.ru/books/tom86/tom86.pdf.

Dostoevskaia, A. G. *Vospominaniia A. G. Dostoevskoi.* Edited by Leonid P. Grossman. Moscow: Gosudarstvennoe Izdatel'stvo, 1925.

Dostoevskaia, A. G. *Vospominaniia A. G. Dostoevskoi.* Moscow: Khudozhestvennaia Literatura, 1971.

Dostoevskaia, A. G. *Vospominaniia 1846–1917: Solntse moei zhizni—Fedor Dostoevskii.* Edited by Irina S. Andrianova and Boris N. Tikhomirov. Moscow: Boslen, 2015.

Dostoyevskaya, A. G. *The Diary of Dostoyevsky's Wife.* Edited by René Fülöp-Miller and Dr. Eckstein. Translated from the German edition by Madge Pemberton. New York: Macmillan, 1928.

Dostoevsky, Anna. *Dostoevsky: Reminiscences.* Translated and edited by Beatrice Stillman. New York: Liveright, 1975.

Dostoevsky, Anna Gregorevna. *Dostoevsky Portrayed by His Wife: The Diary and Reminiscences of Mme. Dostoevsky.* Translated by S. S. Koteliansky. New York: E. P. Dutton, 1926.

Fyodor Dostoyevsky

Dostoevskii, F. M. *Dostoevskii: Materialy i issledovaniia.* 16 vols. Leningrad: Nauka, 1974–2001.

Dostoevskii, F. M. "Dostoevskii v neizdannoi perepiske sovremennikov (1837–1881)." Edited by L. P. Lanskii. *Literaturnoe nasledstvo* 86 (1973): 347–564. http://dostoevskiy-lit.ru/dostoevskiy/pisma-dostoevskomu/neizdannaya-perepiska/vstupitelnaya-statya-lanskogo.htm.

Dostoevskii, F. M. *F. M. Dostoevskii v vospominaniiakh sovremennikov.* Edited by K. I. Tiun'kin and M. Tiun'kina. 2 vols. Moscow: Khudozhestvennaia Literatura, 1990.

Dostoevskii, F. M. *Neizdannyi Dostoevskii: Zapisnye knizhki i tetradi 1860–1881.* Edited by I. S. Zil'bershtein and L. M. Rozenblium. Moscow: Nauka, 1971.

Dostoevskii, F. M. *Polnoe sobranie sochinenii v tridtsati tomakh.* 30 vols. Leningrad: Nauka, 1972–1990.

Dostoevsky, Fyodor. *The Adolescent.* Translated by Andrew McAndrew. New York and London: W. W. Norton, 1971.

Dostoevsky, Fyodor. *The Adolescent.* Translated by Richard Pevear and Larissa Volokhonsky. New York: Knopf Doubleday, 2007.

Dostoevsky, Fyodor. *The Brothers Karamazov.* Translated by Richard Pevear and Larissa Volokhonsky. New York: Farrar, Straus and Giroux, 1990.

Dostoevsky, Fyodor. *Complete Letters.* 5 vols. Edited and translated by David A. Lowe and Ronald Meyer. Ann Arbor, MI: Ardis, 1988–1991.

Dostoevsky, Fyodor. *Crime and Punishment.* Translated by Richard Pevear and Larissa Volokhonsky. New York: Vintage Books, 1992.

Dostoevsky, Fyodor. *The Double* and *The Gambler.* Translated by Richard Pevear and Larissa Volokhonsky. New York: Vintage Books, 2007.

Dostoevsky, Fyodor. *The Gambler with Polina Suslova's Diary.* Translated by Victor Terras. Edited by Edward Wasiolek. Chicago: University of Chicago Press, 1972.

Dostoevsky, Fyodor. *The House of the Dead.* Translated by David McDuff. London: Penguin Books, 1985.

Dostoevsky, Fyodor. *The Idiot.* Translated by Richard Pevear and Larissa Volokhonsky. New York: Vintage, 2003.

Dostoyevsky, Fyodor. *Netochka Nezvanova.* Translated by Jane Kentish. London: Penguin Books, 1985.

Dostoevsky, Fyodor. *The Notebooks for* The Idiot. Edited by Edward Wasiolek. Translated by Katharine Strelsky. Mineola, NY: Dover, 2017.

Dostoevsky, Fyodor. *Notes from Underground.* Translated by David Magarshack. New York: Perennial Classics, 2004.

Dostoevsky, Fyodor. *The Possessed.* Translated by Constance Garnett. New York: Barnes & Noble Classics, 2005.

Dostoevsky, Fyodor. *The Unpublished Dostoevsky: Diaries and Notebooks (1860–81).* Edited by Carl R. Proffer and Robert L. Belknap. 3 vols. Ann Arbor, MI: Ardis, 1973–1976. Translation of *Neizdannyi Dostoevskii: Zapisnye knizhki i tetradi 1860–1881.*

Dostoevsky, Fyodor. *Winter Notes on Summer Impressions.* Translated by David A. Patterson. Evanston, IL: Northwestern University Press, 1997.

Anna and Fyodor Dostoyevsky

Dostoevskii, F. M., and A. G. Dostoevskaia. *Perepiska.* Edited by S. V. Belov and V. A. Tunimanov. Leningrad: Nauka, 1976.

Dostoevskii, Fedor, and A. G. Dostoevskaia. *Pis'ma F.M. Dostoevskogo k zhene.* Moscow: Gosudarstvennoe Izdatel'stvo, 1926.

Belinsky, V. G. *Selected Philosophical Works.* Moscow: Foreign Languages Publishing House, 1948.

Belov, S. V., ed. *F. M. Dostoevskii v zabytykh i neizvestnykh vospominaniiakh sovremennikov.* Saint Petersburg: Andreev i Synov'ia, 1993.

Chernyshevsky, Nikolai. *What Is to Be Done?* Translated by Michael R. Katz. Ithaca, NY, and London: Cornell University Press, 1989.

Clyman, Toby W., and Judith Vowles, eds. *Russia Through Women's Eyes: Autobiographies from Tsarist Russia.* New Haven, CT, and London: Yale University Press, 1996.

Dershau, F. "Iz zapsok igroka" [From the notes of a gambler]. *Russkoe slovo* 4 (1859): 54–69.

Dolinin, A. S. *F. M. Dostoevskii: Stat'i i materialy.* 2 vols. Moscow and Leningrad: Mysl', 1924.

Dostoevskaia, Liubov' Fedorovna, and S. V. Belov. *Dostoevskii v izobrazhenii svoei docheri*. Saint Petersburg: Andreev i Synov'ia, 1992.

Dostoyevsky, Aimée. *Fyodor Dostoyevsky: A Study*. London: William Heinemann, 1921.

Herzen, Alexander. *My Past and Thoughts: The Memoirs of Alexander Herzen*. Translated by Constance Garnett. New York: Alfred A. Knopf, 1928.

Izmailov, A. A. "U A. G. Dostoevskoi (k 35-letiiu so dnia konchiny F. M. Dostoevskogo)." In *F. M. Dostoevskii v zabytykh i neizvestnykh vospominaniiakh sovremennikov*, ed. S. V. Belov, 189–95. Saint Petersburg: Andreev i Synov'ia, 1993.

Khvoshchinskaia, N. D. *Povesti i rasskazy*. Moscow: Khudozhestvennaia Literatura, 1963.

Kovalevsky, Sonya. *Her Recollections of Childhood*. Translated by Isabel F. Hapgood. New York: Century, 1895.

Kovrigina, Z. S. "Poslednie mesiatsy zhizni A. G. Dostoevskoi." In A. S. Dolinin, *F. M. Dostoevskii: Stat'i i materialy*, vol. 2, 583–90. Moscow and Leningrad: Mysl', 1924.

Pavlova, Karolina. *A Double Life*. New York: Columbia University Press, 2019.

Pushkin, Alexander. *Eugene Onegin*. Translated by James E. Falen. Oxford: Oxford University Press, 1995.

Saraskina, Liudmila. *Vozliubliennaia Dostoevskogo: Apollinariia Suslova: Biografiia v dokumentakh, pis'makh, materialakh*. Moscow: Soglasie, 1994.

Sekirin, Peter. *The Dostoevsky Archive: Firsthand Accounts of the Novelist from Contemporaries' Memoirs and Rare Periodicals*. Jefferson, NC, and London: McFarland, 1997.

Shilov, F. G. *Zapiski starogo knizhnika*. Moscow: Kniga, 1990. (Issued in a dual publication with P. N. Martynov, *Polveka v mire knig*.)

Stoiunina, M. N. "Iz vospominanii M. N. Stoiunina ob A. G. Dostoevskoi." In A. S. Dolinin, *F. M. Dostoevskii: Stat'i i materialy*, vol. 2, 578–82. Moscow and Leningrad: Mysl', 1924.

———. "Moi vospominanii o Dostoevskikh." In *F. M. Dostoevskii v zabytykh i neizvestnykh vospominaniiakh sovremennikov*, ed. S. V. Belov, 196–202. Saint Petersburg: Andreev i Synov'ia, 1993.

Suslova, A. P. *Gody blizosti s Dostoevskim. Dnevnik—povest'—pis'ma*. Moscow: Izdanie M. i S. Sabashnikovykh, 1928.

Turgenev, Ivan. *Smoke*. Translated by Michael Pursglove. Richmond, UK: Alma Classics, 2013.

SECONDARY SOURCES

Andrianova, Irina Sviatoslavovna. "Anna Dostoevskaia: Pis'ma muzhu." *Vestnik Baltiiskogo Federal'nogo Universiteta im. I. Kanta*, no. 8 (2013): 106–11. https://cyberleninka.ru/article/n/anna-dostoevskaya-pisma-muzhu/viewer.

———. *Anna Dostoevskaia: Prizvanie i priznaniia*. Petrozavodsk: PetrGU, 2013.

———. "Aspiration for Independence: Anna Dostoevskaia's Publishing Commerce." *Canadian-American Slavic Studies* 50, no. 3 (2016): 299–312.

———. "The Assistant and Co-author of Fyodor Dostoevsky." *Studia Slavica Academiae Scientiarum Hungaricae* 61, no. 2 (2016): 437–44.

———. "Dostoyevsky's First Bibliographer." *Slavic and East European Information Resources* 17, no. 1–2 (2016): 4–15.

———. "Epistoliarnyi roman F. M. i A. G. Dostoevskikh." *Neizvestnyi Dostoevskii*, no. 1 (2015): 3–11.

———. "Epistoliarnyi zhanr v tvorchestve A. G. Dostoevskoi." *Uchennye zapiski Petrozavodskogo Gosudarstvennogo Universiteta* 1, no. 138 (2014): 70–73.

———. "'Ia prishla rabotat', a ne dlia znakomstva': Fedor Dostoevskii i Anna Snitkina." *Neizvestnyi Dostoevskii*, no. 3 (2016): 128–43.

———. "Iz neizvestnykh memuarov. Anna Dostoevskaia o startse amvrosii (po rasskazam F. M. Dostoevskogo i F. N. Ornatskogo)." *Neizvestnyi Dostoevskii*, no. 1 (2016): 94–107.

———. "Kontseptsiia zhanra dnevnika A. G. Dostoevskoi." *Problemy istoricheskoi poetiki* 10 (2012): 224–40.

———. *"Muzei pamiati F. M. Dostoevskogo": istoriia i perspektivy projekta*. Petrozavodsk: PetrGU, 2013.

———. "'Neprochitannoe' literaturnoe nasledie zheny F. M. Dostoevskogo (s prilozheniem tekstov ee neopublikovannykh proizvedenii)." *Neizvestnyi Dostoevskii*, no. 4 (2018): 224–60. https://cyber leninka.ru/article/n/neprochitannoe-literaturnoe-nasledie-zheny-f-m-dostoevskogo-s -prilozheniem-tekstov-ee-neopublikovannyh-proizvedeniy/viewer.

———. "Pis'ma Dostoevskogo k zhene: Problema tsenzurnykh ispravlenii." *Neizvestnyi Dostoevskii*, no. 1–2 (2014): 66–72.

———. "'Velikii Gosudar'! Ia nichego ne proshchu dlia sebia lichno . . .': Vdova Dostoevskogo i imperatorskii dom." *Vestnik slavianskikh kultur* 42 (2016): 52–70.

Belov S. V. *F. M. Dostoevskii i ego okruzhenie: Entsiklopedicheskii slovar'*. 2 vols. Saint Petersburg: Aleteiia, 2001.

———. *Zhena pisatelia: Posledniaia liubov' F. M. Dostoevskogo*. Moscow: Sovetskaia Rossiia, 1986.

———, A. E. Vrangel', and Apollinariia Suslova. *Dve liubvi F. M. Dostoevskogo*. Saint Petersburg: Andreev i Syynov'ia, 1992.

Blake, Elizabeth. "Sonya, Silent No More: A Response to the Woman Question in Dostoevsky's 'Crime and Punishment.'" *Slavic and East European Journal* 50, no. 2 (Summer 2006): 252–71.

Bowers, Katherine, Connor Doak, and Kate Holland, eds. *A Dostoevskii Companion: Texts and Contexts*. Boston: Academic Studies Press, 2018.

Briggs, Anthony. *Brief Lives: Fyodor Dostoyevsky*. London: Hesperus Press, 2011.

Briggs, Katherine Jane. "Dostoevsky, Women, and the Gospel: Mothers and Daughters in the Later Novels." *Dostoevsky Studies*, n.s. 13 (2009): 109–20.

———. *How Dostoevsky Portrays Women in His Novels: A Feminist Analysis*. Lewiston, NY: Edwin Mellen Press, 2009.

Brooks, Jeffrey. *When Russia Learned to Read: Literacy and Popular Literature, 1861–1917*. Evanston, IL: Northwestern University Press, 2003.

Budanova, N. F., and G. M. Fridlender, eds. *Letopis' zhizni i tvorchestva F. M. Dostoevskogo, 1821–1881*. 3 vols. Saint Petersburg: Gumanitarnoe Agentstvo Akademicheskii Projekt, 1993–1995.

Campanella, Anthony P. "Garibaldi and the First Peace Congress in Geneva in 1867." *International Review of Social History* 5, no. 3 (1960): 456–86. https://www.cambridge.org/core/services/aop -cambridge-core/content/view/S0020859000001693.

Catteau, Jacques. *Dostoyevsky and the Process of Literary Creation*. Translated by Audrey Littlewood. Cambridge: Cambridge University Press, 1989.

Christofi, Alex. *Dostoevsky in Love: An Intimate Life*. London: Bloomsbury, 2021.

Clements, Barbara Evans. *A History of Women in Russia: From Earliest Times to the Present*. Bloomington: Indiana University Press, 2012.

Connolly, Julian W. "A World in Flux: Pervasive Instability in Dostoevsky's *The Gambler*." *Dostoevsky Studies*, n.s. 12 (2008): 67–79.

Corti, Egon Caesar, Conte. *Der Zauberer von Homburg und Monte Carlo: 1841–1872*. Frankfurt: Societäts-Verlag, 2008. (Issued in a dual publication with Eva Schweiblmeir, *Die Rückkehr des Glücks 1872–2008*.)

Dennison, Tracy, and Steven Nafziger. "Living Standards in Nineteenth-Century Russia." *Journal of Interdisciplinary History* 43, no. 3 (Winter 2013): 397–441.

Dostoevskii, F. M. *Dostoevskii: Materialy i issledovaniia*. Edited by Georgii Fridlender, V. G. Bazanov, et al. Leningrad: Nauka, 1974–2001.

———. *Stat'i i materialy*. Edited by A. S. Dolinin. 2 vols. Leningrad and Moscow: Mysl', 1924.

Engel, Barbara Alpern. *Mothers and Daughters: Women of the Intelligentsia in Nineteenth-Century Russia*. Cambridge: Cambridge University Press, 1983.

Erhard, Robert. *Aus der Chronik der Kaiserallee: Geschichte und Geschichten vom Promenade-, Konversations- und Kurhaus*. Baden-Baden, Germany: Kurhaus, 2005.

Forrester, John. "On Dostoevsky's 'The Gambler': Transference and the Stenographer." *Paragraph* 3 (April 1984): 48–82.

Frank, Joseph. *Dostoevsky: The Seeds of Revolt, 1821–1849*. Princeton, NJ: Princeton University Press, 1979.

———. *Dostoevsky: The Years of Ordeal, 1850–1859*. Princeton, NJ: Princeton University Press, 1983.

———. *Dostoevsky: The Stir of Liberation, 1860–1865*. Princeton, NJ: Princeton University Press, 1986.

———. *Dostoevsky: The Miraculous Years, 1865–1871*. Princeton, NJ: Princeton University Press, 1995.

———. *Dostoevsky: The Mantle of the Prophet, 1871–1881*. Princeton, NJ: Princeton University Press, 2002.

———. *Dostoevsky: A Writer in His Time*. Princeton, NJ: Princeton University Press, 2010.

———. Foreword. In David I. Goldstein, *Dostoyevsky and the Jews*. Austin and London: University of Texas Press, 1981.

Frankel, Valerie E. *From Girl to Goddess: The Heroine's Journey Through Myth and Legend*. Jefferson, NC: McFarland, 2010.

Freeborn, Richard. *Dostoevsky (Life and Times)*. London: Haus Publishing, 2005.

Fung, Paul. *Dostoevsky and the Epileptic Mode of Being*. New York: Routledge, 2015.

Gordon, Lyndall. "Women's Lives: The Unmapped Territory." In *The Art of Literary Biography*, ed. John Batchelor, 87–98. Oxford: Clarendon Press, 1995.

Grossman, Leonid. *Dostoevsky: A Biography*. Translated by Mary Mackler. Indianapolis and New York: Bobbs-Merrill, 1975.

———. *Seminarii po Dostoevskomu: Materialy, bibliografiia, kommentarii*. Moscow and Petrograd: Gosudarstvennoe Izdatel'stvo, 1923.

Grossmann, Ol'ga. *Russkii mir Drezdena: Progulki po istoricheskim adresam*. 3rd ed. Saint Petersburg: LIK, 2018.

———, and Gizbert Grossman. "Progulki po staromu Drezdenu s chetoi Dostoevskikh." Unpublished article.

Heldt, Barbara. *Terrible Perfection: Women and Russian Literature*. Bloomington: Indiana University Press, 1992.

Helfant, Ian M. *The High Stakes of Identity: Gambling in Life and Literature of Nineteenth-Century Russia*. Evanston, IL: Northwestern University Press, 2002.

———. "His to Stake, Hers to Lose: Women and the Male Gambling Culture of Nineteenth-Century Russia." *Russian Review* 62, no. 2 (2003): 223–42.

Hielscher, Karla. *Dostojewski in Deutschland*. Frankfurt am Main: Insel Verlag, 1999.

Hoisington, Sona Stephan, ed. *A Plot of Her Own: The Female Protagonist in Russian Literature*. Evanston, IL: Northwestern University Press, 1995.

Iarsheva, Irinia Sviatoslavovna. "Pomoshchnitsa i soavtor Dostoevskogo." *Znanie. Ponimanie. Umenie* 2 (2011): 141–44.

Indzinskaia, Anna Vladimirovna. "'Vsia vasha i s kostyliami E. Shtakenshneider': Perepiska E. A. Shtakenshneider i A. G. Dostoevskoi." *Neizvestnyi Dostoevskii*, no. 4 (2015): 34–39. https://cyber leninka.ru/article/n/vsya-vasha-i-s-kostlyami-e-shtakenshneyder-perepiska-e-a-shtakenshneyder-i-a-g-dostoevskoy/viewer.

Kornilova, Irina V., and Timur A. Magsumov. "Emancipation in Educational System: Formation of Women's Higher Education in Russia." *European Journal of Contemporary Education* 6, no. 2 (2017): 352–66.

Kuznetsov, P. G. "Na Sluzhbe u Dostoevskogo v 1879–1881." *Literaturnoe nasledstvo* 86 (1973): 332–36. http://www.litnasledstvo.ru/site/download_article/id/1690.

Lantz, Kenneth. *The Dostoevsky Encyclopedia.* Westport, CT: Greenwood Press, 2004.

Latsch, Johannes. "'Schlimmer als Sibierien': Dostojewskij am Schicksalsrad—Der 'Spieler'-Dichter 1867 in Homburg." *Aus dem Stadtarchiv: Vorträge zur Bad Homburger Geschichte.* Bad Homburg, Germany: Gotisches Haus, 2009.

Leatherbarrow, William J., ed. *Dostoevsky's* The Devils: *A Critical Companion.* Evanston, IL: Northwestern University Press, 1999.

Levy, Michele F. "D. H. Lawrence and Dostoevsky: The Thirst for Risk and the Thirst for Life." *Modern Fiction Studies* 33, no. 2 (1987): 281–88.

Lindert, Peter H., and Steven Nafziger. "Russian Inequality on the Eve of Revolution." *Journal of Economic History* 74, no. 3 (2014): 767–98.

Marullo, Thomas Gaiton. *Heroine Abuse: Dostoevsky's* Netochka Nezvanova *and the Poetics of Codependency.* Dekalb: Northern Illinois University Press, 2015.

Mathewson, Rufus W. *The Positive Hero in Russian Literature.* 2nd ed. Stanford, CA: Stanford University Press, 1975.

McReynolds, Louise. *Russia at Play: Leisure Activities at the End of the Tsarist Era.* Ithaca, NY: Cornell University Press, 2003.

Mikhailova, V. "Chto prostaia zhenshchina smogla sdelat' dlia geniia? 'Byt' Dostoevskoi.'" https://fedordostoevsky.ru/research/biography/031/.

Mikhailovskii, N. K. "Dostoevskii—zhestokii talant." In *F. M. Dostoevskii v russkoi kritike: Sbornik stat'ei,* ed. A. A. Belkin, 306–84. Moscow: Khudozhestvennaia Literatura, 1956.

Mironov, Boris N. "Wages and Prices in Imperial Russia, 1703–1913." *Russian Review* 69, no. 1 (January 2010): 47–72.

Mirsky, D. S. *A History of Russian Literature from Its Beginnings to 1900.* Evanston, IL: Northwestern University Press, 1999.

Mochulsky, Konstantin. *Dostoevsky: His Life and Work.* Translated by Michael A. Minihan. Princeton, NJ: Princeton University Press, 1967.

Morson, Gary Saul. "Dostoevsky's Anti-Semitism and the Critics: A Review Article." *Slavic and East European Journal* 27, no. 3 (1983): 302–17.

Moss, Walter G. *Russia in the Age of Alexander II, Tolstoy and Dostoevsky.* London: Anthem Press, 2002.

Nakoriakova, K. M. *Ocherki po istorii redaktirovaniia v Rossii 16–19 vekov: Opyt i problemy.* Moscow: VK, 2004.

Nasedkin, N. N., ed. *Dostoevskii Entsiklopediia.* Moscow: Algoritm, Eksmo, Oko, 2008.

Nazirov, R. G. "K voprosu ob avtobiografichnosti romana F. M. Dostoevskogo *Igrok.*" *Nazirovskii arkhiv* 1 (2013): 8–93.

Paniukova, Tatiana Viktorovna. "Primechaniia A. G. Dostoevskoi k proizvedeniiam F. M. Dostoevskogo (dve redaktsii)." *Neizvestnyi Dostoevskii,* no. 2 (2016): 70–80.

———. "'Redkoe sushchestvo, po umu, po serdtsu, po kharakteru' (rodstvennitsa dostoevskogo iz sibiri)." *Neizvestnyi Dostoevskii,* no. 3 (2020): 175–200.

Petrovna, Anna Viktorovna. "Tetradi s kritikoi: esche odno delo A. G. Dostoevskoi." *Neizvestnyi Dostoevskii,* no. 1 (2019): 107–18.

Popoff, Alexandra. "Sophia Tolstaia's and Anna Dostoevskaia's Autobiographical Writing." *Aspasia: The International Yearbook of Central, Eastern, and Southeastern European Women's and Gender History* 7, no. 1 (2013): 19–41.

———. *The Wives: The Women Behind Russia's Literary Giants.* New York: Pegasus Books, 2012.

Pushkareva, Natalia. *Women in Russian History: From the Tenth to the Twentieth Century*. Translated by Eve Levin. Armonk, NY, and London: M. E. Sharpe, 1997.

Radzinsky, Edvard. *Alexander II: The Last Great Tsar*. Translated by Antonina W. Bouis. New York: Free Press, 2005.

Razdiakonov, Vladislav Stanislavovich. "Neizvestnoe pis'mo A. G. Dostoevskoi k N. P. Vagneru." *Neizvestnyi Dostoevskii*, no. 4 (2015): 28–33.

Riazanovsky, Nicholas V. *Nicholas I and Official Nationality in Russia, 1825–1855*. Berkeley: University of California Press, 1969.

Rosenshield, Gary. "Gambling and Passion: Pushkin's 'The Queen of Spades' and Dostoevsky's 'The Gambler.'" *The Slavic and East European Journal* 55, no. 2 (Summer 2011): 205–28.

Rozanov, Vasily V. *Dostoevsky and the Legend of the Grand Inquisitor*. Translated by Spencer E. Roberts. Ithaca, NY: Cornell University Press, 1972.

Ruane, Christine. *Gender, Class, and the Professionalization of Russian City Teachers, 1860–1904*. Pittsburgh: University of Pittsburgh Press, 1994.

Ruttenburg, Nancy. *Dostoevsky's Democracy*. Princeton, NJ: Princeton University Press, 2008.

Safronova, Elena Iurievna. "Obraz Germanii v sibirskikh proizvedeniiakh F. M. Dostoevskogo." *Imagologiia i komparativistika* 12 (2019): 113–41.

Sanju, George. "From the Gambler Within: Dostoyevsky's *The Gambler*." *Advances in Psychiatric Treatment* 18, no. 3 (2012): 226–31.

Savage, D. S. "Dostoevski: The Idea of 'The Gambler.'" *The Sewanee Review* 58, no. 2 (April–June 1950): 281–98.

Scanlan, James P. *Dostoevsky the Thinker*. Ithaca, NY, and London: Cornell University Press, 2002.

Semukhina, Irina A. "'... slovno v ruletku proigralsia': Motivno-tematicheskii kompleks azartnoi igry v romane I. S. Turgeneva 'Dym.'" *Filologicheskii klass* 1, no. 51 (2018): 25–32.

Sergievsky, Nicholas N. "The Tragedy of a Great Love. Turgenev and Pauline Viardot." *American Slavic and East European Review* 5, no. 3/4 (November 1946): 55–71.

Slonim, Marc [Mark]. *Three Loves of Dostoevsky*. New York: Rinehart, 1955. Translation of *Tri liubvi Dostoevskogo*.

———. *Tri liubvi Dostoevskogo*. New York: Izdatel'stvo imeni Chekhova, 1953.

Sosnovskaia, Oksana Aleksandrovna. "Professora stenografii P. M. Ol'khin i Iu. V. Tseibig, znakomye F. M. i A. G. Dostoevskikh." *Neizvestnyi Dostoevskii*, no. 4 (2018): 206–23.

———, and Irina Sviatoslavovna Andrianova. "Neizvestnye stenograficheskie zapisi v dnevnike A. G. Dostoevskoi, ili chto ne rasshifrovala Ts. M. Pomeshchanskaia." *Neizvestnyi Dostoevskii*, no. 3 (2019): 140–56.

Steinberg, Mark D. *Petersburg Fin de Siècle*. London: Yale University Press, 2013.

Stites, Richard. *The Women's Liberation Movement in Russia: Feminism, Nihilism, and Bolshevism, 1860–1930*. Princeton, NJ: Princeton University Press, 1978.

Straus, Nina P. *Dostoevsky and the Woman Question: Rereadings at the End of a Century*. New York: St. Martin's Press, 1994.

Strelsky, Katharine. "Dostoevsky in Florence." *Russian Review* 23, no. 2 (1964): 149–63.

Tepperman, Lorne, Patrizia Albanese, Sasha Stark, and Nadine Zahlan. *The Dostoevsky Effect: Problem Gambling and the Origins of Addiction*. Don Mills, ON: Oxford University Press, 2013.

Terras, Victor, ed. *Handbook of Russian Literature*. New Haven, CT: Yale University Press, 1985.

Todd, William M. "'To Be Continued': Dostoevsky's Evolving Poetics of Serialized Publication." *Dostoevsky Studies* 18 (2014): 23–33.

Tsypkin, Leonid. *Summer in Baden-Baden*. Translated by Roger Keys. New York: New Directions, 2003.

Tuliakova, Anastasia. "Skol'ko zarabatyvali russkie pisateli?" *Arzamas*, July 8, 2016. https://arzamas .academy/mag/315-money.

Volgin, Igor. *Poslednii god Dostoevskogo*. Moscow: Sovetskii Pisatel', 1986.

Wachtel, Andrew Baruch, and Ilya Vinitsky. *Russian Literature*. Cambridge, UK, and Malden, MA: Polity Press, 2009.

Walicki, Andrzej. *A History of Russian Thought: From the Enlightenment to Marxism*. Translated by Hilda Andrews-Rusiecka. Stanford, CA: Stanford University Press, 1979.

Williams, Christopher. *Health and Welfare in St. Petersburg, 1900–1941: Protecting the Collective*. London and New York: Routledge, 2018.

Yarmolinksy, Avrahm. *Dostoyevsky: A Life*. New York: Harcourt, Brace, 1934.

Zirin, Mary F., Irina Livezeanu, Christine D. Worobec, and June P. Farris. *Women and Gender in Central and Eastern Europe, Russia, and Eurasia: A Comprehensive Bibliography*. London and New York: Routledge, 2015.

INDEX

Petrovna, Ekaterina. *See* Dostoyevskaya, Ekaterina Petrovna
Philosophical Letters (Chaadayev), 146
Pirogov, Nikolai, 8–9
Plekhanov, Georgi, 68
pochvennichestvo, 24, 87–88
poets/poetry, 6–7, 72, 80, 103, 107, 179–80, 215, 218, 220, 241, 258, 260, 274
Poor Folk, x–xi, xxi, 8, 21, 116, 144
populists/populism, 24, 226, 256
Possessed, The, xxiv, 215; Anna on, 191; Anna publishes limited edition of, 210–13, 217, 224; autobiographical aspect of, 184–85; based on Nechayev murder, 182–85; caricature of Turgenev in, 149; censored parts of, 207, 290, 297; creates public firestorm, 207–8; critical acclaim of, 183; Dostoyevsky on, 184, 190–91, 208; and Dostoyevsky's gambling, 191–92; and Dostoyevsky's hostility toward liberals, 104, 183; Dostoyevsky's spiritual/philosophical ideas in, 184; early drafts/notebooks for, 199–200, 290; ideological/critical debates over, 207–8; secret revolutionaries in, 152, 182–85; serial publication of, 188, 199; theme/plot of, 182–85, 207–8
Prague, 179
printing shops, 209–11, 215, 217, 224, 230, 252, 291
progressives, 145, 216; Anna's views on, 153; Dostoyevsky's views on, 147, 266; journals of, 218, 221; women as, xiv, xv, xx, 11, 15–16, 71–72
"Prophet, The" (Pushkin), 254
prostitutes, xv, 20, 63, 124, 157, 220
Prosvieshchenie publishing house, 295
publishing: all-woman cooperative for, 11; Anna's pioneering role in, xxiv, 220, 295; and exploitative/unscrupulous publishers, xxiv, 48, 213, 292, 297; and 1910 copyright law, 294; speculators of, xix, 26
publishing business (Dostoyevskys'), 219–21; and Anna's business acumen, 217, 224, 232, 239–40, 292; book distribution of, 251–52, 282–84; and book printing costs, 291; after Dostoyevsky's death, 281–85, 287–91; financial straits of, 291–96; issues Dostoyevsky's complete works, 284–85, 289–91, 293–94, 296; launched by Anna, xxiv, 205, 208–15, 292; and 1910 copyright law, 294;

reissues early Dostoyevsky works, 224; run by Anna, 198, 230–34, 277, 281–85, 287–91, 295; and sale of copyrights, 294–95; serves out-of-town customers, 251–52; success of, 217, 224, 247–48, 251–52. *See also specific book titles*
Pushkin, Alexander, 33, 44; Anna reads works by, 39–40, 61, 72; "The Demons" (poem), 182; Dostoyevsky recites poem of, 254; as Dostoyevsky's favorite writer, 39–40, 151; as father of modern Russian literature, 258; literary event honoring, 258–64, 293
Pushkin Celebration (Moscow): Dostoyevsky speaks at, 258–64, 266–67, 286; event missed by Anna, 258–59, 263–64; Turgenev speaks at, 258–61, 263

radical intelligentsia, 70, 72, 150; advocates revolution, xxi; attacks Turgenev novel, 145; and Chernyshevsky's *What Is to Be Done?*, 67–68; Dostoyevsky warns readers about, 64; and Dostoyevsky's *The Brothers Karamazov*, 247–48; Dostoyevsky's distrust/dislike of, xxi, 23, 113, 216, 231; and Dostoyevsky's *Time* journal, xxi, 23–24; infuriated by *The Possessed*, 208; inspiration to feminists, 16, 67; leading journal of, 67–68; and rift with conservatives, 259; theories of, xxi, 64
Recommendation (play), 214
religion: Anna's beliefs in, 93–94, 105–6, 143, 207, 225, 304–5; Anna's upbringing and, 5, 12, 70; Dostoyevsky's beliefs in, 22, 39, 61–62, 147, 151, 246–47, 270; Dostoyevsky's upbringing and, 231. *See also* Christianity; Russian Orthodox Church
Reminiscences (Anna Dostoyevskaya), xvii, 11–12, 65, 83–84, 244, 247–48, 286, 290, 295, 299
Resurrection Monastery (Moscow), 12, 276
revolutionaries: assassination of Alexander II, 276, 286; disparaged by Dostoyevsky, xxi, 152, 159–60, 182–83, 208, 216; in Dostoyevsky's fiction, 152, 183–84, 208, 226; Dostoyevsky's warnings about, 300, 303–4; violent uprisings of, 291, 293–94, 300–304; women as, 300–301. *See also* radical intelligentsia
Roman Catholic Church, 151